STUDIES IN LINGUISTICS

Edited by
Laurence Horn
Yale University

A ROUTLEDGE SERIES

Studies in Linguistics

Laurence Horn, *General Editor*

The Phonetics and Phonology of Gutturals
A Case Study from Ju'hoansi
Amanda Miller-Ockhuizen

True to Form
Rising and Falling Declaratives as Questions in English
Christine Gunlogson

Lexical, Pragmatic, and Positional Effects on Prosody in Two Dialects of Croatian and Serbian
An Acoustic Study
Rajka Smiljanic

Lenition and Contrast
The Functional Consequences of Certain Phonetically Conditioned Sound Changes
Naomi Gurevich

The Inflected Infinitive in Romance Languages
Emily Scida

Syntactic Form and Discourse Function in Natural Language Generation
Cassandre Creswell

The Syntax-Information Structure Interface
Evidence from Spanish and English
Eugenia Casielles-Suárez

The Ups and Downs of Child Language
Experimental Studies on Children's Knowledge of Entailment Relationships and Polarity Phenomena
Andrea Gualmini

Category Neutrality
A Type-Logical Investigation
Neal Whitman

Markedness and Faithfulness in Vowel Systems
Viola Miglio

Phonological Augmentation in Prominent Positions
Jennifer L. Smith

Enriched Composition and Inference in the Argument Structure of Chinese
Ren Zhang

Discourse Adjectives
Gina Taranto

Structural Markedness and Syntactic Structure
A Study of Word Order and the Left Periphery in Mexican Spanish
Rodrigo Gutiérrez-Bravo

Negation and Licensing of Negative Polarity Items in Hindi Syntax
Rajesh Kumar

Syllable Weight
Phonetics, Phonology, Typology
Matthew Kelly Gordon

Reassessing the Role of the Syllable in Italian Phonology
An Experimental Study of Consonant Cluster Syllabification, Definite Article Allomorphy and Segment Duration
Kristie McCrary Kambourakis

Telicity and Durativity
A Study of Aspect in Dëne Sųłiné (Chipewyan) and German
Andrea Wilhelm

TELICITY AND DURATIVITY
A Study of Aspect in Dëne Sųłiné (Chipewyan) and German

Andrea Wilhelm

Routledge
New York & London

Routledge
Taylor & Francis Group
711 Third Avenue y2
New York, NY 10017

Routledge
Taylor & Francis Group
2 Park Square
Milton Park, Abingdon
Oxon OX14 4RN

First issued in paperback 2013

© 2007 by Taylor & Francis Group, LLC
Routledge is an imprint of the Taylor & Francis Group, an informa business

International Standard Book Number-10: 0-415-97645-6 (Hardcover)
International Standard Book Number-13: 978-0-415-97645-9 (Hardcover)
International Standard Book Number-13: 978-0-415-54228-9 (Paperback)

No part of this book may be reprinted, reproduced, transmitted, or utilized in any form by any electronic, mechanical, or other means, now known or hereafter invented, including photocopying, microfilming, and recording, or in any information storage or retrieval system, without written permission from the publishers.

Trademark Notice: Product or corporate names may be trademarks or registered trademarks, and are used only for identification and explanation without intent to infringe.

Library of Congress Cataloging-in-Publication Data
Wilhelm, Andrea.
Telicity and durativity : a study of aspect in Dene Suline (Chipewyan) and German / by Andrea Wilhelm.
p. cm. -- (Studies in linguistics)
Includes bibliographical references and index.
ISBN 0-415-97645-6 (alk. paper)
1. Chipewyan language--Aspect. 2. German language--Aspect. 3. Chipewyan language--Temporal constructions. 4. German language--Temporal constructions. 5. Chipewyan language--Grammar, Comparative--German. 6. German language--Grammar, Comparative--Chipewyan. 7. Grammar, Comparative and general--Aspect. I. Title. II. Series: Studies in linguistics (New York, N.Y.)
PM850.C2W55 2006
497'.2--dc22   2006013031

Visit the Taylor & Francis Web site at
http://www.taylorandfrancis.com

and the Routledge Web site at
http://www.routledge-ny.com

Für Markus und Ella.

Contents

List of Tables   ix

List of Maps   xi

List of Abbreviations   xiii

Acknowledgments   xv

Chapter One
Introduction   1
   1. Basic Research Question   1
   2. Method   9
   3. Findings: Preview   10
   4. Theoretical Assumptions   10
   5. Outline   20

PART I: DËNE SŲŁINÉ

Chapter Two
Viewpoint Aspect and Its Influence on Situation Type in Dëne   23
   1. Introduction to Dëne Sųłiné   23
   2. The Dëne Viewpoints   34
   3. Perfectivity and Telicity   53
   4. Conclusion   67

Chapter Three
Telicity Is Not Grammatized in Dëne   69
   1. Verb Theme Categories   70

2. Conjugation Markers	77
3. CM's Do Not Mark Telicity (but Perhaps Durativity)	90
4. Objects	119
5. Discussion	125

PART II: GERMAN

Chapter Four
Telicity in German — 135
1. Telicity Is Easily Distinguished — 136
2. Telicity in the Morphosyntax I: Well-Known Facts — 139
3. Telicity in the Morphosyntax II: Particle Verbs and Telicity — 149
4. Conclusion — 163

Chapter Five
Viewpoint Aspect and Durativity in German — 165
1. Viewpoint Aspect in German? — 166
2. Durativity Is Not Grammatized — 190

Chapter Six
The Grammatization of Aspectual Notions — 203
1. Introduction — 203
2. The Different Natures of Telicity and Durativity — 205
3. Grammatization — 210
4. Non-Grammatization — 217
5. Implications, Consequences, Further Work — 221

Appendix One	229
Appendix Two	259
Appendix Three	291
Notes	295
Bibliography	315
Author Index	327
Subject Index	331

List of Tables

Table 1:	(Cold Lake) Dëne consonants	25
Table 2:	(Cold Lake) Dëne vowels	26
Table 3:	Dëne verb template	27
Table 4:	Ahtna verb theme categories according to Kari (1979)	71
Table 5:	Nonstative Koyukon verb theme categories according to Axelrod (1993)	73
Table 6:	Modes of the Dëne verb according to Li (1946)	76
Table 7:	Lexical aspectual classes in Dëne according to Bortolin (1998)	79
Table 8:	Test results for four verb themes	98
Table 9:	CM patterns and situation type (nonstative)	100

List of Maps

Map 1: Indigenous Languages of Western Canada   24

List of Abbreviations

1	first person
2	second person
3	third person
4	fourth person
ACC	accusative
adv	adverbial element
ar	areal
Asp	(viewpoint) Aspect
assert	assertion marker
C	consonant
cl	classifier
CM	conjugation marker
comp/C	complementizer
cont	continually
DAT	dative
delim	delimiting/delimited
distr	distributive
dl	dual
ep	epenthetic
fut	future/prospective marker
gd	gender
GEN	genitive
H	high tone
impf	imperfective
incept	inceptive
indef	indefinite
inf	infinitive
M	modal

N	nasal, noun
O	object
opt	optative
P	adposition
part	particle
perf	perfective
pl	plural
pres	present
pret	preterite
prog	progressive
REL	relative pronoun
S	subject
sem	semelfactive
ser	seriative
Spec	specifier
s/sg	singular
T	Tense
th	thematic
tr	transitive
TSit	situation time
TT	topic time
TU	time of utterance
unspec	unspecified
V	verb, vowel
vcd	voiced
vl	voiceless

Acknowledgments

This book examines the relevance of two components of predicate meaning, telicity and durativity, to the grammatical system of natural language. It is a slightly revised version of my dissertation, completed at the University of Calgary's Linguistics department in 2003. Throughout my doctoral studies, I experienced a stimulating, fun, and incredibly supportive environment in this department, and for this I am deeply grateful to all its members—profs, fellow students, and staff alike. Four people deserve special mention:

First, Ed Cook was a member of this department when I first came to Calgary. He is the one who introduced me to and "hooked" me on Athapaskan, he brought me back to academia through a joint paper when I was busy but not content being a stay-at-home mom, and he has generously shared his expertise on Dëne with me, including making a manuscript grammar of the language (since published as Cook 2004) available to me.

Next, my supervisor, Betsy Ritter, not only encouraged me to embark on the doctoral program, she walked with me all along. Without her belief in the validity of my ideas, I would have given up early on. Equally valuable was the sharpening of these ideas and their articulation that happened in countless hours of discussion with someone of acute perception and deep reflection on the topics addressed in this dissertation. Betsy, you truly are my *Doktormutter*, and a kind and patient one at that.

Then Hotze Rullmann, to whom I owe everything I know about Semantics with a capital S, and to whom I went with the numerous "Semantics questions" that came up in writing this dissertation. Not only that, Hotze brought me calm and clarity whenever I could not see the forest for the trees.

And finally, Amanda Pounder of the eagle eye and the quiet but oh-so-probing questions. Amanda caught mistakes and inconsistencies in my arguments no-one else did, and the discussions with her challenged me to think about the most basic and almost unconscious theoretical assumptions I was making.

Among linguists from other places, the influence of Carlota Smith's work on mine is obvious on almost every page of this book. Her approach to aspect has informed my own, and her astute comments on my dissertation were invaluable. Of course this does not mean that she (or any of the other people mentioned here) necessarily agrees with what I end up saying.

Since I first contacted Manfred Krifka, I have marveled at how approachable he is. He takes time to meet, to discuss my data and questions, he gives good advice, and in 2001 sponsored a research semester at the ZAS (Zentrum für Allgemeine Sprachwissenschaft) in Berlin. Also at the ZAS, I benefited much from discussions with Veronika Ehrich, with whom—providentially—I shared an office.

I want to thank Doris Payne for being a friend at the University of Oregon and Holden Härtl for being one at the ZAS, Su Urbanczyk for making me love phonology, Carol Tenny and Nomi Shir for discussion at decisive moments, and Keren Rice, Leslie Saxon, Siri Tuttle, and Sharon Hargus for welcoming me into the community of Athapaskan researchers.

My research on Dëne would not have been possible without the support of Sally Rice, another Athapaskanist, who let me piggyback onto her project on Cold Lake Dëne, and gave me access to her offices, computers and other resources there. Thank you! And of course, I cannot even begin to express my thanks to the kind Dëne speakers who shared their language (and homes) with me: Shirley Cardinal, Ernest Ennow, John Janvier, Nora Matchatis, Valerie Wood. I owe you so much. Likewise, thanks to the Cold Lake First Nations for permitting me to conduct fieldwork among them.

My research was funded by a SSHRC Doctoral Fellowship (No. 752–99–1946), a University of Calgary Thesis Research Grant (No. 994409), and a California Indian Language Center Grant. The stay at the ZAS was funded by a DAAD short-term research grant.

Now to the nonlinguists. They may look with bemusement on my "esoteric" endeavours, but they cheered me on nonetheless, because that's part of me, and they love me. Made sacrifices, too. My husband Markus and my daughter Ella, my parents and my brothers in Germany, my in-law family in North America, and my friends on both continents: especially Micha, Uli & Michael, Siv & family, Kathryn, Beate. Many more: you know who you are.

Finally, I give thanks and praise to the source of all goodness in my life, which includes but goes far beyond all of the above: God the Father, Son, and Holy Spirit.

Chapter One
Introduction

> Was ist überhaupt ein sprachliches Faktum, das von der Grammatikbeschreibung zu erfassen ist?
>
> —Renate Steinitz (1981:25)

1. BASIC RESEARCH QUESTION

1.1. The Linguistic Characterization of Verbal Predicates

This dissertation asks a very fundamental question about the linguistic characterization of verbal predicates, such as *laugh, knock at the door, write a letter*. Verbal predicates denote situations in a world, and these situations have certain characteristics. In the philosophical literature, predicates are often characterized according to what types of situations they denote (e.g., Ryle 1949, Kenny 1963, Taylor 1985, all exploring ideas originating with Aristotle). And linguists have often looked to the philosophical literature for criteria or classes to use in the *linguistic* characterization of predicates.

One philosopher whose work has become particularly influential in modern linguistics is Zeno Vendler, who in an essay titled "Verbs and Times" divided English verbs (actually, verb phrases) into four temporal-aspectual classes, the well-known *states, activities, accomplishments* and *achievements* (Vendler 1957).

(1) states: *know, love (somebody), have, want, be married*
activities: *run, push a cart, write, work, walk*
achievements: *die, recognize (someone), reach the top, win a race, spot the plane*
accomplishments: *run a mile, draw a circle, write a letter, paint a picture, build a house*

Vendler's criteria for these four classes are loosely semantic, involving how a verb (or VP) can be used, and what kinds of entailment patterns it has. In the rich linguistics literature that followed Vendler's paper, these verb classes have been defined and revised in various ways, and formal accounts of them have been developed (e.g., Mourelatos 1978, Dowty 1979, Carlson 1981, Bach 1986, Hinrichs 1985, Moens 1987, Parsons 1990, Piñón 1995). Importantly, much of this work, and most work on tense/aspect, assumes that the Vendler predicate classes, or the characteristics that underlie them, are universal (Comrie 1976, Mourelatos 1978, Dowty 1979, Bach 1981, 1986, Smith 1991, Ehrich 1992, ter Meulen 1995, Musan 2002, etc.). Moreover, a Vendler-type classification is assumed in virtually all work which tries to establish links between temporal-aspectual characteristics of predicates and their grammatical representation. Thus, many theories of argument linking and verb diathesis use lexical semantic or syntactic structures which represent the Vendler predicate classes in some way (e.g., Grimshaw 1990, Jackendoff 1990, 1996, Pustejovsky 1991, Fagan 1992, van Valin 1990, 1993, Tenny 1987, 1994, Borer 1994, 1998, Rapp 1997a,b, Rappaport Hovav and Levin 1998, Ritter and Rosen 1998, 2000, van Hout 2000, Ramchand 2002). To quote Rappaport Hovav and Levin (1998:106):

> in most current theories, the aspects of [verb] meaning which are grammatically relevant usually are those which define the various ontological types of events, which correspond roughly to the recognized Vendler-Dowty aspectual classes of verbs.

Thus, almost unnoticed, Vendler's philosophical and semantic categories have become *grammatical* categories, and universal ones at that. What falls by the wayside in this literature is the fundamental question of whether Vendler's predicate types really form distinct grammatical classes, in all languages. This often forgotten question is the central concern of my dissertation. I believe it is of crucial importance to ensure that the semantic notions used as the basis of *grammatical* theories have "grammatical reality." This leads to the following general research question, which is the focus of this dissertation:

(2) *General Research Question*
How are temporal-aspectual characteristics of predicates grammatized in natural language?

In the following two sections, I will explain what I mean by "temporal-aspectual characteristics" and by "grammatized," and sharpen my research question.

Introduction 3

1.2. *Temporal-Aspectual Characteristics*

"Temporal-aspectual characteristics" refer to the characteristics underlying the Vendler verb/predicate classes given in (1), or, in Vendler's words, how verbs' meaning "presupposes and involves the notion of time" (Vendler 1967:97). I now briefly introduce these characteristics, postponing a more careful theoretical discussion until section 4.1.2.

Telicity. The characteristics and associated tests identified by Vendler himself are somewhat unclear (cf. Verkuyl 1989), and subsequent authors, in attempting to streamline Vendler's ideas, have typically focused on different subsets of Vendler's characteristics. However, there is a broad consensus that one characteristic is telicity; it indicates that a situation has an inherent endpoint or culmination which issues in a result state. The situation itself cannot continue past the inherent endpoint or culmination. For example, the inherent endpoint of the situation denoted by *write a letter* is the completion of a letter (which results in the existence of said letter). The situation denoted by *walk* has no such inherent endpoint—a walking event can be stopped at an arbitrary point, it is not completed or finished, and there is no result state. Accomplishments and achievements are telic; activities and states are atelic. In English, a convenient telicity test is compatibility with time span adverbials such as *in an hour* (e.g., √ *Susi wrote a letter in an hour* but # *Susi walked in an hour*[1]).

Durativity. There is less agreement on what distinguishes achievements from accomplishments; it might be the presence of a process, it might be durativity, or even agentivity. Vendler himself mentions all three criteria: accomplishments but not achievements are "processes," i.e., they contain "successive phases following one another in time" (Vendler 1967:99); achievements but not accomplishments "occur at a single moment," i.e., do not have duration (Vendler 1967:103); and, although of secondary importance, accomplishments involve an agent/volition while many achievements do not (Vendler 1967:105f). All three of these are found in other work as well. For example, Dowty (1979) describes the difference between accomplishments and achievements in terms of "temporally consecutive subsidiary changes" (p. 181) and/or a causing event (p. 183) present in the former but not the latter. Process is also the notion chosen by Pustejovsky (1991) to distinguish accomplishments from achievements, and states from activities. Smith (1991), on the other hand, proposes that the relevant characteristic is durativity, i.e., whether a situation takes time (has duration) or occurs in an instant. For example, *write a letter* (accomplishment) usually denotes a situation that takes some time, whereas *recognize someone* (achievement) denotes a situation that happens in an instant. In English, durative predicates are compatible with a duration adverbial such as *for an hour* or with the verb *stop*: √ *Susi stopped writing a letter* but # *Susi stopped recognizing him*.

Following Smith (1991), I choose durativity rather than process or agentivity as the relevant characteristic. I make this choice because durativity is a truly temporal notion which can be clearly defined and easily tested. Agentivity arguably is not a temporal-aspectual notion but a thematic one, having to do with the presence of a volitional, sentient, possibly causing, event participant rather than with the temporal contour of an event. As far as I am aware, authors which mention agentivity do point out that it is not really aspectual (e.g., Vendler 1957, Pustejovsky 1991), and I will disregard agentivity in this study.

I also reject the characteristic of process, for the following reasons. First, process is a mixed notion which has to do with agentivity and causation, thus overlapping with the thematic domain. This is best seen by looking at attempts to define process. For example, Dowty's (1979:109 and 118) definitions in terms of *CAUSE* and *DO* invoke causation and agentivity, respectively, and for Pustejovsky the presence of a process in accomplishments correlates with agentivity rather than with something inherently aspectual (1991:59). Second, it is difficult to come by tests for process which do not interact with agentivity, particularly in German (see Wilhelm 2000), one of the languages studied here. Thus, using the notion of process may not give very clear results. Finally, the characteristic of process, or successive phases, is not always easy to perceive. For example, what is the process component in the accomplishments *wilt* or *decide*? Similarly, many activities do not have a perceptible process, compare *sleep* (Dowty 1979), *enjoy* (Smith 1999), *fall, float*. Because of the difficulty of identifying successive stages, Smith (1999) proposes to formalize this component (which she calls dynamism, but which in my view is indistinguishable from process) in terms of its mapping onto time. In other words, Smith appeals to a temporal definition, a definition in terms of durativity.

In conclusion, process apparently cannot be described, defined, or tested without reference to agentivity/causation or durativity. I therefore choose the simpler and more clearly temporal-aspectual notion of durativity in my study on the grammatization of temporal-aspectual characteristics of predicates. As we shall see in the course of this dissertation, the study of durativity gives clean and interesting results.[2]

Stativity. Finally, although Vendler puts states in a class with achievements, because purportedly they both lack a process and are true of a single

Introduction 5

moment, it has since become clear that states are a class all by themselves. As opposed to nonstative situations, also called events, stative situations have no dynamics—they continue without input of energy, and have no internal temporal structure—they consist of undifferentiated moments. This difference becomes clear when comparing stative *know (French)* and nonstative *walk* or *write a letter*. There is a vast literature on states, types of states, and their semantic and syntactic representation (Carlson 1977, Dowty 1979, Kratzer 1995, Parsons 1990, Smith 1991, to name just a few).

The temporal-aspectual predicate classes and underlying characteristics I thus arrive at are based on Smith (1991) and summarized in (3). Smith calls the predicate classes "situation types," and I will follow this terminology, but sometimes call nonstative situations "events" (Mourelatos 1978, Parsons 1990). Notice that Smith departs from Vendler in making a durativity distinction not only among telic, but also among atelic situations. Activities are atelic and durative, semelfactives are atelic and nondurative. Such a differentiation among atelics is only consistent, and I assume the existence of the situation type "semelfactive" in this dissertation.

(3) Temporal-aspectual classification of predicates, based on Smith (1991)

SITUATION TYPE	STATIVE	DURATIVE	TELIC	ENGLISH EXAMPLES
State	+	+	n/a	*know the answer, own*
Activity	–	+	–	*run, read*
Accomplishment	–	+	+	*build a house, read a book*
Semelfactive	–	–	–	*tap, knock*
Achievement	–	–	+	*find the key, reach the top*

To keep this dissertation manageable, I will put aside states and stativity, and focus on durativity and telicity, which distinguish the different types of nonstative situations from each other. I thus sharpen my research question as follows:

(4) *Revised Research Question*
     How are telicity and durativity grammatized in natural language?

1.3. Grammatization

By "grammatized" I mean that the explanation of some grammatical phenomenon or contrast must require reference to these characteristics, i.e., to telicity or durativity. Thus, I am not primarily interested in how temporal-aspectual characteristics of predicates are represented in lexical or sentential meaning in general, but in which characteristics form the basis of a morphological or a syntactic phenomenon or contrast. In other words, I mean by "grammatical" something that can be seen in the forms of words or phrases of a given language. I will assume the following definition of "grammatization:"

(5) *Grammatization*
A semantic notion/feature evident in a productive morphosyntactic contrast is grammatized.

Here "morphosyntax" is used in a wide sense, referring to either a morphological or a syntactic contrast.[3] The contrast has to be productive, however, i.e., it cannot just be an isolated, irregular or frozen phenomenon. For example, it is sometimes suggested that German has a pair of verbal suffixes *-l/-r* which impart durative, or rather iterative, meaning on a verb, as in *klappern* 'rattle, clatter' < *klappen* 'fold rigid object (lid, door)' (Abraham, p.c., Duden 1984, Flämig 1965). However, it is far from clear what the meaning of these suffixes is, or whether they are productive synchronically. As to meaning, *-l/-r* have a range of semantic effects, of which durative/iterative meaning is only one. For example, in many cases, they have more of a diminutive meaning (*lächeln* 'smile' < *lachen* 'laugh,' *hüsteln* 'give a little cough' < *husten* 'cough'), or no clearly identifiable meaning at all: *frömmeln* 'be sanctimonious' < *fromm* 'pious' (adj.). As to productivity, many members of the small set of verbs with *-l* or *-r* have no corresponding base form synchronically, e.g., *stolpern* 'stumble,' *wackeln* 'be wobbly, loose.' Suffixation with *-l/-r* is thus not an instance of a productive morphosyntactic contrast, and cannot be said to grammatize durativity (or iterativity).

A much better example of a productive morphosyntactic contrast reflecting a semantic notion, and thus of grammatization, is tense inflection. For example, German *-te* is a productive suffix and transparently marks a past tense interpretation. But it is not only inflectional processes that can constitute productive morphosyntactic contrasts; certain types of word formation or derivation are also productive. Of course, the distribution of a derivational process is usually more restricted than that of an inflectional process, but it can still be considered a productive process if it is associated consistently with a specific meaning and if new words are formed with it (e.g., Bauer 2001).

Finally, it should be noted that my concept of grammatization is not to be confused with *grammaticalization*, which refers to the development of a lexical element into a grammatical element through semantic bleaching (e.g., Lehmann 1982, Traugott and Heine 1991, Bybee et al 1994). My account is synchronic, not diachronic. However, the interest in grammatically relevant aspects of meaning has a long tradition (Dowty 1979, Bierwisch 1983, Pinker 1989, Jackendoff 1990, Smith 1991, Pustejovsky 1995, Levin and Rappaport Hovav 1995, Mohanan and Wee 1999, etc.). My research stands in this tradition, and more generally, in the tradition of research on the (morpho-)syntax/semantics interface.

Now, why is the grammatization criterion important? In other words, why do I focus on the grammatization of telicity and durativity? There are two reasons.

First, the philosophical, and even the semantic characterization of a predicate must be constrained in some way, because it is in principle infinite, i.e., one can come up with an ever more detailed list of the possible meanings of a predicate. Looking to the characteristics of a situation denoted by a predicate will not help, because those are also infinite. As Klein (1994:76) writes, a situation has "many temporal features [. . .]. It may be short or long, may include many subactivities or substates, some of them overlapping, others sequential, etc." For this reason, most linguists try to keep the meaning, or lexical content, of a predicate as general and minimal as possible. For example, Klein (1994) proposes the following:

(6) Maxim of minimality: (Klein 1994:75)
    Put as little as possible into the lexical content!

In the structuralist tradition, on which most of modern linguistics is based, there is a strong criterion for what should be included in the characterization of a linguistic entity, be it phonological, morphological or semantic: to be included, a feature or notion must in some way be responsible for a contrast with another linguistic entity. For example, simplifying somewhat, although [±anterior] is part of the universal inventory of phonological features, it is not part of the feature inventory of those languages which do not have a contrast between dental/alveolar (= [+anterior]) and alveopalatal (= [-anterior]) sounds. The type of contrast I am using as a criterion is a grammatical contrast. Grammatical contrasts are more tangible and easier to discover than lexicosemantic contrasts, and thus are more likely to lead to satisfactory results.

The second reason for using the grammatization criterion is even more important: if a semantic notion is to be used as a grammatical category, the evidence must also be grammatical. As discussed in section 1.1, this evidence is often lacking or only based on English. And yet many linguists assume that durativity and telicity, or the verb classes these two notions yield, are grammatized universally (e.g., Dowty 1979, Ehrich 1992, Rapp 1997a,b, Levin and Rappaport Hovav 1998, Ramchand 2002). On the other hand, some linguists dispute the claim that durativity is a linguistically relevant notion at all. For example, Verkuyl (1989), Tenny (1994), and Klein (1994) dismiss durativity as extra-linguistic. Again, the grammatization criterion puts this debate in perspective. Perhaps durativity is a semantic universal, but not universally grammatized. In fact, this is the position I will argue for in this dissertation.

1.4 Proposal

My answer to the question how telicity and durativity are grammatized in natural language is as follows:

(7) *Preliminary Grammatization Hypothesis*

> If *durativity* is grammatized, it is grammatized in the IP domain
>
> (through viewpoint aspect).
>
> If *telicity* is grammatized, it is grammatized in the VP domain.

This hypothesis makes two important claims. First, it claims that telicity and durativity are not universally grammatized. Such a claim may seem surprising for telicity, since other than in the work of Smith (1991, 1996), telicity is thought to be a universal category. However, in Chapter Three I will give an example of a language (related to Navajo, which Smith examined) in which telicity is not grammatized. My dissertation supports Smith's view that the grammatization of telicity and durativity may vary across languages. I predict that some languages grammatize both notions, some grammatize only one of the two, and some grammatize neither (see Chapter Six). Such a view also sheds considerable light on the debate about the status of durativity: durativity is a universal linguistic entity on the *semantic* level, but it is not *grammatized* in every language.

This is reminiscent of the difference between phonetics and phonology. For example, although Pawnee contains alveolar and palatal consonants phonetically, the difference between them is not contrastive (Parks 1976). Therefore (simplifying somewhat), the feature [±anterior] is not part of the representation of phonemes in Pawnee, even though it must be part of the phonetics.[4] Similarly, durativity may be present semantically but not grammatically in a language. Thus, just as the articulatory feature [±anterior] must be part of UG to account for the range of possible human language sounds, the semantic feature of durativity must also be a UG determined option. And just as [±anterior] is not part of the phonology of every language, so durativity is not part of the morphosyntax of every language.

The second important claim made in (7) concerns the locus of grammatization. Just like [±anterior], durativity has a certain place in the grammar. Assuming a feature-geometric model, [±anterior] is a minor place feature, dependent on the coronal place node, which in turn depends on the place node. Likewise, durativity has a certain position in the grammar. (7) says that durativity can only be grammatized through viewpoint aspect, an inflectional category represented in IP. In other words, durativity is only associated with a grammatical contrast in a language which has grammatical viewpoint aspect.

Concerning telicity, (7) says that the place of telicity in the grammar is the VP. This will be shown in Chapters Four and Six.

2. METHOD

The hypothesis in (7) is based on the study of telicity and durativity in two genetically and typologically very different languages, German and Dëne Sųłiné (Chipewyan; Dëne for short), a Northern Athapaskan language. In both languages, I collected a number of verbs (50 in Dëne and 85 in German) and tested them for durative and telic meaning (see Appendices One and Two). The German test results reflect primarily my own native speaker judgements, but in cases where I was uncertain they were doublechecked with other speakers. For Dëne Sųłiné, I worked mainly with three native speakers, from whom I first elicited verb paradigms and then, based on Dëne Sųłiné examples, elicited judgements on telicity and durativity tests for each verb. The tests used for German and Dëne Sųłiné are discussed in the respective chapters.

I next examined whether any morphosyntactic facts corresponded to the presence vs. absence of durativity, and likewise with telicity. Chapter Two looks at durativity and Chapter Three at telicity in Dëne; Chapter Four discusses telicity and Chapter Five durativity in German.

3. FINDINGS: PREVIEW

What I found was that in Dëne Sųłiné, morphosyntactic facts correlate with durativity but not telicity, while in German the opposite is the case: morphosyntactic facts correlate with telicity but not with durativity. Thus, Dëne Sųłiné grammatizes durativity but not telicity, whereas German grammatizes telicity but not durativity.

My results strongly suggest a universal pattern. This is expressed in (7). In Chapter Six, I provide a conceptual motivation for the universality of this grammatization pattern. Briefly, I argue as follows: since durativity is a temporal characteristic of a situation, it must be expressed in a grammatical domain dedicated to the temporal meaning of situations. This is viewpoint aspect, or, in generative syntactic terms, IP (AspP, to be more precise). Next, since telicity is not in fact a temporal notion but is rather a force-dynamic one, affecting argument structure, it must be grammatized in an atemporal projection in which arguments are merged: VP. My reasoning here parallels that in phonology: [±anterior] necessarily is a dependent of the place node, and more specifically of the coronal place node, because it defines a tongue position with respect to the coronal area, while a feature like [spread glottis] must hang from the laryngeal node, since it specifies something about the larynx articulator.

My findings and their implications are discussed in Chapter Six.

4. THEORETICAL ASSUMPTIONS

Here I spell out the main theoretical assumptions and biases underlying my research, as far as I am aware of them. This discussion also provides the necessary background knowledge for the following chapters.

4.1. Temporal-Aspectual Meaning

My examination of the grammatization of durativity and telicity assumes a certain semantic organization of temporal-aspectual meaning in natural language. I follow influential linguistic work in dividing temporal-aspectual meaning into three domains or levels: tense, viewpoint aspect, and situation type (Comrie 1976, 1985, Smith 1991, Klein 1994, etc.).

Introduction

4.1.1. Three Levels of Temporal-Aspectual Meaning

The division of temporal-aspectual meaning into tense and aspect is well-established. Tense temporally locates an event on a time line, usually with respect to the time at which a sentence is uttered (time of utterance); it is a deictic category. Aspect, on the other hand, is concerned with the internal temporal contour of a situation (Comrie 1976, 1985). For example, the difference between *Susi is singing* and *Susi was singing* is one of tense: in the first example, the singing event is described as taking place at the time of utterance; the singing event in the second sentence is described as having taken place before the time of utterance. The former sentence has present tense meaning, the latter has past tense meaning, which here corresponds to a present vs. past form of the auxiliary *be*.

Aspectual meaning does not locate a situation with respect to the time of utterance; it is not a deictic category. The meaning difference between *Susi was singing* and *Susi sang* is one of aspect. In the former example, the situation is "viewed from within" and as ongoing. In the latter, the situation is viewed from the outside, in its totality (Comrie 1976, Smith 1991). This is the difference between an imperfective and a perfective aspectual viewpoint, expressed by a progressive versus a simple verb form in English. The idea of viewing a situation from different perspectives, or of viewing different portions of a situation (entire situation, versus internal portions), is a helpful metaphor for this type of aspectual meaning. Following Smith (1991), I call this type of aspectual meaning viewpoint aspect.

However, there is a second level of aspectual meaning, namely *situation type*.[5] It refers to the temporal-aspectual structure of the situation itself, and is the level upon which viewpoint aspect operates. As discussed above, I follow Smith (1991) in assuming that there are five situation types (states, activities, semelfactives, accomplishments, achievements), which are based on the temporal-aspectual notions of stativity, durativity and telicity. For example, *sing* denotes an activity situation (nonstative, durative, atelic), *die* denotes an achievement situation (nonstative, nondurative, telic). It is well established that situation type is not determined by the verb alone, but that at least the internal arguments also affect it. For example, *write* and *run* are atelic but *write a letter* and *run into the house* are telic. Smith calls the linguistic unit which realizes situation type a "verb constellation," but differs from me in including subjects/external arguments as well. The role of objects and subjects will be taken up in Chapter Four, section 2.2.

It is not always clear in the literature that there are two levels of aspectual meaning; for example, in much of the traditional literature on aspect in German, telic situations are called "perfective" and atelic situations are called "imperfective" (see Chapter Five for discussion and references). I follow here Smith (1991), who argues explicitly and convincingly that aspectual meaning is composed of the two independent, but interacting levels of viewpoint and situation type.

4.1.2. Formal Semantic Representations

Tense and viewpoint aspect. Much of the recent literature assumes that both tense and viewpoint aspect relate times, where times are sets of adjacent time points (Smith 1991, Klein 1994, Giorgi and Pianesi 1998, Kratzer 1998, Demirdache and Uribe-Etxebarria 2000, Musan 2002). Viewpoint aspect relates a "reference time" to the time of the situation. The reference time corresponds to the "point of view" used in the aspect metaphor. It is the time that adverbials and adverbial clauses often specify, for instance, in (8) and (9) below. Following Klein (1994), I will call the reference time "topic time" or "TT" and the time of the situation "situation time" or "TSit." Imperfective (/progressive) viewpoint, as in *Susi was singing*, (properly) includes TT in TSit; perfective viewpoint, as in *Susi sang*, includes TSit in TT. This successfully formalizes the intuition that the event is viewed from within in the imperfective, and from outside or in its totality in the perfective.[6]

Tense is defined as relating the "reference time" (topic time, TT) to a "privileged point or interval of time" (Chung and Timberlake 1985:203), usually the time of utterance (TU).[7] The most common relations for tense meanings are "TT precedes TU" (past tense), "TT follows TU" (future tense) and "TT overlaps TU" (present tense).

(8) and (9) illustrate two possible interactions of viewpoint aspect and tense:

(8) imperfective viewpoint and past tense: English past progressive
Susi was writing a letter (when I arrived).

(8') $TT \subset TSit \ \& \ TT < TU$

$----\{_{TSit}----[_{TT}--]----\}------[_{TU}---]------>$

(9) perfective viewpoint and future tense: English simple future
Susi will write the letter tomorrow.

(9') $TSit \subseteq TT \ \& \ TU < TT$

$----[_{TU}--]------[_{TT}-\{_{TSit}-------\}-]-------->$

In many languages, a given morphological form expresses a combination of a viewpoint and a tense meaning. For example, the English simple past tense (as in *Susi wrote a letter*) expresses not only past tense, but also perfective viewpoint: TSit ⊆ TT & TT < TU (see Kratzer 1998, and also the complex definitions of the English "tenses" in Reichenbach 1947). Calling such forms "tenses," as is often done in Indo-European languages, is in effect a misnomer. This highlights the importance of distinguishing between the name of a linguistic form and the name of a semantic concept. From now on, I will use capital letters for language-specific *forms* (e.g., English Simple Past) and lower-case letters for non-language specific temporal-aspectual meanings (e.g., present tense, imperfective viewpoint).

Situation type. The formal representation of situation type is not as straightforward as the representation of tense and viewpoint; there are several partially overlapping approaches. I will briefly sketch these in broad terms. The first way of representing situations has its roots in philosophy and model-theoretic semantics. Davidson (1966) argued that situations, or "events," should be treated as referential entities in the logical description of sentences, and he introduced the variable *e* to do so. This proposal has been adopted and refined in important semantic work on situations (Higginbotham 1985, Parsons 1990, Kratzer 1995, 1996). (11) illustrates the logical form of a simple sentence on this approach (abstracting away from tense and viewpoint aspect).

(10) *Susi wrote a letter.*

(11) ∃e [write(e) & Agent(e, Susi) & Theme(e, a letter)]

(11') "There is an event of writing whose agent is Susi and whose theme is a letter."

Some authors propose differentiating between different kinds of situations and use different variables for these. Most notably, Parsons (1990) assumes a basic semantic distinction between *states* and *events*, and Kratzer (1995) argues that permanent, or individual-level, state predicates differ from predicates denoting other types of situations (including nonpermanent, or stage-level, states) in having no event argument at all in the semantics. These types of distinctions open the door to making even more distinctions among predicates, for example, by representing all of the Vendler or Smith classes with different variables. Kratzer (1996:122) speculates about the different situation types, which she calls "Aktionsarten": "I'd like to think of them as originating from selectional restrictions for the Event Argument [. . .]. Event Arguments may be restricted to actions, states, events proper, and so on. An action predicate like *wash the clothes*, then, expresses a partial function that is only defined for actions." However, as far as I am aware, this idea has not been taken up, and the only distinctions widely used are those between states and events, and/or between stage-level and individual-level predicates. Moreover, events (and states) are treated as atomic entities; they are not decomposed into sub-events or other components.

The one exception to this is that I am aware of is Pustejovsky (1991, 1995). Pustejovsky assumes that sentences may denote one of three types of events: states, processes and transitions. Of these, the latter two are themselves composed of events: processes consist of "a sequence of events identifying the same semantic expression;" a transition is defined as "an event identifying a semantic expression, which is evaluated relative to its opposition" (Pustejovsky 1991:56), i.e., a transition minimally denotes a change of state, such as from the door's state of 'not closed' to the state of 'closed' in *The door closed*. We thus see that not only the difference between states and events, but also the difference between activities (processes) and telic situations (accomplishment or achievement) finds formal expression. However, it is unclear how much formal status the difference between accomplishments and achievements (or between activities and semelfactives) has in this approach.

An explicit representation of all five situation types is found in Smith (1991), a second semantic approach. While Smith assumes that all sentences license a Davidsonian event or state entity (represented as e), she also explicitly specifies in the formal semantic representation for each event argument its situation type. The situation type is a shorthand for certain intensional properties of the respective e. These properties are paraphrased in (12) below (assume that a situation S obtains at an interval I made up of time points t; see Smith 1991:169–171 for a more explicit statement of these properties):

(12) Activity: I includes more than one t; the final t is arbitrary

   Semelfactive: I includes only one t

   Accomplishment: I includes more than one t; the final t is natural; a resultant state of S obtains (and S does not obtain) at the time point following the final $t \in I$

   Achievement: I includes only one t; a resultant state of S obtains (and S does not obtain) at the time point following the final $t \in I$

State: I includes more than one t; the time at which the change into the state occurs precedes t; the time at which the change out of the state occurs follows t

We can see that durativity corresponds to the presence of more than one time point in I, and that telicity is defined via a resultant state which obtains after the situation has ended. The final t ∈ I of telic situations is "natural" in that the change into the resultant state occurs (or culminates) there. As we shall see below, the change of state property of telic situations is also represented in predicate decomposition approaches.

Smith points out that some aspectual properties, most notably telicity, "have truth-conditional force," while others "shape presentation" (Smith 1991:192), but that both are part of the meaning of a discourse and therefore should be represented in a semantic approach to aspect. Smith's approach is couched in Discourse Representation Theory.

A third semantic approach assumes that events are atomic entities in the semantics (but see Ramchand 1997, Krifka 1998 for extensions) and focuses on the different part structures of these events. It turns out that telic and atelic situations have different part structures, as reflected in the different truth-conditional entailment characteristics of telic and atelic predicates (e.g., Bach 1981, 1986, Krifka 1989, 1992). To illustrate: a statement like *Susi sang from 3 to 4 o'clock* entails that for any time between 3 and 4 o'clock Susi sang, but such an entailment does not hold for telic predicates like *Susi wrote a letter from 3 to 4 o'clock* (e.g., Vendler 1967, Dowty 1979). Informally, we can say that atelic situations are homogeneous: they consist (to a certain extent) of situations of the same kind. Telic predicates, on the other hand, do not consist of "smaller" events of the same kind. Krifka (1992) defines this difference in terms of how a predicate refers: a predicate has "cumulative reference" if the joining of two events denoted by it constitutes another event denoted by the same predicate. For example, two events denoted by *sing* constitute together an event denoted by *sing*. A predicate has "quantized reference" if no proper part of the event that it denotes may also be denoted by the same predicate. For example, no proper part of the event denoted by *write a letter* constitutes an event which can be denoted by *write a letter*.[8]

Now, as pointed out by Smith (1999), it is important to realize that this mereological approach characterizes not only the difference between telic and atelic predicates, but is more general than that. For example, activities (atelic) explicitly temporally limited by an adverbial such as *for 2 hours* also have quantized reference: no proper part the event denoted by *She worked for 2 hours* constitutes an event which can also be referred to by *She worked for*

2 hours. And accomplishments (telic) in a progressive or imperfective viewpoint have cumulative reference: informally, the situation denoted by *She was writing a letter* does contain "smaller parts" of the same kind. Following Depraetere (1995), Smith draws a distinction between "bounded" situations (which have quantized reference) and "unbounded" situations (which have cumulative reference) in addition to the telicity distinction. While telic situations are often bounded, and atelic situations often unbounded, boundedness and telicity are not interchangeable, as the above examples show.

The approaches discussed so far are semantic ones. They do not say anything about the interaction of telicity—and durativity, to the extent that this characteristic is represented—with the morphosyntax. I now turn to approaches which do make claims about the grammatization of telicity and durativity as well.

Predicate decomposition approaches, which have their roots in Generative Semantics, are concerned with those elements of lexical meaning which are grammatically (morphosyntactically) relevant. Grammatically relevant aspectual meaning is represented in terms of subsituations[9] and various operations on these (Dowty 1979, Jackendoff 1990, Pinker 1989, Rapp 1997a,b, Rappaport Hovav and Levin 1998). The operations are usually expressed as sublexical predicates like *BECOME* (a change of state) and *CAUSE* (an event/state causing another event/state). For example, telic situations are represented as a change into a state and thus consist of at least one subsituation. Thus, *die* is represented as something like *BECOME dead(x)*. Each subsituation has at least one semantic argument, and these arguments are associated with syntactic arguments according to various linking principles; thus, there is a connection between temporal-aspectual meaning and argument structure. Such an approach works very well to represent stativity and telicity; it works less well to represent durativity, although there are some attempts, e.g., Rapp (1997a,b), who distinguishes between nondurative *BECOME* and durative *DEV* (from "develop"). It is also difficult to represent nonstative situations which are not telic, i.e., the basic difference between activities and semelfactives. Usually a predicate like *ACT* or *DO* is used for activities, but how to define this predicate is less clear (see extensive discussion in Dowty 1979).

Pustejovsky (1991, 1995), which was discussed earlier, presents a hybrid between predicate decomposition and model-theoretic approaches. He makes use of the insight of the former that certain events or situations consist of subsituations. Thus, telic situations ("transitions") are represented as change of state, with two subsituations. As far as I can tell, "state" and "process" are his most important subsituations. On the other hand, Pustejovsky also treats certain (sub)situations as Davidsonian referential entities:

both states and processes are (distinct) arguments in the predicate logical representation of sentences.

Finally, claims about the grammatization of telicity and durativity are most direct in syntactic approaches to situation type. Travis (1991, 1994), Borer (1994, 2004), Kratzer (2004), Ramchand (1997), and Ritter and Rosen (1998, 2000) have proposed that a language may have an extra functional projection which is responsible for the telic interpretation of a sentence. This projection contains a telicity and/or an objective case feature which must be checked by movement of the direct internal argument. Going even further in reducing the lexical burden, Butt and Ramchand (2001) and Ramchand (2002) propose expressing the information represented in predicate decomposition theories in the syntax. They argue that a verb's meaning is derived from syntactic projections corresponding to each of the three predicates *CAUSE*, *DO*, and *BECOME*. For example, a telic predicate contains all three projections, an atelic predicate lacks the projection indicating change of state/resultativity.

We thus see that there are a variety of formal approaches to situation type. Some are strictly semantic, but others lie at the syntax-semantics interface or are even primarily syntactic. For the purposes of this study, I am making no assumptions about a (possible) syntactic representation of telicity and durativity, or about the nature of the mapping from telic or durative meaning to morphosyntax, since these questions are precisely the topic of my study: by examining the grammatization of telicity and durativity in two very different languages, I hope to gain new insight into the relationship between semantics and syntax. This will be taken up in Chapter Six.

I do, however, make certain assumptions on the *semantics* of durativity and telicity. I assume that durative predicates denote situations which map to time intervals which consist of more than one time point. For telicity, I assume a "narrow" definition: telic predicates not only have quantized reference; in addition telic predicates denote a change from one state into a different, resultant state. This change of state marks the "inherent" or "natural" endpoint which distinguishes telic from (externally) "bounded" predicates.

4.2. *Syntax, Morphology, and the Lexicon*

I assume a clause structure which is consistent with current Minimalism/Principles and Parameters Theory (Chomsky 1995, 2000; see also Chapter Six). All internal arguments of the verb are merged inside the VP. A projection vP immediately dominates VP. Following Kratzer (1996), I assume that vP introduces the external argument of the verb (i.e., the subject argument) and the predicate's event argument. VP and vP together constitute what I shall call the VP-domain (this corresponds to a phase in Chomsky 2000). Finally, I assume that above vP, there are functional projections for tense and other verbal inflections. I shall call these functional projections the IP domain.

I depart from the Minimalist framework in my assumptions about the relation between syntax, morphology, and the lexicon. Generative syntax is in essence a lexicalist theory (Chomsky 1970), with word formation occurring presyntactically in the lexicon, and, at least in the Minimalist Program, inflectional morphology happening presyntactically as well. I agree in principle with the assumption that morphology (word formation, inflection) and syntax are separate components. In particular, I am convinced by the arguments put forward in Anderson (1992), Zwicky (1985, 1992), and others that syntactic movement of morphemes (e.g., Lieber 1992, Baker 1988) is unable to account for the intricate and frequently opaque morphological processes occurring in natural language. Indeed, the concept of a morpheme as an isolatable, meaning- or function-carrying "piece" of language which combines with other "pieces" of language seems somewhat dubious, particularly in light of rich systems of synthetic morphology. For these reasons, I am sympathetic to a view of the grammar which separates the morphological from the syntactic component.

However, both Dëne and German pose challenges to a strict lexicalist hypothesis, according to which "words" are formed in the lexicon and "phrases" are formed in the syntax (DiSciullo and Williams 1987). Dëne, like all Athapaskan languages, is polysynthetic. Traditionally, the verb is described as consisting of a stem and many prefixes, with the prefix order regulated by a template (e.g., Young and Morgan 1987, Kari 1989, Rice 1989, Cook 2004). The challenge posed by the Dëne/Athapaskan verb is that lexical-derivational elements are interspersed with inflectional elements. There is no ordering of inflection outside of derivation. Moreover, certain elements, called "thematic" in the traditional Athapaskan literature, cannot even be considered (transparently) derivational. They simply must be part of the lexical entry of the verb (the "verb theme"), which is thus discontinuous, at least on the surface. For example, the lexical entry for 'pick objects (e.g., berries)' is *ʔu–ne–Ø–ye/–yá*, with inflectional elements occurring between *ne*–and the imperfective/perfective stems –*ye/–yá*. Neither the prefixes *ʔu*–and *ne*– nor the stems have an independent meaning synchronically, and the fact that the voice/valence morpheme is Ø (rather than *ł*–, *l*–, or *d*–) is unpredictable and thus must also be listed in the lexicon. As Rice (2000) suggests, many lexical entries for verbs resemble much more an English idiom like *kick the bucket* than a simple English verb like *die*.[10]

German, like other Germanic languages, contains so-called particle verbs, which will be the object of study in Chapters Four and Five. They consist of a base verb preceded by a particle, e.g., *aus-trinken* 'drink up, finish' which literally is 'out-drink.' Crucially, particle verbs have characteristics of words as well as of phrases. Particles can be separated from the base verb in the syntax as well as by some morphemes, as shown in (13), and the meaning of a particle verb often is not completely transparent, as, for example, in *umbringen* 'kill,' lit. 'over-bring.'

(13) a. Susi *trinkt* den Kaffee *aus*.
 Susi drinks the coffee out
 'Susi is finishing the coffee.'
 b. *ausgetrunken* (perfect participle form)
 aus-ge-trunken
 out-perfect participle-drunk

For these reasons, there exists a debate about the status of particle verbs: are they formed in the lexicon/morphology or in the syntax? See, for example, Neeleman and Weerman 1993, Stiebels and Wunderlich 1994, Stiebels 1996 for a lexical-morphological view, and Hoekstra 1988, Wurmbrand 1998 for a syntactic view.

It seems that there are two ways out of problems such as those presented by Dëne and German complex verbs. One can abandon the assumption that the lexicon is only the domain of "words," and permit phrasal constructions to be listed in the lexicon as well (e.g., Goldberg 1995, Jackendoff 1997, Booij 2002a,b). Or one can abandon the assumption that the lexicon is a single, presyntactic component, as is done in Distributed Morphology (Halle and Marantz 1993, Marantz 1997, Harley and Noyer 1999). On this view, the heads which the syntax merges are either abstract roots or bundles of grammatical features (component 1 of the traditional lexicon). Phonological content ("vocabulary items," component 2), as well as meaning ("encyclopedia," component 3), are associated with roots and feature bundles post-syntactically ("late insertion"). Whether the output of a structure is a morphological word or a syntactic phrase (consisting of several morphological words) depends on which vocabulary items best match that structure or its feature combination. Nontransparent meaning is independent of lexical word status, it is instead restricted to certain structurally defined domains. I do not have an empirical or conceptual preference for either of these two solutions. I assume the Distributed Morphology (DM) approach here simply because it fits better with minimalist syntax, and because an account of German particle verbs has been worked out in this approach (Zeller 2001).[11] The respective Dëne and German structures will be introduced in Chapters Two (Dëne) and Four (German) and taken up again briefly in Chapter Six. However, my key findings are not dependent on a certain view of the syntax-morphology-lexicon interface.

5. OUTLINE

Chapters Two and Three examine the grammatization of durativity and telicity in Dëne. In Chapter Two, I argue that durativity is grammatized through (imperfective) viewpoint aspect in Dëne. In Chapter Three, I show that telicity is not grammatized at all. Chapter Two also contains a basic introduction to Dëne, and a detailed examination of the semantics and pragmatics of the Dëne viewpoints. Chapter Three includes a review of the literature on situation type, and the controversy on the status of telicity in Athapaskan. In Chapter Four, I turn to German and show the pervasive grammatization of telicity in this language. This pulls together insights scattered throughout the German literature; I also present, as a new contribution, an examination of the effect of particle verb formation on telicity. Chapter Five examines the grammatization of durativity in German. I provide evidence from particle verb formation, as well as from the tense system of the language, that durativity is not grammatized. Chapter Six interprets my findings in terms of the grammatization hypothesis presented in (7) above. I give a motivation of the patterns observed in the two languages, explore in detail the notion of "grammatization," and discuss the impact of my findings on linguistic theories of temporal-aspectual characteristics of predicates. Appendix One gives the Dëne data and Appendix Two the German data on which my arguments are based.

Part I
Dëne Sųłiné

Two things will emerge in my examination of Dëne Sųłiné (Chipweyan; Dëne for short): first, telicity is elusive in this language, and only durativity is grammatized; second, this pattern is intricately linked to the viewpoint aspect system of the language. Throughout my fieldwork, I have been struck by the pervasiveness of viewpoint aspect in Dëne, and by how the inescapable viewpoints make it rather difficult, if not impossible, to "get at" certain situation type aspectual notions, most notably telicity.

Dëne has two viewpoints, the Imperfective and the Perfective. Unless a verb is in irrealis mode, it usually occurs in either Imperfective or Perfective form.[1] The Imperfective has durative force, and therefore only verbs denoting durative situation types (states, activities and accomplishments, but not achievements and semelfactives) are felicitous in the Imperfective. I propose that durativity is grammatized through the Imperfective viewpoint.

Next, the Perfective viewpoint has a strongly completive meaning: it entails that a situation is completed and over. I argue that through its completive meaning, the Dëne Perfective overlaps considerably with telicity. Not only has it the same discourse function that telicity has in languages without grammatical viewpoint aspects, it also suggests that an event has been completed, something that is usually suggested by telic meaning. As a consequence, recourse to telicity is unnecessary in Dëne in most circumstances. The Perfective viewpoint, I propose, eliminates the need to grammatize the notion of telicity. Telicity is all but obscured in the language.

Now, it is important to recall that I am not claiming that telicity, or certain situation types, cannot be expressed *semantically* in Dëne. Indeed, the proposed universal situation types resulting from the underlying notions of telicity, durativity and stativity can largely be distinguished in the language through semantic aspectual tests. However, I will argue that telicity (and thus situation type distinctions based on telicity) is not part of the basic organization of the *grammar* of Dëne. Telicity does not underlie morphosyntactic contrasts in Dëne. Thus, while both semantic-aspectual and morpho-lexical categories exist in Dëne, they do not correlate in terms of telicity.

In the literature on Athapaskan languages, a variety of claims have been put forward about the relationship between aspect and grammar. Most studies have developed language-specific morphological and lexical verb classes and assigned them aspectual labels (e.g., Kari 1979 for Ahtna, Axelrod 1993 for Koyukon). These careful studies usually do not attempt to match the language-specific aspectual classes found with proposed universal aspectual classes, and do not contain explicit semantic evidence.

Those which do attempt a connection to current aspectual theory come to varying conclusions. For example, Smith (1991, 1996) argues that in Navajo telicity is not grammatized, while Midgette (1996) comes to the opposite conclusion for the same language. Both authors utilize semantic as well as morphosyntactic evidence, but they weigh this evidence differently. Importantly, they differ in the interpretation of viewpoint aspectual facts, which I claim are at the heart of understanding aspect, at least in Dëne.

Two recent studies, Bortolin (1998) and Rice (2000), propose that basic verbal morphology found in Dëne and Slave, respectively, encodes the five situation types. These studies thus argue for a grammatization of all situation types in Athapaskan, including telicity. However, the additional observations made in my examination of Dëne point to a need to review the conclusions arrived at by Rice and Bortolin.

A careful examination of more than prototypical members of each class, utilizing morphological as well as semantic diagnostics, reveals that the proposed correlation between morphology and situation aspect does not hold in Dëne. It is possible to classify Dëne verbs based on semantic situation type classes and based on morphology, but the classes simply do not overlap enough to justify a grammatical correlation between them. More precisely, there is no correlation between morphology and telic situation types.

My discussion of Dëne comprises the next two chapters. In Chapter Two, after a brief introduction to Dëne, I present the viewpoint aspects and their central role in the grammatization (or nongrammatization) of aspectual notions, particularly durativity, in the language. In Chapter Three, I focus on telicity in Dëne. Comparing semantic and morphological patterns, I show that the typical Athapaskan morphology-based verb classes, as far as they exist, do not correlate with telicity in Dëne. Instead, Dëne has some finer subsituation aspectual categories which serve to complement the very general distinctions made by the two viewpoints.

Chapter Two
Viewpoint Aspect and Its Influence on Situation Type in Dëne

In this chapter I present evidence from Dëne for my central idea that viewpoint aspect influences what kinds of situation aspectual distinctions are found in a language. We will see that durativity is grammatized through the Imperfective viewpoint, and that the Perfective viewpoint, which has completive force in Dëne, fulfills many of the functions which telicity has in other languages.

1. INTRODUCTION TO DËNE SŲŁINÉ

1.1. Geographic and Genetic Information

Dëne Sųłiné belongs to the Northern branch of the Athapaskan language family and is spoken in northwestern Canada. The Dëne territory stretches from the southern shore of the Great Slave Lake (Northwest Territories) east to Churchill, Manitoba and south to central Alberta/Saskatchewan. The map on the next page shows the general Dëne (= Chipewyan) area, as well as surrounding languages. Of these, Sarsi (or Tsúut'ína), Beaver, Slavey, Dogrib and all the languages northeast of these (except Inupiatun) also belong into the Northern Athapaskan branch.

Dëne is estimated to have about 15,000 speakers altogether (Cook, p.c.)[2], and children are still acquiring the language (Rice and Wood 2002). My fieldwork was conducted at Cold Lake First Nations around Cold Lake, Alberta, a community south of the southern tip of the triangle formed by Chipewyan on the map, and somewhat isolated from other Dëne and Athapaskan communities. Perhaps partly due to this isolation, the Cold Lake dialect is very conservative with a particularly rich morphology.

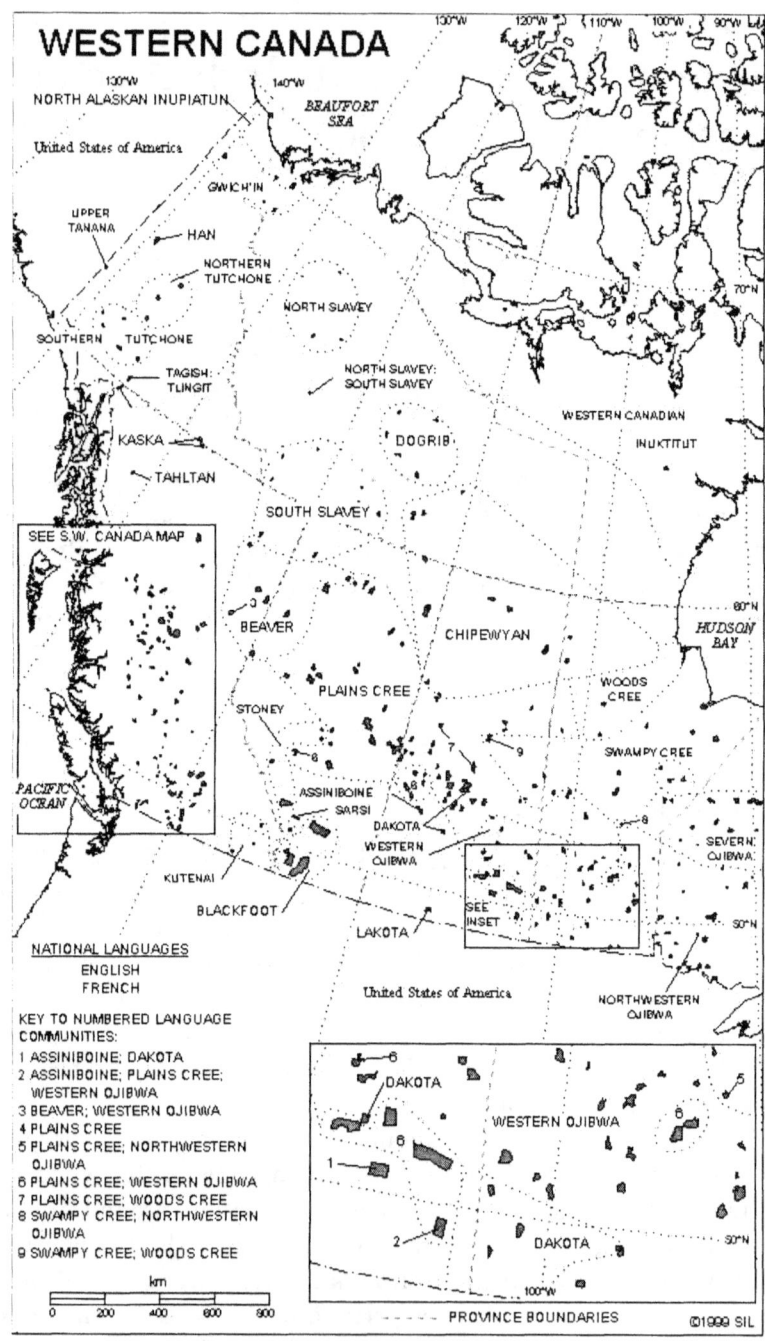

Map 1. Indigenous Languages of Western Canada. Source: *http://www.ethnologue.com*

Cold Lake First Nations numbers about 2,100 members; almost 1,200 of these live on-reserve (Government of Alberta 2004). Less than 10% are speakers of Dëne, and the youngest speakers are in their forties (Rice and Wood 2002). The Cold Lake variety of Dëne seems moribund and is in urgent need of documentation.

The data presented in this dissertation were obtained in interviews with five native speakers of the language (whose ages ranged from the mid-forties to early eighties), often in sessions with two, sometimes with three speakers present. Data from one-on-one sessions were doublechecked in subsequent sessions. The majority of the aspectual data were obtained in Dëne-English or Dëne-Dëne elicitation. Speakers would check Dëne sentences suggested by me for grammaticality/acceptability, interpretation, and better alternatives, and give English translations.

The following tables show the phonemes of Dëne in orthographical symbols, which are also used in this book. Where these symbols are not self-explanatory, the IPA symbol is given underneath. The reader should take care to note that voiced stop symbols represent plain (i.e., unaspirated) *voiceless* stop phonemes, which is the convention in Athapaskan phonology. Also, Dëne is a tone language, distinguishing between high and low tone. In the orthography, high tone is marked with an acute accent above the vowel, e.g., *tsá* 'beaver.'

Table 1. (Cold Lake) Dëne consonants (following Cook, 2004)								
	labial	dental	lateral	inter-dental	alveolar	alveo-palatal	velar	glottal
plain vl. stops	b	d	dl	ddh /dð/	dz	j /dʒ/	g	
aspirated stops		t	tł	tth /tθ/	ts	ch /tʃ/	k	
glottalized stops		t'	tł'	tth' /tθ'/	ts'	ch' /tʃ'/	k'	ʔ
vl. continuants			ł /ɬ/	th /θ/	s	sh /ʃ/	x	h
vcd. continuants	w	(r)	l	dh /ð/	z	zh, y /ʒ ~ j/	gh /ɣ/	
sonorants	m	n						

Table 2. (Cold Lake) Dëne vowels (following Cook, 2004)

Note: nasality is indicated by a cedille, e.g., ą.

	front	central	back
high	i, į		u, ų
mid	e, ę		o, ǫ
reduced		ë /ə/	
low		a, ą /a/	

I will now offer a very short structural description of the language. For more detailed grammatical descriptions of Dëne, see Li (1946) and Cook (2004), see also Rice (1989) for the description of a closely related language, Slave, and Rice (2000) for an account of the structure of the Athapaskan verb.

1.2 Structural Sketch

Dëne is an SOV and head-final language. The verb bears the majority of the grammatical information of a sentence. A sentence is complete without NPs[3]; the richly inflected verb on its own may constitute a sentence. However, isolated sentences usually include full NPs and/or PPs. Nouns and postpositions may show pronominal inflection for the possessor and the object, respectively.

The Dëne verb has a complex structure consisting of a stem (at the right edge) and various prefixes. The easiest way to represent the verb is in the form of a template, i.e., a grid of ordered morpheme positions. I give such a template in table 3, with numbering for easy reference. The numbering proceeds right to left, starting at the stem, i.e., from inner to outer morphemes. It should be kept in mind, however, that this template is just a representational device, not associated with any theoretical claim. In fact, I follow Rice (2000) in assuming that the Athapaskan verb represents an entire clause (see section 1.3 below). I differ from her in assuming that the syntax manipulates only abstract roots and (bundles of) features, which are associated with vocabulary items and to which phonology is applied only post-syntactically (see Chapter One for discussion of this "Distributed Morphology" view).

Table 3. Dëne verb template (based on Cook, 2004)

11	10	9	8	7	# 6
postposition (+ object prefix)	adverbial element	distributive prefix	iterative prefix	incorporated noun	object prefixes
k'e# 'on,' yé# 'in,' ka# 'for,' …	shé#, teghá#, … da# 'up,' dzi# 'around,' xa# 'out,' … ná# continuative	dá#	na#	e.g., la# 'hand,' dhá# 'mouth,' ts'ah# 'hat,' tł'uł# 'rope,' …	se– 1sO ne– 2sO nuhe– 1 or 2dl/plO Ø, be– 3O ye– 4O ʔe– unspecified O ʔede– reflexive ʔete– reciprocal ho– areal

5	4	3	2	1	0
nonlocal subject prefixes	thematic (lexical) prefix	"conjugation marker" (viewpoint & mode)	local subject prefixes	classifier (voice/valence)	stem
ts'e– unspecified subj. he– third person dual ho– areal (Ø 3s)	de–, ne–, ho– gender te–/he– inceptive i– seriative u– seriative (conative?) é–, i– semelfactive	the– (impf/perf) ne– (impf/perf) ghe– (perf) wa– (optative)	s–, i– 1s ne–/N 2s id– 1dl/pl uh– 2dl/pl	l– l– d– Ø	

Based on their morphophonological behaviour, prefixes can be divided into two groups, "disjunct" and "conjunct" prefixes. The latter are typically small, consisting of two segments or less, occur closer to the stem, and are fused to it and to each other. The former occur further away from the stem, may be larger (CVC, two syllables) and undergo little fusion.

The disjunct prefixes behave more like derivational or full lexical items than do the conjunct prefixes, which have more inflectional characteristics (see Rice 2000). The morphophonological boundary between the two prefix domains is called the "disjunct boundary," and is marked by the symbol # in the template.[4] I will cite disjunct prefixes with # rather than with a hyphen (e.g., *na#* instead of *na-* for the "iterative" prefix).

As to the stem, it has been proposed that the Athapaskan verb stem consists of a root and suffix (e.g., Kari 1979, Rice 2000). Since Dëne has more highly fused stems than the languages for which this has been proposed, a systematic analysis of Dëne stems into roots and suffixes has, to my knowledge, not been attempted. I will treat the Dëne stems as unanalyzable units (see Chapter Three for discussion).

1.3. The Dëne Verb as a Clause

While traditionally, the Dëne verb is treated as a single verb with templatic morphology, this view leads to a number of conceptual problems (Speas 1990, Rice 2000). One problem, mentioned in Chapter One, is that inflection is not outside of derivation. Consider again table 3: the conjunct, inflection-type prefixes occur between the disjunct, derivation-type prefixes and the stem. For reasons such as these, Rice (2000) proposes to abandon the traditional view of the Athapaskan verb, and instead to treat it as a syntactic clause. On this view (see also Hale 2001), the disjunct prefixes are lexical items, whereas the conjunct prefixes represent inflectional material/ functional heads. The voice/valence markers ("classifier") are assumed to be *v* heads, the stems are V heads.

The problem of the unusual order of [lexical items (disjunct)–inflectional items (conjunct)–stem] is solved as follows: underlyingly, the stem, as well as the voice/valence marker, are dominated by the conjunct prefixes (as already suggested in Speas 1990). The lexical elements are VP adjuncts. While the motivation for this view of the Athapaskan verb is mostly theoretical rather than empirical, it does have strong conceptual appeal, to be discussed immediately.[5]

We thus arrive at the following general clause structure for Athapaskan:

(1) General Athapaskan clause structure, based on Rice (2000)

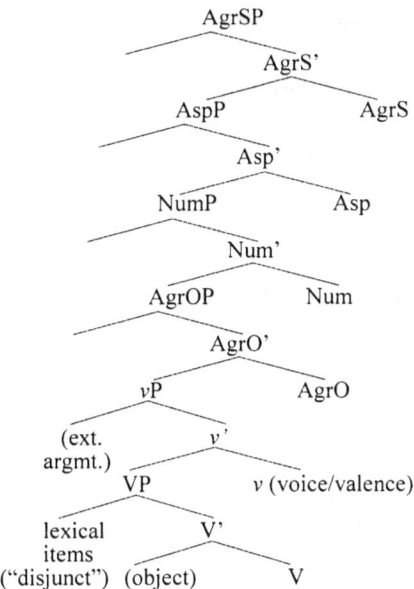

This type of structure is compatible with what we know about cross-linguistic morpheme orders and clause structures (Bybee 1985, Baker 1985): first, lexical items are below functional items. Second, the voice/valence marker is the functional element closest to the VP. Finally, the subject markers are now above the object markers and thereby also further away from the stem than the latter. The surface order is obtained by movement of the verb (+ classifier) to the top of the tree.[6]

I adopt this general structure for the Dëne verb. However, following the Distributed Morphology approach, I assume that the syntactic component contains only abstract roots (l-morphemes) and feature bundles (f-morphemes). The output of syntactic operations is then associated with the phonological "lexical" material (vocabulary items) that matches the feature specifications most closely. Meaning is assigned to structures post-syntactically as well. Importantly, certain syntactic domains can be domains for special meaning. Marantz (1997) assumes that v' is such a domain.

Please note that while these are my theoretical assumptions about the Dëne verb, I will continue to use the traditional terms of various "prefixes" and "positions," "stem" and "verb theme" (see section 1.4), in order to keep what follows as general and simple as possible.

1.4. "Thematic" Elements

Certain Dëne prefixes are called "thematic." This is the label for prefixes which must occur with a certain stem in order for this stem to form a verb with a certain meaning. Thematic prefixes by themselves in many cases lack a clear meaning or function, and often the stem without such a prefix does not constitute a word of the language. Although many thematic prefixes occur in position 4 (thus the label "thematic" of this position), elements in other positions of the template may also be "thematic" (i.e., be an obligatory component of a given verb/clause). Examples (2) and (3) show verbs which contain a thematic disjunct prefix. We can also see, in (2c) and (3b), that without the disjunct prefix, these are not words of the language.

(2) a. łeghániłthër   'I killed it'

   łeghá$_{10}$#ne$_3$–i$_2$–ł$_1$–dhër$_0$
   th#CM-1s-cl-stem: sg experiencer[7]

   b. ts'enidhër   'I woke up'

   ts'e$_{10}$#ne$_3$–i$_2$–Ø$_1$–dhër$_0$
   th#CM-1s-cl-stem: sg experiencer

   c. *niłthër, *nidhër

(3) a. yaghiłti   'I talked/prayed'

   ya$_7$#ghe$_3$–i$_2$–ł$_1$–ti$_0$
   th#CM-1s-cl-stem: ?

   b. *ghiłti

In these examples, the verb stem by itself or the disjunct prefix by itself is pretty much devoid of meaning, and it is only the *combination* of these two elements (plus the respective classifier and conjugation marker) which yields the meanings 'kill sg O,' 'sg wake up,' and 'talk/pray.' Traditionally, this translates into discontinuous lexical entries called "verb themes" for Athapaskan verbs (cf. Kari 1979, Cook 2004). Rice (2000) assumes that thematic elements and the verb stem constitute phrasal idioms.

The conjugation markers in (2) and (3) indicate Perfective viewpoint, but the form of the conjugation marker is often not predictable and must also be specified for a particular verb theme (see section 1.5 for discussion of the conjugation marker). The classifier indicates transitivity in (2): Ø for the intransitive theme in (2b), ł–for the transitive/causative theme in (2a) (see Rice 2000 for details). However, the choice of classifier for a verb theme is also often not predictable, for example, the occurrence of a ł–classifier with an intransitive theme in (3) is unexpected. In fact, the only completely predictable element in these examples is the subject inflection (position 2).

The verb themes for these examples must therefore look something like this (ignoring conjugation marker specifications, argument structure, etc.):

(4) a. łeghá$_{10}$#ł$_1$–dhër$_0$ 'kill sg O'

   b. ts'e$_{10}$#Ø$_1$–dhër$_0$ 'sg wake up'

   c. ya$_7$#ł$_1$–ti$_0$ 'talk/pray'

In the DM approach that I follow, the three vocabulary items of which each theme consists are inserted under the appropriate nodes post-syntactically, when all other nodes of the clause are filled as well. Meaning, including special meaning, is also assigned post-syntactically. The encyclopedic meaning component lists for each vocabulary item the special meanings it has in certain contexts.

Note that sometimes it is difficult to determine the exact morphosyntactic and semantic content of a thematic element. This is the case with the disjunct prefixes above. We know that they are disjunct by their lack of fusion with the following conjunct prefixes. However, we cannot isolate their meaning and function because they occur in few verb themes and never independently. *ya#* may be an adverb or an old incorporated noun, and *łeghá* and *ts'e* are also probably adverbs. It is fairly common to discover that thematic material in an Athapaskan verb cannot be fully categorized, for the very reason that it is not semantically or morphologically independent. The existence of considerable homophony[8] among prefixes further complicates the identification of morphemes.

The next two verb themes show additional types of thematic prefixes.

(5)   bek'eniyéz   'I broke it in two'
      be–k'e$_{11}$#ne$_3$–i$_2$–Ø$_1$–yéz$_0$
      3O-P#CM-1s-cl-stem: break

(6)   yehełt'us   's/he punched him/her/it out'[9]
      ye$_6$–he$_4$–H(<the)$_3$–ł$_1$–t'us$_0$
      3O-th/incept-CM-cl-stem: fist action

(5) contains a thematic postposition (position 11) plus object prefix, (6) a thematic inceptive prefix (position 4). We judge these prefixes to be thematic because they are obligatory and their semantic contribution to the verb meaning is not transparent. Thus, there is no apparent trace in (5) of the usual meaning 'on' of the postposition k'e, or 'start to V' of the inceptive prefix he-in (6).

A verb theme minimally consists of a stem and a classifier.[10] This is shown in (7), where the conjugation marker and the subject prefix represent inflectional material.

(7)   thiłbes   'I boiled it'
        the$_3$–i$_2$–ł$_1$–bes$_0$
        CM-1s-cl-stem: boil

Summing up, a Dëne verb theme consists of a stem, a classifier, and often additional obligatory "prefixes." Verb themes may be discontinuous on the surface, with nonthematic prefixes (e.g., subject and object inflection in positions 2 and 6) sandwiched between the thematic ones. In section 1.3, I discussed a syntactic/Distributed Morphology approach to Dëne verbs and verb themes.

In order not to distract from the main point of this chapter, I will not discuss each prefix position. The template given in table 3 is fairly self-explanatory, and the reader should refer to it when examining examples. Suffice it to say that Dëne verbs inflect for subject and object (positions 2 and 6), and for viewpoint aspect and mode (position 3). Since I am concerned here with aspect, I will discuss position 3 prefixes in detail.

1.5. The Conjugation Markers

There are four prefixes which occur in the aspect/mode position (position 3). The traditional term for them is "conjugation marker" (CM), and I will use this semantically neutral term as well. Paradigms illustrating CM's are given in (8) and (9) below, with the CM's underlined.[11] Note that one of the CM's marks a mood, the so-called "optative," the others are viewpoint aspect morphemes.[12] The optative CM has several allomorphs, for example wa, wu, or u in (8c) and (9c). All of these are surface forms of the same underlying morpheme, which is assumed to be something like wa- or, more conservatively, ghwa-. The surface forms include a labial segment, but vary otherwise. The optative is used in irrealis contexts, for example in direct questions and imperatives, in modal sentences, and to express a desire or wish. Thus, although it is marked in the same prefix position as viewpoint aspect, the optative is a mood or mode rather than an aspect, and I will have nothing more to say about it.[13]

(8) verb theme: $ya_7\#ł_1-ti_0$ (inc.N?#classifier-stem) 'talk, pray' (Cook 2004)

   a. yasti $ya_7\#\emptyset_3-s_2-ł_1-ti_0$ 'I am talking/praying'   IMPF
       yahílti $ya_7\#\emptyset_3-íd_2-ł_1-ti_0$ 'we (two) are talking/praying'
       yanełti $ya_7\#\emptyset_3-ne_2-ł_1-ti_0$ 'you (sg) are talking/praying'
       yołti $ya_7\#\emptyset_3-uh_2-ł_1-ti_0$ 'you (two) talk!/you (two) are talking'
       yałti $ya_7\#\emptyset_3-ł_1-ti_0$'s/he is talking/praying'

   b. yaghiłti $ya_7\#\underline{ghe}_3-i_2-ł_1-ti_0$ 'I talked/prayed'   PERF
       yaghílti $ya_7\#\underline{ghe}_3-íd_2-ł_1-ti_0$ 'we (two) talked/prayed'
       yaghįłti $ya_7\#\underline{ghe}_3-ne_2-ł_1-ti_0$ 'you (sg) talked/prayed'
       yaghuhłti $ya_7\#\underline{ghe}_3-uh_2-ł_1-ti_0$ 'you (two) talked/prayed'
       yaghįłti $ya_7\#\underline{ghe}_3-N-ł_1-ti_0$'s/he talked/prayed'[14]

   c. yawasti $ya_7\#\underline{wa}_3-s_2-ł_1-ti_0$ 'may I talk/pray?'   OPT
       yawųłti $ya_7\#\underline{wa}_3-ne_2-ł_1-ti_0$ 'you (sg) may talk'

(9) verb theme: $ł_1-bes_0$ (classifier-stem) 'boil O'

   a. hesbes $\emptyset_3-s_2-ł_1-bes_0$ 'I am boiling it (e.g., meat)'   IMPF
       hílbes $\emptyset_3-íd_2-ł_1-bes_0$ 'we (two) are boiling it'
       nełbes $\emptyset_3-ne_2-ł_1-bes_0$ 'you (sg) are boiling it'
       hułbes $\emptyset_3-uh_2-ł_1-bes_0$ 'you (two) are boiling it'
       yełbes $ye_6-\emptyset_3-ł_1-bes_0$'s/he's boiling it'

   b. thiłbes $\underline{the}_3-i_2-ł_1-bes_0$ 'I boiled it'   PERF
       thílbes $\underline{the}_3-íd_2-ł_1-bes_0$ 'we (two) boiled it'
       thįłbes $\underline{the}_3-ne_2-ł_1-bes_0$ 'you (sg) boiled it'
       thułbes $\underline{the}_3-uh_2-ł_1-bes_0$ 'you (two) boiled it'
       yéłbes $ye_6-H\leq\underline{the}_3-ł_1-bes_0$'s/he boiled it'

   c. wiłbes $\underline{wa}_3-ne_2-ł_1-bes_0$ 'boil it!' (2sg)   OPT
       yułbes $ye_6-\underline{wa}_3-ł_1-bes_0$'s/he might boil it'

The other morphemes occurring in position 3 mark viewpoint aspect. (8b) shows the morpheme *ghe-*, (9b) *the-*. Both mark Perfective viewpoint, but each is used with a different class of verbs (hence the label CM). As exemplified in (8a) and (9a), these two verb classes do not have an overt CM for the Imperfective; it is simply Ø. A third class of nonstative verbs has a CM *ne-* in the Perfective as well as in the Imperfective. (Certain stative verbs show yet another distribution of *the-* and *ghe-*.) These verb classes are discussed in detail in Chapter Three.

Many Dëne verbs also have different stem shapes in the Imperfective and Perfective (and sometimes also in the Optative). The stems may differ in tone, nasality, vowel quality, syllable type, or a combination of these:

(10) IMPF   PERF
      nes?į 'I am looking at it'   nighił?į 'I looked at it'
      híził xa 's/he is going to scream (once)'   thezël 's/he screamed (once)'
      hesda 'I am eating it (small animal)'   ghesdagh 'I ate it (small animal)'
      hest'éth 'I'm baking/roasting it'   thiłt'e 'I baked/roasted it'

I will return to the stem changes by viewpoint (and mode) and the other viewpoint morphology in Chapter Three.[15]

Summing up so far, Dëne verbs have at their disposal a large number of prefixes, many of them derivational or lexical ("thematic"). Most, but not all derivational prefixes occur outside of the inflectional material. Dëne verbs are inflected for mode, viewpoint aspect, subjects and objects, and number (but at least one so-called number marker, $dá_9\#$, is not inflectional; see footnote 13). The two viewpoint aspects are Imperfective and Perfective.

I will now turn to a detailed examination of the semantics of the viewpoint aspects, and the consequences for situation aspect. Please note that throughout, the situation type assigned to a particular verb theme is based on semantic tests explained in Chapter Three, section 3.1. The tests for each verb theme can be looked up in Appendix Three. Also note that I did not examine the semantic and morphological properties of stative verbs, since stativity is not in the scope of this dissertation. Other than some observations about positional stative verbs in section 2.3.3, I will have nothing to say about stative verbs.

2. THE DËNE VIEWPOINTS

The most apparent and pervasive aspectual marking in Dëne is that of the viewpoints, Imperfective and Perfective. Examples were given in (8), (9) and (10) above. These two viewpoints are well-established for Dëne since Li

(1946), and for Athapaskan in general (Krauss 1969). However, most discussion in Athapaskan has focused on the formal (i.e., morphological) expression of the viewpoints, and except for Smith (1991), work on Navajo (e.g., Young and Morgan 1987), and Axelrod's (1993) work on Koyukon, I am not aware of any careful study of their semantics and pragmatics.

The present discussion attempts to provide such a careful study of the Döne viewpoints. In doing so, some very interesting facts are revealed. In particular, we will see that the Döne Imperfective has durative force, and serves as the main locus of grammatization of durativity. I will also show that the Perfective entails event completion in Döne, and that this is the key factor in the obliteration of telicity as a grammatical category in Döne. Thus, viewpoint and situation aspect are interdependent.

2.1. Semantics and Pragmatics—General Remarks

Recall that, according to Klein (1994) and subsequent work, viewpoint aspect relates the time of the situation (TSit) to a topic time (TT; the time span which is the topic of the utterance). Perfective aspect indicates that TT includes TSit; imperfective that TT falls within TSit. Tense relates a topic time to a time of utterance (TU; the time at which the utterance is made): in Past Tense, TU follows TT, in Present Tense, TU is within TT.

(11) repeats some typical Imperfective-Perfective verb pairs of the language. All viewpoint marking is underlined.

(11) a. yasti $ya_7\#\underline{\varnothing}_3-s_2-ł_1-ti_0$ 'I am talking/praying'
        yaghiłti $ya_7\#\underline{ghe}_3-i_2-ł_1-ti_0$ 'I talked/prayed'

    b. hesbes $\underline{\varnothing}_3-s_2-ł_1-bes_0$ 'I am boiling it (e.g., meat)'
        thiłbes $\underline{the}_3-i_2-ł_1-bes_0$ 'I boiled it'

    c. hest'éth $\underline{\varnothing}_3-s_2-ł_1-\underline{t'éth}_0$ 'I'm baking/roasting it'
        thiłt'e $\underline{the}_3-i_2-ł_1-\underline{t'e}_0$ 'I baked/roasted it'

At first blush, the distinction in these pairs may appear to be one of present vs. past tense, rather than one of imperfective vs. perfective aspect. However, this is just an artifact of the translation into English, a language with obligatory tense. The following facts demonstrate that the contrasts illustrated in (11) mark viewpoint and not tense. First of all, the Imperfective can also be used in a past context, i.e., TU can follow TT. If it were a present tense, this should be impossible (abstracting away from phenomena like the narrative present).[16]

(12) tthidziné k'e jis nánasdą́ nį . . .
tthidziné k'e jis ná–na#s–ł–dą́   nį
yesterday mitt adv-?#-1s-cl-mend O past
'Yesterday I was patching the mitt . . . (when something else came up);
yesterday I patched the mitt for a while . . . (when . . .)'

In (12), the verb is in the Imperfective form (the Perfective form is *nánathiłdą́*, with the *the-* CM). The use of the Imperfective viewpoint lets us see the situation denoted by the verb theme as open-ended, ongoing (TT within TSit), and the most natural continuation of (12) would be another event (likely expressed by a Perfective verb) taking place while the mitt-patching was going on.

The second argument against the idea that these prefixes mark tense is the fact that Dëne has a separate set of postverbal particles or clitics, which, among other things, mark time. The past marker, *nį*, can be seen in (12). There is also a future/prospective enclitic *xa* or *ha*, and a present/assertive/emphatic enclitic *sį*. (Other enclitics do not have temporal function, but rather mark notions like negation or question.)

I conclude that the Dëne Imperfective and Perfective are indeed viewpoint aspects, as in (13), and not tenses.

(13) a. Imperfective

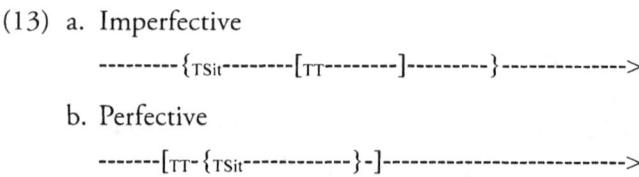

b. Perfective

Let us now explore these two viewpoints in more detail.

2.2. Semantics and Pragmatics of the Imperfective Viewpoint

The imperfective expresses that TT is located within TSit, as diagrammed in (13a). This has several consequences in Dëne. First, the Imperfective is only compatible with situations or TSit's which are durative and/or have internal stages. Second, the Dëne Imperfective is primarily used with events that have not been completed. Third, the Imperfective is used in discourse to describe a (backgrounded) situation occurring simultaneously with some other situation.

2.2.1. Durativity

As already shown in Smith (1991:112ff), TT can only be located within TSit if TSit consists of more than one time point, i.e., if the situation is durative.

In Dëne, this is certainly the case. Nondurative verbs are infelicitous in the Imperfective viewpoint. An Imperfective form of such verbs can usually only be used with a future enclitic, thus forming future tense rather than imperfective viewpoint. When I suggested bare Imperfective forms (without future enclitic), these were either rejected, or a coerced prospective/future rather than an imperfective interpretation was given. This is reminiscent of the English Progressive, which is either rejected or has an 'about to' interpretation with nondurative predicates: *#she is spotting the plane, #she is reaching the top.* Such instances of aspectual coercion make an inherently nondurative predicate durative by including a preliminary stage, which is not really part of the meaning, into TSit.

Here are two Dëne examples. In order to prevent circularity, I also present independent evidence that these predicates are not durative.

(14) verb theme: é–Ø–ził (impf), Ø–zël (perf)
      sem-cl-scream   cl-scream once perf 'scream once'
                                                                                      (NONDURATIVE)

   a. héssił xa.   'I'm going to scream once.'
      h–é–Ø–s–Ø–ził   xa
      ep-sem-CM-1s-cl-scream fut

   b. héssił.   'I'm going to scream once.,'
      h–é–Ø–s–Ø–ził   * 'I'm screaming once.'
      ep-sem-CM-1s-cl-scream

   c. # ʔiłághe ts'údzáhi k'étł'á thizëł.
      ʔiłághe ts'údzáhi k'étł'á   the–i–Ø–zëł
      one   hour   duration.of   CM-1s-cl-sceam perf

The incompatibility with 'for/in one hour,' (14c), establishes independently that the verb theme 'scream once' is not durative (see Chapter Three for this and other durativity tests). When attempting to elicit Imperfective forms, speakers would give me (14a) instead, which represents future tense. When I suggested (14b), again a future interpretation was given.

Example (15) is similar, except that here the bare Imperfective form was judged ungrammatical. (Incompatibility with 'for/in one hour' again establishes nondurativity independently.)

(15) verb theme: ná#ne–Ø–kár   'slap O once' (NONDURATIVE)
     adv/th#th-cl-stem: flat hand action

    a. náneskár xa.   'I'm gonna slap him/her/it once.'

        ná#ne–Ø–s–Ø–kár   xa
        adv/th#th-CM-1s-cl-stem fut

    b. * náneskár.

    c. # ʔįłághe ts'údzáhi k'e nánighikár.

        ʔįłághe ts'údzáhi k'e   ná#ne–ghe–i–Ø–kár
        one   hour   P   adv/th#th-CM-1s-cl-stem

Durative predicates, on the other hand, are perfectly acceptable in the Imperfective viewpoint. Consider the following examples. Here, compatibility with 'for/in one hour' shows independently that these predicates are durative.

(16) verb theme: ł–t'éth, –t'e (impf/opt, perf) 'cook O (by roasting, baking)'
                                                                            (DURATIVE)

    a. łue hest'éth sį.   'I am roasting fish.'

        łue he–Ø–s–ł–t'éth   sį
        fish ep-CM-1s-cl-cook O impf assert

    b. ʔįłághe ts'údzáhi k'e běr thiłt'e.

        ʔįłághe ts'údzáhi k'e běr   the–i–ł–t'e
        one   hour   P   meat CM-1s-cl-cook O perf

        'I cooked the meat for one hour./It took me one hour to cook the meat.'

(17) verb theme: d–yën   'sing' (DURATIVE)

    a. hesjën.   'I'm singing.'

        he–Ø–s–d–yën
        ep-CM-1s-cl-stem: sing

    b. ʔįłághe ts'údzáhi k'e ghesjën.   'I sang for an hour.'

        ʔįłághe ts'údzáhi k'e ghe–s–d–yën
        one   hour   P   CM-1s-cl-stem: sing

Abstracting away from aspectual coercion, we thus have in Dëne the following correlation:

(18) *Viewpoint correlation*
The Dëne Imperfective viewpoint requires a durative predicate.

Thus, Dëne contains a very pervasive morphological category which, so to speak, has a selectional restriction to durative predicates. This is so because of the meaning of this category (i.e., TT *within* TSit). In other words, Dëne contains a morphosyntactic contrast which accesses the durativity of a predicate. I conclude that durativity is grammatized in Dëne, through the Imperfective viewpoint. While some may consider this mediation by the imperfective semantics a rather "weak" grammatization device, I maintain that this is the most direct way in which durativity may be grammatized (see Chapter Six).

2.2.2. Event Incompletion

Smith (1991:91ff) argues that viewpoints make the situation expressed in a sentence "visible," i.e., only the part of a situation focused by a viewpoint is asserted, and available for truth-conditional entailments. For the imperfective, shown in (13a) above, this means that the initial and final bounds are not visible, i.e., not asserted and not available for entailments etc. For example, the English Progressive, which is a type of imperfective (Comrie (1976), Smith (1991)), does not make an assertion about event completion. Therefore, a progressive accomplishment sentence as in (19), which denies completion of the event, is not contradictory.

(19) Mary was walking to school but she didn't actually get there.
(Smith 1991:99)

Although an accomplishment situation like the one denoted by [walk to school] implies an inherent endpoint, this endpoint requirement is not "visible" in the progressive (see also Landman 1992 and references therein). In brief, imperfective viewpoints leave open when TSit will end, i.e., when—and whether—the event will be completed.

This is the case in Dëne as well, and there is ample evidence for it. First, an Imperfective sentence in Dëne is compatible with a subsequent sentence which cancels event completion, as in the English example (19) above. (20) and (21) are Imperfective sentences with cancelled event completion. Imperfectivity is indicated by the Ø CM, and in (21) also by the Imperfective stem –*ye* (the Perfective stem of this verb theme is –*yą*). Translations are as given by the speakers.

(20) √ tthidziné k'e jis nánasdą́   kúlú ʔanasdhën–íle.
    tthidziné k'e jis ná–na#Ø–s–ł–dą́   kúlú ʔa–na#(the–)s–l–dhën ʔíle
    yesterday mitt th-th#CM-1s-cl-stem but th-th#CM-1s-cl-stem not
    'Yesterday I was mending my mitts but I'm not finished it.'

(21) √ jíe ʔuneshe   kúlú ʔanast'e–íle.
    jíe   ʔu–ne–Ø–s–Ø–ye   kúlú ʔa–na#s–Ø–t'e   ʔíle
    berry th-gd/th-CM-1s-cl-stem   but th-th#1s-cl-stem not
    'I'm picking berries but I'm not finished it/with them (I'll finish at a later date).'

Since these sentences involve complex verb themes with several thematic prefixes, no specific meaning can be assigned to the stem. The theme *ná–na#ł–dą́* means 'mend,' and *ʔu–ne–Ø–ye* means something like 'pluck/pick small round objects (berries).' Both themes are transitive, and take *jis* 'mitt' and *jíe* 'berries,' respectively, as complement. The two themes *ʔa–na#ł–dhën* and *ʔa–na#Ø–t'e* mean 'finish' here.[17]

Next, the Imperfective contrasts with the Perfective in terms of event completion. Consider the following minimal pair of past sentences.[18]

(22) a. ʔįłá néné k'étł'á   yoh[19] hołtsį   nį̀.   IMPF
    ʔįłá néné k'étł'á   yoh   ho–Ø–ł–tsį   nį̀
    one year duration.of house gd-CM-cl-make O past
    'S/he was making a/the house for a year.'
    <u>implied</u>: the house is not finished

  b. ʔįłá néné k'étł'á   yoh   hółtsį   nį̀.   PERF
    ʔįłá néné k'étł'á   yoh   ho–the–ł–tsį   nį̀
    one year duration.of house gd-CM-cl-make O past
    'S/he built a/the house for a year/over a year.'
    <u>implied</u>: the house is finished

This minimal pair suggests that the Perfective form denotes an event which has been completed, while the Imperfective form does not. The respective (in-)completion reading associated with each viewpoint is also exploited in texts. Cook (2004) cites three examples from narratives to illustrate this point. (Morphemic breakdown of the verbs given on the right is mine.)

(23) . . . Dëne tsąba łą deɬtsi nį. . . .   de–ł–tsi
       man money much make past   th-cl-make sg O impfv
       . . . 'The man made a lot of money.' . . .

(24) . . . Yeba húk'é   theda łį. . . .   the–Ø–da
       4O-for empty-home sit   habit   CM-cl-sg sit impfv
       . . . 'She used to babysit for him.' . . .

(25) . . . Yegá   néda   nį. . . .   ne–H–Ø–da
       4O-beside sat down past   th-CM-cl-sg sit down perf
       . . . 'She married him.' (lit., 'she sat down beside him') . . .

Cook points out that (23) means that the man made money and was probably still making money at the time of the utterance; had he finished making money, the Perfective would have been used. Similarly, in (24) the babysitting was ongoing on several occasions; for just one instance of babysitting the Perfective would have been chosen (cf. Comrie 1976 on habitual meaning of imperfective viewpoint). In (25), however, the Perfective is used to denote the completed action of marrying someone.

Summing up, textual examples, minimal pairs and cancellation tests provide ample evidence that the Imperfective viewpoint of Dëne presents events as uncompleted. The final bound of a situation/TSit is not located inside the TT picked out by the Imperfective.

2.2.3. Simultaneity/Backgrounding

The "incomplete" flavour of the Imperfective is exploited pragmatically as well. Usually, the situation denoted by an Imperfective sentence is interpreted as simultaneous with the situation denoted by a subsequent sentence. If the subsequent sentence is in the Perfective, it will be foregrounded. Thus, in Dëne the Imperfective is used consistently in clauses which describe events going on around some other, focused (typically Perfective) event, such as the ringing of the phone in the examples below. The Imperfective is used as a backgrounding device, similar to the French Imparfait (cf. Kamp and Rohrer 1983).

(26) [tthidziné k'e hestsagh–ú]   tsątsąnaze déłtsër.
     tthidziné k'e he–s–Ø–tsagh   ʔú   tsątsąnaze déłtsër
     yesterday   ep-1s-cl-cry   comp   phone/bell perf-ring
     '[Yesterday while I was crying] the phone rang.'

(27) [tthidziné k'e naskui–ú]   tsątsą́naze déɬtsĕ́r.
    tthidziné k'e na#s–kui   ʔú   tsątsą́naze   déɬtsĕr
    yesterday   ʔ#1s-vomit comp   phone/bell   perf-ring
    '[Yesterday while I was vomiting] the phone rang.'

While the complex topic of temporal modification by subordinate clauses is beyond the scope of this dissertation, we can safely assume that the subordinate clause has the same function as a temporal adverbial, namely to specify a time of the matrix clause: TSit, TT, or TU (see Musan 2002). I assume here that the subordinate Imperfective clause specifies the TT of the Perfective main clause. Thus, the matrix TT coincides with part of the vomiting event denoted by the subordinate clause. Since the matrix clause is Perfective (TT includes TSit), it follows that the subordinate TSit includes or "surrounds" the matrix TSit—it provides the background for the main clause event.

The close association of the Imperfective with incompletion and event simultaneity/backgrounding leads to pragmatic oddity of isolated past Imperfective sentences: (28a) is infelicitous because there is no other situation for which the crying event could serve as background.

(28) a. # tthidziné k'e hestsagh.   IMPF
         tthidziné k'e he–s–Ø–tsagh
         yesterday   ep-1s-cl-cry

    b. √ tthidziné k'e ghitsagh.   PERF
         tthidziné k'e ghe–i–Ø–tsagh
         yesterday   CM-1s-cl-cry
         'Yesterday I cried.'

As we can see in (28b), the Perfective is preferred in such isolated past sentences.

Summing up, the Dëne Imperfective locates TT within TSit. This has several consequences. The Imperfective is used to denote incomplete situations, and, in discourse, to describe a backgrounded situation going on simultaneously with some other, foregrounded situation. Most important for the purpose of this study, the semantics of the Imperfective viewpoint requires access to the durativity of a predicate: it can only be used with durative predicates. Since Dëne contains a morphosyntactic contrast (Imperfective vs. Perfective) which requires access to the durativity of a predicate, we can say that durativity in Dëne is a semantic feature which is accessible to the grammar, or, in other words, durativity is grammatized. More specifically, the Imperfective grammatizes durativity in Dëne.

2.3. Semantics and Pragmatics of the Perfective Viewpoint

The Dëne Perfective is compatible with all situation types. However, it does have a special meaning which is not typical of perfectives in general: it suggests and, as I will show, entails event completion, irrespective of situation type. I will argue that this sense of event completion goes beyond the usual "boundedness" or "closed viewpoint" meaning of perfectives. Finally, the situations described by a sequence of Perfective sentences receive a sequential interpretation in Dëne.

2.3.1. All (Eventive) Situation Types

Recall the general schema for perfective viewpoint, repeated from (13) above:

(29) Perfective
  -------[$_{TT}$-{$_{TSit}$------------}-]------------>

Locating TSit within TT, the perfective puts no requirements on the nature of TSit. TSit may be durative or not, telic or not—the Perfective is always acceptable in Dëne.[20] To illustrate, I repeat here the nonstative verb themes from examples (14)-(17) above as (30)-(33), this time in the Perfective viewpoint.[21]

(30) verb theme: é–Ø–ził (impf), Ø–zëł (perf)
 sem-cl-scream cl-scream once perf 'scream once'
 (NONDURATIVE)
 thizëł   'I screamed once'
 the–i–Ø–zëł
 CM-1s-cl-scream

(31) verb theme: ná#ne–Ø–kár 'slap O once' (NONDURATIVE)
  adv/th#th-cl-stem: flat hand action
 nánighikár 'I slapped him/her/it once'
 ná#ne–ghe–i–Ø–kár
 adv/th#th-CM-1s-cl-stem

(32) verb theme: ł–t'éth, –t'e (impf/opt, perf) 'cook O (by roasting, baking)'
 (DURATIVE)
 thiłt'e 'I cooked (baked/roasted) it'
 the–i–ł–t'e
 CM-1s-cl-stem

(33) verb theme: d–yën   'sing'   (DURATIVE)
     ghesjën   'I sang'
     ghe–s–d–yën
     CM-1s-cl-stem

2.3.2. Event Completion

In the perfective, TT includes TSit, from beginning to end. This makes all of TSit "visible" to semantic interpretation, as Smith (1991) puts it. Since the endpoint of TSit is also visible, the use of perfective viewpoint entails that the situation is over. Smith (1991) therefore calls the perfective a "closed" viewpoint. However, perfectives do not necessarily put special emphasis on the endpoint of a situation. Also, perfectives per se do not usually specify whether a situation has simply *stopped* (by reaching an arbitrary endpoint) or whether it has been *completed* (by reaching an inherent endpoint); this part of the meaning of a perfective sentence is contributed by the situation type of the predicate (atelic: arbitrary endpoint, telic: inherent endpoint).

The perfective found in Athapaskan languages certainly is a closed viewpoint, entailing that the situation is over. In fact, in many Athapaskan languages the perfective is described as denoting a "completed" event or situation (e.g., Axelrod (1993), Cook (2004), Young (2000)). That is, Athapaskan perfectives seem to put special emphasis on the fact that a situation is over. In Dëne, too, there is ample evidence for this "completive" force of the Perfective. First, reconsider the minimal pair given in (22) above, repeated here as (34).[22]

(34) a. ʔı̨łá něné kʼétłʼá   yoh   hołtsı̨ nı̨.   IMPF
        ʔı̨łá něné kʼétłʼá   yoh   ho–Ø–ł–tsı̨   nı̨
        one year duration.of house gd-CM-cl-make O   past
        'S/he was making a/the house for a year.'
        <u>implied:</u> the house is not finished

     b. ʔı̨łá něné kʼétłʼá   yoh   hółtsı̨ nı̨.   PERF
        ʔı̨łá něné kʼétłʼá   yoh   ho–the–ł–tsı̨   nı̨
        one year duration.of house gd-CM-cl-make O   past
        'S/he built a/the house for a year/over a year.'
        <u>implied:</u> the house is finished

Obviously, here the Perfective forms the counterpart to the Imperfective in that it implies event completion, i.e., the reaching of an inherent endpoint. The same is true for the textual examples given in Cook (2004) and discussed in section 2.1.1 above.

To see the strong association of the Perfective with event completion, it is also very instructive to look at spontaneous translations of Perfective sentences: they often contain an extra English expression like *finished* indicating event completion.

(35) a. bekáthiłt'e   kú . . .   'I'm ready, I finished cooking . . .'

   be–ká#the–i–ł–t'e   kú
   3O-P#CM-1s-cl-cook O   perf and/now

b. ʔuneghiyą̨.   'I'm finished picking berries.'

   ʔu–ne–ghe–i–Ø–yą̨
   th-gd/th-CM-1s-cl-pick (berries) perf

(36) a. k'ájëne bekáthiłt'e.   'I'm just about finished cooking.'
   k'ájëne be–ká#the–i–ł–t'e
   almost 3O-P#CM-1s-cl-cook O perf

b. k'ájëne thiłtsį.   'I just about finished making it.'/
   k'ájëne the–i–ł–tsį   'I'm almost done making it.'
   almost CM-1s-cl-make O

Moreover, Perfective verbs cannot be combined with the completive verb theme *ʔa–na#Ø–t'e* 'stop/finish.' I first show this verb with an Imperfective complement (as indicated by the Ø CM), which is the standard construction in which it occurs:

(37) nánasdą́   ʔanast'e.   'I'm finished patching it.'
   ná–na#Ø–s–ł–dą́   ʔanast'e
   th-th#CM-1s-cl-stem th-th#1s-cl-stem

Combining *ʔa–na#Ø–t'e* with a Perfective clause represents a tautology and is therefore consistently rejected. Speakers would even comment that *ʔa–na#Ø–t'e* is unnecessary and should be omitted in a Perfective context.

(Speakers did not specify whether these examples are ungrammatical or semantically deviant.)

(38) a. #/* nánathiłdą̂   ʔanastʼe.
           ná–na#the–i–ł–dą̂   ʔa–na#s–Ø–tʼe
           th-th#CM-1s-cl-mend O   th-th#1s-cl-stem

    b. #/* yoh   thiłtsį   ʔanastʼe.
            yoh   the–i–ł–tsį   ʔa–na#s–Ø–tʼe
            house CM-1s-cl-make sg O   th-th#1s-cl-stem

    c. #/* yaghiłti   ʔanastʼe.
            ya#ghe–i–ł–ti   ʔa–na#s–Ø–tʼe
            th-CM-1s-cl-talk/pray   th-th#1s-cl-stem

Summing up so far, the fact that the Perfective has completive force in Dëne can be seen by comparing it with the (noncompletive) Imperfective, from speakers' translations of Perfective sentences into English, and from the fact that a Perfective verb plus a completive verb like *ʔa–na#Ø–tʼe* results in a tautology.

It is important to note that in general, perfective viewpoint does not necessarily have completive meaning, as already briefly mentioned above. In introducing perfective aspect, Comrie (1976:18f) points out that

> the use of 'completed' [. . .] puts too much emphasis on the termination of a situation, whereas the use of the perfective puts no more emphasis, necessarily, on the end of a situation than on any other part of the situation, rather all parts of the situation are presented as a single whole. [. . .] Indicating the end of a situation is at best only one of the possible meanings of a perfective form, certainly not its defining feature.

He cites as evidence, among other things, the existence of contrasts between a simple perfective and a special completive form in some languages. I illustrate with Russian, (39), and Mandarin, (40).

(39) a. imperfective: *užinatʼ*   'have supper'
     b. perfective: *my požinali posle polunoči* 'we had supper after midnight'
     c. completive: *my tolʼko čto otužinali*   'we've just finished supper'
                                                    (Comrie 1976:19)

(40) a. perfective: *Wo zuotian xie-le   yifeng xin, keshi mei xie-wan.*
I   yest'day write-LE oneCL letter, but not write-finish
'I wrote a letter yesterday but I didn't finish it.'

b. completive: *Wo zuotian xie-wan-le   yifeng xin.*
I   yest'day write-WAN-LE oneCL letter
'Yesterday I wrote (and finished) a letter.'
(Smith 1991:108)

In light of these facts it is interesting that the Dëne Perfective does have completive meaning. I will next show that the notion of event completion associated with the Perfective is very strong indeed: it is an entailment rather than a mere implicature.

2.3.3. Event Completion Entailed

In order to determine whether a reading is an implicature or an entailment, one attempts to cancel it. Only implicatures can be cancelled (cf. Grice 1975, Levinson 1983). Attempting to cancel an entailment results in a contradiction, i.e., in semantic ill-formedness. For example, the English sentence *Katie has two daughters* carries the implicature that Katie has no more than two daughters (Horn 1972). This implicature can be cancelled: *Katie has two daughters; in fact, she has three.* Our example sentence also entails that Katie has children, and this is not cancellable: # *Katie has two daughters, but in fact, she does not have children.*

In Dëne, the event completion reading cannot be cancelled. I tested most verbs in my database for this, and consistently found that attempting to cancel the completion reading resulted in a contradictory and hence ill-formed sentence.

The clauses I used to cancel event completion are shown in (41), and (42) is a representative list of failed cancellation. The translations in (42) are mine and are only given to illustrate what such a sentence might mean, but speakers consistently termed these sentences "nonsense."

(41) meaning: 'but I'm not finished (it)' / 'but I didn't finish (it)'

a. kúlú ʔanastʼe–íle
   kúlú   ʔa–na#s–Ø–tʼe   ʔíle
   but   th-th#1s-cl-stem   not

b. kúlú ?anasdhën–íle (used after a transitive clause)
kúlú ?a–na#(the–)s–l–dhën ?íle
but th-th#CM-1s-cl-stem not

(42) a. tthidziné k'e bër thiłbes # kúlú ?anasdhën–íle.
tthidziné k'e bër the–i–ł–bes
yesterday meat CM-1s-cl-boil O
('Yesterday I boiled some meat [but I'm not finished it].')

b. ts'ëre nánathiłdą # kúlú ?anasdhën–íle.
ts'ëre ná–na#the–i–ł–dą
blanket th-th#CM-1s-cl-stem
('I mended the/a blanket [but I'm not finished it].')

c. yaghiłti # kúlú ?anast'e–íle.
ya#ghe–i–ł–ti
th#CM-1s-cl-stem
('I talked/prayed [but I didn't finish].')

d. bër ghit'adh # kúlú ?anasdhën–íle.
bër ghe–i–Ø–t'adh
meat CM-1s-cl-stem:cut perf
('I cut (the) meat [but I'm not finished it].')

e. Tsádhekųę níniya # kúlú ?anast'e–íle.
Tsádhekųę ní#ne–i–Ø–ya
Edmonton adv/th#CM-1s-cl-stem: sg go perf
('I arrived in Edmonton [but I didn't finish (arriving)].')

f. thizël # kúlú ?anast'e–íle.
the–i–Ø–zël
CM-1s-cl-scream once perf
('I screamed once [but I didn't finish].')

Interestingly, event completion is entailed with all eventive situation types. According to semantic tests, (42a) and (42b) are accomplishments, (42c) and (42d) are activities, (42e) is an achievement, and (42f) is a semelfactive.

The fact that completion is also entailed with activities is somewhat unusual. In many languages, the "perfective may vary in meaning according to the endpoint of a situation: telic events have natural endpoints, atelic events have arbitrary endpoints" (Smith 1991:105). This means that only perfective accomplishments are interpreted as completed (inherent endpoint reached); perfective activities are interpreted as stopped or terminated (arbitrary endpoint reached), rather than as completed. Consider the English examples in (43) and (44): only telic sentences are incompatible with cancelled event completion. (Smith (1991:106–107) makes the same point, but does not give activity examples.)

(43) Accomplishments
  a. # I built a house but I did not finish building it.
  b. # Mrs Ramsey wrote a letter, but she didn't finish writing it. (Smith 1991:107)

(44) Activities
  a. I sang but I did not finish singing (the song), rather, I stopped.
  b. I walked in the park but I did not finish walking (my routine path) because I met a friend.

Since here the situation type determines whether completion—as opposed to termination—is entailed, this entailment is attributed to the telicity/inherent endpoint of an accomplishment situation rather than to the perfective viewpoint. The perfective simply presents the situation in its entirety—including the inherent endpoint which leads to the completion reading. However, such an analysis is unable to explain why activities, which do not have an inherent endpoint, also entail event completion, and not only termination, in Dëne. For Dëne, we are forced to attribute the completion entailment to the Perfective viewpoint rather than to telicity.

This is confirmed by a second test, based on the clause, 'and am/is still V-ing,' which is only compatible with situations which are not completed. According to Midgette (1996), in Navajo this clause can only be combined with atelic perfective sentences. She attributes this pattern to the fact that telic but not atelic verbs in the perfective viewpoint entail event completion. Here are two of Midgette's Navajo examples:

(45) Kintahgóo bichidí yinı́łbą́ą́z **áádóó t'ahdii ńléígóó   TELIC
town-to his-car he-drove-it and still there-toward
                                                           yoołbąs.
                                                           he-is-driving-it-along
'He drove his car to town **and he's still driving it there' (Midgette 1996:317)

(46) Awéé' yícha áádóó t'ahdii yicha sha'shin   ATELIC
'The baby cried and I guess s/he's still crying.' (Midgette 1996:317)

Interestingly, in Dëne verbs of any situation type are unacceptable with 'and am/is still V-ing,' so event completion is independent of situation type. I will give a few activity examples here to illustrate the contrast with Navajo. The first clause is Perfective, the 'still V-ing' clause is Imperfective.

(47) # yághelgus–ú ʔąłų́ yálgus.
       yá#ghe–l–gus   ʔú   ʔąłų́ yá#l–gus
       th#CM-cl-stem:jump and still th#cl-jump
       ('He finished jumping and he's still jumping.')

(48) # hughikĕr–ú ʔąłų́ heskĕr.
       hu–ghe–i–Ø–kĕr   ʔú   ʔąłų́ he–s–Ø–kĕr
       ser-CM-1s-cl-stem:pat and still ep-1s-cl-stem:pat
       ('I patted it and I'm still patting it.')

The only interpretation on which such sentences become acceptable is if there was some interruption, so 'I V-ed for a while, then I stopped, and now I'm V-ing again.' This is illustrated by the next example:

(49) ghitsagh–ú   ʔąłų́ hetsagh.
     ghe–N–Ø–tsagh   ʔú   ʔąłų́ he–Ø–tsagh
     CM-N-cl-stem:cry and still ep-cl-stem:cry
     'S/he cried and s/he's still crying.' (after an interruption, s/he is crying again)

These activity examples provide further evidence that the entailment of event completion is associated with the Perfective viewpoint, and not only with telicity.

The fact that the meaning of a perfective clause does not vary by telicity is marked, but not unheard of. For example, there are also languages in which (simple) perfective clauses entail only event termination and never event completion, irrespective of telicity: Mandarin Chinese (Smith 1991) and Hindi (Singh 1991) are two examples.[23]

To sum up: In the Dëne Perfective, activities have the same completion interpretation as accomplishments. Now, since the event completion reading in accomplishments is due to the presence of an inherent endpoint/telicity, the logical conclusion seems that the Dëne Perfective contributes something like an inherent endpoint or telicity to atelic situations. I will say that the Dëne Perfective has "quasi-telic" meaning.

How might we represent this quasi-telic meaning? It is theoretically undesirable that a viewpoint aspect contribute actual situation aspectual meaning. In other words, we do not want a representation which says, informally, that the Dëne Perfective adds an inherent endpoint to any situation (which does not already have one). But we do want a representation which has a very similar effect, a representation which accounts for the Perfective's strongly completive, or quasi-telic, meaning.

I propose that, unlike unmarked perfectives, the Dëne Perfective focuses not only the entire situation time, but also a posttime of the situation (the necessity of "posttimes" is independently justified in Klein (1994), and Parsons (1990) has a similar notion of "post-state"). Let me illustrate with a diagram:

(50) Unmarked perfective

-------[$_{TT}$-{$_{TSit}$------------}-]------------->

(51) Dëne completive Perfective

------[$_{TT}$-{$_{TSit}$---------}+++++]-------->
                        posttime

Locating not only TSit, but also a posttime of TSit within TT, gives a natural explanation for the meaning of the Dëne Perfective. At a posttime of TSit, the situation is already over. This yields the notion that Dëne Perfective situations are over. More importantly, by including a posttime, every TT contains a change of state, namely from ϕ (as denoted by the lexical verb, and true throughout TSit), to $\neg \phi$ (true throughout the posttime, and part of the denotation of the Perfective verb). Changes of state are a characteristic of telicity. It is thus not surprising that the Dëne Perfective, which also includes a change of state (from ϕ to $\neg\phi$), has quasi-telic meaning, and in particular that it entails event completion.[24]

And what happens to the telicity of a situation? It is still there: TSit of telic predicates contains two states[25], TSit of atelic predicates contains only one state. However, this distinction is not so important anymore, since due to the Perfective's scope over a posttime, every perfective situation contains two states anyway.

This proposal is in the spirit of Smith (1999), who argues explicitly that in "activity sentences the perfective viewpoint actually *adds* information, conveying a temporally bounded unit" (Smith 1999:503; emphasis mine) through the addition of implicit initial and final temporal bounds. However, these implicit temporal bounds need not coincide with the actual beginning and ending of an activity situation, so they do not necessarily convey a sense of event completion. My posttime account goes even further. The presence of a posttime ensures that the situation cannot continue, i.e., that the actual end of an activity situation is reached. This, I argue, derives the completive, quasi-telic meaning of the Dëne Perfective.

Independent evidence for the inclusion of a posttime comes from the morphology and semantics of positional stative verbs ('sit,' 'lie,' etc.) in Dëne. These verbs inflect for Imperfective and Perfective: the CM pattern is *the-/ghe-*, and the stem may also change. But interestingly, positional statives with Imperfective meaning are morphologically Perfective, and denote the result state of a completed action or event. For example, compare the stative and nonstative uses of the stem 'sg sit,' particularly (53a) and (52b):

(52) a. <u>nonstative</u>

    nesdá   'I'm sitting down'   IMPF
    ne–Ø–s–Ø–dá   (in the process of)
    th-CM-1s-cl-stem:sg sit

  b. nida   'I sat down'   PERF
    ne–(the–)i–Ø–da
    th-CM-1s-cl-stem:sg sit

(53) a. <u>stative</u>

    thida   'I am sitting'   IMPF
    the–i–Ø–da   (I sat down and am now sitting)
    CM-1s-cl-stem:sg sit

b. ghidá   'I sat/was sitting'   PERF
   ghe–i–Ø–dá   (now I don't anymore)
   CM-1s-cl-stem:sg sit

The Imperfective stative form has the same stem and the same CM (although invisible here[26]) as the Perfective nonstative form; thus it is morphologically a Perfective (cf. Li 1946, Kari 1979). The meaning of the Imperfective stative verb, in particular the paraphrase 'I sat down and am now sitting,' supports this: the verb denotes the result, or posttime, of a sitting-down event. I propose that this derivation of certain Dëne stative verbs is possible and motivated through the special meaning of the Dëne Perfective, which includes a "posttime" of the situation.

Moreover, the meaning of the Perfective stative verb (really a Perfective of a Perfective), (53b), also supports the posttime analysis. It does not simply denote a situation in which I sat, it also denotes that I am now (i.e., at TT) no more in a state of sitting. This means that here, too, TT includes a posttime of the situation.

I conclude that in Dëne, unlike in more familiar languages, the perfective viewpoint is associated by entailment with the notion of event completion, independent of situation type. This strong completive or quasi-telic sense, which is marked for perfectives cross-linguistically, comes about because the Perfective includes a posttime of a situation.

3. PERFECTIVITY AND TELICITY

By entailing that a situation has been completed, the Dëne Perfective adds a kind of meaning to a predicate that comes very close to a situation type meaning. In other words, the Dëne Perfective strongly overlaps in meaning with telicity: while telic situations are inherently bounded by virtue of denoting a transition into a result state, the Dëne Perfective bounds both telic and atelic situations by including the transition between TSit and a posttime. As a consequence, the type of final bound or endpoint of the situation (inherent vs. arbitrary) simply seems not to matter much in Perfective viewpoint.

The semantic overlap between perfectivity and telicity in Dëne represents a mixing of two levels of aspectual meaning which are usually kept separate: situation type and viewpoint. Why can such a mixing or overlap of levels occur?

In fact, this semantic overlap is not as surprising as it may first appear. There is a general semantic and pragmatic overlap of perfective viewpoint and telic situation type in natural language. First of all, as already said, both aspectual devices serve to bound a situation (in different ways, admittedly). Second, due to their bounding function, both aspectual devices share an important discourse-related function: both have the capability of specifying the temporal relationship between situations in a discourse as sequential (Comrie 1976, Hopper 1982, Kamp and Rohrer 1983, Partee 1984, Dahl 1985, ter Meulen 1995, Smith 1999). Let me explain this point further.

3.1. Event Ordering in Narrative

When presented not with isolated sentences, but with a narrative of several sentences or clauses, each denoting one situation, speakers need to know the temporal relationships between these situations: which of them are to be understood as occurring simultaneously, and which ones are to be understood as happening before or after other situations?

3.1.1. Perfective Indicates Sequential Events

A major device for specifying these temporal relationships is through viewpoint aspect.[27] We already saw that the Imperfective invites an interpretation of one situation as simultaneous to another (section 2.2.3). The Perfective, on the other hand, invites a sequential interpretation. Consider the following Perfective/Imperfective minimal pair:

(54) a. tthidziné k'e łue theɬt'e   -ú ʔenétthëdh.   PERF
        tthidziné k'e łue the–Ø–ɬ–t'e   ʔú ʔenétthëdh
        yesterday fish CM-cl-cook O perf and it(fire)-went-out
        'Yesterday s/he cooked fish and then the fire went out.'/
        'Yesterday after she cooked fish the fire went out.'

   b. tthidziné k'e łue heɬt'éth   -ú ʔenétthëdh.   IMPF
      tthidziné k'e łue he–Ø–ɬ–t'éth   ʔú ʔenétthëdh
      yesterday fish ep-cl-cook O impf and it(fire)-went-out
      'Yesterday while s/he cooked/was cooking fish the fire went out.'

(54a) cannot receive a simultaneous interpretation; the subordinating clitic ʔú cannot be translated as 'while.' To express a simultaneous relationship, the Imperfective must be used, as in (54b).

Similarly, in narratives the Perfective is used for those events which happen one after another; the Imperfective relates backgrounded situations. Regrettably, there are no published Dëne texts with interlinear glosses, or any text studies. However, two short texts whose use of viewpoint aspects I examined show the predicted pattern. Here is just one typical passage.

(55) Sentence 1 from *Setá chu Tsá ghą Náiddhër* 'My Father and I were Looking For Beavers' (from Cook (2004), whose glosses and translation I follow)

Setá   chu tsá   ka–níta   xa dzí–rít'áis   t'á,
1s-dad and beaver P-1pl-look for for around-1pl-walk impf with(= while)
                   IMPF   IMPF

nághaye   tsá   ghą   nádhër   k'é ghą   nít'as.
wolverine beaver P   3s-stay impf M   P/while 1pl-dl arrive perf
                        IMPF   PERF

'While my father and I were *walking around* (IMPF) for that we *look for* (IMPF) a beaver, we *came upon* (PERF) a wolverine which was *staying by* (IMPF) (= trying to catch) a beaver.'

We can see that the main event, the coming upon a wolverine, is in the Perfective. The verbs in the first line, which sets up the context for the main event, are in the Imperfective, and so is the embedded (relative) clause in line 2 which describes what the wolverine was engaged in doing. All three of these Imperfective predicates describe situations which are simultaneous with the main event.

A study of the function of aspect in a Koyukon text (Axelrod 1993, Chapter Six) finds that the imperfective is used for backgrounded events and simultaneous situations, while the perfective is used in foregrounded events, and is particularly frequent in the most dramatic sections of the story, which consist of action sequences.[28]

Summing up, the temporal ordering of situations in discourse is a central function of viewpoint aspect, and the Perfective has the function of rendering events sequential in Dëne narratives.

3.1.2. Telicity Indicates Sequential Events

In languages which have little or no viewpoint aspect, situation aspect is an important means for specifying temporal relationships between situations.

German is such a language; it has no grammatical viewpoint aspect contrasts (see Chapter Five). And in German, the default interpretation of telic situations is sequential, while the default interpretation of atelic situations is simultaneous. Consider (56), which gives two mini-texts which only differ in telicity of the second sentence. Event ordering in sentences 2 and 3 differs accordingly.

(56) a. Susi *wollte* den alten Apfelbaum beschneiden. Sie *sägte* einen morschen
Susi *wanted* the old apple-tree prune she *sawed* a dead
ATELIC   TELIC

Ast   ab. Es *fing an* zu regnen.
branch *off* it *started* to rain
             TELIC/inceptive

'Susi wanted to prune the old apple tree. She sawed off a dead branch. It started raining.' (implicated: it started raining after Susi had sawed off the dead branch.)

b. Susi *wollte* den alten Apfelbaum beschneiden. Sie *sägte* eifrig (an einem
Susi *wanted* the old apple-tree prune she *sawed* eagerly (at a
ATELIC   ATELIC

morschen Ast). Es *fing an* zu regnen.
dead branch it *started* to rain
              TELIC/inceptive

'Susi wanted to prune the old apple tree. She was sawing eagerly (at a dead branch). It started raining.' (implicated: it started raining while Susi was sawing off the dead branch.)

These effects of situation type have been noted by researchers working in various theoretical frameworks. For example, Bohnemeyer and Swift (2004) use these facts to argue that telicity in viewpoint-less languages is associated with a *default* perfective viewpoint. In other words, the default function of telic situations in discourse is like that of perfective viewpoint, namely to specify sequential events. Ter Meulen (1995) develops the categories "plug" and "hole" to describe event ordering in discourse. A predicate that is a plug does not allow for further information on the event described by it; it "plugs" the information flow regarding this event, and subsequent clauses have to be about other, later events. A hole predicate does allow for further information on the event described by it; events described in following sentences can expand the hole or happen simultaneously. Activities (atelic) are classed as holes and achievements (telic) are classed as plugs. Accomplishments (telic) may function as plugs or holes, but are plugs by default. Thus, ter Meulen exploits the effect of telicity on event ordering. Finally, in light of the pragmatic similarity between telicity and perfectivity it is not surprising that German delimiting particles (and prefixes) such as *ab* in *absägen* 'saw off' have often been called "perfective" or "perfectivizing" in traditional descriptions (e.g., Behagel 1907, Paul 1959, Duden 1984).

There is a difference between perfectivity and telicity, however.[29] The sequential interpretation of telic situations can easily be overridden. (57) shows an accomplishment situation in two contexts which force a simultaneous interpretation. The sentences are not ungrammatical or pragmatically odd.

(57) a. Susi *sägte*   einen morschen Ast   *ab*, als   es anfing zu regnen.
Susi *sawed* a   dead   branch *off* when it started to rain
TELIC
'Susi was sawing off a dead branch when it started raining.'

b. Während Susi einen morschen Ast   *absägte*, fing es an   zu regnen.
while   Susi a   dead   branch *off-sawed* start$_1$ it start$_2$ to rain
TELIC
'While Susi was sawing off a dead branch, it started raining.'

One could say with Bohnemeyer and Swift (2004) that here a telic situation is presented in imperfective viewpoint rather than in the default perfective viewpoint. This is possible because German has no overt imperfective-perfective distinction.

Overriding the sequential interpretation of a sentence overtly marked for perfective viewpoint is not so easy. In (54) above, a simultaneous interpretation is only available if the verb is Imperfective, not if it is Perfective. (Also notice that English must use the Progressive in (57).)

Summing up, then, perfectivity and telicity share the important properties of bounding an event, and of inviting a sequential interpretation of events in narrative discourse. Thus, there is a semantic and pragmatic overlap between perfectivity and telicity. I will argue next that this overlap explains some curious facts about telicity in Dëne.

3.2. *The Perfective Supplants Telicity in Dëne*

If telicity and perfectivity overlap in such important ways, one might expect to find languages which use only one of the two. Indeed, we just got a glimpse of German, a language that employs only telicity, or situation type in general, to fulfill these functions. Viewpoint aspect is absent from this language as a productive morphosyntactic category. But are there also languages which utilize only viewpoint aspect? I propose that Dëne is just such a language. In Dëne, the viewpoints are omnipresent, and the Perfective has a marked completive, quasi-telic meaning, as we saw above. Due to this, there is a stronger overlap between perfectivity and telicity in Dëne than in many other languages. This makes the expression of telicity unnecessary in all those circumstances where perfectivity covers telicity functions. And since those circumstances are so abundant, telicity is virtually obscured in Dëne. In other words, the Perfective supplants telicity in Dëne.

I will now present evidence that telicity is indeed obscured in Dëne. The evidence comes from the curious fact noted in several Athapaskan languages that there is a lack of expressions which are sensitive to telicity. Since those are the expressions standardly used to test for telicity, the most common and standard telicity tests are also unavailable in Dëne (and in Athapaskan languages in general, as far as this has been examined; see Smith (1991) and Midgette (1996) on Navajo and Bortolin (1998) on a different dialect of Dëne).

3.2.1. 'in an hour' vs. 'for an hour'

The most common expression sensitive to telicity is a time expression which means 'in an hour' (Vendler 1957, Dowty 1979, Smith 1991). Only telic predicates can be felicitously combined with 'in an hour' on the reading that 'one hour passed from the beginning of the event until its natural endpoint was reached' (completion reading). A time expression which means 'for an hour' is compatible with atelic predicates (semelfactives receive a shifted iterative interpretation) and with some accomplishments. (58a) shows an English accomplishment, (58b) an activity. We can see that the activity plus 'in an hour' is very strange—because an event completion reading is excluded.

(58) a. She wrote the letter {√ *in an hour* / ? *for an hour*}.   TELIC

   b. She laughed {# *in an hour* / √ *for an hour*}.   ATELIC

In Dëne, however, there is only one general time adverbial which covers both the 'in an hour' and the 'for an hour' meaning. Therefore, the telicity test based on the 'in/for an hour' contrast also is not available. The general Dëne time adverbial which covers both of these meanings consists of an NP denoting a time period plus the postposition *k'e*:

(59) a. ʔįłághe ts'údzáhi k'e   '(for/in) one hour'
        one   hour   P

    b. ʔįłághe dziné   k'e   '(for/in) one day'
        one   day   P

    c. ʔįłághe sa   k'e   '(for/in) one month'
        one   sun/month P

The postposition *k'e* is often glossed as 'on,' but it is semantically very bleached and is translated as whatever is most appropriate in the given context:[30]

(60) a. [ʔįłá dziné k'e] nánasdá xa.   '*One of these days* I'll patch it.'
        one day P 1s-patch fut

    b. [tthidziné k'e] shíghestį.   '*Yesterday* I ate.'
        also-day P 1s-perf-eat

In less conservative speech, *k'e* is optional (see (61b-c), (62) below). This confirms that the postposition does not make a semantic contribution to the sentence, but is more of a case marker which has been lost in innovative Dëne. Thus, the only semantic contribution comes from the NP, and it does not specify its temporal relationship to the situation at all. It is therefore not surprising that [NP *k'e*] can be interpreted as both 'in X time' and 'for X time.' The general meaning of [NP *k'e*] is shown by speakers' translations into English in (61)-(63). (61) gives activity predicates, (63) accomplishments, and (62) a predicate whose situation type I have not been able to determine. (Omission of *k'e* is indicated by Ø.)

(61) Activities

    a. [ʔįłághe ts'údzáhi k'e] ghesjën.
        one   hour   P   perf-1s-sing
       'I sang *for* an hour.'

    b. [ʔįłá dziné Ø] dighitł'ís.
        one day   perf-1s-write
       'I wrote *for* one day/*in* one day.'

    c. [ʔįłá dziné Ø] honi dighitłʼís.
       one day   story perf-1s-write
       'I finished writing the/a story *in* a day.'

    d. tthidziné kʼe [ʔįłághe tsʼúdzáhi kʼe] nathesku.
       yesterday one   hour P perf-1s-vomit
       'Yesterday I was vomiting *for* one hour.'

(62) <u>Activity or Accomplishment (not sure)</u>
    a. [ʔįłághe sa Ø] łés sųłiné dagį ghą shíghetį.
       one   month bread authentic only P   perf-1s-eat
       'S/he ate only bannock *for* one month.'

    b. [ʔįłághe tsʼúdzáhi Ø] łés ghą shíghetį.
       one   hour   bread P perf-1s-eat
       'It took him/her one hour to eat the bread.' (=> '*in* one hour' reading)

(63) <u>Accomplishments</u>
    a. [ʔįłághe tsʼúdzáhi kʼe] thiłbes.
       one   hour   P perf-1s-boil
       'I boiled it *for* one hour.'

    b. [ʔįłághe tsʼúdzáhi kʼe] bekathełtʼe.
       one   hour   P perf-cook perf
       'S/he cooked it *in/for* an hour.'

    c. sechële [ʔįłá něné Ø] yoh thełtsį.
       1s-younger brother one year   house perf-make
       'My younger brother made a house *in* one year.'

    d. tthidziné kʼe [ʔįłághe tsʼúdzáhi kʼe] jis nánathiłdą́.
       yesterday one   hour P mitten perf-1s-patch
       'Yesterday I patched the mitt *for* one hour.'

We can see that both 'in' and 'for an hour' translations occur, sometimes for the same sentence, e.g., (61b) and (63b).[31] There is also no clear translation pattern by situation type: both 'in' and 'for' translations occur with both activities and accomplishments. These latter two facts—that there is no systematic split in readings by situation type, and that both readings can occur for the same sentence—confirm that [NP *k'e*] is unspecified or "general" regarding the 'in' and the 'for' meaning.[32] They also suggest that the predicates themselves are not distinguishable by telicity, the characteristic which this time expression is supposed to bring out.

Thus, the lack of an 'in' vs. 'for (an hour)' distinction supports the idea that telicity is obscured in two ways. First, by illustrating a lack of sensitivity to the telicity of a predicate, and second, by suggesting that predicates themselves may be indeterminate in terms of telicity.

3.2.2. 'finish' vs. 'stop'

A parallel argument can be made based on another pair of meanings, 'finish' vs. 'stop.' English contains separate lexical expressions for these, and this lexical contrast is used for another common telicity test: Both activities and accomplishments are compatible with the expression meaning 'stop,' but the item meaning 'finish' is only compatible with accomplishments (see, among others, Dowty (1979) for this test):

(64) a. She {√ *finished* / √ *stopped*} writing the letter.   TELIC
    b. She {# *finished* / √ *stopped*} laughing.   ATELIC

As in the case of 'for/in an hour,' Dëne has no separate lexical items for 'stop' and 'finish.' And therefore, the 'stop/finish' contrast can also not serve as a telicity test in Dëne.

There are several lexical items which can be translated as either 'stop' or 'finish.' Of these, the one most like an aspectual verb is *?anat'e*, which follows an Imperfective VP.[33] (65) shows *?anast'e* (the 1s Imperfective form of this verb) with activity predicates, (66) shows it with accomplishment predicates.

(65) Activities

    a. hesjën   ?anast'e.
       1s-sing
       'I'*m done* singing.'

    b. yasti   ?anast'e.
       1s-speak/talk/pray
       'I *finished* praying/speaking, I *stopped* praying/*quit* talking.'

c. yásgus   ʔanastʼe.
      1s-jump(cont)
      'I*'m done* with jumping (*for now*).'

(66) Accomplishments
   a. ʔuneshe   ʔanastʼe.
      1s-pick(berries) impf
      'I*'m finished* picking berries (containers all filled up).'

   b. nánasdą́   ʔanastʼe.
      1s-patch O
      'I*'m finished* patching it.'

   c. yoh hołtsį   ʔanatʼe.
      house make O
      'S/he made the house and *finished* it.' / 'S/he *quit* making the house.'

   d. hesbes   ʔanastʼe.
      1s-boil O
      'I*'m finished* boiling (it).'

These examples clearly illustrate that *ʔanastʼe* covers both the 'stop' (or 'quit') and the 'finish' (or 'be done') meaning. Moreover, while with accomplishments *ʔanastʼe* is fairly consistently translated as 'finish,' there are also instances, (65b) and (66b), where both translations occur for the same predicate, whether it is an activity or an accomplishment. This suggests again that the predicates themselves may be somewhat indeterminate as far as telicity is concerned.

3.2.3. Noun Quantization

In this context it is interesting to look at Dëne NPs. It has often been observed that the atelic/telic distinction in verbs (or VPs) is paralleled by a similar distinction in nouns (e.g., Bach 1986, Krifka 1989). For example, both English mass nouns and atelic verbs/VPs have the property of cumulative or nonquantized reference. Take the mass noun *sand*. If I have *sand* and add *(some more) sand*, the combination of these two will still correctly be referred to as *sand*. A predicate has cumulative reference, then, if the joining of two objects or events denoted by a predicate constitutes another object or event denoted by the same predicate. To give an example of a verb, two events of talking (atelic) constitute together an event of talking.

Both English count nouns and telic verbs/VPs have the property of quantized reference. This means that no proper part of the object or event that such a predicate denotes may also be denoted by the same predicate. For example, no proper part of an object denoted by the count noun *dog* constitutes an object that may also be denoted by *dog*, and no proper part of the event of eating an apple (telic) constitutes an event of eating an apple.

Now, in languages where telicity is not obscured, a connection has been observed between the semantics of the direct object and the telicity of the VP: a quantized direct object seems to be required in order to get a telic VP (e.g., Krifka 1989, 1992). For example, in English *eat* forms a VP with telic reference only in combination with a quantized DP like *an apple* or *the apple*. With a cumulative DP such as *porridge* or *apples*, an atelic interpretation results:

(67) a. She *ate an apple* (√ in five minutes).   VPs with telic/
 b. She *ate the apple* (√ in five minutes).   quantized reference
 c. She *ate the apples* (√ in five minutes).
 d. She *ate the porridge* (√ in five minutes).

(68) a. She *ate porridge* (# in five minutes).   VPs with atelic/
 b. She *ate apples* (# in five minutes).   cumulative reference

Note that in English, the morphosyntax of the DP indicates whether a nominal constituent has quantized or cumulative reference. Take first number inflection: Count nouns have distinct singular and plural forms. Singular count nouns are quantized precisely because they are singular. Mass nouns cannot be inflected for number and thus cannot be marked as quantized by this process. The second grammatical device interacting with quantization is definiteness. All definite nominals, be they mass or count, have quantized reference, presumably because the definite determiner selects all instances of an entity in a given context (cf. Link 1983, Chierchia 1998 for details). Nominals with an indefinite determiner (= *a*) are singular and thus also quantized. Mass nouns and plural count nouns can occur without determiner, and then have cumulative reference, as in (68). Quantized reference can be achieved by counting and/or measuring them:[34]

(69) a. She ate *two bowls of* porridge (√ in five minutes).
 b. She ate *two* apples (√ in five minutes).

Interestingly, in Dëne, there is no NP morphosyntax to signal the distinction between quantized and cumulative reference. Nominal constituents usually consist of only a bare noun; there is no number morphology and no determiners. Plurality can be marked by verbal prefixes (*he-* in position 5 for a 3dl subject, *dá#* in position 9 for a plural/distributive subject or object), but Cook (2004) shows that this marking is optional in nonisolated sentences. In the absence of number inflection, Dëne count nouns are not specified for singular or plural. They may denote a single instance of an entity, or several instances, as shown in (70).

(70) a. dzół xěł senádé.   (Wilhelm 2005)
     ball with several play impf
     'They (several) are playing with a ball/with balls.'

  b. Bal łue nághéłnígh.
     Val fish perf-buy
     'Val bought fish.' [speaker comment: "it doesn't say how many"]

But this means that they have cumulative reference: the joining of two objects denoted by *dzół*, for example, will also be denoted by *dzół*. Mass nouns, of course, are also cumulative. For example, the sum of two instances of *běr* 'meat' is also an instance of *běr* 'meat.' Combined with the absence of determiners, the result is that all Dëne nouns have cumulative reference, unless they are counted and/or measured, as in (71).

(71) a. náke łue hesbes.
     two fish 1s-boil O
     'I'm boiling two fish.'

  b. solághe nedádhi běr   (Wilhelm 2005)
     five   pound   meat
     'five pounds of meat'[35]

In sum, the lack of morphosyntactic processes like number inflection and definiteness marking means that nominal quantization is not grammatized in Dëne. This is no accident in light of the fact that telicity is not grammatized either. The quantization of nominals simply is not as important as in a language like English, where it contributes to telicity. But in Dëne, telicity, and therefore also quantization, are unimportant.

3.2.4. Summary

The proposal that telicity is indeed obscured in Dëne (through the completive Perfective) finds independent support in the lack of expressions which are sensitive to telicity: neither the 'in/for an hour' contrast not the 'stop/finish' contrast are lexicalized, and nominals are not overtly quantized.

Now, what exactly does it mean to say that telicity is "obscured" in Dëne? After all, I did class predicates as accomplishments vs. activities in some examples given above. I do *not* mean that telicity is not part of the semantics of the language, and that, for example, speakers cannot express certain situation types. Rather, what I mean is that telicity is not *grammatized* in Dëne, i.e., grammatical processes do not have access to (and are insensitive to) telicity. I will argue for this claim at length in the next chapter. But first, let me show that telicity is part of the semantics of Dëne, and that in most cases one can determine whether a predicate is telic or not.

3.2.5. 'Almost'

As just pointed out, the facts presented thus far do not mean that Dëne does not distinguish between telic and atelic predicates. To illustrate, I will present a lexical item which clearly distinguishes accomplishments, *k'ájëne* 'almost.' The interpretation of 'almost' is a well-known accomplishment test (Dowty 1979). 'Almost' plus an activity results in an event onset reading. Accomplishments have an additional event completion reading. I illustrate with English examples:

(72) She *almost* laughed. (activity)

    (i) √ She never laughed/never even started laughing. (ONSET)

    (ii) # She started laughing but did not finish laughing. (COMPL.)

(73) She *almost* wrote the letter. (accomplishment)

    (i) √ She never wrote the letter/never even started writing it. (ONSET)

    (ii) √ She started writing the letter but did not finish it. (COMPL.)

In Dëne, the different readings for the two situation types are striking. If not rejected altogether, activities show the expected event onset reading, while for accomplishments the event completion reading is salient. (Recall that English translations were provided by Dëne speakers.)

(75) Activities
   a. k'ájëne ghitsagh.
      almost perf-1s-cry
      'I almost cried (never started).'

   b.? k'ájëne ghesjën.
      almost perf-1s-sing
      'I just about sang (but didn't).' (pragmatically a bit odd)

   c. k'ájëne yághesgus.
      almost perf-1s-jump(cont)
      'I almost jumped (continuously) (but didn't).'

   d. k'ájëne thanakóthi nighił?į́.
      almost car   perf-1s-look at O perf
      'I almost looked at the car (but never did).'
                       (. . . nághesnígh xa)
                       (1s-buy   fut)
                       (. . . 'so I could buy it')

(76) Accomplishments
   a. k'ájëne bĕr   thiłbes.
      almost meat perf-1s-boil O
      'I'm almost done cooking the meat by boiling it.'/ 'I'm almost finished boiling the meat.'

   b. k'ájëne bekáthiłt'e.
      almost perf-1s-cook perf
      'I'm just about finished cooking.'

   c. k'ájëne thiłtsį.
      almost perf-1s-make O
      'I just about finished making it.'/ 'I'm almost done making it.'

   d. k'ájëne nánathiłdą́.
      almost perf-1s-patch O
      'I just about mended it.' (event reading)

The 'almost' facts confirm that there is a semantic distinction between atelic and telic predicates, at least as far as activities and accomplishments are concerned. It should be noted, however, that 'almost' cannot distinguish achievements from semelfactives. This is because they are both punctual, and with punctual predicates 'almost' can only get an onset reading, irrespective of telicity. In fact, 'almost' seems more sensitive to event complexity than to telicity per se. Accomplishments are the only complex situation type, being both durative and telic (containing both a process and a change of state). So, we are still left with the fact that Dëne has very few expressions which are sensitive to telicity alone, which I have taken as evidence that telicity is obscured in Dëne.

4. CONCLUSION

In this chapter, I have explored the semantics and pragmatics of the Dëne viewpoints, the Imperfective and the Perfective. We have seen that the Imperfective has durative force, as is most clearly shown by its incompatibility with nondurative verbs. Because the Imperfective, a morphosyntactic category of the language, requires access to the durativity of a predicate, I have argued that durativity is grammatized through the Imperfective in Dëne. In terms of pragmatics, the Imperfective is used to express a situation which is simultaneous with another, and to background situations in discourse.

The Dëne Perfective has a strong completive meaning: it entails that a situation is over, and even completed. This marked type of Perfective is represented in terms of TT including not only TSit, but also the posttime of TSit. But the Perfective overlaps not only semantically, but also pragmatically, with telicity. Cross-linguistically, both telicity and perfectivity may serve to bound situations, and to express a sequential temporal relationship between situations. I showed that in Dëne, the Perfective fulfills these functions. This makes recourse to telicity unnecessary in most circumstances. The semantic and pragmatic overlaps, combined with the pervasiveness of the Perfective, eliminate the need to grammatize the notion of telicity, and telicity is all but obscured in the language. A lack of expressions sensitive to telicity provided independent evidence that telicity is obscured in Dëne.

I concluded that telicity is not grammatized in Dëne. This is a weaker and more plausible claim than saying that telicity is not even a semantic notion in the language. The latter claim is doubtful on conceptual grounds, as it amounts to a Sapir-Whorfian view of language. It is also doubtful empirically, as there is some evidence (the interpretation of *k'ájëne* 'almost') that atelic and telic situations are distinct semantically. The view that telicity is not grammatized in Dëne concurs with Smith's (1991, 1996) findings on Navajo.

In the next chapter, I take up in detail my claim that telicity is not grammatized in Dëne. I will show that productive morphosyntactic contrasts of Dëne do not represent or access telicity. I will focus on those processes and categories which have been proposed in the literature to be loci of grammatizing telicity in Athapaskan. A careful synchronic study of Dëne will reveal that these processes and categories are not productive or not attested, or not correlated with telicity.

Chapter Three
Telicity Is Not Grammatized in Dëne

In the last chapter, we saw that Dëne has a very pervasive viewpoint system, and I proposed that the completive Perfective viewpoint obscures telicity in Dëne. More precisely, I propose that telicity is not grammatized in Dëne. In this chapter, I present evidence for this proposal.

Let us begin by reviewing what I mean by grammatization: a semantic notion is grammatized in a language if it is evident in a productive morphosyntactic contrast or category. This is in the spirit of Klein (2002), who uses the same criterion to distinguish between the "descriptive component" of the lexical content and that component which contains grammatically relevant elements.

To show that telicity is not grammatized in Dëne, I thus have to show that there is no productive morphosyntactic contrast or category which accesses telicity. Since I cannot possibly discuss all productive morphosyntactic processes and categories of Dëne, I will focus on those which have to do with the aspectual system of the language. I will do this by reviewing important proposals on the aspectual significance of certain morphological categories found in Athapaskan languages. Some of these categories have been argued to be sensitive to telicity or a very similar notion. I will show that in fact there is no evidence for a correlation between these categories and telicity in Dëne synchronically. This becomes particularly clear if one starts out, as I do, with a semantic rather than a morphological classification of Dëne verbs, and then examines whether the semantic classification (into situation types) correlates with productive morphological contrasts or categories.

I will begin with a discussion of the traditional idea of verb theme categories (section 1), and then (in sections 2 and 3) look at the conjugation markers (CM's) which we already encountered in Chapter Two. Finally I will examine direct objects (section 4), which have not received as much attention in the literature as the verb theme categories and the CM's. As just stated, we will see that none of these correlate with telicity in Dëne.

1. VERB THEME CATEGORIES

The longest-standing and most influential proposal about the grammatization of aspectual notions in Athapaskan is the idea of verb theme categories, first developed by Kari (1979) for Ahtna, and taken up for such diverse Athapaskan languages as Slave (Rice 1989), Koyukon (Axelrod 1993) and Navajo (Midgette (1996); but see Smith (1996) for a different view). Verb theme categories are lexical classes of verbs (i.e., verb themes), and they are distinguished by the types of derivations they can undergo.[1] While derivational morphology is the criterion for distinguishing these classes, the claim is that they have a semantic basis in aspectual distinctions reminiscent of the situation types: which roots can undergo which derivations depends on the situation type they denote. Thus, the claim is that productive derivational morphology expresses situation type notions, including telicity.

However, there generally is no clear semantic testing or evidence for this claim. Morphologically determined classes are assigned semantic labels, and the reality of these labels is not examined. Moreover, it is doubtful whether Dëne even has a morphological system of verb theme categories, as I will show below.

In order to assess whether situation type, and in particular telicity, is indeed grammatized through verb theme categories in Dëne, I will introduce Kari's (1979) and Axelrod's (1993) categorizations. To my knowledge, these two represent the most detailed works on verb theme categories. I shall begin with Kari (1979), who developed the idea of verb theme categories.

1.1. Kari (1979)

Kari (1979) is a very detailed examination of lexical classes in Ahtna, an Alaskan Athapaskan language. Ahtna is morphologically more conservative and allows more complex syllables than Dëne; thus it is easier to analyze the verb stem into a root plus a suffix. In doing this, Kari discovered systematic stem suffixation paradigms, called *stem suffixation formulae*, by viewpoint aspect and mode: different verb classes in Ahtna take different suffixes in the Imperfective, Perfective, Optative (as well as the Future and the Perfective Negative; both nonexistent as stem alternations in Dëne). Altogether there are 27 different stem suffixation formulae, thus 27 verb classes. Kari proposes that these verb classes represent different "aspects" (henceforth: Aspects) in which an Ahtna verb may appear.

However, not all of these Aspects are basic; some contain only verb themes which are formed via derivational (thematic) prefixes from more basic verb themes. Kari thus superimposes on the 27 Aspects a more general categorization which looks at only the most basic Aspect in which each stem is found (the derivational elements of the most basic Aspect in which a stem is found are called "primary aspectual string"). Normally a theme in a basic Aspect consists of just the stem (root + suffix) and the CM (a cognate of the respective Dëne CM). Altogether, Kari arrives at ten general *verb theme categories*, each with its own basic imperfective/perfective CM pattern and suffixation formula. Table 4 gives Kari's ten categories.

Table 4. Ahtna verb theme categories according to Kari (1979)			
verb theme category LABEL	basic CM pattern	semantics of basic themes	example (and name of basic "Aspect")
(i) nonstative (active[a]*):*			
MOTION themes	**n-/n-**	characterize movement; e.g., momentaneous movement	**n**iya· (perf) 's/he arrived, came to a point' ("Momentaneous Aspect")
SUCCESSIVE themes	**Ø/gh-**	multiple/repeated events	i**gh**itse·tl' (perf) 's/he chopped it repeatedly' ("Durative Aspect")
OPERATIVE themes	**Ø/gh-**	perform action duratively	**gh**adna' (perf) 's/he worked' ("Durative Aspect")
CONVERSIVE themes	**Ø/s-**	complete a process	yi**z**dle·dz (perf)[b] 's/he cooked it' ("Conclusive Aspect")
(ii) stative (neuter):			
EXTENSION themes	**n-/gh-**	'be'	**n**i'a· 'it extends' (impf)
CLASSIFICATORY themes	**s-/gh-**	shape/texture/ animacy/ number of an entity	**z**ta·n (impf) 'stick-like O is in position'
POSITIONAL themes	**s-/gh-**	be in x position	**z**da· (impf) 's/he is sitting, staying'
STATIVE themes	**s-/gh-**	(various states)	de**z**q'ats' (impf) 'it's cold'

Table 4.—*(continued)*			
DIMENSIONAL themes	Ø/gh-	shape/size/quality/ color of single argument	deldel (impf) 'it is red'
DESCRIPTIVE themes	Ø/gh-	"catch-all Ø-neuter grouping" (p. 174)	k'ila·n (impf) 'it is abundant'
a. In the Athapaskan literature, the term "active" means "nonstative" (rather than "not passive"). "Neuter" means "stative." b. I assume that the segment *z* reflects the CM *s*-.			

Each of these categories has its own derivational potential, in terms of which other Aspects beyond the basic one the stems/themes may occur in. The motion theme category is the most productive: by varying the CM's and adding derivational material, hundreds of verb themes are created in about a dozen other Aspects such as "momentaneous-customary," "momentaneous-distributive-customary," "reversative," "continuative." Other verb theme categories are of varying productivity; the least productive ones contain only a small number of verb themes in few if any other Aspects.

As already mentioned above, Kari implies that the categories in table 1 are the lexical aspectual classes of Ahtna (and of Athapaskan in general). Obviously, some of Kari's semantic characterizations are very suggestive, and it is tempting to try and match them with the better-known situation types. For example, there clearly is a division between stative and nonstative verb themes in Ahtna, and among the nonstative themes conversive(-conclusive) themes might correspond to accomplishments, (momentaneous) motion themes to achievements, durative operative and successive themes to activities, and semelfactive successive themes to semelfactives. Thus, if translated into modern terminology, it seems that the morphologically-determined lexical verb classes of Ahtna correspond to situation type, and effectively grammatize the five situation types, including the telic-atelic distinction.

However, we have to keep in mind that these are primarily morphological rather than semantic classes. In the absence of shared phonological characteristics, it was logical to look for semantic characteristics of the verb theme categories. Certainly, prototypical members of each category, as given in table 1, may exhibit clear semantic characteristics, but each category also contains many verb themes which are less clear or even surprising semantically. For example, under motion themes in momentaneous Aspect (≈ achievements), we also find themes like *ɬdaniya* 's/he walked a long time' (p.83), *naniya* 's/he went across' (p. 83), *ye' ughiya* 's/he went all over the place' (p. 85). Judging from their gloss, these could just as likely be activities or accomplishments. And conversive themes in conclusive Aspect (≈ accomplishments) like *hwełna·n* 's/he won,' *naquzka·q'* 's/he installed rafters,' *nastqoy* 's/he vomited' (p. 148) could be achievements or activities.[2] But Kari does not provide any explicit semantic evidence, and to my knowledge the semantics of this primarily morphological classification has not yet been investigated for Ahtna. Based on Kari's (1979) work, I speculate that the Ahtna verb theme categories are more like the noun classes of Bantu languages: while they have a (perhaps historical) semantic basis, each class also contains a large number of semantically arbitrary members (see Corbett 1991 and references therein).

1.2. Axelrod (1993)

Working on another Alaskan Athapaskan language, Koyukon, Axelrod (1993) develops a verb theme categorization very similar to that of Kari's. However, she justifies the categories in a slightly different manner, which gives interesting insights into the categorization. Like Kari, she proposes, on morphological grounds, a number (fifteen) of Aspects, which are obligatory categories of the verb. Unlike Kari, she bases verb theme category membership not on a verb theme's "primary aspectual string," but on its aspectual derivational potential, i.e., on which Aspects a verb theme can occur in. Table 5 illustrates for the nonstative categories:

Table 5. Nonstative Koyukon verb theme categories according to Axelrod (1993)

verb theme category LABEL	possible Aspect oppositions (cf. p. 123–25)						diagnostic Aspect (cf. p. 25–26)
	Semelfactive	Consecutive	Conclusive	Durative	Momentaneous	other motion Aspects[a]	
MOTION					√	√	Momentaneous
OPERATIVE			√	√			Durative
CONVERSIVE		√	√	√			Conclusive
SUCCESSIVE	√	√	√	X	√		Semelfactive

a. These are the Perambulative, the Continuative, the Persistive, and the Reversative (Axelrod 1993:20), which all provide different contours to a motion event.

Again, the semantic description of the verb theme categories is very suggestive of situation type: members of the successive category are characterized as denoting "punctual actions that can be performed once or as a series of single actions" (p. 25), conversive themes as denoting telic situations, "focusing [. . .] on the goal or completion of the action" (p.25), operative themes as denoting "processes, activities that take place over a period of time" (p. 25–26), and motion themes as denoting "movement performed in a particular direction, manner, or time frame" (p. 26). Based on these semantic descriptions, we could identify the operative category with activity situations, the conversive category with accomplishments, and the successive category with semelfactives. Only achievements do not correspond to a verb theme category, but are a subclass of motion themes, namely motion themes in Momentaneous Aspect. Nonetheless, the picture that emerges for Koyukon even more clearly than for Ahtna is that the broad lexical-derivational categories of this language correspond (roughly) to the universal situation types. This would be a clear case in which aspectual-derivational morphology represents—and thus grammatizes—situation type notions, including telicity.

But are the verb theme categories really morphosyntactic, i.e., formal expressions of situation type meanings, i.e., is there really a match between formal and semantic categories? Axelrod says (p. 26) that verb theme categories in Koyukon are "not precise descriptions of categories with clear-cut parameters," but rather "a means of abbreviating or symbolizing the structural, semantic and distributional characteristics of a group of verb themes." She does not provide semantic tests for verb theme category membership, but points out that there is semantic overlap between categories, and that each category has more and less prototypical members. For these reasons, we cannot be sure that these morphology-based categories really are formal expressions of the situation types.

Summing up, the aspectual-derivational morphology (particularly the stem suffixation patterns) of conservative Athapaskan languages provides evidence for lexical verb classes called verb theme categories. These formal categories are believed to have a semantic basis in situation aspect, but the explicit semantic evidence to support this idea does not yet exist. Having introduced verb theme categories, I will now turn to the question whether such a categorization also exists in Dëne.

1.3. Verb Theme Categories in Dëne?

Recall that the major criterion for establishing verb theme categories is which Aspects a verb theme may occur in. The Aspects, in turn, are identified based on the stem sets or stem suffixation patterns which occur in the perfective, imperfective, optative (and other "modes" the language may have).

For example, the suffixation pattern of Conclusive Aspect in Koyukon looks as follows (Axelrod 1993:79): open roots show Ø imperfective, *-nh* (=[ŋ]) perfective, *-ł* future, *-ł* optative. For the root *tsee* [tsi] 'make sg/dual object,' a cognate of the Dëne stem *tsi̯*, the resulting Conclusive stem set is *tsee, tseenh, tseeł, tseeł* (cf. (1a) below). Reduced-vowel closed roots have the suffixation pattern Ø, *-ŋ*, Ø, Ø, which results in unvaried stem sets, (1b). Most full-vowel obstruent-closed roots have this same pattern, but because the obstruent coda of full-vowel roots spirantizes unless blocked by a suffix, the resulting stem set looks different, (1c). Finally, some full-vowel closed roots are exceptional because spirantization does not occur, (1d). Thus, for the Conclusive Aspect there are three stem sets by syllable type, plus one exceptional stem set. I give an example of each (from Axelrod 1993:79):

(1)	syllable type and root	impf	perf	fut	opt	gloss
a.	CV: *tsee*	*tsee*	*tseenh*	*tseeł*	*tseeł*	'make sg/dl O'
b.	CəC: *ləts*	*ləts*	*ləts*	*ləts*	*ləts*	'urinate'
c.	CVT³: *ts'oots*	*ts'oos*	*ts'oos*	*ts'oos*	*ts'oos*	'dry up'
d.	(exception) *baats*	*baats*	*baats*	*baats*	*baats*	'boil'

This example of the Conclusive Aspect illustrates two things: first, the stem suffixation patterns are a very complex process, which depends on root shape and has exceptions; second, the final consonant is crucial to determining stem suffixation patterns and therefore the Aspects.

Now, the syllable structure of Dëne is more restrictive than that of Koyukon or Ahtna. The only permissible codas are single sonorants or fricatives; the many noncontinuant obstruents are not allowed (Cook 2004). This wreaks havoc with the stem suffixation patterns of closed syllables. For example, the root 'boil' in Dëne, cognate with the Koyukon root 'boil' given in (1), is invariable: it is always *bes* (impf), *bes* (perf)[4], *bes* (opt), while in Koyukon the Conversive stem set given in (1d) is different from the Momentaneous stem set *baas, baats, bestl, baas* (Axelrod 1993:54). But in Dëne, there is only stem set/Aspect of 'boil,' or if there were two, they would be indistinguishable. Moreover, Dëne has simply lost root-final consonants or affixes. For example, the cognate stem set for 'make sg/dl O' in Dëne is simply *tsi* (impf), *tsi̯* (perf), *tsi̯* (opt), without trace of the suffixes *-ł* or *-nh*.

For these reasons, it is very difficult to determine in Dëne which Aspect a given verb theme is in. In fact, it is impossible to distinguish morphologically most of the Aspects found in Koyukon and Ahtna. It is my impression that, due to phonological simplification and morpheme loss, the Aspects are greatly impoverished in Dëne, and one cannot really speak of a system of Aspects in this language. This is supported by the fact that neither Li (1946) nor Cook (2004), the most detailed descriptions of the language, have come up with a system of Aspects comparable to that proposed for Ahtna or Koyukon. I will briefly discuss Li's attempt because it illustrates how impoverished the Dëne system is.

1.3.1. Li (1946)

Li (1946), predating Kari by some thirty years, noted a morphological relationship between certain verb stems in Dëne. He says that there are five potential derivations or "modes" (henceforth: Modes) available to the verb stems of the language, and gives these Modes aspectual labels, as shown in table 6 below. (In addition, verbs of each Mode may occur in the imperfective, perfective or "future" (= optative).) Perhaps these Modes are comparable to the Ahtna or Koyukon Aspects?

Table 6. Modes of the Dëne verb according to Li (1946)		
(surface ɛ and r replaced by underlying e and d, respectively)		
MODE	SEMANTICS, as stated by Li (1946:405)	EXAMPLE THEME (with impf/perf/opt stems)
Neuter	"state or [...] position"	Ø–tį̄, –tį̄, –té '(living being) in lying position'
Momentaneous	"a rapid action or transition from one state to another"	ne–téih, –tį̄, –té '(living being) get into lying position'
Continuative	"activity which lasts for a certain length of time"	ná#te, –tį̄, –té '(living being) lie continually' > 'dream'
Customary	"action which is customary or repeated"	dzé–dé–ł–teih, –teih, –teih 'handle living being customarily/repeated-ly' > 'carry (living being) around'
Progressive	"activity which is kept on particularly while one is moving along"	da–ł–teł, –teł, –teł 'keep on handling a living being' > 'hold (living being)'
Abstract stem	e.g., "handle a living being"	— (no underlying form suggested)

Li's classification represents a mixture of verb theme categories and Aspects, and probably also some additional categories: Li's Neuter Mode seems to coincide with two of Kari's stative theme categories: stative-positional and classificatory. This is supported by the fact that these have cognate imperfective/perfective CM's: *the-/ghe-* (Dëne) and *s-/gh-* (Ahtna). The Momentaneous Mode in table 3 corresponds to the basic Aspect of motion themes in Koyukon and Ahtna, the Momentaneous. Li's customary and progressive Modes are called "super-aspects" in Axelrod (1993) because they are not mutually exclusive with the Aspects and each other. It seems, then, that only one of the Modes identified by Li corresponds to an Aspect, namely the Momentaneous. Interestingly, this is the Aspect that is most easily identified morphologically in Dëne.

Thus, even in a documentation of Dëne from almost 80 years ago[5], we can see that the system of "Aspects" and verb theme categories is much more rudimentary than that of Ahtna or Koyukon. First of all, the number of classes found by Li is much smaller than that found by Kari. Second, Li's Modes represent a mix of different types of categories in the more conservative languages (Aspect, verb theme category, superaspect). Third, the morphological relations between the different Modes of a stem are "highly irregular" (Li 1946:408); underlying abstract stems and suffixation formulae cannot be given. In many cases it cannot be asserted without doubt that verbs represent related Modes of a single stem. Fourth, only a small number of stems can occur in all five Modes. From the examples given by Li, it seems that only the small set of "classificatory" verb stems, i.e., stems which denote some physical characteristic of its absolutive argument ('living being,' 'stick-like,' 'fabric-like,' 'round and solid,' etc.) occur in all five Modes. It is thus doubtful whether the idea of abstract stems in different Modes (or Aspects) holds for the majority of Dëne verbs.

Summing up, Li (1946) attempts a verb theme categorization, but he focuses on stative and motion themes, which often contain related stems and which have a wide derivational potential. Other types of themes do not seem to be part of the categorization, and there is no Aspect system comparable to that of Ahtna or Koyukon. I conclude that a verb theme categorization, if it does exist in Dëne, cannot be based on an Aspect-type system.

This leaves us with the conjugation markers as possible morphological criteria for verb theme categories, and thus as potential candidates for grammatizing telicity. I discuss CM's next.

2. CONJUGATION MARKERS

As discussed in Chapter Two, Dëne has four prefixes (*the-, ghe-, ne-,* Ø), called conjugation markers or CM's, which are involved in marking Imperfective and

Perfective viewpoint.[6] Their distribution, i.e., which of the four prefixes marks the Imperfective and which marks the Perfective for a given verb theme, is traditionally thought to be determined by lexical verb class. There are four broad CM patterns, Ø-imperfective/*the*-perfective, Ø-imperfective/*ghe*-perfective, *ne*-imperfective/*ne*-perfective, and *the*-imperfective/*ghe*-perfective. These four morphological patterns define four broad verb classes. Now, a group of researchers has explored whether these CM-based verb classes have an aspectual semantic foundation (Midgette 1996, Bortolin 1998, Rice 2000).[7] For example, if these lexical classes corresponded to the five situation types, then we could say that the language marks situation type overtly in its morphology, and more specifically that situation type is grammatized through the CM patterns.

This interesting idea is also already foreshadowed in the work of Kari (1979). Recall that the "primary aspectual strings" on which Kari bases the Ahtna verb theme categories in large part, differ in the CM patterns they display (see table 4 above). The cognate Dëne CM's can be used for a morphological classification similar to Kari's. In fact, the inflected examples Li (1946:406) gives of each of his proposed five "modes" differ in CM's as well. I repeat Li's examples to illustrate (Impf. and Perf. CM's are underlined, nonovert Impf. CM's are indicated by an added Ø. Surface ε is replaced by underlying *e*):

(2) Neuter: θi-tį 'I am lying,' ɣi–tį 'I had lain (no longer lying),' ɣwa-s-té 'I shall lie'

Momentaneous: ne-s-téih 'I am lying down,' ni·-tį 'I have lain down,' nu-s-té 'I shall lie down'

Continuative: ná-Ø-s-té 'I dream,' ná-θi·-tį 'I have dreamt,' ná-ɣwa-s-té 'I shall dream'

Customary: dzéré-Ø-s-teih 'I am carrying it around,' dzéré-ɣi-ł-teih 'I have carried it around,' dzéré-ɣwa-s-teih 'I shall carry it around'

Progressive: da-ye-s-teł 'I am holding it,' da-ɣi-ł-teł 'I have been holding it,' da-ɣwa-s-teł 'I shall hold it up'

We saw above that Li's "modes" represent a mix of categories. Bortolin (1998) establishes five more basic classes of verb themes in Dëne based on the CM prefixes they require. These five classes correspond to Kari's major theme categories: to the four active theme categories, plus one class (with two subclasses) for all stative theme categories. Bortolin argues that these classes have a semantic basis and correspond to Smith's (1991) five situation types.

Telicity Is Not Grammatized in Dëne 79

Importantly, she supports her claim with principled semantic evidence. Here is her classification. ("Seriative" refers to verb themes of the successive-semelfactive category which denote an open-ended series of punctual events.)

Table 7. Lexical aspectual classes in Dëne according to Bortolin (1998), with traditional terminology added

Group	Situation Types (= lexical aspect)	Traditional terminology	Morphology (= CM's)	
			Imperfective	Perfective
Active		Active		
	activity	operative	Ø	ghe-
	achievement	motion/momentaneous	ne-	ne-
	accomplishment	conversive/conclusive	Ø	the-
	semelfactive	successive-semelfactive	Ø	the-
	(seriative)	successive-seriative	Ø	ghe-
Stative		Neuter		
	stative-attributive		Ø	N/A
	stative-positional		the-	ghe-

Bortolin proposes that the situation type or lexical aspect of a verb determines which CM's are chosen. For example, *ya#l–ti* 'talk, pray' is an activity and thus has a Ø-imperfective/*ghe*-perfective pattern. *l–bes* 'boil O' is an accomplishment, with Ø-imperfective and *the*-perfective. Note that activity and seriative verb themes use the same CM pattern (Ø/*ghe*-), as do accomplishments and semelfactives (Ø/*the*-).[8] I will shortly give examples for each verb class. But before I do so, I want to discuss Rice (2000), which takes Bortolin's proposal yet a step further.

Rice (2000), using Slave as the primary language of investigation, suggests that CM's do not mark viewpoint at all (viewpoint is marked by stem changes and by extra material following the CM, as discussed in section 2.1 below), but that their sole function is to indicate situation type. In Rice's (2000:253) words, "situation aspect is overtly marked, or grammaticalized, in Athapaskan languages." She proposes the following associations between situation type and CM, in Perfective nonstative verbs:

(3) activity: *gh* (Rice 2000:257)
accomplishment: *s* (= *the*- in Dëne)
achievement: *n*
semelfactive: *s* (= *the*- in Dëne)

The syncretism between accomplishment and semelfactive marking is explained as follows: in the perfective, not only semelfactives but also accomplishments are viewed as single punctual events. This neutralizes the differences in duration and telicity between them. Because they represent, in the perfective, a single semantic situation type category, they are marked by the same CM *s*. In nonperfective viewpoints, semelfactives show a "subsituation aspect" prefix *i-* (= position 4 in Dëne) which distinguishes them from other situation types.[9]

Rice (2000) does not apply any semantic tests to show that *gh-*marked verbs are indeed activities, *n-* marked verbs achievements, etc. Rather, she presents morphological evidence that has to do with regular cooccurrence of the predicted CM with further aspectual and derivational prefixes. For example, verb themes with an "inceptive" prefix, which focus on the early part of an event ('start to V') pattern like accomplishments and take the *s* CM.

In summary, several Athapaskan studies either associate the CM's themselves with semantic force (Young and Morgan 1987, Rice 2000), or they use the different CM patterns found in a language as the major criterion for morphological verb classes, which are then correlated with lexical aspectual classes (Kari 1979, Bortolin 1998, to some extent Li 1946). These proposals represent a significant step in the attempt to understand the aspectual organization of Athapaskan languages. Moreover, core examples of each verb class indeed provide support for the proposed correlation between morphology and aspectual meaning.

However, a careful morphological and semantic examination of verbs/CM patterns in Dëne reveals that the correlation between morphology and semantics is not as consistent as initially thought. I will discuss this in sections 2.1 and 3 below. In section 2.1, I address morphological problems that some of these proposals face in Dëne. In section 3, I class Dëne verbs based on situation type *meaning* and show that these semantic classes do not correlate with the morphological classes.

2.1. *Morphological Problems*

Below are Dëne examples to illustrate each of the situation type verb classes proposed by Rice (2000) and Bortolin (1998). (I ignore stative verbs.) To keep things simple, only first and third person singular forms are given. Optative forms are included because they are relevant to the discussion that follows. Conjugation markers are underlined.[10]

(4) CM pattern: Ø/ghe- ; proposed situation type: ACTIVITY
verb theme: ya#ł–ti (?#cl-stem) 'talk, pray' (Cook 2004)
   a. yasti   ya#Ø–s–ł–ti   'I am talking/praying'   IMPF
      yałti   ya#Ø–ł–ti   's/he is talking/praying'
   b. yaghiłti ya#ghe-i–ł–ti 'I talked/prayed'   PERF
      yaghiłti ya#ghe–N–ł–ti 's/he talked/prayed'
   c. yawasti ya#wa–s–ł–ti   'may I talk/pray?'   OPT
      yawułti ya#wa–ne–ł–ti   'you (sg) may talk'

(5) CM pattern: Ø/the- ; proposed situation type: ACCOMPLISHMENT
verb theme: ł–bes (cl-boil) 'boil O'
   a. hesbes   Ø–s–ł–bes   'I am boiling it (e.g., meat)' IMPF
      yełbes   ye–Ø–ł–bes   's/he's boiling it'
   b. thiłbes/z[11] the-i–ł–bes/z   'I boiled it'   PERF
      yé–ł–bes/z   ye–the(>H)–ł–bes/z 's/he boiled it'
   c. wułbes   wa–ne–ł–bes   'boil it!' (2sg)   OPT
      yułbes   ye–wa–ł–bes   's/he might boil it'

(6) CM pattern: ne-/ne- ; proposed situation type: ACHIEVEMENT
verb theme: ghá#ł–chu (impf), –chú (perf), –chu (opt) (from Cook 2004)
      P#cl-fabriclike 'to give fabric-like O to'
   a. beghá̜neschu   be-ghá̜#ne–s–ł–chu   'I am giving him/her   IMPF
                                          fabric-like O'
      yeghá̜iłchu   ye-ghá̜#ne–ł–chu   's/he is giving him/her
                                          fabric-like O'
   b. beghá̜niłchú   be-ghá̜#ne-i–ł–chú   'I gave him/her   PERF
                                          fabric-like O'
      yeghá̜iłchú   ye-ghá̜#ne–ł–chú   's/he gave him/her
                                          fabric-like O'
   c. beghá̜waschu   be-ghá̜#wa–s–ł–chu   'I should give him/her   OPT
                                          fabric-like O'
      beghá̜nuschu   be-ghá̜#ne–wa–s–ł–chu   (alternate form)
      yeghá̜yułchu   ye-ghá̜#(ye?)–wa–ł–chu   's/he should give
                                             him/her fabric-like O'

(7) CM pattern: *ne-/ne-* ; proposed situation type: ACHIEVEMENT
verb theme: *ne–Ø–dá* (impf), *–da* (perf), *–dá* (opt)
   CM/th-cl-sg sit 'sg[12] sit down'

a.	nesdá	<u>ne</u>–s–Ø–dá	'I am (in the process of) sitting down'	IMPF
	nedá	<u>ne</u>–Ø–dá	's/he is (in the process of) sitting down'	
b.	nida	<u>ne</u>–the–i–Ø–da	'I sat down'	PERF
	néda	<u>ne</u>–the(>H)–Ø–da	's/he sat down'	
c.	nusdá	<u>ne</u>–<u>wa</u>–s–Ø–dá	'I should sit down'	OPT
	nudá	<u>ne</u>–<u>wa</u>–dá	's/he should sit down' (Cook 2004)	

(8) CM pattern: *Ø/the-* ; proposed situation type: SEMELFACTIVE
verb theme: *é–ł–yúł* (impf, opt), *ł–yúł* (perf)[13]
   sem/th-cl-blow 'blow O once'

a.	héshúł	é–Ø–s–ł–yúł	'I am going to blow it once'	IMPF
	yíshúł	ye–é–Ø–(i–?)ł–yúł	's/he is going to blow it once'	
b.	thishúł	<u>the</u>–i–ł–yúł	'I blew it once'	PERF
	yéshúł	ye–<u>the</u>(>H)–ł–yúł	's/he blew it once'	
c.	húshúł	é–<u>wa</u>–s–ł–yúł	'may I blow it once?'	OPT
	húghúlyúł	é–<u>ghwa</u>–íd–ł–yúł	'(you and I) let's blow it (out)'	

(9) CM pattern: *Ø/ghe-* ; proposed situation type: SERIATIVE
verb theme: *ł–yúł* (cl-blow) 'blow on O continuously'[14]

a.	heshúł	Ø–s–ł–yúł	'I am blowing it (continuously), I keep blowing at it'	IMPF
	yeshúł	ye–Ø–ł–yúł	's/he keeps blowing at it'	
b.	ghishúł	<u>ghe</u>–i–ł–yúł	'I had kept blowing at it'	PERF
	yeghįshúł	ye–<u>ghe</u>–N–ł–yúł	's/he had kept blowing at it'	
c.	t'és ghúlyúł	<u>ghwa</u>–íd–ł–yúł	'(you and I) let's blow the coals (*t'és*)'	OPT

A closer inspection of these examples reveals two morphological problems in the proposed correlation between CM's and verb classes, which I will discuss now.

2.1.1. Which Elements Mark Viewpoint?

Part of the proposal found in Rice (2000) is that the CM's are pure situation type markers, i.e., that they do not mark viewpoint at all. Instead, it is suggested that there are other elements, probably in an additional position between positions 2 and 3, which mark viewpoint. Indeed, many Dëne verbs, including those given in examples (4)-(9) above, do show additional changes in the Perfective which are not easily explained. I will discuss these changes here and argue that they cannot replace the CM's as viewpoint markers.

The changes in question are located somewhere between the CM's and subject prefixes (perhaps in an additional position in the template), and may show up in first person singular and/or in third person: first, verbs with a ł- or Ø classifier have *i*- rather than *s*- as first person singular subject marker in the Perfective. Second, some verbs show a nasal element in the Perfective, often only in third person, and finally, some Perfective verbs show a high tone, again often only in third person.

Third person high tone.

(10) *3rd person Perfective high tone (=H)*

yélbes/z	ye–H–ł–bes/z	's/he boiled it'
	4O-?-cl-stem	
heyélbes/z	he–ye–H–ł–bes/z	'they (two) boiled it'
	dl-4O-?-cl-stem	

The third person high tone only occurs in paradigms with a *the*-CM, and is in complementary distribution with *the*-. H occurs in third person forms after a conjunct prefix, *the*- occurs elsewhere. This is stated in Cook (2004) and also found in my data (with only two exceptions in twenty *the*-perfective verbs). Now, if H were to mark perfective viewpoint and *the*- situation type only, the two should be able to cooccur. However, they are in complementary distribution. Thus, the existence of H does not support the idea that the CM's do not mark viewpoint.

In fact, Cook (2004) argues that H and *the*- represent the same morpheme, namely that H is a reflex of a *the*- CM deleted after a conjunct prefix. The historical development of the alternation between H and *the*- is proposed to be the following: the vowel of *the*- is deleted (in third person) but causes a high tone to appear. This is followed by gradual weakening of *th*- to zero, leaving only H in third person forms. The intermediate stage, where H cooccurs with vowelless *th-*, is indeed attested in old forms, e.g. *tunéthda* 's/he drowned' (cited by Cook from Li 1946).

It is debatable whether *the-* and many other conjunct prefixes really have the shape *Ce*, or whether perhaps they consist of a consonant only, and the vowel is epenthetic (cf., e.g., Speas 1984, Hargus and Tuttle 1997). Therefore it is also possible that this H is an independent morpheme rather than an allomorph of *the-*. But even if H is an independent morpheme, it still occurs in complementary distribution with *the-*, which is surprising if H is a perfective marker and *the-* a situation type marker. Thus, irrespective of whether H derives from deleted *the-* or not, we cannot maintain that it, rather than *the-*, is a viewpoint marker in Dëne.

First person i- and third person nasality.

(11) a. *1sg i- (instead of s-) before Ø/ł-classifier in a Perfective verb:*

thiłbes/z	the–i–ł–bes/z	'I boiled it'
	CM-1s-cl-stem	
	(cf. hesbes 'I am boiling it' (impf))	
yaghiłti	ya#ghe–i–ł–ti	'I talked/prayed'
	th#CM-1s-cl-stem	
	(cf. yasti 'I am talking/praying' (impf))	
ts'enidhër	ts'e#ne–i–Ø–dhër	'I woke up'
	adv#CM-1s-cl-stem	
	(cf. ts'enesthi 'I am (in the process of) waking up' (impf))	

b. *3rd person nasality (=N) in a Perfective verb:*

yaghiłti	ya#ghe–N–ł–ti	's/he talked/prayed'
	th#CM-?-cl-stem	
	(cf. yałti 's/he is talking/praying' (impf))	
dáyaheghiłti	dá–ya#he–ghe–N–ł–ti	'they pl talked/prayed'
	distr-th#dl-CM-?-cl-stem	
	(cf. dáyałti 'they pl are talking/praying' (impf))	
ts'enidhër	ts'e#ne–N–Ø–dhër	's/he woke up'
	adv#CM-?-cl-sg stem	
ts'ënidé	ts'e#ne–N–Ø–dé	'they woke up'
	adv-CM-?-cl-pl stem	

1sg *i-* instead of *s-* before Ø/ł- classifiers (11a) is a completely regular, well-known alternation in Dëne. The third person nasal feature (11b) occurs before Ø/ł-classifiers in verbs with a *ghe-* or *ne-* CM (Cook 2004). Cook does not state how regularly N occurs in third person forms before Ø/ł- classifiers, but in my sample of verbs this correlation is very regular, with only five possible exceptions in 42 *ghe-* or *ne-* Perfective verbs. Cook suggests that both *i-* and N may be different reflexes of a historical nasal *ɲ. In the spirit of Rice (2000) one could say that this *ɲ is the perfective marker, and that *ghe-* and *ne-* mark situation type.

However, there are some problems with this analysis as well. They turn on the fact that there are conspicuous gaps in the distribution of this hypothetical perfective nasal. Let us look at the distribution as summarized in (12) below. The highlighted fields indicate gaps in the distribution.

(12) *Distribution of hypothetical perfective* *ɲ

   a. in verbs with Ø or ł-classifier

		Person				
		1sg	1dl/pl	2sg	2dl/pl	3 (*Ce* is the CM morpheme)
CM	the-	*i* < *s*+*ɲ	*id* < *id*+*ɲ	*ne-*	*uh-*	*Ce* < CM+Ø
	ghe-	*i* < *s*+*ɲ	*id* < *id*+*ɲ	*ne-*	*uh-*	*Cį* < CM+*ɲ
	ne-	*i* < *s*+*ɲ	*id* < *id*+*ɲ	*ne-*	*uh-*	*Cį* < CM+*ɲ

   b. in verbs with *d-* or *l*-classifier

		Person				
		1sg	1dl/pl	2sg	2dl/pl	3 (*Ce* is the CM morpheme)
CM	the-	*s*	*id* < *id*+*ɲ	*ne-*	*uh-*	*Ce* < CM+Ø
	ghe-	*s*	*id* < *id*+*ɲ	*ne-*	*uh-*	*Ce* < CM+Ø
	ne-	*s*	*id* < *id*+*ɲ	*ne-*	*uh-*	*Ce* < CM+Ø

Let us first look at verbs with a Ø or ł-classifier. The underlying presence of *ɲ is phonologically plausible in first person singular, and in the third person of verbs with a *ghe-* or *ne-* CM. Note that nasalization in third person also causes raising of the preceding vowel. This raising is a regular process in Dëne that is, for example, always seen in second person singular conjunct (i.e., nasalized) forms. However, no nasalization and raising occurs in the third person of verbs with a *the-* CM. This is the first gap in the distribution of *ɲ.

Second, there is also no trace of nasalization in second person forms. The 2sg form plus *ɲ should be *nį* rather than *ne*, the 2dl/pl form should be something like *ų̀h*. But the second person morphemes/verb forms look identical in the Imperfective and the Perfective (except for the CM and some stem changes). Thus, second person forms represent a further gap in the distribution of *ɲ.

What about the 1dl/pl forms? Here one could hypothesize that *ɲ vocalizes to *i*, just as in 1sg forms, merges with the identical vowel of the 1dl/pl subject prefix and thus is invisible.

Let us now consider verbs with a *d-* or *l-*classifier. Here the only possible trace of underlying *ɲ can be found in 1dl/pl forms. Not even first and third person forms show any changes that could be attributed to *ɲ. In fact, Perfective verbs with a *d-* or *l-*classifier look the same as their Imperfective counterparts (except for the CM and some stem changes).[15]

From the gaps in the distribution of *ɲ in Perfective verbs, most notably in second person and in verbs with a *d-* or *l-*classifier, I conclude that we cannot shift the function of perfective marking away from the CM's and onto a hypothetical morpheme *ɲ, at least not in the current synchronic state of the grammar.[16]

More generally, the proposal that CM's do not mark viewpoint but only situation type, while very interesting and suggestive, is at this stage just a proposal, without solid evidence. It requires further elaboration and justification even in Slave. For example, while Rice (2000:178) says that "there are morphemes that mark perfective aspect," she does not give an underlying representation of these morphemes. Although the examples she gives in the chapter on aspect (chapter 11) are in third person, where N, H, etc. occur most often, the glosses usually indicate a portmanteau morpheme that consists of viewpoint marking and a CM. Thus, the proposed viewpoint morphemes remain elusive in Rice (2000).

Therefore, I will assume that while there may be (irregular) perfective marking through material such as H and N, this is in addition to the perfective marking of the conjugation markers (and stem variation, of course). In particular, I will not follow Rice (2000) in assuming that the conjugation markers indicate situation type, and situation type only.

2.1.2. The Status of ne-

The second problem with CM's as situation type markers has to do with *ne-*. The behavior of *ne-* casts some doubt on whether it is a conjugation marker like *ghe-* and *the-*. First, *ne-* occurs only in the achievement (= "motion/

momentaneous") class, whereas the other markers occur in more than one class. Second, in the achievement class *ne-* occurs in both viewpoints, while the other markers occur in one viewpoint only (in nonstative verbs). This unique patterning of *ne-* already suggests that it is different from the other markers. Third, more differences become apparent upon closer inspection of example (7), repeated here for convenience:

(13) CM pattern: *ne-/ne-* ; proposed situation type: ACHIEVEMENT

verb theme: *ne–Ø–dá* (impf), *–da* (perf), *–dá* (opt)

CM/th-cl-sg sit 'sg[17] sit down'

a. nesdá	ne–s–Ø–dá	'I am (in the process of) sitting down'	IMPF
nedá	ne–Ø–dá	's/he is (in the process of) sitting down'	
b. nida	ne–the–i–Ø–da	'I sat down'	PERF
néda	ne–the(>H)–Ø–da	's/he sat down'	
c. nusdá	ne–wa–s–Ø–dá	'I should sit down'	OPT
nudá	ne–wa–dá	's/he should sit down'	(Cook 2004)

Note that here *ne-* occurs not only in the Imperfective and the Perfective, but also in the Optative. Even in (6c) above, there is an alternate Optative form which includes *ne-*: *beghánuschu* along with *begháwaschu* for 'I should give him/her fabric-like O.' Usually, a verb is marked for only one of Perfective, Imperfective and Optative, and the respective markers are in complementary distribution. The fact that *ne-* is not in complementary distribution with Optative *wa-* suggests that it is not a CM. This is confirmed by (7/13b), where *ne-* cooccurs with another CM, *the-*perfective. *The-* is difficult to see here because it deletes without trace in most persons. However, it has imparted a high tone on the preceding syllable in the third person (as discussed in section 2.1.1), and it occurs overtly in the first person dual form *nithíke* 'we two sat down.' In light of these facts it makes more sense to analyze *ne-* as a thematic prefix (position 4) of the verb theme 'sit down,' and *Ø/the-/wa-* as its impf/perf/opt CM's (position 3). This verb theme then follows the *Ø/the-* CM pattern of viewpoint marking.

More generally, the status of *ne-* as a conjugation marker of achievement or motion/momentaneous verb themes is questionable. Already Li (1946) notes the cooccurrence of *ne-* with Optative *wa-* in some verbs. He solves this problem by stipulating a homophonous thematic prefix *ne-* 'completive' in addition to the CM *ne-*. About this thematic *ne-* he writes: "It requires often the momentaneous stems, the *θε-* perfective, and is used in all three aspects [= impf., perf., opt.], differing from the momentaneous [CM] *nε-*, which is used only in the imperfective and perfective." (Li 1946:415). And according to Cook (2004), the main CM pattern for momentaneous themes in Dëne is *Ø/the-(>H)/wa-* while *ne-* is thematic. Cook suggests that in some verbs (in innovative dialects), where there is *the-*deletion in the Perfective and *ne-*deletion in the Optative, *ne-* comes to be in complementary distribution with the other CM's, and may for a while be reanalyzed as a CM, until it vanishes from the paradigm altogether due to spreading *ne-*deletion. Based on the evidence discussed here, I will follow Cook (2004) in assuming that *ne-* is thematic rather than a CM.

2.2. Consequences

In this section I have presented morphological evidence against the proposal that the CM's mark situation type rather than viewpoint. I showed that the presence of another element in the conjunct domain marking perfective is doubtful, and that thus we must consider the CM's to mark viewpoint at least in addition to situation type. I then presented evidence that the morpheme *ne-* is not a CM at all in Dëne. Now, if *ne-* is not a CM but a thematic prefix, Bortolin's and Rice's classification, which assumes that *ne-* marks achievements, needs to be developed further. I propose the following: achievements are morphologically a mixed and compositional category; they may contain a unique thematic prefix (*ne-*) and follow the accomplishment CM pattern (*Ø/the-*). Semelfactives, which also have the CM pattern *Ø/the-*, are grouped with accomplishments and achievements. This yields the following attractive—but, as we shall see in section 3, problematic—proposal which condenses the CM patterns even further than Rice (2000) and at the same time eliminates morphological syncretism and irregularities:

(14) *Condensed situation type-CM pattern correlation in Dëne nonstative verbs*

quantized: *the-*

nonquantized/cumulative: *ghe-*

This elegant analysis uses the concept of quantization (Krifka 1989, 1992) rather than the more common situation types. Recall from Chapter One that a predicate has quantized reference if no proper part of the object or event it denotes may also be denoted by the same predicate. This is true for accomplishments, achievements and semelfactives.[18] For example, no proper part of the event of cooking a fish (accomplishment) constitutes an event of cooking a fish; no proper part of arriving at a certain place (achievement) constitutes an event of arriving there; and no proper part of blowing a candle out with one puff of air (semelfactive) or of doing one jump (semelfactive) constitutes an event of blowing a candle out with one puff of air or of doing one jump, respectively. Conversely, a predicate has cumulative reference if the joining of two objects or events denoted by a predicate constitute another object or event denoted by the same predicate. For example, two events of talking (activity) constitute together an event of talking, and two events of blowing repeatedly (seriative) or jumping repeatedly (seriative) constitute together another event of blowing repeatedly or jumping repeatedly.

This is indeed an exciting proposal. It would mean that quantization, a notion that characterizes telic predicates but also semelfactives, is grammatized in Dëne verbs. Moreover, it would shed light on some other facts observed in Dëne. First, if quantization is marked on verbs, it is less surprising that nouns are not marked for quantization in Dëne. We could say that in this head-marking language, the verb rather than the noun fulfills this task (cf. Krifka 1992 on overt quantization in Czech verbs vs. nouns).

Second, the fact that the Imperfective (in nonstative verbs) is always marked with the CM Ø would fall out naturally, as follows: the semantic distinction between cumulative vs. quantized reference, which is marked by *ghe-* vs. *the-*, does not matter in the Imperfective, because in a way, in the Imperfective even quantized/telic predicates have "cumulative-type" reference. Recall that in the imperfective, TT is included in TSit, and that only the part of the TSit coextensive with TT is available for truth-conditional judgements. An imperfective telic predicate can thus be conceived of being true of a proper part of an event of which the corresponding perfective predicate is true. To take an English example, if Sue *wrote a letter* (= perfective) in an hour, say from 3 to 4 o'clock, then it is true that she *was writing a letter* (= imperfective) from, say, 3:15 to 3:45.[19] Since in the imperfective, all predicates have "cumulative-type" reference, the distinction between cumulativity and quantization need not be marked: the Imperfective is neither *the-* nor *ghe-*, it is Ø.[20]

Finally, (14) is also compatible with the CM pattern observed in positional stative verbs such as 'sit.' Recall the CM pattern of these verbs: *the-/ghe-* (cf. Chapter Two, section 2.3.3). According to (14), this pattern means that Imperfective positional stative verbs are quantized and Perfective positional stative verbs are cumulative. The latter is unproblematic, but why should Imperfective positional statives have quantized reference (and why should the reference type of these verbs differ by viewpoint)? In Chapter Two we observed that Dëne positional stative verbs such as 'sit' morphologically are Perfective forms of corresponding nonstative—and telic—verbs such as 'sit down.' We might speculate that the CM *the-* is due to the fact that underlyingly, Imperfective positional statives are Perfective quantized predicates that have come to denote the result state of the original event. Thus, the quantization marker *the-* makes sense diachronically if not synchronically.

However, in spite of these promising aspects of the proposal given in (14), it has a serious empirical problem: in my careful semantic testing, I have found numerous exceptions in Dëne to the proposed correlation between the CM patterns and quantization. For example, there are accomplishments with a *ghe*-perfective and activities with a *the*-perfective. Overall, my findings indicate that it is difficult to predict CM choice based on quantization, as proposed in (14), or based on situation type, as proposed in Bortolin (1998), Rice (2000). This is especially true for telic/quantized situation types. I will present these findings in section 3.

2.3. Summary

Summing up, Dëne, like other Athapaskan languages, exhibits morphological verb classes (verb theme categories). In the absence of transparent root suffixation patterns, a major determinant of each class in Dëne is the conjugation marker pattern associated with it. Several researchers, beginning with Kari (1979), have proposed that CM patterns, and hence verb classes, are based on semantic, and, more precisely, on aspectual characteristics. Modern analyses (Bortolin 1998, Rice 2000) claim that Athapaskan verb classes correspond to universal categories of situation type. If this is true, both durativity and telicity are grammatized in Athapaskan. I suggested in section 2.2. that there are only two CM patterns in Dëne nonstative verbs, and that these patterns grammatize the distinction between cumulative and quantized reference. However, there are also voices, at least for Navajo, which say that only telicity is represented by verb classes (Midgette 1996, see section 5), or that telicity is not represented by verb classes in Navajo (Smith 1991, 1996). In the next section, I will add the findings of my semantic testing in Cold Lake Dëne to this discussion. They support the view that telicity (or quantization) is not grammatized in Dëne.

3. CM'S DO NOT MARK TELICITY (BUT PERHAPS DURATIVITY)

I will now take a close semantic look at the proposed correlation between situation type (or quantization, see sections 3.2.6, 3.4 below) and CM's in Dëne. I will pay particular attention to the notions of telicity and durativity, applying semantic tests rather than relying on English translations of verb meaning.[21] I will show that while Dëne does contain activity, accomplishment, achievement and semelfactive predicates, not all of these situation types show systematic morphosyntactic correlations. In particular, there is no consistent morphosyntactic encoding of telicity by CM's. CM patterns and the associated verb classes do not correlate with all five situation types and, in particular, do not distinguish telic from atelic predicates. Durativity, however, is associated quite consistently with the Ø/ghe- CM pattern. Thus, if any situation type notion is grammatized through CM patterns, it is durativity, not telicity.

My findings on the semantic correlates of CM patterns constitute a departure from Bortolin (1998) and Rice (2000), who propose grammatization of all five situation types. At the end of this chapter, I will discuss what makes such different views of closely related languages possible. But first I will present examples of all nonstative situation types and test their correlation with CM patterns.

3.1. Situation Types and Semantic Tests

Here I present example predicates for each situation type. Importantly, I will introduce and apply semantic tests as evidence for situation type. Recall from Chapter One the notions underlying the five situation types: stativity, durativity, and telicity. The semantic tests use expressions sensitive to one of these three notions.

(15)

		UNDERLYING NOTIONS		
		Stative	Durative	Telic
SITUATION TYPES	State	+	+	n/a
	Activity	–	+	–
	Accomplishment	–	+	+
	Semelfactive	–	–	–
	Achievement	–	–	+

Since the primary foci of my study are telicity and durativity, I have not used stativity tests. See Bortolin (1998) and Smith (1991) for an examination of stativity.

3.1.1. Durativity

Durativity can be tested in Dëne in several ways: through manner adverbs, time span expressions, terminative expressions, and Imperfective viewpoint.

Manner adverbs. Certain adverbs such as 'quickly' or 'slowly' imply duration of the predicate they are combined with (see Smith 1991:57). This is because they modify the manner in which the situation proceeds. I call this reading of manner adverbs the *process reading*. Nondurative predicates are not compatible with these adverbs, or only on a special *onset reading*, i.e., one in which they modify the length of time until the situation begins.

I used *ʔįghą́* 'quickly' (like Bortolin (1998)) and sometimes *ts'ethię̀* 'slowly, carefully, with ease' for manner adverbs. In Dëne, durative predicates are compatible with these and have a process reading. If nondurative predicates are at all compatible with these manner adverbs, they have an onset reading.

Time span expressions. Time span expressions are also useful durativity tests. They explicitly state a stretch of time during which the situation held or holds, and thus imply duration.

I used *ʔįlághe ts'údzáhi k'e* 'for/in an hour,' and sometimes *ʔįlághe ts'údzáhi k'étł'á* 'for a whole hour' (see below for morpheme-by-morpheme glosses). Both of these are postpositional phrases, but while the postposition *k'étł'á* has lexical meaning, emphasizing entirety of an object or time span, from beginning to end (*tł'á* literally means 'buttocks,' i.e., 'end'), the postposition *k'e* is fairly devoid of lexical meaning and functions more as a (case) marker of a nonargument NP (see Chapter Two, section 3.2.1). Less conservative speakers often omit *k'e* without loss of meaning or grammaticality (e.g., (16b) below). In Dëne, nondurative predicates are not compatible with these time span expressions.

Terminative expressions. Expressions such as 'stop' or 'finish' can only be applied to situations which have some duration. Nondurative situations are always over in an instant, and it is thus senseless to apply terminatives to them.

I used two related verbs, *ʔanast'e* 'I am finished, I stopped/quit' and *ʔanasdhën* 'I finished O, I am done/finished.' Of these, *ʔanast'e* acts more like an aspectual verb or auxiliary (it takes a verbal complement, it has no Perfective forms), and it is the one I used most often. Only durative predicates are combinable with these terminatives.

Imperfective viewpoint. Finally, as we saw in Chapter Two, nondurative verb themes do not easily occur in the Imperfective viewpoint in Dëne. An Imperfective form of these verbs can only have a prospective/future interpretation. In some cases, they require a future enclitic, thus forming future tense. Verb themes which do occur in the Imperfective form, with an imperfective/present interpretation, are durative. Therefore, the Imperfective viewpoint can be used as a durativity test.[22]

Two examples of durative verb themes are given in (16) and (17). The (a) sentences contain a manner adverb, the (b) sentences a time span expression, the (c) sentences contain a terminative, and the (d) sentences are in the Imperfective viewpoint (as indicated by the Ø CM and, in (17), the stem shape). We can see that these two verb themes are compatible with manner

Telicity Is Not Grammatized in Dëne

adverbs on a process reading, with time span and terminative expressions, and may occur in the (nonfuture) Imperfective viewpoint. I therefore conclude that they are durative.

(16) verb theme: *ya#ł–ti* (?#cl-stem) 'talk, pray' (DURATIVE)

    a1. ʔı́ghą́ yasti.

        ʔı́ghą́   ya#Ø–s–ł–ti

        quickly ʔ#CM-1s-cl-talk/pray

        'I'm talking quickly.'

    a2. ʔı́ghą́ yaghiłti.

        ʔı́ghą́   ya#ghe–i–ł–ti

        quickly ʔ#CM-1s-cl-talk/pray

        'I talked quickly.'

    b. ʔı̨łághe ts'údzáhi yaghiłti.

       ʔı̨łághe ts'údzáhi ya#ghe–i–ł–ti

       one   hour   ʔ#CM-1s-cl-talk/pray

       'I spoke for one hour.'

    c. yasti ʔanast'e.

       ya#Ø–s–ł–ti   ʔa–na#Ø–s–Ø–t'e

       th#CM-1s-cl-talk/pray th-th#CM-1s-cl-stem

       'I finished praying/speaking, I stopped praying, I quit talking.'

    d. cf. (16a1)

(17) verb theme: *ł–t'éth, –t'e* (impf/opt, perf) 'cook O (by roasting, baking)'
                                                                                 (DURATIVE)

    a. ʔı́ghą́ bĕr thiłt'e.

       ʔı́ghą́   bĕr   the–i–ł–t'e

       quickly meat CM-1s-cl-cook O perf

       'I cooked the meat fast (it didn't take me long to cook it).'

    b. ʔı̨łághe ts'údzáhi k'e bĕr thiłt'e.

       ʔı̨łághe ts'údzáhi k'e bĕr   the–i–ł–t'e

       one   hour   P meat CM-1s-cl-cook O perf

       'I cooked the meat for one hour, it took me one hour to cook the meat.'

c. bĕr hest'éth ʔanasdhën.
    bĕr   he–Ø–s–ł–t'éth   ʔa–na#(the)–s–l–dhën
    meat ep-CM-1s-cl-cook O impf   th-th#CM²³-1s-cl-stem
    'I finished cooking meat.'

d. łue hest'éth sį.
    łue he–Ø–s–ł–t'éth   sį
    fish ep-CM-1s-cl-cook O impf assert
    'I am roasting fish.'

Verb such as those in (18) and (19) are not durative, as their behaviour in durativity tests shows:

(18) verb theme: é–Ø–ził (impf), Ø–zël (perf)
                 sem-cl-scream   cl-scream once perf   'scream once'
                                                       (NONDURATIVE)²⁴

a. # ʔíghą́ thizël.
       ʔíghą́ the–i–Ø–zël
       quickly CM-1s-cl-sceam perf

b. # ʔiłághe ts'údzáhi k'étł'á thizël.
       ʔiłághe ts'údzáhi k'étł'á   the–i–Ø–zël
       one   hour   duration of CM-1s-cl-sceam perf

c. # héssił ʔanast'e.
       h–é–Ø–s–Ø–ził   ʔa–na#Ø–s–Ø–t'e
       ep-sem-CM-1s-cl-scream   th-th#CM-1s-cl-stem

d.   héssił xa.
       h–é–Ø–s–Ø–ził   xa
       ep-sem-CM-1s-cl-scream   fut
       'I'm going to scream once'

e.   héssił.
       h–é–Ø–s–Ø–ził
       ep-sem-CM-1s-cl-scream
       'I'm going to scream once,' * 'I'm screaming once'

The adverb, the time span expression, and the terminative are infelicitous with the verb theme 'scream once.' For (18a), speakers suggested that this sentence would only be acceptable in a context where it meant 'I screamed all of a sudden'; however, in such a context a different adverb (e.g., 'suddenly') would be more appropriate. Thus, (18a) has only a very marginal onset reading, if any reading at all. (18b) is ill-formed because, as speakers suggested, *thizël* means "just one little scream," which cannot last for an hour.[25] (18c) was rejected as well. (18d) and (18e) show that the Imperfective of this verb is marked; it requires an overtly future form, (18d) or, at the least, a future/prospective interpretation, (18e).

(19) verb theme: *ne–Ø–dá, –da, –dá* (impf, perf, opt)
  th-cl-sg sit 'sg sit down' (NONDURATIVE)

  a. ʔíghą́ nesdá.
      ʔíghą́ ne–Ø–s–Ø–dá
      quickly th-CM-1s-cl-sg sit impf
      'I'm going to sit down right away.' (onset reading)

  b. # ʔiłághe tsʼúdzáhi kʼe nida.   (OK here: *ghidá*)
       ʔiłághe tsʼúdzáhi kʼe ne–(the–)i–Ø–da   ghe–i–Ø–dá
       one   hour   P th-CM[26]-1s-cl-sg sit perf CM-1s-cl-sg sit perf

  c. # nesdá ʔanastʼe.
       ne–Ø–s–Ø–dá   ʔa–na#Ø–s–Ø–tʼe
       th-CM-1s-cl-sg sit impf th-th#CM-1s-cl-stem

(19a) shows two things. First, the manner adverb has an onset reading, which suggests nondurativity (compare (16a) above). Second, the preferred interpretation of the Imperfective is an (immediate) future reading. This is further evidence that Dëne 'sit down' is nondurative. The next piece of evidence comes from the time span expression, which is incompatible with Perfective *nida*, (19b). Speakers suggested as felicitous alternative to combine the time span adverbial with stative *ghidá*, which would mean 'I sat for one hour.' Finally, terminatives are also incompatible with this verb theme, (19c).

Summing up, manner adverbs, time span expressions, terminatives, and Imperfective viewpoint can be used as durativity tests in Dëne. (Section 3.2 below contains lists of verb themes by situation type. All verb themes, with tests, are listed in Appendix One.)

3.1.2. Telicity

Unlike languages such as English and German, Dëne has only one reliable telicity test, the interpretation of the adverb *kʼájëne*[27] 'almost.' (See Chapter Two, section 3.2, for the notorious scarcity of telicity tests in Athapaskan.) However, this test only distinguishes the telicity of durative predicates (i.e., it distinguishes between accomplishments and activities only): as discussed in Chapter Two, 'almost' has two interpretations with accomplishments, an onset and a completion reading. With activities and punctual predicates, 'almost' has only an onset interpretation. It can therefore not be used to distinguish between achievements and semelfactives. In fact, this test does not so much test telicity per se, as whether a predicate represents a *complex* situation type. By complex I mean the fact that a situation type possesses both durativity and telicity (a process and a change of state). Only accomplishments are complex in this way.

The following examples illustrate the 'almost' test in Dëne. Note that the translations are left unedited as provided by the speakers. (20) is the only example with a completion reading, and in fact the completion reading is very salient. This is the typical pattern of accomplishments with 'almost' in Dëne: the completion reading is salient, and it is almost impossible to obtain an onset reading. The salience of the completion reading makes accomplishments very easy to distinguish from other situation types, which, as expected, only show the onset reading, (21)–(23).

(20) verb theme: *ł–t′éth*, (impf/opt), *ł–t′e* (perf) 'cook O (by roasting/baking)'
 cl-cook O cl-cook O (ACCOMPL./COMPLEX)
 k′ájëne k′ásba thiłt′e sı̨.
 k′ájëne k′ásba the–i–ł–t′ e sı̨
 almost chicken CM-1s-cl-cook O perf assert
 'I'm just about done cooking the chicken.' (completion reading)

(21) verb theme: *ya#ł–ti* 'talk, pray'
 ?#cl-stem (NON-ACCOMPL.)
 k′ájëne yaghiłti sı̨.
 k′ájëne ya#ghe–i–ł–ti sı̨
 almost ?#CM-1s-cl-talk/pray assert
 'I was going to speak but I didn't (I didn't get a chance to make my speech).' (onset reading)

(22) verb theme: *é–Ø–ził* (impf), *Ø–zël* (perf) 'scream once'
 sem-cl-scream impf, cl-scream perf (NON-ACCOMPL.)
 k′ájëne thizël.
 k′ájëne the–i–Ø–zël
 almost CM-1s-cl-sream perf
 'I just about screamed (but did not at all).' (onset reading)

(23) verb theme: *ne–Ø–dá* (impf), *–da* (perf), *–dá* (opt)   'sg sit down'
         th-cl-sg sit   (NON-ACCOMPL.)
k'ájëne nida.
k'ájëne ne–the–i–Ø–da
almost th-CM-1s-cl-sg sit perf
'I just about sat down (but didn't).' (onset reading)

The lack of other telicity tests makes it difficult to distinguish between semelfactives and achievements in Dëne. Ironically, the only (partially satisfactory) way out of this dilemma is to resort to durativity tests: according to Smith (1991), achievements, which denote a change of state, are conceptualized in some languages as including the stages leading up to this transition. Certain circumstances then allow focusing of these preliminary stages. As an example, consider the English sentence *She was leaving (when the phone rang)*. In an effort to find an interpretation for the progressive, speakers focus on the preliminary stages of the event, such that this sentence means something like *She was getting ready to leave/She was about to leave (when the phone rang)*.

This option is not open to semelfactives, which do not denote a change of state. Thus, in English a progressive of a semelfactive is only acceptable on a repetition ('iterative' or 'seriative') reading, which in fact shifts the situation type from semelfactive to activity: *She was coughing (when the phone rang)* can only mean that she was coughing repeatedly, not that she was about to cough, or that she was in the middle of a single cough. Smith (1991:115) suggests that this difference between achievements and semelfactives is "due to the conceptual primacy of changes of state for human beings."

Returning to Dëne, it seems that in this language achievements may also include preliminary stages, while semelfactives may not. This difference comes out in durativity tests such as manner adverbs, terminatives, and Imperfective viewpoint (see also Bortolin 1998). Consider again the verb theme 'sit down.' It contrasts with 'scream once' from (18) above in that it may combine with manner adverbs, (24a, b), and in that it may also occur in the Imperfective viewpoint, (24c).

(24) verb theme: *ne–Ø–dá* (impf), *–da* (perf), *–dá* (opt)   'sg sit down'
         th-cl-sg sit   (ACHIEVEMENT)
   a. ʔíghą́ nida.
      ʔíghą́ ne–the–i–Ø–da
      quickly th-CM-1s-cl-sg sit perf
      'I sat down quickly.' (not sure what kind of reading)

b. ts'ethi̧ę nida.

ts'ethi̧ę   ne–the–i–Ø–da

with ease th-CM-1s-cl-sg sit perf

'I sat down with ease.' (process reading)

c. nesdá.

ne–Ø–s–Ø–dá

th-CM-1s-cl-sg sit impf

'I am (in the process of) sitting down.'

While 'sit down' usually occurs in the Perfective viewpoint, (24c) shows that it is apparently also possible in the Imperfective, on precisely the type of "preliminary stage" reading expected with achievements.

Thus, some durativity tests may reveal a difference between semelfactives and achievements in Dëne. Simply put, achievements act a little bit durative while semelfactives do not. However, we are dealing here with fine nuances in the interpretation of basically nondurative predicates, and in many cases it is much more difficult to distinguish between semelfactives and achievements than in the examples given here.

Summing up, Dëne has only one reliable telicity test, which distinguishes accomplishments, or complex situation type, from all other situation types. Achievements, i.e., punctual and simple telic predicates, are much harder to identify. There is no telicity test per se, but sometimes durativity tests reveal the presence of preliminary stages typical for achievements. The scarcity of good telicity tests, by the way, also suggests that telicity is not grammatized in Dëne (see Chapter Two, section 3.2).

3.1.3. The Five Situation Types in Dëne

With the tests introduced in the previous sections, we are able to determine with some confidence a verb theme's situation type. The following table shows for the verbs above how the combination of tests can be used to determine situation type.

Table 8. Test results for four verb themes

		ya#l–ti 'talk, pray'	l–t'éth, –t'e 'cook (roast) O'	é–Ø–zil, Ø–zël 'scream once'	ne–Ø–dá, –da, –dá 'sg sit down'
Durativity	Manner Adv.	process	process	X	onset/process
	Time Span	√	√	X	X
	Imperfective	√	√	X	(√)

Table 8. Test results for four verb themes (*continued*)

		ya#l–ti 'talk, pray'	l–t'éth, –t'e 'cook (roast) O'	é–Ø–zil, Ø–zël 'scream once'	ne–Ø–dá, –da, –dá 'sg sit down'
Complexity/ Accompl.	'almost': completion	X	√	X	X
=> Notions		durative, simple	durative, complex	nondur., simple	semidur., simple
=> Sit. Type		Activity	Accompl.	Semelfactive	Achievement

The results summarized in this table show that Dëne has predicates representing each situation type. This means that semantically, Dëne speakers are able to express the same aspectual ideas as speakers of English or German. In other words, the semantic categories of situation types, which are believed to be universal, are also found in Dëne. It remains to be seen, however, whether the situation types, or the notions underlying them, are also grammatized in Dëne, i.e., whether they show consistent and productive morphosyntactic correlations, and in particular whether they regularly correspond to certain CM patterns.

With the battery of tests described above, I examined a good fifty Dëne nonstative verb themes in order to determine their situation type (the tests are shown in Appendix One). Once (semantic) situation type was established, I looked for morphosyntactic correlations in terms of CM patterns. In this section I will demonstrate that there are no consistent and productive CM pattern correlations with telicity in Dëne. This is an important piece of evidence in support of my claim that telicity is not grammatized in this language.

3.2. CM Patterns Do Not Correlate with Telicity

Recall that the most important proposals about the grammatization of situation aspect, including telicity (or perhaps quantization), rest on the CM patterns exhibited by different classes of verbs in Athapaskan. The CM patterns define four to five broad lexical verb classes (verb theme categories), and it has been proposed that these classes represent situation types. We thus have, in Athapaskan, a potential correlation between morphology (CM patterns) and semantics (situation type). For convenience, I repeat here the proposed correlation between CM patterns (of nonstative verbs) and situation type (Bortolin 1998, Rice 2000).

Table 9. CM patterns and situation type (nonstative)	
CM pattern (impf/perf)	Situation type
Ø/ghe-	Activity
Ø/the-	Accomplishment, Semelfactive
ne-/ne-[a]	Achievement
a. Recall (section 2.2.1 and 2.2.3) that this needs to be revised to Ø/the- in Dëne.	

In my corpus of Dëne verbs, the only consistent correlation between CM patterns and situation type I found is between activities and the Ø/ghe- CM pattern. I have found no consistent correlation between accomplishments/semelfactives and the Ø/the- pattern or between achievements and either the ne-/ne- or the Ø/the- pattern. I will now present my findings.

3.2.1. Accomplishments

I first present those verb themes which, by the 'almost' test, have clearly been determined to be accomplishments. The few ambiguous examples are not presented here in order not to distract from the main point. They are discussed in footnotes or in following sections. Only Perfective forms, where CM's show up more clearly than in the Imperfective, are given. The CM's are underlined, or given in brackets. 1–3 list themes with CM the-, 4–6 list themes with ghe-, and 7–14 are groups of related themes with varying CM's.

(25) ACCOMPLISHMENT verb themes
  √ completion reading with 'almost'
  √ pass durativity tests

	VERB THEME	GLOSS	TRANSL.	1s PERF FORM
1	ł–bes	cl-stem	'boil O'	thiłbes
2	ná–na#ł–dá̜	adv-?#cl-stem	'mend O'	nánathiłdá̜
3	(ho–)ł–tsi̜	(ar/th-)cl-stem	'make sg O'	thiłtsi̜
4	Ø–da, –dagh	cl-stem	'eat sg animal'	ghesdagh
5	u–ne–Ø–ye, –ya̜	ser/th-gd-cl-stem	'pick (berries)'	ʔuneghiya̜
6	(ho–)ł–gha̜	(ar/th-)cl-stem	'make pl O'	ghigha̜
7	ł–t'éth, –t'e	cl-stem	'roast/bake O'	thiłt'e
8	be-ká#ł–t'éth, –t'e	3O-P#cl-stem	'cook (meal)'	bekáthiłt'e
9	ta#ne–ł–t'éth, –t'e	adv?#th-cl-stem	'cook several O'	taniłt'e (Ø or ne-)
10	tł'o de–Ø–t'áth, –t'adh	N th-cl-stem	'cut grass (hay)'	tł'o deghit'adh
11	ná#Ø–t'áth, –t'adh	adv#cl-stem	'cut O up (into pieces)'	nághit'adh
12	ł–t'éth, –t'adh	cl-stem	'shape O with blade'	thiłt'adh

Telicity Is Not Grammatized in Dëne

13	da#Ø–ʔá, –ʔą, –ʔał	adv#cl-stem	'put round solid O up there'	da<u>thi</u>ʔą
14	ná#Ø–ʔá, –ʔą, –ʔał	adv#cl-stem	'take round solid O down'	ná<u>ghi</u>ʔą

The distribution of the CM's in these verb themes is striking. Of 14 verb themes which clearly pattern as accomplishments, only seven show the expected CM *the-*, but almost as many, six, show *ghe-* (the "activity CM"), and one verb, 9, has either *ne-* or no CM at all. In the latter theme, the prefix *ne-* cooccurs with *wa-* in the Optative form (1sg opt: *betanust'éth* < *be–ta#<u>ne</u>–wa–s–ł–t'éth*), which makes it more likely that *ne-* is thematic rather than a CM (the CM then is Ø). In either case *ne-* indicates that this verb theme belongs to the morphological "momentaneous" (="achievement") class, even though semantically it is an accomplishment.

The themes listed in (25) come from all kinds of verb theme categories, as far as this can be determined in the absence of clear stem suffixation. Relying on CM's and the category of cognate themes in other Athapaskan languages, we can say that there are, in addition to conversive (=accomplishment) themes (1, 2, 3, 7, 8), classificatory motion themes (13, 14), a momentaneous theme (9), successive themes (10–12), an operative theme (6), and what might be further motion/classificatory or operative themes (4, 5).

In sum, the facts emerging from (25) show that there is no correlation between the *Ø/the-* CM pattern and the accomplishment situation type. I now move on to activities.

3.2.2. Activities

In (26), entries 1–12 list activity verb themes with the Perfective CM *ghe-*; 11 and 12 are related themes. Entries 13 and 14 show the CM *the-*.

(26) ACTIVITY verb themes

    X   no completion reading with 'almost'

    √   pass durativity tests

	VERB THEME[28]	GLOSS	TRANSL.	1s PERF FORM
1	ł–yúł/l	cl-stem	'blow O prolonged'	<u>ghi</u>shúl
2	Ø–tsagh	cl-stem	'cry'	<u>ghi</u>tsagh
3	Ø–t'áth, –t'adh	cl-stem	'cut O'	<u>ghi</u>t'adh
4	yá#l–gus	adv#cl-stem	'jump prolonged'	yá<u>ghe</u>sgus
5	u–ł–t'us	ser/th-cl-stem	'punch O repeatedly'	hu<u>ghi</u>ł'us
6	Ø–ził	cl-stem	'scream repeatedly/prolonged'	<u>ghi</u>ził
7	ne–ł–ʔį̀, –ʔį̀, –ʔį́	th-cl-stem	'look at O'	ni<u>ghi</u>ł?į́

8	d–yën	cl-stem	'sing'	ghesjën
9	ya#ł–ti	?#cl-stem	'talk, pray'	yaghiłti
10	dzí#(dé?–)Ø–gha	adv#(?-)cl-stem	'sg walk around'	dzíghigha
11	u–Ø–kár	ser/th-cl-stem	'slap O repeatedly'	hughikár
12	(u–)Ø–kĕr	ser/th-cl-stem	'pat O'	hughikĕr, ghikĕr
13	na#Ø–ku(i)	?#cl-stem	'vomit'	nathesku
14	hú–the–Ø–gha, –ya, –yá	?-CM-cl-stem	'sg travel through/by'	húthiya (Ø or the-)

Equally striking, activity verb themes do show the *ghe-* CM quite consistently. There are only two exceptions, 13 and 14, in fourteen verb themes. Of these two exceptions, the motion theme 'travel through/by,' 14, requires comment. Here *the-* behaves like a CM in that it is deleted with a high-tone reflex in third person. However, it shows up not only in the Perfective but also in the Imperfective. This means that in this verb theme the CM *the-* is thematic, and we may have to posit a Ø nonthematic CM. In either case the CM is not *ghe-*.

In terms of traditional verb theme categories, again based on CM's and cognates, most of the activities in (26) are operative themes (2, 7–9) or successive[29] themes (1, 3–6, 11, 12). *Ghe-*marked successive themes denote a series or succession of semelfactive situations. 'Vomit' (13) is likely a conversive theme, and 10 and 14 represent different types of motion themes.

All in all, in the activity class we find a much more regular (although not perfect) correspondence between semantic type and morphological marking: verb themes which are activities semantically, including themes which denote a succession of semelfactive situations, show the CM *ghe-* in the Perfective. Since activities are durative predicates, this suggests that durativity may be grammatized through the CM pattern in Dëne: Ø/*ghe-* is a productive morphosyntactic process which accesses the durativity of a predicate. However, the correlation between durativity and CM patterns goes only in one direction: durative (atelic) verbs generally show Ø/*ghe-*, but it is not true that nondurative themes generally do *not* show Ø/*ghe-* (see, for example, the achievements and semelfactives in the next two sections). Thus, the Ø/*ghe-* pattern is not part of a true morphosyntactic contrast, which is required by my definition of grammatization. The grammatization of durativity is thus only a weak tendency (see discussion in section 3.4).

3.2.3. Achievements

I now turn to the nondurative situation types, semelfactives and achievements. Recall that the difference between these two situation types is very difficult to determine due to an absence of telicity tests. All one can do is rely on the durativity difference between semelfactives and achievements. This is somewhat problematic because (i) the difference in durativity is very subtle, and (ii) the durativity of achievements is more of a contextual rather than lexical phenomenon—as if they were nondurative by implicature, but context may cancel this. I found more of a continuum rather than a sharp division between the two situation types. Nonetheless, here are the verbs which might be achievements, because they show some durative characteristics. 1 and 2 show the CM *ne-*, 3 and 4 show *ghe-*, and 5 shows *the-*. Examples 5–12 represent pairs of related verb themes with different CM's.

(27) ACHIEVEMENT verb themes
   X   no completion reading with 'almost'
   (√) pass some durativity tests (e.g., nonfuture Imperfective)

	VERB THEME[30]	GLOSS	TRANSL.	1s PERF FORM
1	ts'e#Ø–dhi, –dhër	adv#cl-stem	'sg wake up'	ts'e<u>n</u>idhër
2	ní#Ø–gha, –ya, –yá	adv#cl-stem	'sg arrive'	ní<u>n</u>iya
3	ná#ł–bes	adv#cl-stem	'boil O (too) soft'	ná<u>gh</u>iłbez
4	Ø–ʔį́, –ʔį̀, –ʔį́	cl-stem	'see O'	<u>gh</u>esʔį̀
5	he/te–ł–yú:ł, –yéł	incept-cl-stem	'throw solid round O once'	tish<u>é</u>l (*the-*)
6	k'e#ne–Ø–yís, –yéz	?#th/CM-cl-stem	'break elongated O in two'	k'eniyéz (*ne-* or Ø)
7	ná#Ø–yís, –yéz	adv#cl-stem	'break sg O'	ná<u>gh</u>iyéz
8	ná–dá#Ø–yéz	adv-distr#cl-stem	'break pl O'	nádá<u>th</u>iyéz
9	(O yé) Ø–gha, –ya, –yá	(PP) cl-stem	'sg step (into O)'	(O yé) <u>gh</u>iya
10	he/te–Ø–gha, –ya, –yá	incept-cl-stem	'sg leave (start to go)'	hiya, tiya (*the-*)
11	be–ghá#ne–Ø–ʔá, –ʔą, –ʔał	3O-P#th/CM-cl-stem	'give solid round O to'	begháníʔą (*ne-* or Ø)
12	ni#dí–Ø–ʔá, –ʔą, –ʔał	N?#?-cl-stem	'pick/lift up solid round O'	niríʔą (Ø)

These twelve themes vary subtly in durativity. They do not all pass or fail the same tests, and some pass fewer durativity tests than others. For example, 'break sg O' (7), and 'throw solid round O once' (5), may occur in the Imperfective, but fail all other durativity tests. They are therefore very nearly semelfactives. However, moving them over into the semelfactive category would not affect the results of this study, since only one of them, 5, has the semelfactive CM pattern. Moreover, even without these two themes, not even half of the achievements show the predicted CM pattern *ne-/ne-* (1, 2, and perhaps 6, 11). The other verb themes show everything from the activity pattern Ø/*ghe-* (3, 4, 7, 9), over the accomplishment/semelfactive pattern Ø/*the-* (5, 10) to no

CM's at all, which could be called a Ø/Ø pattern (12, and perhaps 6, 11). The semantic achievement class thus represents a mixed class morphologically.

This is further confirmed by the fact that the verbs represent different verb theme categories, as far as I can tell. Only two of them, 1–2, are momentaneous themes (the prototypical achievements). 9–10 are non-momentaneous motion themes, 5, 11 and 12 are classificatory motion themes, 3 is derived from a conversive (=accomplishment) theme, 4 is a durative theme, and I do not know what 6–8 are.

Worthy of note is the fact that two of these achievements, 5 and 10, show a subsituation aspect *inceptive*, as indicated by the prefix *he-* or *te-*. The basic aspectual meaning of inceptives which are not semantically bleached (as in 10) is the transition into an event. This transition is not conceived of as a point in time but as a short stage, as is typical of achievements. It is therefore not surprising that inceptive themes pattern like achievements semantically. Morphologically, however, inceptives follow the *Ø/the-* CM pattern associated with accomplishments. The inceptive will be discussed further in section 3.3.2.

Summing up, no consistent morphological pattern or class is associated with the verb themes I classified as achievements based on semantic tests. However, we have to remind ourselves that the distinction between semelfactives and achievements is tenuous, as there are no clear telicity tests. Keeping this problem in mind, let us examine the themes that act highly punctual and thus look more like semelfactives.

3.2.4. Semelfactives

These very punctual themes are compatible with 'quickly' only on an onset reading (if at all), they are incompatible with time span expressions, and they may not occur in the nonfuture Imperfective. 1–5 show the CM *the-*, 6 shows Ø or H, 7 and 8 show *ghe-*, and 9 and 10 show Ø or *ne-*.

(28) SEMELFACTIVE verb themes

X no completion reading with 'almost'

X fail all durativity tests

	VERB THEME[31]	GLOSS	TRANSL.	1s PERF FORM
1	é–Ø–t'éth, Ø–t'áth	sem/th-cl-stem, cl-stem	'make one quick cut (e.g., knife slips)'	thit'áth
2	é–Ø–ził, Ø–zëł	sem/th-cl-stem, cl-stem	'scream once'	thizëł
3	é–ł–k'íth, ł–k'éth	sem/th-cl-stem, cl-stem	'shoot O (with gun)'[32]	thiłk'éth

4	hǫ–tthi#de–l–tsa(gh), hǫ–tthi#de–í–l–tsa(gh)	adv-?#th-cl-stem adv-?#th-sem?-cl-stem	'cry out in fear'	hǫtthiríthestsa(gh)
5[33]	é–ł–yúł, ł–yúł	sem/th-cl-stem, cl-stem	'blow O once (e.g., blow out candle)'	thishúł
6	ya#l–gus, –gos	adv#cl-stem	'jump once'	yásgos (Ø or H)
7	ná#ne–ł–t'us	adv#th-cl-stem	'punch O once'	nánighiłt'us
8	ná#ne–(i–)Ø–kár	adv#th-(?-)cl-stem	'slap O once'	nánighikár
9	ní–na#ne–d–gha, –ya, –yá	adv-iter#th-cl-stem	'come back' (lit., 'arrive again/arrive back')	ninesja (Ø or ne-)
10	łeghá#ne–ł–dhi, –dhër	?#th/CM-cl-stem	'kill sg O'	łeghániłthër (Ø or ne-)

Morphologically, these themes fall into at least three distinct classes, with different CM's, and the *the*-CM occurs only five times out of ten. The largest morphological class (1–3, 5) shows a thematic semelfactive prefix in the Imperfective/Prospective/Future, and the Ø/*the*- CM pattern. Next, 'jump once' (6) shows neither a semelfactive prefix nor a standard CM. Since there is a high tone in all Perfective forms, we might say that the CM is H or Ø.[34] Another morphological class is represented by 'punch O once' and 'slap O once' (7–8). These themes are characterized by an adverbial prefix *ná#* which indicates motion across or towards something, by the thematic prefix *ne-* (which often occurs in momentaneous themes), and, surprisingly, by the (activity) CM pattern Ø/*ghe-*. Thus, although they are semelfactives semantically, they certainly are not morphologically. Finally, there are two themes which are morphologically momentaneous, 'come back' (9), and 'kill sg O' (10), as indicated by the adverbial prefix *ní#* and the thematic prefix *ne-* in combination with a motion stem. Nonetheless, these themes fail all durativity tests and therefore are like semelfactives rather than like achievements.

Thus, verb themes which most likely denote semelfactive situations also are morphologically heterogeneous, in CM patterns as well as in their presumed verb theme categories. In particular, there is no support for the idea that semelfactives require the Ø/*the*- CM pattern.

Moreover, examples such as 9–10 show that even the semantic distinction between semelfactives and achievements in the absence of telicity tests is somewhat problematic. It is undisputable that 'arriving back' and 'killing' involve a transition (from 'not there' to 'there,' from 'not dead' to 'dead') and therefore should be telic, i.e. achievements rather than semelfactives. The same could be said of the first theme, which is used in such sentences as *sįlá thit'áth sı̨* 'I cut my hand,' where there is a transition in the theme 'hand' from 'not cut' to 'cut.' Semantically, these themes seem to represent achievements without preliminary stages.

To conclude my study of CM patterns and situation types, I will present a few themes which I was unable to class because the semantic tests were inconclusive.

3.2.5. Unclassed Verb Themes

The themes discussed here may be accomplishments or activities. Recall that these two situation types are normally easy to distinguish, based on the 'almost' test. However, in the cases presented here, the 'almost' test is less conclusive than usual.

The first verb theme to be discussed is *de–Ø–tł'ís* 'write' (originally: 'mark/scratch').

(29) de–Ø–tł'ís   th-cl-stem   'write, make marks'   di<u>ghit</u>ł'ís

This theme is ungrammatical with *k'ájëne* 'almost.' However, it does show a completion reading in a second 'almost' construction which speakers suggested to use with this theme:

(30) honi dighitł'ís t'unéga sı̨.   'I'm just about done writing a story.'
     honi de–ghe–i–Ø–tł'ís   t'unéga sı̨
     story th-CM-1s-cl-write almost? assert

I have not had opportunity to explore the element *t'unéga*, and therefore I do not know if it is a full verb or a particle. I also do not know if *t'unéga* means 'almost' or 'almost done.' I therefore prefer to reserve judgment about the situation type of this verb theme.

The next two themes are unique in allowing both a completion and an onset reading with the 'almost' test.

(31)   1   l-déł, -del   cl-stem   'consume pl O'   <u>ghes</u>del
       2   shé#d-tı̨   N?#cl-stem   'sg eat/dine'   shí<u>ghes</u>tı̨

(32) a. k'ájëne bër ghíldel.
       k'ájëne bër   ghe–íd–l–del
       almost meat CM-1dl/pl-cl-consume pl O
       'We just about ate the meat.' (never did, or almost done but some might be left)

b. k'ájëne shíghestı̨.
   k'ájëne   shé#ghe–s–d–tı̨
   almost   th#CM-1s-cl-sg eat
   'I just about ate.' (but didn't), 'I'm almost done eating.'

While their pattern is not entirely typical of accomplishments, which usually only show the very salient completion reading, they should probably be classed as accomplishments anyway, since for other situation types the completion reading is impossible. It is interesting to note that both themes denote eating situations. Perhaps these themes, denoting frequently occurring situations subject to many social conventions, allow an interpretation unavailable to other accomplishments. Jackendoff (1997:53) makes a similar observation about English. He notes that the "universal grinder" and "universal packager," which convert quantized into nonquantized predicates and vice versa, seem to apply mainly in eating and drinking contexts. Whatever the reason, these two themes sit a bit on the fence semantically between activities and accomplishments.

Finally, there is one theme which may be an activity, but its defective paradigm makes semantic testing difficult. *ní–ya#né–ne–l–ti* (adv-?#th-th-cl-stem) 'stutter' does not have Perfective forms; instead, a complex sentence is given to express perfective/past meaning. The Imperfective CM is Ø or perhaps *ne-*.

(33) a. níyanélti sı̨
       ní–ya#né–ne–l–ti   sı̨
       adv-?#th-th/CM-cl-stem   assert
       's/he is stuttering' (impf)

   b. tthidziné k'e níyanélti ghı̨lé nı̨.
      tthidziné k'e ní–ya#né–ne–l–ti   ghe–N–lé   nı̨
      yesterday   adv-?#th-th-cl-stem CM-N-exist perf past
      'yesterday s/he stuttered (for a reason).' (perf/past)
      lit.: [yesterday [s/he-stutter-impf] it-happened past]

Because of the lack of Perfective forms, the aspectual tests which work better in the Perfective ('almost,' 'quickly') are difficult to apply. The time span test, as well as compatibility with the Imperfective, indicate durativity. But although this verb behaves somewhat like an activity, we cannot determine its situation type with certainty.

Incidentally, the prefixes *ni#* and *ne-* suggest that this is a momentaneous theme (see Cook 2004). The fact that a Momentaneous Aspect form exists for a nonmotion theme, but only in a fossilized, defective paradigm, supports my proposal that Dëne has lost most of the historical Aspect system.

3.2.6. Summary

To sum up my study of CM patterns in Dëne, it has become clear that the only situation type with consistent morphological marking (*ghe*-perfective CM) is 'activity,' which is durative and atelic. The fact that *ghe*- also occurs with derived activities, namely those consisting of a succession of semelfactives, is further evidence that durative situations are marked by *ghe*-. However, the correlation is true only in one direction, from "activity"/"durative" to *ghe*-, not from *ghe*- to "activity"/ "durative," as some semelfactives, achievements, and accomplishments also show *ghe*-. Thus, if there is grammatization of activities (or of durativity) through the CM *ghe*-, it is quite weak.

The three non-activity situation types exhibit a variety of CM patterns, and cover themes from several morphological classes (verb theme categories), as far as this can be determined.[35] These facts are strong evidence for my claim that telicity is not grammatized in Dëne: it is neither possible to associate accomplishments with *the*-, nor is it possible to associate achievements with *ne*-. Moreover, nondurative situation types are almost impossible to distinguish further, due to a lack of telicity tests. This is further evidence for the weak status of telicity. Overall, the facts presented here show that in Dëne, CM patterns cannot be thought of as grammatical markers of the situation types.[36]

Similarly, my earlier proposal that CM patterns grammatize quantized reference is not supported by the facts. Quantized predicates (the accomplishments, achievements, semelfactives just discussed) do not show any systematic CM pattern and certainly are not consistently correlated with *the*-. But what about those with nonquantized/cumulative reference? Again, here it is true that the majority of cumulative predicates in my sample of verbs show the Ø/*ghe*- CM pattern. Unfortunately, a number of quantized predicates also have this pattern. For this reason, I hesitate to say that cumulative reference is grammatized through CM patterns in Dëne.

3.3. Excursus: Morpheme Cooccurrence Patterns?

In this section, I have focused on semantic tests in examining the relationship between morphological (CM pattern) and semantic (situation type) verb classes, and found that such a relationship only exists between activities and the CM *ghe*-. Rice (2000:260ff) focuses on a different kind of evidence for the claim that CM's indicate situation type. She presents cooccurrence patterns of the CM's with certain additional morphemes of the verb, arguing that the meanings of these additional morphemes (re-)determine the situation type of the entire verb/predicate and therefore select a certain CM. The morphemes in question are preverbs (= disjunct prefixes) or subsituation aspect markers (position 4 in Dëne).

3.3.1. Disjunct Prefixes

My central hypothesis that durativity is grammatized in the IP domain and telicity in the VP domain indeed predicts that if there were grammatization of telicity at all in Dëne, it should be through the disjunct prefixes, which are in VP. My hypothesis does not claim any correlation of disjunct prefixes and CM patterns, because CM's are not in the VP domain.

Rice finds evidence for a correlation of certain disjunct prefixes (or "preverbs," in her terminology) and certain CM patterns in Slave. For example, the Slave preverb *ní* "indicates termination or arrival at a point" (Rice 2000:263). Rice argues that *ní* requires the achievement CM *ne-* because this preverb indicates a simple, punctual transition.

Dëne has the cognate preverb or disjunct prefix *ní*, and it does cooccur with the CM *ne-*. However, these cooccurrence patterns do not speak to the fact that there are other verbs in Dëne which semantically are achievements but do not show a *ne-* CM (and similarly for semelfactives and accomplishments). For example, in section 3.2.5 (example (33)) we saw the verb theme 'stutter,' which contains both *ní#* and the CM *ne-* but nonetheless is not an achievement, but an activity (or perhaps an accomplishment).

For several of the preverbs given by Rice I have not been able to find cognates in Dëne. For example, I have not found a morpheme *lí* that corresponds to the Slave preverb *lí* 'stop V-ing,' or a preverb *xa* with the aspectual meaning 'up' (as in English *eat up*). The Dëne adverbial prefix (=position 10) most similar in form is *xá#* 'out,' the one most similar in meaning is *da#* 'up,' but *da#* has locative ('up onto something') rather than aspectual meaning. Cognate Dëne forms of one of the Slave examples with *xa* also do not contain this morpheme:

(34) 'eat plural O' :

a. Slave: O **xa**-d-éh-de.   'S/he ate up pl. O one by one.'

    preverb-qualifier-accomplishment sit. aspect-stem

    (Rice 2000:264)

b. Dëne: łue ghesdel sı̨.   'I ate the (several) fish.'

    łue ghe–s–l–del   sı̨

    fish CM-1s-cl-eat/consume pl O perf assert

    yek'e heldel.   'They ate it (all of whatever they were eating) up.'

    ye–k'e he–l–del

    4O-P ep-cl-eat/consume pl O perf

In Dëne, 'eating up,' i.e., complete consumption of the food items, is part of the meaning of the stem. This meaning can be emphasized by a PP such as *yek'e* which focuses the totality of the food items to be consumed (see singular translation 'it'). In either case, there is no *xa*.

Thus, the preverb and CM cooccurrence patterns found in Slave do not necessarily hold in Dëne. However, my database is too small to determine systematic cooccurrence patterns in Dëne, and I leave this issue for further research. As mentioned above, my central hypothesis predicts the preverbs alone (without CM's), if anything, to be involved in grammatizing telicity.

I will now discuss the role of certain position 4 prefixes with aspectual meaning.

3.3.2. Subsituation Aspects

Aspectual position 4 prefixes also show fairly regular patterns in Slave and other Athapaskan languages. Rice (2000) calls them subsituation aspects, Smith (1991) calls them superlexical aspects. In the section on morpheme cooccurrence patterns, Rice (2000) discusses three subsituation aspects in Slave, the inceptive, the conative, and the egressive.[37] She proposes that each of these "define subsituations within the larger situation structure" (p. 260). These subsituations have their own temporal contour and thus select their own CM. According to Rice, the inceptive and egressive denote durative, telic situations and, as predicted, occur with the CM *s* (= *the-*). The conative denotes a nondurative telic[38] situation and thus occurs with the CM *n* (= *ne-*). Rice takes these patterns as evidence that the CM's indeed mark situation type.

In Dëne, the picture is somewhat different. First, subsituation marking is not very productive, but, as Cook (2004) writes, limited to small subclasses of verbs; moreover, subsituation aspect markers are obligatory in some verb themes. For these reasons, Cook (2004) proposes that subsituation categories and the respective position 4 prefixes are derivational, and largely thematic, i.e., idiosyncratic, in Dëne. Second, the situation type meaning and the CM of a subsituation aspect do not always match up. Let us consider each of the Dëne subsituation aspects.

Inceptive

The inceptive is marked by a prefix *he-* (or *te-* in conservative varieties) in position 4, and by the Ø/*the-* CM pattern (see Cook 2004). The basic aspectual meaning of inceptives is the transition into an event ('start to V').[39] This transition is not conceived of as a point in time, but as a short stage, as is typical of achievements. Indeed, according to semantic tests the

Telicity Is Not Grammatized in Dëne　　　　　　　　　　　　　　*111*

three inceptive verbs in my database pattern like achievements (nondurative, telic) rather than as accomplishments (see also section 3.2.4 above). Their behavior as achievements is shown by their inability to occur in durative contexts. In (35)-(37), we can see that (i) the Imperfective form either requires a future marker or has an 'about to' interpretation, as is typical of achievements, and (ii) that it cannot occur in a sentence which describes an ongoing situation that serves as the background for another situation (translations are unedited). The (d) examples show that the Perfective CM is *the-* (or rather the high tone which occurs when *the-* is deleted following a conjunct prefix).

(35) a. Tsádhekų̈ę ts'ën hegha xasį̈.
　　　　Tsádhekų̈ę ts'ën he–Ø–Ø–gha　　xa sį̈
　　　　Edmonton to　incept-CM-cl-sg go fut assert
　　　　'S/he is gonna leave to [*sic*] Edmonton.'

　　b. Tsádhekų̈ę ts'ën hete?ás sį̈.
　　　　Tsádhekų̈ę ts'ën he–te–Ø–Ø–?ás　　sį̈
　　　　Edmonton to　dl-incept-CM-cl-dl go assert
　　　　'They two are leaving to [*sic*] Edmonton.' (right now)

　　c. # Tsádhekų̈ę ts'ën hessa–ú tsił hejër héja.
　　　　Tsádhekų̈ę ts'ën he–Ø–s–Ø–gha　　?ú
　　　　Edmonton to　incept-CM-1s-cl-sg go and/when
　　　　　　　　　　　　　　　　　tsił　hejër he–H–ja
　　　　　　　　　　　　　　　　　snow ?　　incept-CM-stem
　　　　(intended: 'As I was leaving for Edmonton, it started to snow.')

　　d. tthidziné k'e Tsádhekų̈ę ts'ën téya nį̈.
　　　　tthidziné k'e Tsádhekų̈ę ts'ën te–H(<the)–Ø–Ø–ya　　　nį̈
　　　　yesterday　Edmonton to　incept-CM-3s-cl-sg go perf　past
　　　　'S/he left for Edmonton yesterday.'

(36) a. behest'us xasį̈.
　　　　be–he–Ø–s–ł–t'us　　　xa sį̈
　　　　3O-incept-CM-1s-cl-fist action fut assert
　　　　'I'm going to punch him/it out.'[40]

b. # tthidziné k'e behest'us–ú tsątsąnaze déłtsĕr.

    tthidziné k'e be–he–Ø–s–ł–t'us   ?ú   tsątsąnaze déłtsĕr

    yesterday   3O-incept-CM-1s-cl-fist action and/when phone rang(perf)

    (intended: 'Yesterday when I was punching him/it out the phone rang.')

c. # tthidziné k'e behest'us t'ú tsątsąnaze déłtsĕr.

    tthidziné k'e be–he–Ø–s–ł–t'us   t'ú   tsątsąnaze déłtsĕr

    yesterday   3O-incept-CM-1s-cl-fist action while phone rang(perf)

    (intended: 'Yesterday while I was punching him/it out the phone rang.')

d. yehéłt'us.

    ye–he–H(<the)–Ø–ł–t'us

    3O-incept-CM-3s-cl-fist action

    'S/he punched him/it out.'

(37) a. dzół teshúł xasį.

    dzół te–Ø–s–ł–yúł[41]   xa sį

    ball incept-CM-1s-cl-handle round O with force fut assert

    'I'm gonna throw the ball.' (one throw)

b. dzół teshúł sį.

    dzół te–Ø–s–ł–yúł   sį

    ball incept-CM-1s-cl-handle round O with force assert

    'I am throwing the ball.' (I'm ready to throw it, going through the motions but not thrown yet)

c. # dzół heshúł–ú hutheskĕr.

    dzół he–Ø–s–ł–yúł   ?ú   hu–the–s–kĕr

    ball incept-CM-1s-cl-handle round O with force and/when ?-CM-1s-stem

    (intended: 'As I was throwing the ball, I slipped.')

d. dzół téshĕl sį.

    dzół te–H(<the)–Ø–ł–yél   sį

    ball incept-CM-3s-cl-handle round O with force perf assert

    'S/he threw the ball.'

It is interesting to consider which sentences were offered as alternatives to (37c). They contain either a perfective inceptive verb (with sequential event ordering), or an embedded future/prospective form. This underscores that the bare Imperfective is dispreferred with inceptives.

(38) a. hotié dzółtishĕl-ú hutheskĕr.

   hotié dzół te-(the-)i-ł-yél   ʔú   hu-the-s-kĕr

   precisely ball incept-(CM-)1s-cl-stem (perf) and/when ʔ-CM-1s-stem

   'Just as (after) I threw the ball I slipped.'

 b. dzół heshúł xanú hutheskĕr.

   dzół he-Ø-s-ł-yúł   xa ni̧ ʔú   hu-the-s-kĕr

   ball incept-CM-1s-cl-stem fut past and/when ʔ-CM-1s-stem

   'As I was going to throw the ball I slipped.'

The three inceptive verbs in my database are apparently lexicalized. The common translation for the verb in (35) is 'leave' rather than 'start to go,' and in (36) and (37) the semantic contribution of the inceptive prefix to the meaning of the verb theme is even less transparent. It is probably because of cases such as these that Cook (2004) argues that the inceptive, as all subsituation aspects, is lexical, meaning that it must be part of the lexical entry of a given verb theme whether it contains the inceptive morpheme or not, and which, if any, contribution it makes to the verb's meaning.

Conative u- ?

In Slave, verb themes with the conative affix *ú-* denote an attempted action such as 'shoot at (something)' or 'throw (type of object) at (something).' According to Rice (2000:262), the conative subsituation aspect denotes a punctual change of state (= achievement). Its cooccurrence with the CM *ne-* supports that this CM marks achievements (see footnote 18 above).

In Dëne, a position 4 prefix *u-*, usually without high tone, occurs in a variety of verbs with a variety of meanings and CM's. A conative meaning is not always apparent. This suggests that either there are homophonous *u-* prefixes, or that the conative prefix has undergone semantic bleaching or shift. For example, Cook (2004) only mentions a "seriative (< conative?)" prefix *u-*. Verb themes with a position 4 prefix *u-* show a variety of CM's.

I will first give examples where *u-* contributes to seriative meaning. "Seriative" verbs refer to a series of punctual actions. Usually seriative verb themes also have a semelfactive counterpart.

(39) hughikár si̱.
    h–u̱–ghe–i–Ø–kár si̱
    ep-*u*-CM-1s-cl-slap assert
    'I slapped it repeatedly.,' 'I had gone through the process of slapping.'

cf. nánighikár.
    ná#ne–(i?–)ghe–i–Ø–kár
    adv#th-(?[42]-)CM-1s-cl-slap
    'I slapped it once.'

(40) tthidziné k'e hughiɬt'us.
    tthidziné k'e h–u̱–ghe–i–ɬ–t'us
    yesterday   ep?-*u*-CM-1s-cl-punch
    'Yesterday I punched him/her/it repeatedly.'

cf. nánighiɬt'us.
    ná#ne–(i?–)ghe–i–ɬ–t'us
    adv#th-(?-)CM-1s-cl-punch
    'I punched him/her/it (once).'

cf. tthidziné k'e behiɬt'us ni̱.
    tthidziné k'e be–he–(the–)i–ɬ–t'us   ni̱
    yesterday   3O-incept/th-(CM-)1s-cl-punch past
    'Yesterday I punched him/her/it out.'

However, as we shall see in the next section, not all seriative verb themes contain a prefix *u*-. In another verb theme with seriative meaning, some speakers but not others have a prefix *u*- ((a) and (b) are from two different speakers):

(41) a. ɬi̱chogh ghi̱kĕ̌r.
        ɬi̱chogh ghe–ne–Ø–kĕ̌r
        horse   CM-2s-cl-pat
        'You (sg) patted the horse.'

    b. hughi̱kĕ̌r.
        h–u̱–ghe–ne–Ø–kĕ̌r
        ep-*u*-CM-2s-cl-pat
        'You sg patted it.'

Telicity Is Not Grammatized in Dëne

In all of these cases, the CM is *ghe-*, which is the fairly regular pattern with seriative and other activities, as we saw above.

In the next two related verbs, *u-* has a clearer conative meaning, although there is overlap with seriative meaning in (42b), where we see the CM *ghe-*, as expected. The CM *ne-* cooccurs with *u-* only in the conative/semelfactive verb theme in (42a). This verb theme seems to be punctual, but we do not know if the punctual meaning is due to *u-* or *é-* or both.

(42) a. hónesk′éth ha. (Elford and Elford 1998:279,
 h–é–u–ne–s–ł–k′éth ha Cook 2004)
 ep-sem-*u*-CM/th-1s-cl-shoot with gun fut
 'I will shoot (at it).'

 b. hughiłk′éth.
 h–u–ghe–i–ł–k′éth
 ep-*u*-CM-1s-cl-shoot with gun
 'I continuously shot O, fired at O.'

In other verb themes, *u-* seems to be completely thematic, or lexicalized. In the next two examples, it is impossible to know the meaning or function of *u-*.

(43) húthiya sį.
 h–ú–the–i–Ø–ya sį
 ep-*ú*-CM-1s-cl-sg go assert
 'I passed through.'

(44) ʔuneghiyą.
 ʔ–u–ne–ghe–i–Ø–yą
 epʔ-*u*-gd-CM-1s-cl-stem
 'I picked berries.'

According to semantic tests, (43) is an activity and (44) an accomplishment. The CM's *the-* and *ghe-* do not match up with situation type here.

Finally *u-*, or *ú-*, may cooccur with the inceptive prefix *he-/te-* in verbs of inceptive meaning. These verbs are more transparently "inceptive" than the lexicalized examples with only *he-/te-* given in the previous section. The CM is *ne-*.

(45) a. bĕr húniłbes sį.
   bĕr h–ú–ne–i–ł–bes   sį
   meat ep-*ú*-CM/th-1s-cl-boil O assert
   'I started boiling (the) meat.'

  b. bĕr hunułt'e sį.
   bĕr h–u–ne–uh–ł–t'e   sį
   meat ep-*u*-CM/th-2dl/pl-cl-cook O assert
   'You (two) have started to cook it (meat).'

Unfortunately, I have not tested the situation type of these verbs, and therefore do not know if they are achievements.

In conclusion, the prefix *u-/ú-* (if indeed we are dealing with only one prefix here) has a variety of meanings in Dëne, but most often occurs in seriative verbs. If this prefix originally marked conatives, it has become semantically bleached. In terms of morpheme cooccurence patterns, *u-* cooccurs with a variety of CM's, which are sometimes but not always semantically motivated. The most consistent pattern seems to be cooccurrence with the CM *ghe-* in seriative, i.e., activity, verbs.

I now turn to other ways of marking the seriative/semelfactive opposition.

Seriative and Semelfactive

As already mentioned, some stems occur in related themes, one of which denotes a single short action, while the other denotes an extended action made up of repetitions of the single short action. Morphologically, two such related themes can be distinguished in a variety of ways. (46) summarizes the possible morphological distinctions between semelfactives and seriatives.

(46) VERB THEME[43]	GLOSS	TRANSL.	1s PERF FORM
1a ł–yúł/l	cl-stem	'blow O prolonged'	<u>gh</u>ishúl
1b é–ł–yúł, ł–yúł	sem/th-cl-stem, cl-stem	'blow O once (e.g., blow out candle)'	<u>th</u>ishúl
2a Ø–ził	cl-stem	'scream repeatedly/prolonged'	<u>gh</u>iził
2b é–Ø–ził, Ø–<u>z</u>ël	sem/th-cl-stem, cl-stem	'scream once'	<u>th</u>izël
3a Ø–t'áth, –t'adh	cl-stem	'cut O'	<u>gh</u>it'adh
3b é–Ø–t'ëth, Ø–t'áth	sem/th-cl-stem, cl-stem	'make one quick cut (e.g., knife slips)'	<u>th</u>it'áth
4a <u>u</u>–Ø–kár	ser/th-cl-stem	'slap O repeatedly'	hu<u>gh</u>ikár

Telicity Is Not Grammatized in Dëne 117

4b	ná#ne–(i–)Ø–kár	adv#th-(?-)cl-stem	'slap O once'	nánighikár
5a	u–ł–t'us	ser/th-cl-stem	'punch O repeatedly'	hughiłt'us
5b	ná#ne–ł–t'us	adv#th-cl-stem	'punch O once'	nánighiłt'us
6a[44]	u–ł–k'éth	ser/th-cl-stem	'shoot O continuously, fire at O'	hughiłk'éth
6b	é–ł–k'íth, ł–k'éth	sem/th-cl-stem, cl-stem	'shoot O (with gun)'[45]	thiłk'éth
7a	yá#l–gus	adv#cl-stem	'jump prolonged'	yághesgus
7b	ya#l–gus, –gos	adv#cl-stem	'jump once'	yásgos (Ø or H)

The related themes can be distinguished through a semelfactive position 4 prefix *é-* as in themes 1–3, through a (seriative) position 4 prefix *u-* (themes 4–5, and examples (39) and (40) above), through both (theme 6) or through neither (theme 7).[46] However, from these examples we can also see that the way the semelfactive/seriative contrast is marked is anything but predictable. First, it cannot be predicted whether a semelfactive or a seriative prefix will occur (and which verb theme is more basic). Second, the contrast is also marked by other means: most but not all themes also show a CM contrast between *ghe-* (seriative) and *the-* (semelfactive). In themes 4 and 5, there is not just a seriative prefix *u-*, but also an adverbial prefix *ná#* in the semelfactive themes. In theme 2, the contrast is marked in the Perfective by different CM's and by different stems, in addition to the semelfactive prefix *é-* in the Imperfective. In theme 7, the contrast is marked only by the CM's.

Moreover, several of these stems occur not only in semelfactive/seriative pairs, but in other verb themes as well. For example, in addition to *ná#ne–ł–t'us* 'punch O (with fist) once' and *u–ł–t'us* 'punch O (with fist) repeatedly,' there is *he/te–ł–t'us* 'beat O up (by punching with fist)' (cf. discussion of inceptives above), which is neither semelfactive nor seriative. Even more themes exist for the stems 'cut' and 'shoot (with gun),' making it in effect difficult to determine which, if any, themes should be called the 'semelfactive' and the 'seriative' ones.

In conclusion, while there are specific semelfactive and seriative morphemes in position 4, there is no one-to-one correspondence between these morphemes and semelfactive or seriative meanings respectively. For this reason, Cook (2004) calls the semelfactive and the seriative lexical or derivational aspects. CM's, on the other hand, mark the contrast quite consistently. This supports my earlier findings that durative themes, especially activities, are marked by *ghe-* (and other themes by any CM).

Summary

The marking of subsituation aspect through position 4 prefixes is less than systematic in Dëne, and it is reasonable to assume that position 4 morphemes are in most cases an idiosyncratic part of the verb theme (see also Cook 2004). Cooccurence patterns of specific position 4 prefixes with specific CM's have either not been found, or the CM does not match the verb's situation type. The only fairly consistent pattern is that seriative verbs have the CM *ghe-*, irrespective of position 4 prefix. Therefore, I maintain that, other than *ghe-* marking activities, CM's do not correlate with situation type in Dëne.

3.3.3. End of Excursus: Morpheme Cooccurrence Patterns

I have not found consistent cooccurrence patterns of disjunct prefixes (preverbs) or position 4 prefixes with CM's, in which the CM's also match the predicted situation type. The only consistent pattern is that activities are marked with the CM *ghe-*, irrespective of other morphemes.

But what the examples and discussion in this section have shown is that Dëne has rich morphological means (albeit often lexicalized) to mark aspectual distinctions which are more fine-grained than the four (or five, including states) situation types. The fact that these "subsituation aspects" are often not productive supports my impression that the rich system of Aspects found in Alaskan Athapaskan languages is part frozen, part lost in Dëne.

3.4. Discussion

In this section I have shown that CM patterns do not mark situation type, other than perhaps activities, in Dëne. Similarly, CM's do not mark the difference between quantized and cumulative reference: while it does seem true that cumulative predicates are consistently associated with the *ghe*-perfective CM, quantized predicates (accomplishments, achievements, semelfactives) do not show any consistent morphological patterns, and a number of them even show *ghe-*.

What seems to be the case instead is that there are many fine subtypes of quantization in Dëne (see section 3.3). The standard situation types are too general to capture these fine distinctions. Moreover, it is not possible to predict which meaning—or which stem—will be associated with which kind of morphology. Likely the rich aspectual system that once existed in Athapaskan, and which can still be seen in languages like Ahtna and Koyukon, has been impoverished in Dëne due to the loss of syllable types, followed by morpheme loss, as well as through phonological and morphological mergers.

The fact that telicity/quantization is not grammatized through CM patterns, but that there is a weak correlation with durativity/cumulativity, fits well with my observations on telicity and durativity in the previous chapter. There I found independent evidence that durativity is grammatized but telicity is not, and I suggested that the pervasive viewpoints are the driving force behind this. In particular, I proposed (i) that the Imperfective viewpoint, which has durative meaning, grammatizes durativity, and (ii) that the strong completive meaning of the Perfective makes reference to telicity unnecessary in most circumstances. In light of the viewpoint facts, it is not surprising that the Dëne CM patterns are not sensitive to telicity/quantization, but are perhaps sensitive to durativity/cumulativity.

In the next section, I will discuss a last piece of evidence for my claim that telicity is not grammatized in Dëne: the behavior of (direct) objects.

4. OBJECTS

In Chapter Two (section 3.2.3) I showed that Dëne NPs are not marked overtly for quantization, and that they all have cumulative reference (in the absence of a numeral and/or measure phrase). I argued that this is to be expected if telicity is not grammatized: if it is not important to know whether a VP is telic, the contribution of the direct object to telicity, in the form of quantization, is also not important, and therefore quantization-marking processes can be absent.

More generally, we do not expect to find in Dëne a morphosyntactic object marking process, such as case marking or object affix choice, to be sensitive to telicity. For example, we do not expect to find alternations as in Finnish, where only objects of telic VPs get accusative case (see, e.g., Kiparsky (1998)), or in German, where the difference between a telic and an atelic VP can be reflected in a direct object vs. PP (accusative vs. "conative") alternation:

(47) Finnish (Kiparsky 1998:279)

    a. Matti   ost-i   maido-n   (tunni-ssa).
       Matti-SgNom buy-Pst3Sg milk-Sg**Acc** (hour-Iness)
       'Matti bought the milk (in an hour).'

    b. Matti   ost-i   maito-a   (tunni-n).
       Matti-SgNom buy-Pst3Sg milk-Sg**Part** (hour-Acc)
       'Matti bought milk (for an hour).'

(48) German (cf. Filip 1989)

    a. Susi hat (in einer Stunde) **ein**   Gedicht geschrieben.
       Susi has (in one hour)   **a-ACC** poem   written
       'Susi has written/wrote a poem (in an hour).'

b. Susi hat (#in einer Stunde) **an einem** Gedicht geschrieben.
   Susi has (in one hour)   **at a-DAT** poem   written
   'Susi has written at a poem/was writing a poem (#in one hour).'

Dëne exhibits two of the object-related alternations which have been discussed elsewhere as affecting telicity: the indefinite (or unspecified) object prefix, and plural-stem verbs. I will begin with the former.

Midgette (1996:321–22) suggests that if a Navajo verb has an indefinite or "unspecified" object, as indicated by the object prefix *a-* (rather than Ø or *yi-*), an atelic interpretation results, rather than the usual telic interpretation. For example: <u>sis</u> sétł'ǫ́ 'I wove a <u>belt</u>' (telic) vs. <u>a</u>sétł'ǫ́ 'I did some weaving' (atelic) (p. 320). Although Dëne does have the cognate "unspecified" object prefix ʔe–, I have not found corresponding telicity alternations in my Dëne data. First of all, the morphological aspect marking of the verb does not change if the object is "unspecified."[47] This is shown in examples (49) and (50). Second, the semantic situation type does not change either, as shown by the 'almost' test in examples (51) and (52). However, I do not have many examples with ʔe–in my data, and the behaviour of verbs with ʔe–needs to be examined better in further research.

(49) a. nánathiłdą́.
       ná–na#Ø–the–i–ł–dą́
       th-th#<u>3O</u>-CM-1s-cl-mend
       'I patched O (specific thing), I patched it.'

   b. nána<u>ʔe</u>thiłdą́.
       ná–na#ʔe–the–i–ł–dą́
       th-th#<u>unspecO</u>-CM-1s-cl-mend
       'I patched (a nonspecific thing).'

(50) a. honi dighitł'ís.
       honi Ø–de–ghe–i–Ø–tł'ís
       story <u>3O</u>-th-CM-1s-cl-mark
       'I wrote a story.'

   b. ʔerighitł'ís.
       ʔe–de–ghe–i–Ø–tł'ís
       <u>unspecO</u>-th-CM-1s-cl-mark
       'I wrote.'

(51) a. k'ájëne nánathiɬdą́.
   k'ájëne ná–na#Ø–the–i–ɬ–dą́
   almost th-th#3O-CM-1s-cl-mend
   'I just about mended it.' (just about done)

b. k'ájëne nánaʔethiɬdą́.
   k'ájëne ná–na#ʔe–the–i–ɬ–dą́
   almost th-th#unspecO-CM-1s-cl-mend
   'I almost finished sewing/patching it.'

(52) a. # k'ájëne honi dighitɬ'ís.
   k'ájëne honi Ø–de–ghe–i–Ø–tɬ'ís
   almost story 3O-th-CM-1s-cl-mark

b. # k'ájëne ʔerighitɬ'ís sį̀.
   k'ájëne ʔe–de–ghe–i–Ø–tɬ'ís   sį̀
   almost unspecO-th-CM-1s-cl-mark assert

If ʔe–corresponded to an atelic and Ø to a telic interpretation, then (51a) and (52a) should have a completion reading with 'almost,' and (51b) and (52b) should have an onset reading or they should be unacceptable (as sometimes happens with activities). But the situation type obviously does not vary with the object marker.

I now turn to the second potentially telicity-sensitive alternation, plural-stem verbs. We noted in Chapter Two, section 3.2.3, that Dëne does not have nominal number marking.[48] Instead, Dëne expresses number concepts, including entity number, on the verb. This is an instance of *verbal number* (see Durie 1986, Mithun 1988, Corbett 2000 (chapter 8), and Bar-el et al 2001). One way in which Dëne and other Athapaskan languages do this is by having different stems for singular and plural objects. Thus, –tsį̀ means 'make sg O,' but –ghą means 'make pl O' (see below for examples). Both Kari (1979) and Axelrod (1993) suggest that plural-stem verbs are atelic and durative (in their terms, operative themes or (nonsemelfactive) successive themes), while singular-stem verbs are accomplishments (i.e., conversive themes) or semelfactives. Moreover, several of Rice's (2000) accomplishment examples are singular-stem verbs, while several of the activity examples are plural-stem verbs (p. 257ff). Does this mean, then, that object number influences telicity after all?

In my semantically tested classification, I did not find an effect of object number, as encoded by verb stems, on telicity. Several Dëne cognates of both singular *and plural* verbs behave as accomplishments. I give here some of the relevant examples, with the 'almost' test.

(53) a. k'ájëne łue ghesdagh sį́.

    k'ájëne łue ghe–s–Ø–dagh   sį́

    almost fish CM-1s-cl-eat sg animal assert

    'I just about ate the fish.' (just about done)

  b. k'ájëne bër ghíldel.

    k'ájëne bër   ghe–íd–l–del

    almost meat CM-1dl/pl-cl-consume pl O

    'We just about ate the meat.' (never did, or almost done but some might be left)[49]

(54) a. k'ájëne thiłtsį́.

    k'ájëne the–i–ł–tsį́

    almost CM-1s-cl-make sg O

    'I just about finished making it/I'm almost done making it.'

  b. k'ájëne ke sųłiné ghighą sį́.

    k'ájëne ke sųłiné   ghe–i–Ø–ghą   sį́

    almost moccasin CM-1s-cl-make pl O assert

    'I have just about completed the pair of moccasins.'

(55) a. k'ásjëne dzół nághi?ą́.

    k'ásjëne dzół   ná#ghe–i–Ø–?ą́

    almost   ball adv#CM-1s-cl-handle sg round O perf

    'I just about got the ball down.' (almost finished)

  b. ? k'ájëne dzół nághila sį́.

    k'ájëne dzół   ná#ghe–i–Ø–la   sį́

    almost ball adv#CM-1s-cl-handle pl O perf assert

    'I'm just about done taking the balls down.' (I have not yet taken all of them down)[50]

These examples suggest that plural-stem verbs do not necessarily denote atelic situations (activities) in Dëne. It is worthy of note, however, that in all the plural examples given here the plural object seems to have a quantized interpretation: a specific number of objects seem to be involved in the events. This is a semantic cooccurrence which is not marked overtly in the morphosyntax. Also note that the CM's do not follow the pattern predicted in Rice (2000): some singular-stem verbs, and all of the plural-stem verbs, although accomplishments, show the CM *ghe-*.

The tendency that objects of telic VPs often seem to receive a quantized interpretation in Dëne does not contradict my claim that telicity is not grammatized in Dëne.[51] The relationship between object quantization and telicity is of a compositional semantic nature (see Krifka 1989, 1992). It does not depend on overt morphosyntactic marking. Moreover, it has yet to be determined how consistently telicity correlates with a (nonovertly) quantized object in Dëne. I will offer just a few examples where the (semantic) telicity of a VP does *not* seem to be influenced by the (semantic) quantization of the object.

In order to get a contrast in quantization, I chose a mass noun, *bër* 'meat,' and a count noun, *k'ásba* 'chicken(s).' While we know that both mass and count nouns have cumulative reference in Dëne (see Chapter Two, section 3.2.3), it may be easier to impose quantized reference on a count noun. For example, a count noun can be restricted to refer to a single individual quite easily, and a singular reading is quantized, cf. (56b), (57b).

I combined these two nouns with telic verbs and applied the 'almost' test, cf. (56) and (57). In all cases, the result was a telic/accomplishment situation, as indicated by the completion reading of 'almost.' The form of the verb also stayed the same. Judging by the English translations, in all examples except (56a) the objects have a definite and hence quantized interpretation, but even (56a) is an accomplishment.

(56) a. k'ájëne bër thiłt'e sı̨.

      k'ájëne bër the–i–ł–t'e   sı̨

      almost meat CM-1s-cl-perf cook O assert

      'I'm just about done cooking meat.'

   b. k'ájëne k'ásba thiłt'e sı̨.

      k'ájëne k'ásba   the–i–ł–t'e   sı̨

      almost chicken CM-1s-cl-perf cook O assert

      'I'm just about done cooking the chicken.'

(57) a. k'ájëne bĕr nághit'adh sį.

    k'ájëne bĕr ná#ghe–i–Ø–t'adh   sį

    almost meat adv#CM-1s-cl-cut O perf assert

    'I'm just about done cutting up the meat.'

b. k'ájëne k'ásba nághit'adh sį.

    k'ájëne k'ásba ná#ghe–i–Ø–t'adh   sį

    almost chicken adv#CM-1s-cl-cut O perf assert

    'I'm just about done cutting up that chicken.'

The next example is somewhat different because in all cases the objects have a quantized interpretation. However, since a blanket (see (58a)) is a much larger object than a mitten, it is more conceivable that mending a blanket takes longer and, in terms of a real-world situation, is more of an activity than an accomplishment. This is even suggested by the speaker's translation into English ('sewing *on* a blanket'). Nonetheless, the VP patterns like an accomplishment semantically, and the verb as well as the object have the same form as in the more clearly telic examples (except for the distributive prefix *dá#* which indicates that the object is plural in (58b-c)). It seems, then, that the meaning of the object does not influence the situation aspect of the VP.

(58) a. k'ájëne ts'éré nánathiłdą́ sį.

    k'ájëne ts'éré ná–na#the–i–ł–dą́   sį

    almost blanket th-th#CM-1s-cl-stem assert

    'I'm sewing on a blanket and I'm just about done.'

b. k'ájëne sǫlághe jis nádánathiłdą́ sį.

    k'ájëne sǫlághe jis   ná–dá–na#the–i–ł–dą́   sį

    almost five   mitten th-distr-th#CM-1s-cl-stem assert

    'I'm just about done mending these five mitts.'

c. k'ájëne horelyų jis nádánathiłdą́ sį.

    k'ájëne horelyų jis   ná–dá–na#the–i–ł–dą́   sį

    almost all   mitten th-distr-th#CM-1s-cl-stem assert

    'I'm just about done with all of them.' (= all of the mittens)

Summing up, object semantics does not consistently influence telicity in Dëne, nor does the language seem to have object marking alternations which correspond to telic/atelic alternations. The fact that object morphosyntax does not interact with telicity supports my hypothesis that telicity is not grammatized in Dëne.

5. DISCUSSION

In this chapter, I have attempted to show that telicity is not grammatized in Dëne. I have argued in section 1 that Dëne has largely lost the potentially situation-type based verb theme categories and Aspects of more conservative Athapaskan languages. In sections 2 and 3 I showed at length that CM patterns do not grammatize telicity either. Finally, I gave evidence that object morphosyntax does not influence telicity in Dëne (section 4). Taking all these pieces together, the emerging picture is indeed that the morphosyntax of Dëne does not represent telicity, i.e., that telicity is not grammatized in Dëne. (Recall that this does not mean that telicity cannot be semantically expressed.) Thus, in the debate on the grammatization of situation type (or the underlying notions) I come down on the side of Smith (1991, 1996), who finds that telicity is not grammatized in Navajo.

The driving force behind this cross-linguistically surprising finding is the pervasive viewpoint aspect system of Dëne. It represents the one truly productive, grammatical aspectual marking in Dëne. As argued in Chapter Two, the durative force of the Imperfective grammatizes durativity, and the completive force of the Perfective obscures telicity, which consequently is not grammatized in the language. Midgette (1996), in an examination of aspect in Navajo, comes to a very different conclusion about the relationship between viewpoint aspect and situation type. I will present her view briefly and argue that it is not as consistent with the facts as mine.

5.1. Navajo

Examining the Navajo verb theme categories (which are similar to those of Koyukon and Ahtna), Midgette suggests that stativity and telicity are the primary organizing features of the Navajo categories (see (59) below). Durativity is argued to be only of secondary importance. As evidence she cites, besides morphological facts such as CM patterns, a strong inflectional correlation between prototypically telic themes and perfective viewpoint, and prototypically atelic themes and imperfective viewpoint.

However, it is doubtful whether the viewpoint correlation can really be stated in terms of telicity. We saw above (Chapter Two) that in Dëne, the correlation is between imperfectivity and durativity: the Imperfective is restricted to durative verbs, while the Perfective places no such restrictions. This very same analysis is also possible, and even more likely, for Navajo than Midgette's, which I will now demonstrate.

First of all, the correlation between telicity and perfectivity cited by Midgette as evidence does not hold for all verbs. Both telic and atelic members from the "operative" verb theme category may be either imperfective or perfective. To quote Midgette (1996:321): ". . . the specification of the telic property does not affect the choice of inflection [. . .]; verb bases in the operative theme category appear frequently in both Perfective and Imperfective. . . ."

Second, in contradistinction to this exception, the correlation between imperfectivity and durativity does hold consistently in Navajo. This is reported in Smith (1991), and is also suggested by Midgette's own examples. The two types of verb themes consistently preferring the Perfective in Midgette's data are telic motion verb themes in Momentaneous Aspect and telic successive verb themes. Crucially, these are also both punctual: the former correspond to achievements (as, for example, indicated by the Momentaneous Aspect), the latter correspond to semelfactives ("the action occurs one time [. . .] and is also extremely brief in duration," Midgette 1996:318). Rather than saying that they prefer the Perfective because they are telic[52], I would say that they cannot occur in the Imperfective because they are punctual (and thus, they have to occur in the Perfective).

Thus, the correlation between viewpoint and situation type finds a better, exceptionless explanation if it is based on durativity rather than on telicity.

The discussion of momentaneous motion themes and of semelfactives leads me to a further criticism of Midgette (1996), which concerns her more general claims on the role of telicity in the organization of Navajo verbs. According to Midgette, Navajo verbs are organized as shown in (59), with telicity (and stativity) playing a major role.

(59) Navajo Verb Theme Categories and Telicity (based on Midgette 1996:320, fig. 4).

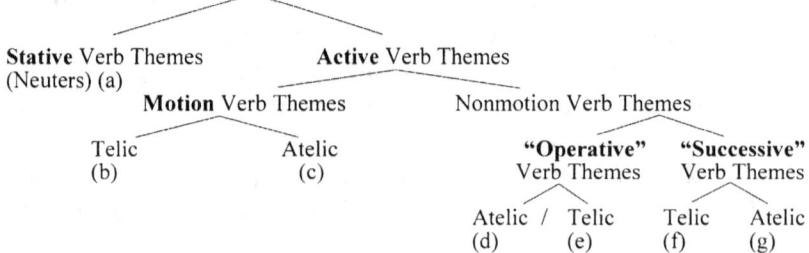

Telicity Is Not Grammatized in Dëne 127

(a) Nisnééz. 'I am tall.'
(b) Kintahgóó níyá. 'I went to town.' (Momentaneous)
(c) Kintahgóó yishááł. 'I'm going along towards town.' (Cursive)
(d) Ashtł'ó. 'Im weaving.', Sis yishtł'ó. 'I'm weaving a belt.'
(e) Asétł'ǫ. 'I did some weaving.', Sis sétł'ó. 'I wove a belt.'
(f) Mósí sétał. 'I gave the cat a kick.' (Semelfactive)
(g) Mósí nánishtał. 'I was kicking the cat.' (Repetitive)

Midgette argues that the major distinction among the active themes is based on telicity: motion themes are prototypically telic while nonmotion themes are prototypically atelic. She furthermore argues that durativity does not form natural classes of verbs in Navajo. However, most of the hierarchy in (59) can be recast in terms of durativity:

(60) Revision: Navajo Verb Theme Catgories and Durativity

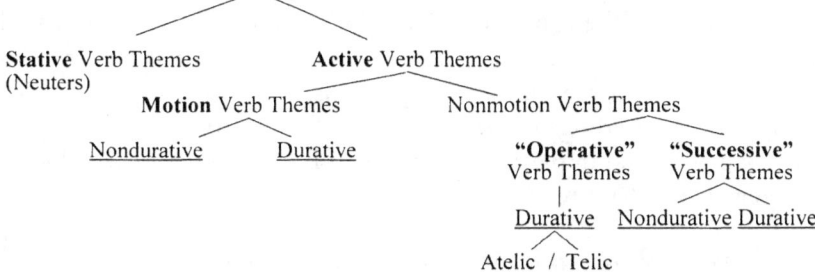

In this revised hierarchy (which successfully predicts compatibility with imperfective viewpoint) telicity has become a lower-level distinction, whereas durativity is responsible for the main distinctions among the active (= nonstative) verb themes.

This reanalysis of Navajo, as well as my findings on Dëne, are in agreement with Smith's (1991, 1996) analysis of aspect in Navajo. Smith argues that while stativity and durativity are grammatized in Navajo, telicity is not. The reason is that a situation type is realized as an entire "array" of verb themes, i.e., there is not a single verb theme for, say, an accomplishment situation, but a number of themes which denote different phases (initial point, endpoint, internal stages) of the situation. Smith writes (1991:392): "The features of dynamism and duration are salient, while the distinction between telic and atelic is not grammatized. The multiple lexicalization pattern neutralizes the difference between telic and atelic situations." (61) is an example of such an array of verb themes:

(61) a. diyógí bi'niitł'ǫ́ (I started to weave a blanket)^(Perf A:Mom) (Smith 1991:415)
b. diyógí nínítł'ǫ́ (I finished weaving a blanket)^(Perf A:Mom)
c. diyógí yishtł'ó (I'm weaving along on a blanket)^(Impf B:Dur)
d. diyógí sétł'ǫ́ (I wove a blanket)^(Impf B:Rep)

Durativity is grammatized in two ways. First, Smith finds a distinction between two types of verb theme categories, "type A" and "type B." I could not make out what precisely the morphological characteristics of each type are, and whether these two types correspond to any of the Athapaskan verb theme categories, but Smith does say that type B verb themes are always durative while type A themes rarely are. This, then, is one way in which durativity is grammatized. Second, durativity is grammatized through the strong association between the Imperfective viewpoint and duration. Smith does not find a correlation between telicity and viewpoint.

Summing up, a close examination of the evidence in Navajo suggests that in this language as well, durativity but not telicity is grammatized. But the discussion of the competing claims in Smith (1991, 1996) and Midgette (1996) raises an important question: how is it possible that there can be such different views on the same language? This question also poses itself when comparing my findings in Dëne to those of Rice (2000) in the neighboring language Slave and in particular to those of Bortolin (1998), who looked at a different Dëne dialect.

5.2. How Much Variation Is There in Athapaskan?

Undoubtedly, there is quite a bit of variation among the Athapaskan languages. For example, the Alaskan Athapaskan languages are unintelligible to a Dëne speaker. Their sound system is quite different; they have no tone, but do have a larger inventory of consonants and of syllable types. I have argued above (section 1) that the aspectual system of Dëne is truly different from that of Alaskan languages such as Ahtna and Koyukon. In Dëne, a simplification of the consonant inventory and syllable types has led to morpheme loss, as well as morpheme and paradigm mergers, especially in the system of Aspects, which relies heavily on stem suffixation patterns. For these reasons, Dëne has only a residue of Aspects and Aspect-based verb theme categories, and we cannot base any claims on the grammatization of situation type features on such an incomplete, frozen system.

But what about Slave and other dialects of Dëne? Here it is less likely that different findings are due to variation among the languages. Cold Lake Dëne is the most conservative of all Dëne dialects, in terms of phonology as well as morphology. Dëne in general allows for more syllable types than Slave (in Slave, the only permissible surface coda is *h*, cf. Rice (1989)). Therefore, we would expect the aspect morphology of Cold Lake Dëne to be at least as full and productive as that found in Rice (2000) and Bortolin (1998). I attribute our different results to the evolution of aspect research in these languages.

Bortolin (1998) and Rice (2000) were the first to examine the grammatization of situation type in an Athapaskan language. They succeeded in recognizing the generalizations behind the unwieldy traditional aspectual classifications found in Athapaskan, and developed an attractive hypothesis in terms of current aspect theory. Moreover, their proposed correlations between morphological classes and situation types are supported by core examples of each morphological class.

Because these proposals were in place, I was able to employ a new methodology which started with semantic classes and searched for morphosyntactic correlates, rather than starting with the morphology and looking for semantic correlates. Hand in hand with this goes my emphasis on explicit semantic testing with language-specific tests.[53] That is, I examined in detail the semantic reality of the Dëne morphological classes (as by CM). My study shows that such a detailed semantic examination may reveal patterns (or the absence thereof) which cannot be deduced from looking at English translation equivalents. Starting with semantic classes, which were determined by semantic tests, is one reason why my findings differ from the previous ones.

By initially ignoring the morphological classes, I was also able to "cast my net" differently, i.e., to build a different data sample. If one looks at a small number of prototypical examples of each morphological class, one is more likely to find a correlation between CM-based classes and situation type, than if one looks at a larger sample which includes less prototypical examples. While my data sample is not particularly large (ca. 50 verbs), I have made an effort to include more than just basic examples. I have done this in part by eliciting several verb themes derived from a single stem. In this way I obtained morphologically simple as well as morphologically more complex verb themes—a range of varied examples whose situation type I was not able to predict or guess at before analysis. And indeed, it was particularly in the examination of the nonbasic examples that the correlation between CM-based morphological classes and situation type broke down.

Let me give just two examples to illustrate this. The first is the stem *t'áth/t'adh* 'action with sharp blade,' from which derive semelfactives, activities, and accomplishments. The second is the stem *gha/ya/yá* 'sg go (on foot),' which has semelfactive, achievement, and activity derivations. When looking at the array of derivationally related themes, it becomes obvious that CM patterns do not match situation types.

(62) t'áth/t'adh 'action with sharp blade'

	Sit. Type	Verb Theme	Gloss	Translation	1s perf Form
1	SEM	é–Ø–t'ëth, Ø–t'áth	sem/th-cl-stem, cl-stem	'make one quick cut' (e.g., knife slips)	thit'áth
2	ACT	Ø–t'áth, –t'adh	cl-stem	'cut O'	ghit'adh
3	ACC	tł'o de–Ø–t'áth, –t'adh	N th-cl-stem	'cut grass (hay)'	tł'o deghit'adh
4	ACC	ná#Ø–t'áth, –t'adh	adv#cl-stem	'cut O up (into pieces)'	nághit'adh
5	ACC	ł–t'ëth, –t'adh	cl-stem	'shape O with blade'	thiłt'adh

(63) gha/ya/yá 'sg go (on foot)'

	Sit. Type	Verb Theme	Gloss	Translation	1s perf Form
1	SEM	ní–na#ne–d–gha, –ya, –yá	adv-iter#th-cl-stem	'sg come back' (lit., 'sg arrive again/back')	ninesja (Ø or ne-)
2	ACH	ní#Ø–gha, –ya, –yá	adv#cl-stem	'sg arrive'	níniya
3	ACH	(O yé) Ø–gha, –ya, –yá	(PP) cl-stem	'sg step (into O)'	(O yé) ghiya
4	ACH	he/te–Ø–gha, –ya, –yá	incept-cl-stem	'sg leave (start to go)'	hiya, tiya (the-)
5	ACT	dzí#(dé?–)Ø–gha	adv#(?-)cl-stem	'sg walk around'	dzíghigha
6	ACT	hú-the–Ø–gha, –ya, –yá	?-CM-cl-stem	'sg travel/ through by'	húthiya (Ø or the-)

Of course, it is highly desirable to expand my database, in order to verify that the tendencies I found are indeed true patterns (or absence of patterns). Expanding my sample would also have the benefit of documenting more verbs of an endangered language for which only a small English-Dëne dictionary exists (Elford and Elford 1998).

A final reason why my findings differ is that I considered the larger context of a phenomenon. I looked not only at the semantics of situation type in Dëne, but also at the semantics of viewpoint aspect. It turned out that the two are intricately linked, and that the viewpoint aspects deeply affect what is going on at the situation type level. This larger context supports my findings on situation type by providing further motivation for them.

Summing up, some of the variation, especially among less closely related languages, is real. Due to loss of phonological and morphological distinctions, the aspectual system of Dëne is quite different from the traditional system which can still be glimpsed in more conservative languages. However, the heterogeneous findings in more closely related languages also have to do with the research focus and methods chosen. Since my primary interest was in the semantic reality of certain morphological classes, the best methodology was semantic (i.e., explicit semantic testing of a diverse set of verb themes). I also considered the larger semantic context in trying to understand the (non-) grammatization of situation type in Dëne.

5.3. Conclusion

In the chapters on Dëne (Chapters Two and Three), I have argued that in this language durativity is grammatized but telicity is not. I have motivated this claim from the function of the Dëne viewpoint aspects, showing that the Imperfective grammatizes durativity, and that the completive, quasi-telic Perfective obscures telicity. In doing this, I have motivated aspectual coding from discourse pragmatic function: one event bounding and sequencing strategy is all a language needs, and in Dëne this is perfective viewpoint. This raises an interesting question: is there a language in which telicity alone fulfills the discourse-pragmatic function? In the next two chapters, I will argue that German is such a language and that, interestingly, durativity is not grammatized in German.

Part II
German

In this part of the dissertation, I examine the aspect system of German. This examination will show two things. First, in German only telicity, but not durativity is grammatized. Second, just as in Dëne Sųłiné, there is a connection between the (non-)grammatization of these notions and viewpoint aspect: crucially, German has no grammatical viewpoint aspect system to speak of. I will argue that the absence of grammatized durativity is a consequence of the absence of viewpoint aspect in German. On the other hand, the grammar of German is highly sensitive to telicity, and contains several systematic mechanisms for changing the telicity of a predicate. I will argue that due to the absence of viewpoint aspect, situation type subsumes important viewpoint functions in this language. Thus, telicity plays such an important role in German because one of its functions is to suggest a perfective viewpoint.

In Chapter Four, I demonstrate that telicity is grammatized through morphosyntactic processes affecting the verb and its internal arguments. Besides bringing together a number of well-known phenomena, I draw attention to particle verb formation, a process whose relevance to telicity has not received much attention previously. I show that there is a group of particles in German which systematically create telic verbs from atelic base verbs, and that they do so by contributing a result state to the predicate. Also in Chapter Four, I motivate the important role telicity plays in the grammar of German from the absence of grammatical viewpoint aspect in the language. This draws on insights on the relationship between telicity and perfectivity developed in Chapter Two.

In Chapter Five, I discuss the tense/aspect system of German and show that there is no grammatical category of viewpoint aspect. Not only does German not have viewpoint aspects per se, such as the English Progressive or the Dëne Imperfective, it also does not make use of tenses to mark viewpoint contrasts indirectly. In principle, all tenses can convey either imperfective or perfective viewpoint in German. This is even true for the Perfect and the Preterite, which are sometimes argued to convey perfective and imperfective meaning, respectively. Moreover, the Perfect is the only past tense marker available in South German dialects, completely supplanting the Preterite. Thus, the choice between Perfect and Preterite cannot be exploited for viewpoint contrasts in South German, and the absence of grammatical viewpoint aspect is even clearer in this variety. Finally, I show that durativity is not grammatized in German. The central evidence comes from particle verb formation. Interestingly, the same process which systematically creates telic verbs affects durativity in a completely arbitrary way. The particle verb may be durative where the base verb is not, or vice versa, or durativity may be unaffected by the addition of a particle. This is independent of which particle or which base verb is used. These facts suggest that durativity is not grammatized in German. Again, my claim is that the absence of viewpoint aspect and the nongrammatization of durativity are no coincidence, because the prime locus of grammatizing durativity is precisely viewpoint aspect.

Chapter Four
Telicity in German

This chapter explores the grammatization of telic situation type in German. Recall that a semantic notion is grammatized if it is evident in a productive morphosyntactic contrast of a language. We will see that, unlike in Dëne, telicity is clearly and pervasively grammatized in German. In section 1, I point out how easy it is to test for telicity in German. While this is a semantic rather than a grammatical fact, it is suggestive nonetheless, in particular in comparison with Dëne, where it is quite difficult to test for telicity. The next two sections are devoted to an examination of telicity-sensitive morphosyntax. In section 2, I review several phenomena that are well-known from the literature on German: the distribution and interpretation of the perfect participle form of the verb, as well as the role of direct internal arguments, of overtly marked nominal quantization, and of accusative vs. dative PPs in telicity. Considered together, these phenomena provide strong evidence that telicity is grammatized in German. In section 3, I turn to another morphosyntactic phenomenon, whose relevance to telicity has not been well studied: particle verb formation. I develop a careful analysis of the aspectual and morphosyntactic properties of three particles, showing that these particles are overt markers of telicity. We will see that particles mark telicity by signaling a result state (a state which results from a change of state). The presence of a change of state, and hence a result state, is widely believed to be the defining characteristic of telic meaning (Dowty 1979, Pustejovsky 1991, Klein 1994, Rappaport Hovav and Levin 1998, Rapp 1997a, Ramchand 2002, etc.). It seems, then, that German shows a fairly direct grammatization of telicity in the form of "resultative" particles.

What will also become apparent is that the grammatical phenomena sensitive to telicity are all located in what I call the VP-domain. By VP-domain I mean the the syntactic projection that contains the verb and its internal arguments, but excludes the subject or external argument (see Chapter Six).

In German, as I will show, direct internal arguments, goal PPs, and resultative particles, which are all constituents of the VP, affect telicity. This will support my claim that telicity is grammatized in the VP-domain.

The German facts represent an important contrast to Dëne Sųłiné, where we found (i) grammatization of durativity rather than telicity, and (ii), that durativity is grammatized by morphosyntactic elements above the VP (in the IP-domain). A comparison of the two languages thus suggests that telicity and durativity are profoundly different in terms of grammatization.

I conclude this chapter by asking why telicity is so important in German (section 4). The answer will come from a comparison with Dëne Sųłiné, where telicity is quite unimportant. The one crucial difference in the tense-aspect system of the two languages is that Dëne has two pervasive viewpoint categories, while German lacks grammatical viewpoint aspect. Because there is no grammatical viewpoint aspect, and specifically not a perfective with a strongly completive meaning, telicity is not obscured in German. Moreover, in the absence of viewpoint aspect, German relies on telicity for those functions expressed by viewpoint in Dëne. The status of viewpoint aspect versus telicity in German, and the consequences for durativity, will be the topic of Chapter Five.

1. TELICITY IS EASILY DISTINGUISHED

Let me begin by pointing out a fact that is often taken for granted. In German, it is very easy to determine whether a predicate is telic or not. There is a range of semantic telicity tests, most very similar to the English tests (see, e.g., Ehrich 1992). In (1) and (2), I illustrate how two very similar telicity tests distinguish telic from atelic predicates.[1]

(1) **telic predicates**, as per compatibility with 'in X time' and 'take X time to'

    a. *den Brief schreiben*

        Susi hat den Brief <u>in einer Stunde</u> geschrieben.
        Susi has the letter in one hour written
        'Susi wrote the letter in one hour.'

        Susi hat <u>eine Stunde gebraucht</u>, um den Brief zu schreiben.
        Susi has one hour needed C the letter to write
        'It took Susi one hour to write the letter.'

b. *ein/das Gemälde stehlen*

Die Diebe haben das Gemälde in 10 Minuten gestohlen.
'The thieves stole the painting in 10 minutes.'

Die Diebe haben 10 Minuten gebraucht, um das Gemälde zu stehlen.
the theives have 10 minutes needed   C the painting to steal
'It took the thieves ten minutes to steal the painting.'

c. *eine/die Katze verjagen*

Die Kinder haben die Katze in fünf Minuten verjagt.
'The children chased off the cat in five minutes.'

Die Kinder haben fünf Minuten gebraucht, um die Katze zu verjagen.
the children have five minutes needed   C the cat to chase-off
'It took the children five minutes to chase off the cat.'

d. *einen/den Ast absägen*

Susi hat den Ast in einer Stunde abgesägt.
'Susi sawed off the branch in one hour.'

Susi hat eine Stunde gebraucht, um den Ast abzusägen.
Susi has one hour   needed   C the branch to-saw-off
'It took Susi one hour to saw off the branch.'

e. *ins Haus rennen*

Das Mädchen ist in wenigen Sekunden ins Haus gerannt.
'The girl ran into the house in a few seconds.'

Das Mädchen hat nur Sekunden gebraucht, um ins Haus zu rennen.
the girl has only seconds needed   C in-the house to run
'It took the girl only seconds to run into the house.'

f. *einschlafen*[2]

Die Kinder sind in einer Stunde eingeschlafen.
'The children fell asleep in one hour.'

Die Kinder haben eine Stunde gebraucht, um einzuschlafen.
the children have one hour needed   C to-fall-asleep
'It took the children one hour to fall asleep.'

(2) **atelic predicates**, as per incompatibility with 'in X time' and 'take X time to V'[3]

    a. *lachen*

        #Susi hat <u>in einer Stunde</u> gelacht.
        ('Susi laughed in an hour.')

        #Susi hat <u>eine Stunde gebraucht</u>, um zu lachen.
         Susi has one hour   needed   C to laugh
        ('It took Susi one hour to laugh.')

    b. *begehren*

        #Die Besucher haben das Gemälde <u>in einer Stunde</u> begehrt.
        ('The visitors coveted the painting in one hour.')

        #Die Besucher haben <u>eine Stunde gebraucht</u>, um das Gemälde zu
         the visitors have one hour   needed   C the painting to
                begehren.
                covet
        ('It took the visitors one hour to covet the painting.')

    c. *jagen*

        #Die Kinder haben die Katze <u>in fünf Minuten</u> gejagt.
        ('The children chased the cat in five minutes.')

        #Die Kinder   haben <u>fünf Minuten gebraucht</u>, um die Katze zu jagen.
         the children have five minutes needed   C the cat   to chase
        ('It took the children five minutes to chase the cat.')

    d. *sägen*

        #Susi hat <u>in einer Stunde</u> (Holz) gesägt.
        ('Susi sawed (wood) in an hour.')

        #Susi hat <u>eine Stunde gebraucht</u>, um (Holz) zu sägen.
         Susi has one hour   needed   C wood to saw
        ('It took Susi one hour to saw (wood).')

e. *(im Haus hin und her) rennen*

#Das Mädchen ist <u>in wenigen Sekunden</u> (im Haus hin und her) gerannt.

('The girl ran (around in the house) in a few seconds.')

#Das Mädchen hat <u>nur Sekunden gebraucht</u>, um (im Haus hin
the girl has only seconds needed C in-the house there

und her) zu rennen.
and here to run

('It took the girl only seconds to run (around in the house).')

f. *schlafen*

#Die Kinder haben <u>in einer Stunde</u> geschlafen. (ok on 'started to sleep' reading)

('The children slept in an hour.')

#Die Kinder haben <u>eine Stunde gebraucht</u> um zu schlafen.
the children have one hour needed C to sleep

('It took the children one hour to sleep.')

If we recall from Chapter Two how difficult it is to test for telicity in Dëne, we will not take the fact that telicity is so easily determined in German for granted. We will rather take it as a first indication that telicity might be grammatized in German: perhaps telicity tests are easily available, and predicates pattern clearly as telic or atelic because in German, telicity is not only a semantic notion, but is also part of the morphosyntax.

I will now turn to those morphosyntactic phenomena of German which do access telicity. In section 2, I point out the significance of several well-known phenomena; section 3 is devoted to an analysis of telic particle verbs.

2. TELICITY IN THE MORPHOSYNTAX I: WELL-KNOWN FACTS

In German, many grammatical contrasts and categories either access telicity or affect it directly. While most of these facts are well-known, they are sometimes mistakenly linked to perfectivity rather than to telicity (see discussion in the next chapter). I follow here Andersson (1972), Ehrich (1992), Abraham (1995), and Rapp (1997a, b), all of whom clearly state the German facts in terms of telicity rather than perfectivity.[4]

We begin with the perfect participle, continue with direct objects, overtly marked nominal quantization, and conclude with accusative case marking.

2.1. The Perfect Participle

Just as in English, verbs in German may occur in the form of a past or perfect participle, often called "participle II" ("Partizip II") in the German literature: the participle is formed with a suffix *-t* or *-en* and may be accompanied by stem changes, such as ablaut, in strong verbs. In addition, an (unstressed) prefix *ge-* immediately precedes the stem, unless another unstressed prefix (e.g., *ver-* or *be-*) is present or the initial syllable of the verb stem is unstressed (as in *telefoNIEren* 'phone'). Note that here I am using the predicates for which (a)telicity was established independently in the previous section.

(3)	infinitive[5]	perfect participle	gloss of infinitive and participle
	schreiben	*geschrieben*	'write,' 'written'
	stehlen	*gestohlen*	'steal,' 'stolen'
	verjagen	*verjagt*	'chase off,' 'chased off'
	absägen	*abgesägt*	'saw off,' 'sawed off'
	rennen	*gerannt*	'run,' 'run'
	einschlafen	*eingeschlafen*	'fall asleep,' 'fallen asleep'
	lachen	*gelacht*	'laugh,' 'laughed'
	begehren	*begehrt*	'covet,' 'coveted'
	jagen	*gejagt*	'hunt/chase,' 'hunted/chased'
	sägen	*gesägt*	'saw,' 'sawed'
	schlafen	*geschlafen*	'sleep,' 'slept'

The first thing to consider is the distribution of the perfect participle. The attributive use of the participle is often cited as a test for telicity (e.g., Andersson (1972), Ehrich (1992), Abraham (1995)). The idea here is that the participle predicates a state of one of its arguments, and that only verbs part of whose meaning is a state allow this. Obviously, telic but not atelic predicates contain a (result) state as part of their meaning. Indeed, precisely the argument of telic predicates which underwent the change of state can occur with the attributive participle (the object in transitive clauses, the subject in intransitive clauses):

(4) *finite clause (telic)*   *attributive perfect participle*

Susi hat den Brief geschrieben 'Susi has written the letter'	der geschriebene Brief 'the written letter'
die Diebe haben das Gemälde gestohlen 'the thieves have stolen the painting'	das gestohlene Gemälde 'the stolen painting'
die Kinder haben die Katze verjagt 'the children have chased off the cat'	die verjagte Katze 'the chased-off cat'
Susi hat den Ast abgesägt 'Susi has sawed off the branch'	der abgesägte Ast 'the sawed off branch'
das Mädchen ist ins Haus gerannt 'the girl has (lit. 'is') run into the house'	das ins Haus gerannte Mädchen 'the into the house run girl'
die Kinder sind eingeschlafen 'the children have (lit. 'are') fallen asleep'	die eingeschlafenen Kinder 'the fallen-asleep children'

However, the participle can also be used attributively with arguments which occur as objects of stative verbs (these, of course, also denote a state), (5), and, as Rapp (1997a) shows, as objects of (nonstative) atelic verbs, (6):

(5) *finite clause (stative)*   *attributive perfect participle*

die Besucher haben das Gemälde begehrt 'the visitors have coveted the painting'	das begehrte Gemälde 'the coveted painting'
alle lieben diesen Lehrer 'all love this teacher'	der (von allen) geliebte Lehrer 'the (by all) loved teacher'
alle kennen diese Frau 'all know this woman'	die von allen gekannte Frau (Rapp 1997a:223) 'the by all known woman'

(6) *finite clause (atelic)*   *attributive perfect participle*

die Kinder haben die Katze gejagt 'the children have chased the cat'	die (von den Kindern) gejagte Katze 'the (by the children) chased cat'
der junge Mann schiebt einen Wagen 'the young man is pushing a cart'	der von einem jungen Mann geschobene Wagen (Rapp 1997a:222) 'the by a young man pushed cart'

finite clause (atelic)	*attributive perfect participle*
die Zuschauer hörten das Lied 'the audience heard the song'	das von den Zuschauern gehörte Lied 'the by the audience heard song' (Rapp 1997a:222)

The only arguments, then, which cannot take an attributive participle are those which occur as subjects of intransitive atelic clauses or as subjects of transitive clauses, even if the latter are telic:

(7) *finite clause* *perfect participle*
    (intrans., atelic) *attributed of subject*

das Mädchen hat gelacht 'the girl has laughed'	*das gelachte Mädchen ('the laughed girl')
das Mädchen ist im Haus hin und her gerannt 'the girl ran (around in the house)'	*das (im Haus hin und her) gerannte Mädchen ('the (around in the house) run girl')
das Mädchen hat gesägt 'the girl has sawed'	*das gesägte Mädchen ('the sawed girl')
die Kinder haben geschlafen 'the children have slept'	*die geschlafenen Kinder ('the slept children')

finite clause *perfect participle*
(trans., telic) *attributed of subject*

Susi hat den Brief geschrieben 'Susi has written the letter'	*die geschriebene Susi/Frau ('the written Susi/woman')
die Diebe haben das Gemälde gestohlen 'the thieves have stolen the painting'	*die gestohlenen Diebe ('the stolen thieves')

Since the participle occurs with object arguments of all transitive clauses, irrespective of telicity (or stativity), the generalization actually is that the attributive perfect participle indicates the presence of a direct internal argument rather than telicity. However, there is still a connection to telicity when only intransitive predicates are concerned, because only arguments of telic but not those of atelic intransitive clauses can take the attributive participle. We can say that the distribution of the attributive perfect participle reflects telicity of intransitives. If we assume that telic intransitives are unaccusative,

Telicity in German 143

i.e., that their subject is a direct object/direct internal argument underlyingly, we can maintain the generalization that the attributive perfective participle indicates direct internal argumenthood.[6]

Now, where telicity does play a crucial role is in the *interpretation* of the attributive perfect participle of transitive verbs: participles derived from atelic predicates have a salient simultaneous interpretation in relation to the finite verb they are derived from, participles derived from telic predicates have only an anterior interpretation (cf. Rapp 1997a:239ff, Musan 2002:27f). This difference in interpretation can be seen when the participle is paraphrased. The simultaneous interpretation may be paraphrased by a present-tense passive with *werden* (the so-called "Vorgangspassiv" or "eventive passive"), the anterior interpretation by a past-tense passive with *ist worden/wurde* or by a resultative passive with *ist* ("Zustandspassiv," roughly corresponding to the English adjectival passive), but never by a present-tense passive with *werden*. This contrast in paraphraseability with a present-tense *werden* passive is shown in (8) versus (9). Note that since passive forms are involved, participles of intransitive verbs cannot undergo such paraphrases.

(8) *perfect participle*   *paraphrase*

der geschriebene Brief — √ der Brief *ist* geschrieben
'the written letter'   'the letter is written'

  # der Brief *wird* geschrieben 'the letter is being written'

das gestohlene Gemälde — √ das Gemälde *ist* gestohlen
'the stolen painting'   (worden)
   'the painting is (has been) stolen'

  # das Gemälde *wird* gestohlen
   'the painting is being stolen'

die verjagte Katze — √ die Katze *ist* verjagt (worden)
'the chased off cat'   'the cat is (has been) chased off'

  # die Katze *wird* verjagt
   'the cat is being chased off'

der abgesägte Ast — √ der Ast *ist* abgesägt worden
'the sawn off branch'   'the branch has been sawn off'

  # der Ast *wird* abgesägt 'the branch is being sawn off'

(9) *perfect participle*   *paraphrase*

    das begehrte Gemälde — √ das Gemälde *wird* begehrt
    'the coveted painting'   'the painting is being coveted'

    die von den Kindern gejagte — √ die Katze *wird* gejagt
    Katze
    'the by the children chased cat'   'the cat is being chased'

In sum, the interpretation, and to an extent also the distribution, of attributive perfect participles is sensitive to telicity in German.[7]

2.2. Direct Objects

In German, telic verbs require a direct internal argument. For example, agentive verbs are either atelic or ungrammatical if there is no object at all. Verbs of creation receive an atelic interpretation, (10)-(11), (causative) verbs of change of state and of directed motion are ungrammatical, (12)-(13), without object:[8]

(10) a. Sie hat (in einer Stunde) ein Kleid genäht.   *telic*
        'She sewed a dress (in an hour).'

     b. Sie hat (#in einer Stunde) genäht.   *atelic*
        'She sewed (#in an hour).'

(11) a. Sie hat (in fünf Minuten) ein Bild gemalt.   *telic*
        'She painted a picture (in five minutes).'

     b. Sie hat (#in fünf Minuten) gemalt.   *atelic*
        'She painted (#in five minutes).'

(12) a. Sie hat (in einer Stunde) den Ast abgesägt.   *telic*
        'She sawed off the branch (in an hour).'

     b. *Sie hat abgesägt.   *
        ('She sawed off.')

(13) a. Sie hat den Wagen (in 10 Sekunden) in die Ecke geschoben.   *telic*
        'She pushed the cart into the corner (in 10 seconds).'

     b. *Sie hat (in die Ecke) geschoben.   *
        ('She pushed (into the corner).')

Intransitive telic verbs, at first blush, seem counterexamples to this claim, since they have a subject only, for example, *die Kinder sind eingeschlafen* 'the children fell asleep.' However, there is evidence that the subject of telic intransitive verbs is an object underlyingly, i.e., that telic intransitive verbs are unaccusative. Recall the distribution of attributive perfective participles discussed in the preceding section. We saw that these participles likely indicate the presence of a direct internal argument. Now, arguments of telic but not of atelic intransitive verbs can take an attributive participle (recall, e.g., *die eingeschlafenen Kinder* 'the fallen-asleep children' vs. **die geschlafenen Kinder* 'the slept children'). This suggests that arguments of telic (but not of atelic) intransitives are direct internal arguments as well.

To sum up, in German only a direct object/internal argument can serve to "measure out" the event, in the sense of Tenny (1987, 1994). German thus supports Tenny's claim that it is a universal property of telic verbs that they require a direct internal argument.[9] The fact that a (quantized, see next section) direct object is necessary for a telic interpretation has led some linguists to propose a syntactic position reserved for objects of telic predicates (e.g., Borer 1994, 1998, Ritter and Rosen 1998, Kratzer 2004).

2.3. Overtly Marked Object Quantization

Strictly speaking, the presence of a direct object is not sufficient to achieve a telic interpretation. As discussed in the influential work of Krifka (1989, 1992) and Verkuyl (1972, 1993), the quantization of a direct object influences the telicity of the VP. It is a distinguishing characteristic of telic verbs that they receive a telic interpretation only with a quantized direct object (cf. (14) below); if the object has nonquantized reference, an atelic reading results (cf. (15) below). Inherently atelic predicates are not sensitive to object quantization—they are always atelic (cf. (16)).

Importantly, quantization of objects—and of all nouns—is indicated by DP morphosyntax in German: bare plurals (i.e., indefinite plurals) and mass nouns, which cannot be pluralized, have nonquantized reference. Nouns preceded by a singular definite or indefinite article or by a plural definite article, as well as mass nouns preceded by a measure phrase, have quantized reference (see Krifka 1989).[10] This contrast is also illustrated in (14) and (15).

(14) *telic verb and quantized object: telic interpretation*

    a. Sie hat (in einer Stunde) [einen$_{sg,\ indef}$ Brief] geschrieben.
       'She wrote (in one hour) a letter.'

b. Sie hat [den$_{sg, def}$ Apfel] (in einer Minute) gegessen.
'She ate the apple (in one minute).'

c. Sie hat [die$_{pl, def}$ Äpfel] (in 10 Minuten) gegessen.
'She ate the apples (in 10 minutes).'

d. Sie hat [[drei Schalen]$_{measure}$ Pudding] (in einer Minute) gegessen.
'She ate three bowls of pudding (in one minute).'

cf. ??Sie hat [drei Pudding/Puddinge] gegessen.[11]
('She ate three pudding/puddings.')

(15) *telic verb and nonquantized object: atelic interpretation*

a. Sie hat (#in einer Stunde) [Briefe]$_{pl, indef}$ geschrieben.
'She wrote (#in one hour) letters.'

b. Sie hat (#in einer Stunde) [Äpfel]$_{pl, indef}$ gegessen.
'She ate (#in one hour) apples.'

c. Sie hat (#in einer Minute) [Pudding]$_{mass}$ gegessen.
'She ate (#in one minute) pudding.'

(16) *atelic verb: atelic interpretation irrespective of object quantization*

a. Sie hat (#in einer Stunde) [Katzen$_{pl, indef}$/die Katze$_{sg, def}$] gestreichelt.
'She petted cats/the cat (#in one hour).'

b. Sie hat (#in einer halben Stunde) [Kunst$_{mass}$/das Gemälde$_{sg, def}$] angeschaut.
'She looked at art/at the painting (#in half an hour).'

Especially in comparison with Dëne, it is significant that German DP morphosyntax signals noun quantization, and that noun quantization interacts with telicity. Recall that in Dëne, telicity is not grammatized, and nominal quantization is not overtly marked.

2.4. Accusative Objects vs. Partitive Adjuncts

Telicity, and, more precisely, the fact that a telic predicate requires a direct object is also reflected in a DP-PP alternation. Direct objects are marked with accusative case in German. If the same (quantized) nominal is presented as an adjunct headed by the preposition *an* 'at,' an atelic interpretation results (cf. Filip 1989). This is shown in (17) and (18):

(17) a. Susi hat *den Brief* (in einer Stunde) geschrieben. (cf. Filip 1989)
'Susi wrote *the.ACC letter* (in one hour).'

b. Susi hat (#in einer Stunde) *an dem Brief* geschrieben.
'Susi wrote (#in one hour) *at the.DAT letter*.'

(18) a. Susi hat (in fünf Minuten) *einen Apfel* gegessen.
'Susi ate (in five minutes) *a.ACC apple*.'

b. Susi hat (#in fünf Minuten) *an einem Apfel* gegessen.
'Susi ate (#in five minutes) *at a.DAT apple*.'

The alternation in (17) and (18) shows that in German, the distinction between an incremental theme (> telicity) and a partitive theme (> atelicity) is overtly marked in the morphosyntax. Only a direct object, in accusative case, can serve to register the change of state which is typical of telic predicates (cf. Krifka 1989, 1992).[12] If the same nominal occurs inside the PP with *an*, it has a partitive interpretation, which leads to an atelic rather than a telic situation.[13]

2.5. Accusative Case vs. Dative Case in PPs

There is another well-known alternation which affects telicity (e.g., Abraham 1995). Certain prepositions, such as *in* 'in' and *unter* 'under,' can assign either dative or accusative case to their complement. This alternation is particularly important for the interpretation of verbs of motion. If the preposition assigns accusative case, the PP is a goal argument, and the sentence is telic, as shown in (19a) and (20a) below. A PP with a dative complement is a locative adjunct, and the sentence is atelic ((19b) and (20b)).

(19) a. Sie sind (in fünf Minuten) *in den Saal* getanzt. (cf. Abraham 1995)
'They danced (in five minutes) *into the.ACC room*.'

b. Sie haben (#in fünf Minuten) *in dem Saal* getanzt.
'They were dancing (#in five minutes) *in the.DAT room*.'

(20) a. Sie hat die Kiste (in fünf Minuten) *unter den Tisch* geschoben.
'She pushed the box (in five minutes) *under the.ACC table*.'

b. Sie hat die Kiste (#in fünf Minuten) *unter dem Tisch* herum geschoben.
'She pushed the box around (#in five minutes) *under the.DAT table*.'

In (19) and (20), the alternation between accusative and dative case corresponds to a difference between a goal argument and a locative PP. With verbs of motion, telicity derives from a change of location, which is achieved by traversal of a bounded path. Only a goal PP, but not a locative PP, is able to denote a bounded path.

It should be noted that this alternation is not only relevant to verbs of motion. Even nonmotion verbs may receive an indirect motion interpretation with an unselected object and an accusative PP. The only difference is that with these verbs, the PP does not represent a goal argument of the verb, but rather acts as a (goal) resultative phrase (see Mezhevich 2003, and also Spencer and Zaretskaya 1998).

(21) a. Susi hat (in einer Stunde) Peter *unter den Tisch* getrunken.

'Susi drank Peter *under the.ACC table* (in an hour).'

b. Susi hat (#in einer Stunde) (*Peter) *unter dem Tisch* getrunken.

'Susi drank (*Peter) (#in an hour) *under the.DAT table*.'

We thus see that constituents of the VP (DPs and PPs) are essential to the telicity of a predicate, and that German expresses the semantic contributions of these constituents through argument vs. adjunct status, which is reflected in case marking as well.

2.6. Summary

It seems, then, that in German, telicity is grammatized in several ways, including the (interpretation of) the perfect participle and the interaction of objects and case with telicity. It is interesting to note that all these phenomena are local to the VP. Direct objects, which go on to receive/check accusative case, and accusative-marked goal PPs are internal arguments, and telic participles denote the result state of their internal argument. Thus, we can observe that the grammatization of telicity in German has to do with the verb, its direct internal argument and other constituents of the VP. In other words, telicity seems to be a VP-domain phenomenon.[14]

Comparing these facts to Dëne, a strikingly different pattern emerges. In Dëne, telicity has no overt correlates in the morphosyntax, and noun quantization is not overtly marked. Moreover, with first and second person subjects the presence of an object need not be overtly marked either: the Dëne object prefix in this case is Ø.

In the next section, I will turn to particle verb formation, a process whose connection to telicity has not been the focus of much study. I will show that particle verb formation is a major mechanism for creating telic predicates in German.

3. TELICITY IN THE MORPHOSYNTAX II: PARTICLE VERBS AND TELICITY

3.1. Introduction

In this section, I will show that particle verb formation is a very productive process of forming telic verbs in German. Particle verbs consist of a simple verb like *fahren* 'drive' and a particle, e.g., *um*, as illustrated in (22). Particles are not always bound to the base verb; in many contexts, such as main clauses, they are separated from the base. For example, in main clauses, (23), the verb is in V2 position and the particle is clause-final. Therefore, they are also called "separable prefixes." I will use the term "particle" in order to avoid confusion with true, inseparable prefixes.[15]

(22) . . . weil sie das Hindernis úmfuhr.   *subordinate clause, verb-final*
 . . . because she the obstacle UM-drove
'. . . because she knocked the obstacle over driving.'

(23) a. Sie fuhr das Hindernis úm.   *main clause, verb-second*
 she drove the obstacle UM
'She knocked the obstacle over driving.'

b. *Sie úmfuhr das Hindernis.

Many but not all particles are homophonous with prepositions. For example, German has a preposition *um*, as in *um das Hindernis* 'around the obstacle.' We know that *um* in (22) is a particle and not a preposition because it precedes the verb and not the DP. Furthermore, the two kinds of *um* differ in meaning. As a preposition, *um* usually means 'around,' but as a particle it often means 'over' in the sense of 'turned over, turned upside down' (i.e., it expresses a change in orientation of the reference object).

As mentioned in Chapter One, particle verbs act sometimes like one word, and sometimes the particle and the (base) verb act like two separate syntactic constituents. "Word"-like characteristics include the (perhaps exaggerated) noncompositionality of particle verb meanings and the fact that they can undergo word formation processes such as nominalization. The status of particles as a syntactic constituent is most apparent in their infamous separability (cf. (23a) above), and in the fact that particles can undergo modification and topicalization, which is a test for syntactic constituency in German (Zeller 2001). Not surprisingly, until recently, accounts of particle verbs either took a basically lexical-morphological or a basically syntactic approach (see, for example, Neeleman and Weerman 1993, Stiebels and Wunderlich 1994, Stiebels 1996 for a lexical-morphological view, and Hoekstra 1988, Wurmbrand 1998 for a syntactic view), but each approach had to devise some diacritics or make some stipulations to account for all the properties of particles. However, all analyses agree that the particle, or particle phrase, is the (morphological or syntactic) *sister of the verb*.

As discussed in the introduction, I will follow the recent proposal of Zeller (2001), who argues that particle verbs require a theory such as Distributed Morphology (DM), which does not strictly separate morphology and syntax (cf. Halle and Marantz 1993, Marantz 1997, Harley and Noyer 1999). With Zeller I assume that particles project a "Particle Phrase" (PartP) which is the sister of V, and that the particle and the verb form a special domain of "structural adjacency" (bolded in (24)), which makes it possible for particle-verb combinations to have special meanings.

(24) Particle verb structure, based on Zeller (2001)

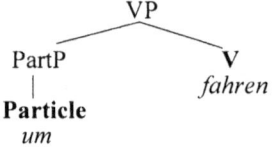

While particles are phrasal (maximal projections), they do not contain functional material above the lexical PartP. This corresponds to the fact that particles cannot be modified, are not referential, and that their category can only be determined by analogy with the category of unbound elements.

Turning now to the effect of particle verb formation on situation type, it is a rather striking fact of German that the number of simplex telic verbs is small, and that most telic verbs are particle or prefix verbs (e.g., Steinitz 1981 and traditional references below). For example, the base verb *schieben* in (25) is atelic, while *umschieben* is telic, as can easily be demonstrated with the 'in an hour' test:

(25) a. Sie hat (#in einer Minute) den Karren *geschoben*.
 she has in a minute the cart pushed
 'She pushed the cart (#in a minute).'

b. Sie hat den Karren (√in einer Minute) *umgeschoben.*
she has the cart   in a   minute over.pushed
'She pushed over the cart (√in a minute).'

This atelicity of simple verbs and the delimiting function of verbal particles and prefixes has been noted in traditional sources[16] (cf. Behagel 1907:56ff on prefix verbs, Paul 1959:65ff on prefix and particle verbs, Flämig 1965, Dal 1966, Duden 1984); it is also discussed in some of the more recent treatments of particle verbs (Krifka 1989, Leiss 1992, Stiebels and Wunderlich 1994, Stiebels 1996, Lüdeling 1998). However, these works mention the delimiting function only in passing, as the aspectual effects of particles are not their primary concern.[17] To the best of my knowledge, no detailed examination of the aspectual effects of particles exists.

In this section, I will present just such a careful examination. It will become apparent that certain particles, such as *ab, aus, um,* always delimit a situation, i.e., derive a telic situation type.[18] This is even the case when the derived verb has an idiomatic or opaque meaning—the aspectual effects survive even in idiomatic/lexicalized cases. Other particles, most notably *mit* and *nach,* do not affect situation type; they are aspectually neutral. I do not discuss aspectually neutral particles in this dissertation.

The delimiting particles to be discussed here are *ab* 'off,' *aus* 'out,' and *um* 'over.' Each particle's meaning is in fact much more varied than these translations suggest, and at first glance their semantic contribution to the complex verb is varied and not always transparent. Upon closer examination, there is evidence that particles are polysemous, and that it depends on the semantic class of the base verb which of the particle's meanings is activated in the interpretation of the complex verb (see Stiebels and Wunderlich 1994, Stiebels 1996, Zeller 2001). If one assumes polysemy and class-based interpretation, the meaning of many "idiomatic" particle verbs can actually be predicted.

What is striking, however, is that certain particles—such as *ab, aus* and *um*—always contribute telicity to the complex verb. In other words, what all the meanings of these particles have in common is something that derives telicity. I will show this, and identify the "telicizing" meaning component of the particles, by examining the effect of these particles on simplex verbs of each situation type, beginning with activity base verbs.

I examined 85 verbs, 29 simplex verbs and the related particle verbs with *ab, aus* and *um* (see Appendix Two). The simplex verbs were chosen fairly randomly; however, I did make sure to include simplex verbs of each (nonstative) situation type, and I did not include verbs for which no related particle verbs exist. The long-standing intuition that certain particles contribute telicity was resoundingly confirmed. Of the 68 telic verbs in my database, 56 are particle verbs and only 12 are simplex, while none of the 17 atelic verbs are particle verbs. In the following sections, I will examine the aspectual effects of telicizing particles by comparing simplex verbs of each situation type and the particle verbs derived from them.

But before doing so, a note on methodology is in order: as discussed above, telicity (and situation type in general) is a characteristic of the entire VP. I will therefore base situation type on the behavior of the entire VP, not the verb alone. We saw above that it is characteristic of telic predicates that object quantization affects situation type (sections 2.2–2.4), and that the same verb may pattern as an accomplishment with a quantized object and as an activity otherwise. Here are some more examples illustrating this property:

(26) a. Sie hat *das Buch* (in zwei Tagen) gelesen. *telic*
 'She read *the book* (in two days).'

 b. Sie hat (stundenlang/#in zwei Tagen) gelesen. *atelic*
 'She read (for hours/#in two days).'

(27) a. Sie hat *die Grube* (in zwei Tagen) gebaggert. *telic*
 'She excavated *the pit* (in two days).'

 b. Sie hat (die ganze Woche/#in zwei Tagen) (in der *atelic*
 Keplerstraße) gebaggert.
 'She has excavated (in the Kepler Street) (all week/#in two days).'

In such cases, the question arises which VP—the one with or the one without object—to consider the more basic one. In other words, are verbs like *lesen* and *baggern* activities or accomplishments in their most basic meaning?

Rapp (1997b) solves this problem by proposing two lexical variants for optionally transitive verbs: an activity and an accomplishment variant. For example, the lexical semantic structure of the accomplishment variant of *lesen* in (26a) would be something like *CAUSE (DO (x), BECOME (BE (y)))*, and the activity variant in (26b) would have the structure *DO (x)*. The latter structure is derived from the former by a systematic rule of detransitivization (deletion of the *y* argument and all associated predicates). Thus, the transitive/accomplishment variant is more basic, but derived *DO (x)* is also a lexically listed meaning of *lesen*. Tenny (1994:43f), who discusses a very similar alternation in English, calls it "unspecified NP deletion," thus also assuming that the transitive/accomplishment variant is more basic. She notes that if the verb is used intransitively, some generic or unspecified object is understood. To use

Tenny's example, *Brian ate* usually means that Brian ate a meal and not, say, a peppercorn. This seems also true for *lesen*. Without context, (26b) means that she read a book or perhaps magazines (standard reading material), but not billboards, letters or recipes.

However, it is questionable whether this is also the appropriate characterization of the alternation between *baggern* and *die Grube baggern* in (27). Intuitively *baggern* seems inherently intransitive/an activity rather than transitive/an accomplishment. This is supported by the fact that no unspecified object is understood in (27b). (27b) simply means that she moved dirt around with heavy equipment, but it does not mean that she excavated a pit, ditch, trench or other kind of hole. Interestingly, the truly understood "object" of *baggern*, namely the substance being moved (e.g., dirt or sand) can never be a syntactic object of this verb. Moreover, as the paraphrase I just gave of (27b) suggests, *baggern* is quite manner-specific, probably because it is derived from the noun *Bagger* which denotes the excavating equipment. From these considerations I conclude that *baggern* is indeed basically intransitive/an activity (i.e., *DO (x)*), comparable to *singen* 'sing' and *tanzen* 'dance.' The object of *baggern* in (27a) then must be a "fake" object like the ones that *singen* and *tanzen* can take.

My classification of base verbs below as intransitive/activities or transitive/accomplishments will be based on considerations such as just discussed. The reader should be warned, however, that these considerations do not always yield conclusive results.

Let us now turn to the effects of particle verb formation on telicity.

3.2. Activity Base Verb —> Accomplishment Particle Verb

A telicizing particle plus an activity base verb often results in an accomplishment particle verb. In the traditional classification of situation types (e.g., Vendler 1957, Smith 1991), activity and accomplishment differ only in telicity. Telicity, in turn, is defined in terms of a transition from one state into a result state. We hypothesize therefore that these particles add a transition and/or result state to an atelic situation.

The following examples illustrate the activity-to-accomplishment pattern. (28) shows that *arbeiten* is atelic and durative, and (29)-(31) illustrate that different particle verbs derived from this verb are all telic and durative; (32)-(33) shows the same correlation for different base verbs and the particle verbs derived from them. (Telicity and durativity tests are italicized.)

(28) arbeiten 'work' (activity)
    a. Susi hat (#*in einer Stunde*) gearbeitet.   atelic
        'Susi worked (#*in an hour*).'

    b. Susi *hat aufgehört* zu arbeiten.   *durative*[19]
       Susi has stopped to work
       'Susi *stopped* working.'

(29) **ab**arbeiten 'work off' (accomplishment)

    a. Susi hat (*in einer Woche*) ihre Schulden abgearbeitet.   *telic*
       'Susi worked off her debts *in one week*.'

    b. Susi *hat aufgehört*, ihre Schulden abzuarbeiten.   *durative*
       Susi has stopped her debts   off-to-work
       'Susi *stopped* working off her debts.'

(30) **aus**arbeiten 'work out' (accomplishment)

    a. Susi hat den Plan (*in einer Woche*) ausgearbeitet.   *telic*
       'Susi worked out the plan *in one week*.'

    b. Susi *hat aufgehört*, den Plan auszuarbeiten.   *durative*
       'Susi *stopped* working out the plan.'

(31) **um**arbeiten 'work over/rework' (accomplishment)

    a. Susi hat das Kapitel (*in einer Woche*) umgearbeitet.   *telic*
       'Susi reworked the chapter *in one week*.'

    b. Susi *hat aufgehört*, das Kapitel umzuarbeiten.   *durative*
       'Susi *stopped* reworking the chapter.'

(32) **sä**gen 'saw' (activity) —> **ab**sägen 'saw off' (accompl.)

    a. Susi hat (#*in einer Stunde*) (Holz) gesägt.   *atelic*
       'Susi sawed (#*in an hour*) (wood).'

    b. Susi *hat aufgehört*, (Holz) zu sägen.   *durative*
       'Susi *stopped* sawing (wood).'

    c. Susi hat den Ast (*in einer Stunde*) abgesägt.   *telic*
       'Susi sawed the branch off (*in an hour*).'

    d. Susi *hat aufgehört*, den Ast abzusägen.   *durative*
       'Susi *stopped* sawing off the branch.'

(33) graben 'dig' (activity)—> **um**graben 'dig (turn over the earth)' (accompl.)

    a. Susi hat (#*in einer Stunde*) (in der Erde) gegraben.   *atelic*
       'Susi dug (#*in an hour*) (in the earth).'

    b. Susi *hat aufgehört*, (in der Erde) zu graben.   *durative*
       'Susi *stopped* digging (in the earth).'

    c. Susi hat das Blumenbeet (*in einer Stunde*) umgegraben.   *telic*
       'Susi dug/turned over the flowerbed (*in an hour*).'

    d. Susi *hat aufgehört*, das Blumenbeet umzugraben.   *durative*
       'Susi *stopped* digging/turning over the flowerbed.'

(34) brüten 'sit on eggs' (activity)—> **aus**brüten 'hatch out' (accompl.)

    a. Die Henne hat (#*in einer Stunde*) gebrütet.   *atelic*
       'The hen sat on the eggs (#*in an hour*).'

    b. Die Henne *hat aufgehört* zu brüten.   *durative*
       'The hen *stopped* sitting on the eggs.'

    c. Die Henne hat die Eier (*in einer Woche*) ausgebrütet.   *telic*
       'The hen hatched out the eggs (*in a week*).'

    d. Die Henne *hat aufgehört*, die Eier auszubrüten.   *durative*
       'The hen *stopped* hatching out the eggs.'

Other particle verbs which fit into this pattern are *ausbrennen* 'burn out,' *abbrennen* 'burn down,' *abbaggern* 'remove by digging (with machine),' *ausbaggern* 'dig out (with machine),' *ausfahren* 'drive/move out,' *ausgraben* 'dig out,' *abjagen* 'get something off someone' (< *jagen* 'hunt, chase'), *abkratzen* 'scratch off'[20], *auskratzen* 'scratch out,' *absägen* 'saw off,' *aussägen* 'saw out,' *absuchen* 'search/look over an area thoroughly' and many more. A large portion of the verbs in my database follow this pattern: of the 38 accomplishment particle verbs, 18 are formed from simplex activity verbs (16 are formed from simplex accomplishments, three from simplex semelfactives, one from a simplex achievement).

In most cases the particle indeed signals a state of the internal argument which results from the activity denoted by the base verb, although not always in a literal sense. In other words, the particle augments the base verb meaning by adding a result state. In lexical theories, such as Jackendoff (1990), Rappaport

Hovav and Levin (1998), Rapp (1997a,b), result states are treated as subevents. In this type of particle verb formation we therefore have a combination of two subevents, a process (base verb) and a result state (particle), shown in bold below. This is illustrated for *ausarbeiten*, in the standard notation of Rapp (1997a,b) in (34), and in the notation of Spencer and Zaretskaya (1998) in (35).

(35) a. *arbeiten*: DO (x); *aus*: **BE (y)**

b. *ausarbeiten*: CAUSE [DO (x), BECOME [**BE (y)**]]

(36) a. *arbeiten*: V (x); *aus*: **W (y)**

b. *ausarbeiten*: CAUSE [ACT (x)], BECOME [**W (y)**], $_{BY}$[V (x)]

Both notations have in common the addition of the result state subevent through the operator *BECOME*. While (35) is simpler, (36) reflects more directly the intuition that the particle "expresses the core semantic predication" and that the base verb is a secondary subordinated predicate which expresses the manner in which the result state comes about (Spencer and Zaretskaya 1998:1).

Either way, the augmentation leads to a difference in argument structure between the base verb and the particle verb: the particle introduces its own argument into the lexical representation. This either leads to the transitivization of intransitive base verbs (*arbeiten*$_{itr.}$ > *ausarbeiten*$_{tr.}$), or to the presence of a direct object which is not selected by the base verb (*Holz/*Ast sägen* > *Ast absägen*). Stiebels (1996) calls the augmentation of a predicate by a new subevent "lexical adjunction."

The resultative function of *ab, aus,* and *um* is not surprising given their adverbial or prepositional origin (cf. Stiebels 1996), which lends itself to indicating a concrete or abstract goal. Of course, their meanings were quite broad to begin with, and have become even broader (i.e., the particles have become more polysemous), e.g., through metaphorical extension. See Stiebels (1996) for a detailed discussion of the range of meanings of *ab*, Benware (1993) for a discussion of the range of meanings of the word *um*, and Hundsnurscher (1968) on particle verbs formed with *aus*.

3.3. Semelfactive Base Verb —> Achievement or Accomplishment Particle Verb

Semelfactive predicates are neither durative nor telic. In German, no formal differences distinguish semelfactives from activities, and in fact semelfactive verbs can get an "iterative" activity interpretation in the right circumstances.

They then denote a succession of punctual events, see (37) below. Particle verbs built on these types of base verbs are either achievements or accomplishments, depending on whether they are built on the base verb's semelfactive or iterative/activity interpretation. So again, the particle creates a telic from an atelic predicate. And again, it does so by contributing a result state (which has its own argument) to the base verb's meaning.

In the following examples, I will use a durative context such as 'for X time' to determine semelfactivity. Only semelfactives (i.e., nondurative atelics) but not underived activities (i.e., durative atelics) have an iterative interpretation in this context (e.g., Smith 1991). At the same time, this test shows that the difference between a semelfactive and an iterative interpretation is not marked overtly, i.e., it is a purely semantic distinction in German. This contrasts with Dëne, where semelfactive and the corresponding "seriative/successive" verb themes differ morphologically. (Tests are italicized.)

(37) <u>husten</u> 'cough' (semelfactive)

    a. Sie hat (#*in fünf Minuten*) gehustet.   *atelic*
    'She coughed (#*in five minutes*).'

    b. Sie hat *fünf Minuten lang* gehustet. => iterative   *nondurative*
    'She coughed *for five minutes* (repeatedly).'

(38) **aus**<u>husten</u> 'cough out/up' (achievement or accomplishment)[21]

    a. Sie hat (*in fünf Minuten*) den Staub/den Krümel ausgehustet.   *telic*
    'She coughed out/up the dust/the crumbs (*in five minutes*).'

    b. ??Sie *hörte auf*, den Krümel auszuhusten.   *nondurative*
    ??'She *stopped* coughing out/up the crumb.'

    c. Sie *hörte auf*, den Staub auszuhusten.   *durative*
    'She *stopped* coughing out/up the dust.'

(39) **ab**<u>husten</u> 'remove by coughing' (accomplishment)

    a. Sie hat den Schleim (*in fünf Minuten*) abgehustet.   *telic*
    'She removed the phlegm by coughing (*in five minutes*).'

    b. Sie *hörte auf*, den Schleim abzuhusten.   *durative*
    'She *stopped* removing the phlegm by coughing.'

When object properties or world knowledge make it likely that more than one cough is needed to achieve the desired result, these particle verbs are durative. This is the case for *abhusten* 'remove by coughing,' probably because the only plausible object is the mass noun 'phlegm,' and also for *aushusten* 'cough out/up' with the (mass) object *den Staub* 'the dust.'[22] If it is plausible that the result is achieved with just one cough, as in *den Krümel aushusten* 'cough out the crumb,' then the VP patterns as nondurative (achievement).

This same pattern is also observed with other particle verbs derived from semelfactive base verbs, for example *abklopfen* 'remove by knocking' and *ausklopfen* 'clean out by knocking' from *klopfen* 'knock, tap,' and *abschlagen* 'remove or deflect by striking,' *ausschlagen* 'knock out (e.g., tooth)'[23], *umschlagen* 'turn over (page, collar)' or 'change suddenly (weather, mood)' from *schlagen* 'strike, hit.'

It seems, then, that while German "semelfactives" may actually be unspecified morphosyntactically as far as durativity is concerned, they are clearly specified for telicity: telicity is represented morphosyntactically—e.g., particle verbs are telic. With semelfactive base verbs, just as with activity base verbs, all the particle does is add a result state (through augmentation, or lexical adjunction), thus creating a telic situation. If durativity is variable in the base verb, then it is also variable in the particle verb, i.e., the particle does not affect durativity.

Let us now turn to cases where the telicizing particles *aus, ab, um* are combined with a telic base verb.

3.4. Accomplishment Base Verb—> Accomplishment Particle Verb

Accomplishments are durative and telic. Interestingly, it is possible and quite common in German to form particle verbs from accomplishment base verbs. These particle verbs are also accomplishments. For example, *bauen* 'build' is an accomplishment, and so are *abbauen* 'deconstruct,' *ausbauen* 'take (by dismantling), extend' and *umbauen* 'remodel, convert.' Other verbs which follow this pattern include *abändern* 'make some changes' and *umändern* 'change around (completely)' from *ändern* 'change,' *ausessen* 'empty (by eating)' from *essen* 'eat,' *umnähen* 'fold over and hem,' *umpflanzen* 'plant somewhere else,' *ausräumen* 'clear out, empty (closet, room),' *umräumen* 'rearrange, store differently,' *umschütten* 'pour into something else,' *abschreiben* 'copy,' *ausschreiben* 'write out,' *umschreiben* 'rewrite,' *abwaschen* 'wash (off),' *auswaschen* 'wash out,' etc. 16 of the 38 accomplishment particle verbs in my database are derived from accomplishment base verbs. To illustrate (tests are italicized):

(40) <u>bauen</u> 'build, construct' (accomplishment)
    a. Sie haben (*in einem Jahr*) ein Haus gebaut.[24]   telic
       'They built a house (*in one year*).'

Telicity in German

    b. Sie *haben aufgehört*, ein Haus zu bauen.   *durative*
       'They *stopped* building a house.'

(41) **ab**bauen 'dismantle, take down' (accomplishment)
    a. Sie hat das Gerüst/die Vorurteile (*in einer Woche*) abgebaut.   *telic*
       'She dismantled the scaffolding/the prejudices (*in a week*).'
    b. Sie *hat aufgehört*, das Gerüst/die Vorurteile abzubauen.   *durative*
       'She *stopped* dismantling the scaffolding/the prejudices.'

(42) **aus**bauen 'take out (by dismantling), extend' (accomplishment)
    a. Sie hat den Motor/das Straßennetz (*in einer Stunde*) ausgebaut.   *telic*
       'She took out the engine/extended the road system (*in an hour*).'
    b. Sie *hat aufgehört*, den Motor/das Straßennetz auszubauen.   *durative*
       'She *stopped* taking out the engine/extending the road system'

(43) **um**bauen 'remodel, convert' (accomplishment)
    a. Sie hat das Haus (*in einem Jahr*) umgebaut.   *telic*
       'She remodeled the house (*in a year*).'
    b. Sie *hat aufgehört*, das Haus umzubauen.   *durative*
       'Sie *stopped* remodeling the house.'

(44) schütten 'pour' (accomplishment)
    a. Sie hat den Sand (*in fünf Minuten*) in den Sandkasten geschüttet.   *telic*
       'She poured the sand into the sandbox (in five minutes).'
    b. Sie *hat aufgehört*, den Sand in den Sandkasten zu schütten.   *durative*
       'She *stopped* pouring the sand into the sandbox.'

(45) **aus**schütten 'pour out' (accomplishment)
    a. Sie hat den Sand (*in fünf Minuten*) ausgeschüttet.   *telic*
       'She poured the sand out (*in five minutes*).'
    b. Sie *hat aufgehört*, den Sand auszuschütten.   *durative*
       'She *stopped* pouring out the sand.'

In these cases, base and particle verbs seem to select roughly the same objects: something that can be built in the *bauen* verbs, something that can be changed in the *ändern* verbs (see Appendix Two), something that can be poured in the *schütten* verbs, etc. What the particle seems to do here, just as in the case of atelic base verbs, is specify a result state. The only difference is that the base verb already denotes a result state. In a particle verb derived from an accomplishment, the result state denoted by the particle takes the place of the result state denoted by the base verb. We can say that the particle "saturates" one of the subevents/predicates of the base verb:

(46) a. *schütten*: CAUSE (DO (x), GO (LOC (y,a), LOC (y,b)));
 aus: ¬**LOC**$_i$ **(y,a)**

 b. *ausschütten*: CAUSE (DO (x), GO (LOC (y,a), ¬**LOC**$_i$ **(y,a)**))

(47) a. *bauen*: CAUSE (DO (x), BECOME (BE (y))); *aus*: ¬**LOC**$_i$ **(y,a)**

 b. *ausbauen*: CAUSE (DO (x), BECOME (¬**LOC**$_i$ **(y,a)**))[25]

The argument structure in these cases does not change. Both *bauen* and *ausbauen* are transitive verbs, which select the same type of object. In *bauen*, the result state is simply existence of the object built. In one reading of *ausbauen*, the result state instead is 'being outside of something one was originally built into.' Both *schütten* and *ausschütten* are verbs with a theme, a source and a goal argument. In the base verb, the result state/location is specified syntactically by the goal (or source) argument, e.g., *Sie hat den Sand (aus dem Sack) in den Sandkasten geschüttet*. 'She poured the sand (out of the sack) into the sandbox.' The particle takes the place of the goal argument, specifying a different result state instead. For example, the result state of *den Sand ausschütten* is that the sand is 'out of its container' (usually on the ground). Evidence that *aus* really replaces the goal and not the source argument comes from its ability to cooccur with a source argument much more felicitously than with a goal argument:

(48) a. Sie hat den Sand *aus dem Sack* ausgeschüttet.
 'She poured the sand out *from the sack*.'

 b. Sie hat den Sand ?*in den Sandkasten*/??*in den Eimer* ausgeschüttet.[26]
 'She poured the sand out ?*into the sandbox*/??*into the bucket*.'

In sum, with accomplishment verbs the particle saturates one of the predicates of the base verb, or, more specifically, it replaces the resultative subevent of the base verb. Stiebels (1996) calls particles in this function "lexical arguments." We will now see that the same patterns are observed with achievement base verbs.

3.5. Achievement Base Verb—> Achievement Particle Verb

Achievements are telic and nondurative. To the extent that achievements can be distinguished from accomplishments in German, particle verbs derived from achievement base verbs tend to be achievements as well. German telic verbs often vacillate between a nondurative (achievement) and a durative (accomplishment) interpretation, so this is a pattern that is not easy to show. However, the verbs *kommen* 'come' and *bringen* 'bring' are fairly clear cases of achievements, and so are the particle verbs derived from them:

(49) <u>kommen</u> 'come' (achievement)

    a. Sie ist (*in fünf Minuten*) gekommen.[27]   *telic*
    'She came (*in five minutes*).'

    b. #Sie *hat aufgehört* zu kommen.[28]   *nondurative*
    'She *stopped* coming.'

(50) **um**<u>kommen</u> 'die' (achievement)

    a. Sie ist (*in fünf Minuten*) umgekommen.   *telic*
    'She died (*in five minutes*).'

    b. #Sie *hat aufgehört* umzukommen.   *nondurative*
    'She *stopped* dying.'

(51) <u>bringen</u> 'bring' (achievement)

    a. Sie hat die Blumen (*in fünf Minuten*) gebracht.   *telic*
    'She brought the flowers (*in five minutes*).'

    b. #Sie *hat aufgehört*, die Blumen zu bringen.[29]   *nondurative*
    'She *stopped* bringing the flowers.'

(52) **um**<u>bringen</u> 'kill' (achievement)

    a. Sie hat den Einbrecher (*in fünf Minuten*) umgebracht.   *telic*
    'She killed the burglar (*in five minutes*).'

    b. #Sie *hat aufgehört*, den Einbrecher umzubringen.   *nondurative*
    'She *stopped* killing the burglar.'

Kommen and *bringen* are verbs of directed motion with an implied goal: unless otherwise specified, the goal is something like 'to the speaker's location.' However, the goal (and/or source) can also be specified overtly, either by a PP (such as *ins Haus* 'into the house') or by a particle. What the particle seems to do is to pick out one very specific result state from among the many conceivable result states of *bringen* and *kommen*, a result state which is a location only in a metaphoric sense. In predicate decomposition a metaphoric location is represented by BE rather than LOC:

(53) a. *ums Leben kommen/umkommen* 'die': BECOME (BE (y))

b. *ums Leben bringen/umbringen* 'kill': CAUSE (DO (x), BECOME (BE (y))

Here the PP *ums Leben* specifies *BE* (y) as '¬alive (y),' and the particle *um* seems to be a shortened version of this. Although the semantic contribution of the particle *um* is not transparent here, the particle predictably contributes a result state.

3.6. Summary

In this section, I examined the role of particles in the grammatization of telicity in German. I showed that certain particles are overt markers of telicity. These "telic" or delimiting particles derive telic verbs. The most productive patterns of particle verb formation are from an activity or from an accomplishment base verb to an accomplishment particle verb (of the 38 accomplishment particle verbs in my database, 18 are formed from activities and 16 from accomplishments). The function of the particle is to contribute a result state to the verb's meaning. Strikingly, in this most productive pattern of particle verb formation, the semantic complexity of a telic (resultative) predicate corresponds to morphological complexity in German.

In the case of telic base verbs, the particle contributes an (overtly marked) more specific result state than that implied in the base verb's meaning, i.e., the particle saturates an existing argument position of the base verb. In the case of atelic base verbs, the particle creates a new argument position through what can be called augmentation (Rappaport Hovav and Levin 1998), lexical adjunction (Stiebels 1996), or lexical subordination (Spencer and Zaretskaya 1998).

The "resultative function" of particles is not surprising given the original goal-type meaning of the particles *ab, aus* and *um*. In fact, *ab* and *aus* often still have goal-type meaning. The less goal-type, literal the particle's meaning, the less transparent the result state contributed.[30] But while the meaning of the particle verb may be transparent or idiomatic, it is consistently telic (see also Spencer and Zaretskaya 1998).

It should be noted that in Germanic languages, resultative constructions are a highly productive device for creating telic predicates (e.g., Hoekstra 1988, van Valin 1990, Spencer and Zaretskaya 1998). The key role of resultatives has been shown in Blom (2002), who argues that the resultative-marking function of particles is the foundation of the stability of particle verbs in the diachrony of complex predicates in the closely related language Dutch.[31]

What also became clear from the examples discussed is that telicizing particles do not affect durativity. Clearly durative base verbs derive clearly durative particle verbs, and likewise with nondurative verbs. If the base verb is unspecified as to durativity, then a particle verb can be built either on the durative or on the nondurative interpretation, or it can also be unspecified, i.e., allow both interpretations.

To conclude this chapter, let me summarize the main points and end with a suggestion of what might motivate the grammatization of telicity in German. A comparison with the profoundly different patterns found in Dëne will help shed light on this issue.

4. CONCLUSION

I have shown in this chapter that the notion of telicity is very pervasive in German, as apparent in the role of certain particles as well as in the role of other VP constituents.

Certain German particles are a type of resultative, a subpredicate which contributes a result state to the meaning of the verb (cf. Spencer and Zaretskaya 1998). Verbs with such particles are telic. Thus, in German the semantic complexity of telicity is reflected in the structural complexity of particle verbs.

Goal PPs also denote an endpoint—a result location—, thereby also contributing to telicity: verbs of motion are telic with an (accusative) goal PP but not with a (dative) locative one (cf. section 2.5). Only accusative PPs are goal arguments; dative PPs are locative adjuncts.

The result state or location of a telic predicate needs to be predicated of an argument, i.e., there needs to be an argument which "measures out" the telic event. As Tenny (1987, 1994) has shown, only direct internal arguments serve this function. In a transitive clause, the direct internal argument appears as an accusative-marked direct object in German. In fact, verbs of creation/destruction and verbs of consumption require just such an object in order to be telic.

Finally, as Krifka (1989, 1992) and others have shown, this direct internal argument needs to be quantized. It is for this reason that German telic verbs select a (quantized) direct internal argument (accusative direct object if verb is transitive).

We also saw that particles, goal (and resultative) PPs, as well as direct internal arguments are constituents of the VP, so telicity is grammatized in the VP domain in German.[32]

In the next chapter, I will turn to durativity and show that this notion is not grammatized in German. Interestingly, we will see that the lack of grammatizing durativity is correlated with a lack of grammatical viewpoint aspect in German.

We can speculate that the salience of (VP-domain) telicity in German is due to the absence of viewpoint aspect. Unlike in Dëne, no pervasive viewpoints obscure situation type/telicity. In German, then, the level of (a)telicity can also be exploited to convey viewpoint-type meaning. As discussed in Chapter Two, telic predicates are by default associated with perfectivity, atelic verbs with imperfectivity. In fact, this (im)perfective "force" of (a)telic predicates has not gone unnoticed in the traditional literature on German. However, more often than not it has led to a confusion of these two levels, as we shall see in the next chapter, where I will briefly review the literature on aspect in German and show that German has no grammatized viewpoint aspect. I will further show that this correlates with the nongrammatization of durativity in German.

Chapter Five
Viewpoint Aspect and Durativity in German

The last chapter explored the expression of telicity in German and found that it is grammatized pervasively. We also saw that the grammatical elements overtly marking or sensitive to telicity (objects and object properties, particles and other resultatives) are all constituents of the VP. I ended the chapter by suggesting that telicity may be so pervasive in German because, unlike Dëne, German is a language without viewpoint aspect, and that German bounds events in the VP domain, through telicity, while Dëne bounds events in the inflectional domain, through perfectivity.

In this chapter I will do two things. First, I will provide detailed evidence for the claim that German does not have grammatical viewpoint aspect (of course other, semantic, means such as adverbs can be used to express viewpoint-type meaning). The absence of viewpoint aspect is clearest in South German dialects, and accordingly, the discussion will focus on South German in those areas where it provides clearer evidence than Standard German. In particular, while neither Standard German nor South German have an inflectional or other obligatory device dedicated to marking viewpoint aspect, it has been claimed by some for Standard German that the choice of a past tense (Perfect vs. Preterite) also conveys viewpoint information, i.e., that some tenses have a secondary viewpoint-related meaning. However, no such indirect viewpoint marking whatsoever exists in South German, as a comparison of past tenses in Standard and South German will show.

Thus, German, and especially South German, is truly a language without grammatical viewpoint marking, and in this respect represents an interesting mirror image of Dëne. In the second part of this chapter, then, I discuss the implications of the absence of viewpoint aspect for durativity, and show that durativity is not grammatized in German.

1. VIEWPOINT ASPECT IN GERMAN?

In this section, I will show that German (and particularly South German) has no grammatical viewpoint aspect. In order to do so, I first have to make sure that what we have been treating as overt markers of telicity are indeed that and not markers of perfectivity/viewpoint aspect. This is an issue because these two levels of aspect have been confused in the literature on German for a long time. After dealing with the difference between viewpoint aspect and situation type in German, I will investigate the grammatical-inflectional categories of the verb, showing that these categories do not represent viewpoint distinctions either, particularly not in South German. To keep the discussion as general as possible, I focus on Standard German unless South German crucially differs (i.e., in the use of past tenses).

1.1. Situation Type vs. Viewpoint Aspect in German

I will not give a detailed review here of the long tradition of aspect research in German philology and linguistics; for an overview, see Andersson (1972), Steinitz (1981), and Leiss (1992). Suffice it to say that, largely due to the influence of the literature on Slavic languages, the oppositions "imperfective"—"perfective" or "durative"—"perfective" are often used to describe situation type meaning. While these are, in modern terminology, viewpoint aspectual terms (cf. Comrie 1976, Smith 1991), in the German literature "imperfective" and "perfective" are treated as "Aktionsarten." The choice of the category "Aktionsarten," which means 'type/manner of action,' is already an indication that here we are really dealing with situation types. Certainly, the other "Aktionsarten" usually listed are subcategories of situation type meaning (subsituation aspect). In (1) I give an overview of the traditional aspectual classification of German verbs. I will then show that "perfective" and "imperfective" really refer to telic and atelic situation types.

(1) Traditional aspectual classification of German verbs

   I. imperfective/durative Aktionsart

   schlafen 'sleep,' *leben* 'live,' *sitzen* 'sit' (Dal 1966)

   blühen 'bloom,' *schlafen* 'sleep,' *frieren* 'freeze/be cold,' *wohnen* 'inhabit,' *sein* 'be' (Duden 1984)

   arbeiten 'work,' *blühen* 'bloom,' *schlafen* 'sleep' (Flämig 1965)

   liegen 'lie,' *schlafen* 'sleep,' *wohnen* 'inhabit' (Paul 1959:65)

II. perfective (punctual/terminative) Aktionsart

besteigen 'climb onto,' *entnehmen* 'take out of,' *verblühen* 'finish blooming,' *erfrieren* 'die by freezing' (Duden 1984)

kommen 'come,' *bringen* 'bring,' *sterben* 'die' (Paul 1959:65)

a. inchoative/ingressive Aktionsart

erblühen 'start blooming' (Leiss 1992)

erblühen 'start blooming,' *aufbrechen* 'break open, set out,' *erblassen* 'pale,' *aufstehen* 'stand up' (Duden 1984)

erblühen 'start blooming,' *erblicken* 'catch sight of,' *ertönen* 'be heard (sound)' (Dal 1966)

erblühen 'start blooming,' *anfahren* 'start driving,' *einschlafen* 'fall asleep,' *grünen* 'become green,' *reifen* 'ripen,' *schwärzen* 'make black,' *öffnen* 'open (tr.)' (Flämig 1965)

b. terminative/effective/egressive/resultative Aktionsart

verblühen 'finish blooming' (Leiss 1992)

verblühen 'finish blooming,' *verblassen* 'fade (of color),' *aufessen* 'eat up,' *ausklingen* 'die away (sound),' *verbrennen* 'burn completely' (Duden 1984)

verblühen 'finish blooming,' *verdorren* 'wilt,' *verklingen* 'fade (of sound)' (Dal 1966)

erschlagen 'beat to death,' *verbrennen* 'burn completely,' *durchbóhren* 'pierce,' *umfáhren* 'drive around sth.,' *úmfahren* 'knock over driving' (Flämig 1965)

c. punctual Aktionsart

antreffen 'meet, run into' (Leiss 1992)

ersteigen 'climb to the top of' (Dal 1966)

finden 'find,' *treffen* 'hit (target), meet,' *brechen* 'break' (Flämig 1965)

(d. factitive verbs)

töten 'kill,' *öffnen* 'open (tr.),' *sättigen* 'fill/satisfy/saturate' (Flämig 1965)

This is apparently a semantic rather than a morphological classification (cf. Steinitz 1981). Imperfective and perfective verbs do not constitute different verb paradigms or even systematic oppositions, as pointed out in Leiss (1992). In particular, the subtypes of "perfective" verbs do not correspond to morphological subclasses: a variety of prefixes and particles is used in each class, and simplex verbs (such as *kommen* 'come') occur as well. It is striking, however, that "imperfective" verbs are simple and that most "perfective" verbs are created by particle verb formation, prefixation or some other derivational process. It is this pattern of simplex verbs vs. derived particle/prefix verbs which has led philologists (e.g., those cited in (1); see Andersson 1972, Steinitz 1981 for detailed references and review) to draw an analogy with the Slavic aspectual system, where in many cases simplex verbs are imperfective and prefixed verbs are perfective.[1] But although the morphology may be vaguely similar to that used in Slavic aspect, there is no reason to believe that this pattern encodes a viewpoint aspectual distinction in German.

As already mentioned, German simple vs. particle/prefix verbs do not constitute cells of an aspectual paradigm. In other words, while most Slavic and Däne verbs can be cited in imperfective-perfective pairs, German so-called imperfective and perfective verbs are separate words. This can be demonstrated in two ways. First, not all German verbs occur in pairs of unprefixed "imperfective" and prefixed/particle "perfective" forms. For example, *pflegen* 'tend (to)' (atelic), *achten* 'mind, respect' (atelic), etc., do not have prefixed/particle "perfective" partners. And most unprefixed/particle-less "perfective" verbs have no "imperfective" partner, although they are derivationally related to other "perfective" verbs, e.g., *töten* 'kill' (telic; *abtöten* 'kill off' is also telic), *bringen* 'bring' (telic; *umbringen* 'kill,' *abbringen* 'get/put off, talk someone out of,' etc. are also telic), *leeren* 'empty' (telic; *ausleeren* 'empty out' is also telic), etc.

Second, and more importantly, it can be shown that the *meaning* of these German "perfective" verbs is telic (or atelic) rather than truly perfective (or imperfective). This was already done by Andersson (1972), who points out that German verbs may have both a perfective or an imperfective viewpoint interpretation:

(2) so-called perfective *zurückkehren* 'return' (Andersson 1972:63)

a. perfective interpretation:

Als   er *zurückkehrte*, fand er ein Telegramm vor, das ihm eine unangenehme
when he returned   found he a telegram   PART that him a   unpleasant

Überraschung bereitete.
surprise   gave/caused

'When he *returned* home, he found a telegram which caused him an unpleasant surprise.'

b. <u>imperfective interpretation</u>:

Schmidt, der auf dem gewohnten Weg von seinem Büro *zurückkehrte*, merkte
Schmidt who on the usual way from his office returned noticed
nicht, dass er die ganze Zeit gegen den Menschenstrom ging.
not that he the whole time against the people-flow went

'Schmidt, who *was returning* from his office on the usual way, did not notice that he was walking against the flow (of people) the whole time.'

(3) <u>so-called imperfective *lieben* 'love'</u> (Andersson 1972:64, citing Roganova 1961, who in turn cites Feuchtwanger)

<u>perfective interpretation</u>:
Gegenüber lag eine kleine Insel, Jean-Jacques *liebte* sie sogleich . . .
across lay a small island Jean-Jacques loved her immediately

'Across there was a small island, Jean-Jacques *loved (fell in love with)* it right away . . .'

If *zurückkehren* were truly perfective, it should not be able to occur with an imperfective interpretation, i.e., (2b) should be impossible. Likewise, if *lieben* were truly imperfective, the perfective interpretation shown in (3) should be impossible. These facts strongly suggest a different analysis, in which *zurückkehren* is not perfective but telic, and *lieben* is not imperfective but atelic. Thus, the German verbal morphology encodes situation type (telicity) rather than viewpoint aspect (perfectivity) distinctions. In Andersson's words, a distinction must be drawn between "Grenzbezogenheit" ('relatedness to a boundary,' i.e., telicity) and the actual reaching of this boundary (i.e., perfectivity), as well as between "Nichtgrenzbezogenheit" ('nonrelatedness to a boundary,' atelicity) and the non-reaching of a boundary (imperfectivity). Andersson's boundary corresponds to the "inherent endpoint" discussed as characteristic of telicity in Chapter One.

Additional evidence that the characterization in terms of perfectivity/viewpoint is incorrect comes from a comparison between German and Russian (and English). According to Andersson, *zurückkehren* is translated into Russian by different verb forms in (2a) and (2b). In (2a), we find the perfective verb *vosvratit'sja* 'return (perf.),' in (2b) we find the imperfective verb *vozvraščat'sja* 'return (impf.).' In English we have the simple past *returned* in (2a) and the progressive *was returning* in (2b). In (3) Russian uses a perfective verb *vljubilsja* 'fell in love (perf.),' and similarly in English. If German verbs also showed overt morphological viewpoint distinctions, we should expect two different forms of *zurückkehren* in (2a) and (2b), or perhaps the use of *zurückkehren* in (2a) and the use of *kehren* in (2b), and a prefixed form of *lieben* in (3). The comparison with Russian and English shows that German does not encode perfectivity (viewpoint) but telicity (situation type).

I conclude, with Andersson, that German prefixes and particles do not show overt morphological viewpoint distinctions. The traditional aspectual classification of German verbs into those of "imperfective Aktionsart" versus those of "perfective Aktionsart" needs to be recast as one of telic versus atelic situation type. It is then the case that simple verbs are usually atelic and that particle verbs (and prefixed verbs) are usually telic. The role of morphology was addressed in the discussion of particle verbs in the previous chapter.

1.1.1. Completion Entailments in German

Andersson's analysis corresponds exactly to that found in Smith (1991). Smith shows that telicity in and of itself does not entail perfectivity/event completion (i.e., the reaching of a boundary, or inherent endpoint). Only a telic predicate in perfective viewpoint entails event completion. Similarly, an atelic predicate entails event termination (i.e., that the situation stopped or ended, the reaching of not an inherent boundary but of an arbitrary end) only in the perfective viewpoint. In the imperfective, telic predicates do not entail completion and atelic predicates do not entail termination. Thus, the two aspectual levels of viewpoint and situation type can be distinguished in terms of their entailments. A completion (or termination) entailment is indicative of perfective viewpoint.

This entailment test can be applied to German verbs to show that they are (a)telic rather than (im)perfective. Let us take some so-called perfective, i.e. telic, verbs and attempt to cancel event completion:

(4) Context: Was hat Susi gestern nachmittag gemacht?
  'What did Susi do/was Susi doing yesterday afternoon?'

   a. Sie hat *einen Brief geschrieben*, aber sie ist noch nicht fertig damit.
    'She *wrote a letter*, but she is not yet done with it.'

   b. Sie hat *einen morschen Ast abgesägt*, aber sie ist nicht fertig geworden.
    'She *sawed off a dead branch*, but she did not get done.'
              (. . . weil es anfing zu regnen)
              ('. . . because it started raining')

c. Sie ist mit dem Fahrrad *zur Uni gefahren*, ist aber nie angekommen.
'She *went* by bike *to the university*, but she never got there.'

(. . . weil sie einen Platten hatte)
(' . . . because she had a flat tire')

Although atelic predicates would fare better in these contexts, the important point is that telic predicates can also be used here. This confirms that an imperfective viewpoint can occur with telic verbs.

It is true, however, that telic verbs usually receive a perfective interpretation, and atelic verbs usually receive an imperfective interpretation. In fact, this preferred association of telicity with perfectivity and atelicity with imperfectivity is precisely what has contributed to the misanalyses in the traditional literature on German. Following Bohnemeyer and Swift (2004), we can say that in the absence of overt viewpoint marking, a telic predicate is associated with perfective viewpoint by "default." I argued above (Chapter Two, section 3.1) that this is motivated by the communicative need to specify event sequencing in discourse. In the absence of overt viewpoint marking, telicity is pressed into a viewpoint-type service, namely to specify events as sequential in discourse. However, since telicity is a situation type feature, the sequential (or perfective) interpretation is only an implicature and can be cancelled. Examples (2b) and (4a)-(4c) above are all instances of a cancelled sequential/perfective interpretation.

In conclusion, the labels "imperfective" and "perfective" commonly used in the aspectual characterization of German verbs are a misnomer. Instead, German verbs should be characterized as atelic vs. telic. We saw in the previous chapter that telicity is overtly encoded in German in several ways. However, both telic and atelic German predicates are unspecified in terms of viewpoint: while there are default associations between a particular situation type and viewpoint, German predicates can fundamentally denote a situation from an imperfective *or* a perfective viewpoint. The viewpoint aspectual interpretation of a predicate is normally determined by default rules precisely because German does not have overt grammatical marking for viewpoint.

Having demonstrated that derivational morphology (particles and prefixes) does not encode viewpoint aspect but situation type, I now turn to evidence that viewpoint aspect is not encoded elsewhere in the morphosyntax of German either.

1.2. No grammatical Viewpoint in German

The goal of this subsection is to demonstrate that viewpoint aspect as a grammatical category is absent from German. This is shown in two steps. First, the relevant inflectional forms of the German verb are tenses rather than viewpoints (section 1.2.1). Second, going beyond strictly synthetic inflection, there are no grammatized periphrastic viewpoint constructions like the English progressive either (section 1.2.2). Again, the discussion here focuses on Standard German, but South German patterns identically. A comparison of the potential viewpoint functions of tense in Standard versus South German is postponed until section 1.3.

1.2.1. German Verbs Do Not Inflect for Viewpoint Aspect

If viewpoint aspect were a grammatical category of German, the most natural place to look for it would be among the verb's inflectional forms. Now, in most sources one can read that German verbs have six tense forms, but there is no mention of viewpoint aspects[2] (e.g., Behagel 1907, Dal 1966, Duden 1984, Flämig 1964/65, Paul 1959, Wunderlich 1970). A sample paradigm is given in (5). As one can see, there are no forms like an imperfective or a perfective, and no viewpoint-sensitive contrasts such as the English progressive versus simple forms. Thus, while German has the category tense, it has no inflectional forms which are primarily and obligatorily used to express viewpoint aspect. This is radically different from Dëne Sųłiné, where viewpoint aspect is a pervasive and obligatory category of the verb.

(5) the indicative forms of *lieben* 'love,' second person singular

    a. du liebst 'you love'   *Präsens* (Present)

    b. du liebtest 'you loved'   *Präteritum* (Preterite)

    c. du hast geliebt 'you have loved'   *Perfekt* (Perfect)

    d. du hattest geliebt 'you had loved'   *Plusquamperfekt* (Pluperfect/Past Perfect)

    e. du wirst lieben 'you will love'   *Futur I* (Future)

    f. du wirst geliebt haben 'you will have loved'   *Futur II* (Future Perfect)

However, one question needs to be addressed before we can make the generalization that German has no grammatical viewpoint aspects. The question is: does German perhaps use some other grammatical device to express viewpoint aspect? Two possibilities are (i) progressive paraphrases and (ii) contrasting uses of certain tenses, like the French Imparfait vs. Passé Composé. The remainder of section 1 explores these possibilities.

1.2.2. Progressive Paraphrases

I will begin with a discussion of progressive paraphrases (tenses are discussed in section 1.3). We will see that German does not have periphrastic constructions which can be considered to grammatize perfectivity or imperfectivity.

German is, of course, not unable to express imperfective or progressive meanings. In this section, I will consider the devices commonly mentioned as expressing such meanings. I will show that these devices do not constitute grammatizations of imperfectivity/progressivity, since they are not obligatory grammatical forms. The devices or constructions with a progressive-like meaning are presented in (6).

(6) German paraphrases of the progressive:

    a. *gerade* 'right now, just now, currently' (Adv)

    b. *am V-en sein* : at.the + nominalized Inf + be
       'be in the process of V-ing'[3]

    c. *dabei sein zu* + Inf: there + be + to + Inf 'be in the process of V-ing'

The first thing to be noted is that the items in (6) are only discussed as paraphrases of the *progressive*. I am not aware of a discussion anywhere of paraphrases of *imperfective* viewpoint. For example, Dahl (1985) does not list German among the languages with imperfective/perfective categories. This gap I take to mean that if there are paraphrases or other devices expressing (im)perfectivity per se in German, they are too varied to be considered systematic or grammatical in any way.

Next, none of the progressive paraphrases in (6) are obligatorily used in progressive contexts; they are alternatives to the Present or the Preterite, which may also be used in these contexts. This is illustrated in (7) and (8) with contexts in which, according to Dahl (1985), progressive forms prototypically occur.

(7) Context: (Father to child) Please do not disturb me, . . .

    a. . . . ich schreibe *gerade* einen Brief.
       '. . . I am (currently) writing a letter.'

    b. . . . ich *bin am/beim* Briefeschreiben.
       '. . . I am in the process of letter-writing.'

    c. . . . ich *bin dabei*, einen Brief zu schreiben.
       '. . . I am in the process of/involved in writing a letter.'

d. . . . ich schreibe einen Brief.
      '. . . I am writing a letter.'

(8) Context: A: I talked to my brother on the phone yesterday.
              B: What was he doing?
   a. . . . er kochte *gerade*/hat *gerade* gekocht.
      '. . . he was (at that moment) cooking.'
   b. . . . er *war am/beim* Kochen.
      '. . . he was in the process of cooking.'
   c. . . . er *war dabei* zu kochen.
      '. . . he was in the process of/engaged in cooking.'
   d. . . . er kochte/hat gekocht.
      '. . . he was cooking.'

In both (7) and (8), progressive sentences without any progressive device (the (d) examples) are completely acceptable. It depends on personal preference, style, and dialect which option is chosen. That the unparaphrased forms are an equal and perhaps even a better choice can also be seen from translating the question asked by "B" in (8) into German (as is done in Dahl 1985): *Was hat er gemacht?*[4].

Of the progressive paraphrases shown in (6), the *am* construction (6b) seems quite similar in form to the English progressive. However, unlike the English progressive, this construction is not productive or obligatory in most dialects (including Standard and South German).[5] Part of the reason for this may be that, syntactically, the construction is restricted to bare verbs, as in (8b) above, and N-V compounds, as in (7b) (cf. Delisle 1985). If the VP contains a noncompounded object or an adjunct, the construction is impossible. This can be seen in the following examples.

(9) a. *Max war [am/beim im   Garten Arbeiten], als . . .
        Max was at.the   in.the yard   work   when . . .
        ('Max was in the process of working in the yard/garden when . . .')

    b. Max war im   Garten [am/beim Arbeiten], als . . .
       Max was in.the yard   at.the   work   when
       * (i) 'Max was working in the yard when . . .'
       √ (ii) 'Max was in the yard, working, when . . .'

c. *Er war [die Rosen am/beim Gießen], als . . .
   he was the roses at.the water when . . .
   ('He was in the process of watering the roses when . . .')

d. *Sie war [ihrer Mutter am/beim Helfen], als . . .
   she was her mother at.the help when . . .
   ('She was in the process of helping her mother when . . .')

The reason for the ungrammaticality is that this construction requires a noun (*am* and *beim* consist of a P plus determiner). Bare verbs can be interpreted as nominalized, thus nouns, and so can N-V compounds, but when additional structure precedes the verb, the nominal interpretation breaks down.

Summing up, then, German contains neither an obligatory periphrastic device nor an inflectional category for viewpoint aspectual meanings such as "perfective," "imperfective," or "progressive" (see also Musan 2002:6–9). I now turn to possibility (ii) mentioned above, namely that of indirect viewpoint marking via tense.

1.3. Tenses Do Not Have Viewpoint Function in (South) German

Having found neither a synthetic inflectional nor a periphrastic viewpoint aspect category in German, the next question is whether perhaps some other category is appropriated to convey viewpoint notions as a secondary function of that category.

A secondary viewpoint-marking function of tense is conceivable wherever more than one form is available to express a certain tense meaning. Originally, Old Germanic had a two-way tense distinction between past and nonpast (Dal 1966). Past tense was expressed by the Preterite form of a verb, nonpast (i.e., present and future) tense by the present form of a verb. Both of these forms have survived into Modern German, for example, Present *ich singe* 'I sing/am singing' and Preterite *ich sang* 'I sang/was singing.' Modern Standard German has an additional form to convey past tense meaning, the Present Perfect, e.g. *ich habe gesungen* 'I sang/have sung,' as well as additional forms for future meanings (Future: *ich werde singen* 'I will sing'; Future Perfect: *ich werde gesungen haben* 'I will have sung') and remote past meaning (Past Perfect: *ich hatte gesungen* 'I had sung').[6]

It has indeed been suggested that in Modern Standard German, the Preterite as well as the Present have secondary imperfective meaning (e.g.,

Ehrich 1992, Flämig 1965, see also Duden 1984), i.e., that they convey an imperfective viewpoint besides their primary tense meaning.[7] However, I will show that this proposal does not have strong empirical support.

Moreover, in South German, there is again only one form available for nonpast[8] and for past time reference, respectively. The Present Perfect has completely supplanted the Preterite as the sole past tense, and the Present is used for both present and future time reference (the latter is probably the case in colloquial German in general). I will show that South German presents even clearer evidence than Standard German that tenses do not have secondary aspectual meanings, and that viewpoint aspect is not grammatized.

I begin with an examination of the Present Tense (section 1.3.1), followed by a discussion of the Preterite and Present Perfect in Standard and South German (section 1.3.2). But before doing so, I want to briefly review the terminology used below.

Recall from Chapter One that in many modern theories, tenses and viewpoint aspects are defined through relations between times: the time of the situation (TSit), the topic time (or reference time) TT, and the utterance time (TU) (e.g., Reichenbach 1947, Klein 1994, Kratzer 1998). Tense represents an ordering of TU and TT; thus, past tense orders TT before TU, future tense orders TT after TU, and present tense orders TT at TU or overlapping it. The ordering of TT and TSit is the domain of viewpoint aspect (imperfective: TT within TSit, perfective: TSit within TT). Of importance for our discussion is that whenever the meaning of a tense also says something about the ordering of TSit, it has an additional viewpoint aspectual meaning.

1.3.1. Present (vs. Future)

The Standard German Present is taken by some to have imperfective meaning. For example, Flämig (1965) classes the Present as an imperfective tense which represents "time as ongoing" ("Darstellung der Zeit als Verlauf," p. 3). And Ehrich (1992) defines the intrinsic meaning of the Present as an "association" relation between TSit and TT. "Association" between a time X and a time Y means that X neither completely precedes nor completely follows Y (p. 67), i.e., it is an overlap relation. Note that this relation does not hold between TT and TU, the normal domain of tense, but between TSit and TT, which is usually thought of as the domain of viewpoint aspect.

According to Ehrich, the "present tense" meaning comes about because there also exists a default association/overlap relation between TT and TU for

Viewpoint Aspect and Durativity in German

the Present. However, the overlap of TT and TU is not part of the intrinsic meaning of the Present, and furthermore, being only a default relation, it may be shifted by context (Ehrich 1992:70).

(10) Imperfective definition of Present (Ehrich 1992)

    TSit,TT & TU,TT => TSit,TU   (, = association)

The claim that the Present has a secondary use as imperfective viewpoint is somewhat problematic because there is no contrasting nonpast tense available to consistently express perfective viewpoint. Indeed, others define the German Present as a true tense that is aspectually neutral. For example, Musan (2002:15) defines the Present as locating TT "not properly before" TU, i.e., TU included in TT or TT after TU. This is a "nonpast" tense definition of the Present.

(11) Aspectually neutral definition of Present (Musan 2002)

    TT $\neg<$ TU   ($\neg<$ = not before)

Note that this definition of the Present says nothing about the relation between TT and TSit and thus has no viewpoint aspectual component.

Now, if the Present were to have imperfective force, it would be expected that certain predicates, in particular predicates with a nondurative situation type meaning, could not occur in the Present. The reason for this restriction is that imperfective viewpoints order TT within TSit (TT $\subset$ TSit). But if TSit is only a point, as is the case in nondurative situations, no other time can be included in it. For example, recall that in Dëne, one test for durativity is compatibility with the Imperfective: nondurative verbs (i) may not occur in Imperfective form at all or (ii) may only occur in a future/prospective reading of the Imperfective (see Chapter Two, section 2.2.1 and Chapter Three, section 3.1.1).

With respect to (i), there are no verbs in German which cannot occur in the Present Tense form. This is a first indication that the Present is not an imperfective. But is there perhaps evidence in German for the second, weaker, criterion (ii)? Indeed, it has been claimed that a future interpretation is more readily available or perhaps even preferred over a present tense interpretation for certain verbs. Thus, Wunderlich (1970) says that "clearly punctual" verbs (especially in the context of a first or second person subject) usually have a future meaning in the present tense. The verbs in (12) are achievements (punctual and telic).

(12) future reading of present-tense verbs

    a. Ich *treffe* meinen Freund Emil.   (Wunderlich 1970:133)
       I meet-PRES my friend Emil
       'I'm meeting/going to meet my friend Emil.'

    b. Kasparov *gewinnt*.   (Ehrich 1992:69)
       Kasparov win-PRES
       'Kasparov is winning/is going to win.'

However, this future reading is in no way obligatory. As Löbner (1988), Ehrich (1992) and Musan (2002) point out, a present tense reading is always available. For example, (12a) can also mean that my meeting Emil takes place at the time of utterance ("right now"), and likewise for (12b).[9] Moreover, with semelfactive verbs, which are also punctual, the present tense reading is preferred:

(13) a. Susi *hustet*.
      Susi cough-PRES
      'Susi is coughing (once/repeatedly).'

    b. Susi *klopft* an die Tür.
      Susi knock-PRES at the door
      'Susi is knocking at the door (once/repeatedly).'

As Ehrich (1992:69) writes, "die Gegenwartsbedeutung ist immer möglich, unabhängig von der Aktionsart des Verbs und der adverbialen Modifikation" ('the present tense meaning is always possible, independent of the verb's aktionsart [= situation type] and adverbial modification').

However, the future interpretation is not always readily available. Ehrich (1992) and Musan (2002) agree on the following generalization: telic verbs can get a future (in addition to a present) reading without contextual triggers; atelic verbs can get a future reading only with a contextual trigger such as a future adverbial, otherwise they only have a present reading.

This accords with my judgements as well, even though in South German, the Present is the only tense available for expressing future meaning. *Werden* + infinitive, the Standard German Future, is only used with modal meaning in South German. Thus, *sie wird singen* does not mean 'she will/is going to sing,' but 'she is probably singing,' and likewise for all situation types.[10] But it is nonetheless true in South German that the Present form of atelic verbs has a future reading only in a future context, and a present reading in neutral contexts. (14) and (15) illustrate:

(14) telic predicates

    a. Die Susi *sägt* den Ast *ab*.
       √ 'Susi is sawing off the branch (right now).'   √ Present reading
       √ 'Susi will saw off the branch   √ Future reading
        (soon/at an appointed time).'

    b. Die Susi *gewinnt*.
       √ 'Susi is winning (right now).'   √ Present reading
       √ 'Susi is going to win (soon).'   √ Future reading

(15) atelic predicates

    a. Die Susi *schafft* im Garten.
       √ 'Susi is working in the yard (right now).'   √ Present reading
       # 'Susi is going to work in the yard (soon).'   # Future reading

    b. Die Susi *klopft* an die Tür.
       √ 'Susi is knocking at the door (right now).'   √ Present reading
       # 'Susi is going to knock at the door (soon).'   # Future reading

(16) atelic predicates and future adverbial

    a. Die Susi *schafft* morgen im Garten.
       √ 'Susi is going to work in the yard tomorrow.'   √ Future reading

    b. Die Susi *klopft* morgen an deine Tür.
       √ 'Susi is going to knock on your door tomorrow.' √ Future reading

Since in principle, present readings are available for all situation types, I conclude that the core meaning of the Present in both Standard and South German is indeed 'TT not before TU,' as in Musan (2002), and not imperfective 'TT overlaps TSit,' as in Ehrich (1992). Thus, the Present is not a viewpoint aspect, but a tense.

The pattern seen in (14)-(16) can then be derived straightforwardly, assuming that the default viewpoint of telic situations is perfective rather than imperfective (Bohnemeyer and Swift 2004), while the default viewpoint of atelic situations is imperfective. In the present tense, we thus have TT ¬< TU & (per default) TSit ⊆ TT for telic predicates and TT ¬< TU & (per default) TT ⊂ TSit for atelic predicates. Both of these constellations still allow for various kinds of orderings of TSit and TU (recall that this ordering is not specified as part of the present tense meaning per se). But crucially, there are fewer ways to derive the ordering TSit after TU, which corresponds to a future interpretation, with atelic than with telic predicates. Specifically, as long as TU within TT (a subcase of TT ¬< TU), TU may precede TSit only in telic—default perfective—predicates. This contrast is illustrated in (17) vs. (18). TU is within TT in both (17a), present interpretation, and (17b), future interpretation.

(17) present-tense telic predicates: TU ⊂ TT & (per default) TSit ⊆ TT
(see (14) above)

    a. ------[$_{TT}$-{$_{TSit}$-[$_{TU}$-]----}-]------->   present interpretation
    or
    b. ------[$_{TT}$-[$_{TU}$-]-{$_{TSit}$---}-]------->   future interpretation[11]

If TSit is really short, as with achievements, the ordering of TSit around TU is less likely than the ordering of TSit after TU. This explains the tendency towards a future reading found with achievements.

Now, in the cases of TU within TT, the ordering TU before TSit is precluded for atelic predicates in default imperfective viewpoint, which requires TT within TSit. This is shown in (18).

(18) present-tense atelic predicates: TU ⊂ TSit & (per default) TSit ⊂ TSit
(see (15) above)

    -----{$_{TSit}$-[$_{TT}$--[$_{TU}$-]----]-}------->   present interpretation

The "future" ordering TU before TSit is only possible if the default imperfective ordering (TT within TSit) is overridden, (19a), or if TT is explicitly located after TU. Both of these effects can be achieved by a future adverbial or similar device.

(19) present-tense atelic predicates (and future adverbial): (see (16) above)

    a. TT ¬< TU & TSit ⊆ TT
    ------[$_{TT}$-[$_{TU}$-]-{$_{TSit}$---}-]------->   future interpretation
    b. TT > TU & TSit ⊆ TT[12]
    -----[$_{TU}$-]--[$_{TT}$-{$_{TSit}$---}-]------->   future interpretation

Viewpoint Aspect and Durativity in German 181

In conclusion, the German data do not support the claim that the Present Tense has a secondary imperfective meaning. First, there is no systematic contrast with another, perfective, present tense which could bring out this meaning. Second, the Present Tense shows present readings with all situation types. This means that the German Present Tense does not pattern like a (secondary) imperfective viewpoint, which is not compatible with nondurative situations (semelfactives and achievements). Thus, the Present does not represent a grammatization of imperfective viewpoint in German.

1.3.2. Preterite (vs. Perfect)

As far as I can tell, all treatments of the Preterite versus the Perfect are based on Standard German. However, Standard German is a somewhat artificial language that is used mostly in writing and in official circumstances such as political speeches or newscasts. In colloquial German, and especially in South German dialects, there is very little use of the Preterite. I will illustrate this difference by a separate discussion of Standard German and South German. I will also show that even in Standard German, the viewpoint aspect function of the Perfect-Preterite contrast is negligible.

Standard German. Flämig (1965:3,7) says that just like the Present, the Preterite is a "Verlaufsstufe"-tense, i.e., a tense which represents time as ongoing. The other past tense, the Perfect, is a perfective tense which represents a "completed event" ("vollzogenes Geschehen," p. 3). Flämig thus suggests that there is an aspectual difference between the Perfect and the Preterite.

Similarly, many modern analyses assign the two tenses different meanings. For example, in Ehrich (1992), the Perfect is defined through an inherent anteriority[13] relation between TSit and TT, while the Preterite is defined through an inherent association or overlap relation between TSit and TT. Again, an overlap between TSit and TT is typical of imperfective viewpoint rather than of (past) tense. In addition, each of the two tenses also specifies the relation between TT and TU; however, this is only a default relation and may be shifted by context (Ehrich 1992:70). The default for the Perfect is association/overlap between TT and TU; in the Preterite TT is by default anterior to TU. This yields the following results for the Perfect and Preterite:

(20) Perfect

TSit < TT & TT,TU and thus TSit < TU (< = anteriority; , = association)

(21) Preterite

TSit,TT & TT < TU and thus TSit < TU

Schematically, this can be represented as follows (for the sake of concreteness, I represent Ehrich's association relation as an inclusion relation, but association could also be represented as a partial overlap of the respective times):

(22) Perfect

------{TSit----}----[TT---[TU----]---]-------->

Preterite

-----{TSit-[TT-----]-}------[TU----]-------->

This account yields two interesting results. First, the two tenses comprise both viewpoint aspectual and tense meaning: the Preterite is an "imperfective past tense," the Perfect a "perfect present tense." Second, although the two tenses have a different structure and correspond to different viewpoints, they nonetheless often (i.e., in the default cases) have the same result TSit < TU. This is how Ehrich derives a kind of past tense interpretation for each of these tenses. Note, however, that technically, only the Preterite is a past tense (TT < TU), while the Perfect is a present tense (TT and TU overlap).

Of importance to our discussion is that an analysis such as Ehrich's effectively assigns the Preterite an imperfective viewpoint. This amounts to saying that in Standard German, the Preterite does have a secondary viewpoint aspectual meaning. Does this perhaps mean that in Standard German the choice of Preterite versus Present Perfect can be exploited to express an imperfective vs. perfect/perfective contrast?

It is indeed the case in Standard German that the Preterite and the Present Perfect cannot always be substituted for each other without a change in meaning or a decline in acceptability (Ehrich (1992), Musan (2002), among many others). In several of these instances, one could attribute the nonsubstitutability to a difference in viewpoint aspect between the two tenses. Let us consider these examples.

(23) shows that only the Preterite but not the Perfect can be used for a simultaneous past situation in an embedded clause. The reasoning here assumes that simultaneity typically requires an imperfective viewpoint, and since only the Preterite works in a simultaneous context, the Preterite but not the Perfect has imperfective meaning. In (24), we see that only the Perfect but not the Preterite can be used to refer to a completed future situation. Thus, the Perfect is preferred in a perfective context.

(23) simultaneous past situations—Standard German   (Ehrich 1992:69)

    a. Hans wußte, daß es *regnete*   (*geregnet hat*).
       Hans knew that it rain-PRET (*rained has)
       'Hans knew that it was raining.'

    b. Hans wachte früh auf. Heute *war*   (**ist . . . gewesen*) sein Geburtstag.
       Hans woke early up today be-PRET (*is . . . been) his birthday
       'Hans woke up early. Today was his birthday.'

(24) completed future situation—Standard German   (Ehrich 1992:68)

    Sie bekommen die Ware,   wenn Sie *bezahlt haben* (**bezahlten*).
    you receive   the merchandise when you paid   have (*paid-PRET)
    'You'll receive the merchandise when you('ll) have paid (*paid-PRET).'

Examples such as (23) and (24) may lead us to think that the Preterite has secondary imperfective, and the Present Perfect secondary perfective meaning. However, this would be incorrect. For one thing, both tenses are compatible with all situation types, (25) and (26), whereas we know that imperfective viewpoint is in principle restricted to situations which are durative, either inherently or by coercion.

(25) Preterite

    a. Susi sägte einen Ast ab.   *durative (accomplishment)*
       'Susi sawed/was sawing off a branch.'

    b. Susi arbeitete.   *durative (activity)*
       'Susi worked/was working.'

    c. Susi war müde.   *durative (state)*
       'Susi was tired.'

    e. Susi kam gestern an.   *nondurative (achievement)*
       'Susi arrived yesterday.'

    f. Susi nieste (einmal).   *nondurative (semelfactive)*
       'Susi sneezed (once).'

(26) Perfect

    a. Susi hat einen Ast abgesägt.   *durative (accomplishment)*
       'Susi sawed/was sawing off a branch.'

    b. Susi hat gearbeitet.   *durative (activity)*
       'Susi worked/was working.'

    c. Susi ist müde gewesen.   *durative (state)*
       'Susi was tired.'

    d. Susi ist gestern angekommen.   *nondurative (achievement)*
       'Susi arrived yesterday.'

    e. Susi hat (einmal) geniest.   *nondurative (semelfactive)*
       'Susi sneezed (once).'

Moreover, it is easy to find examples where each tense conveys the opposite viewpoint aspect. Thus, in (27), the italicized Preterite is used in a context inviting a perfective viewpoint, and in (28), the italicized Perfect is used in a context inviting an imperfective viewpoint:

(27) perfective Preterite

    a. Als   er *zurückkehrte*, fand   er ein Telegramm vor, das   ihm
       when he returned   found he a   telegram   PART that him
       eine   unangenehme   Überraschung bereitete.
       a   unpleasant   surprise   gave/caused
       'When he *returned* home, he found a telegram which caused him an unpleasant surprise.' (Andersson 1972:63, repeated from section 1.1 above)

    b. Als   Hermine   den Zaubertrank zubereitete, *trat*   Harry *ein*.
       when Hermione the magic-potion prepared   stepped Harry in
       'When Hermione was preparing the magic potion, Harry *entered*.' (Musan 2002:7)

(28) imperfective Present Perfect

    a. Susi hat sich verletzt, als   sie Fussball *gespielt hat*.
       Susi has self hurt   when she soccer   played has
       'Susi injured herself when she *was playing* soccer.'

b. Hans *hat* im Garten *gearbeitet* und das Telefon nicht gehört.

Hans has in.the yard worked and the telephone not heard

'Hans *was working* in the yard and didn't hear the phone.'
(Musan 2002:93)

These examples show that even in Standard German, both tenses can express either imperfective or perfective viewpoint. This suggests that both the Preterite and the Present Perfect are unspecified for viewpoint aspect, at least as far as the imperfective-perfective contrast is concerned (e.g., Musan 2002). Of course, the Present Perfect by its very nature does express *perfect* meaning. In many accounts, perfect meaning forms a poststate or posttime of the time of the situation, and it is this time which is then used in further temporal ordering through viewpoint aspect or tense (e.g., Parsons 1990, Klein 1994, Stowell 1996, Musan 2002). For example, a "perfective perfect" would locate a poststate/posttime (call it TPost) of the situation, rather than TSit, within TT. An "imperfective perfect" would locate TT within TPost (see Musan 2002 for such an account of the German Perfect). Thus, on many influential accounts, the presence of a perfect is compatible with both imperfective and perfective viewpoints, and the perfect is not a true viewpoint aspect (see also Comrie 1976 and Smith 1991 on the latter point).[14] In any case, imperfective and perfective perfects must be possible in principle because English has perfect progressive (i.e., imperfective) forms along with perfect "simple" (i.e., perfective) forms:

(29) a. Susi *has been writing* a letter.

b. Susi *has written* a letter.

In sum, although the Present Perfect and the Preterite are not synonymous, and certainly not freely interchangeable in Standard German, there is no conclusive evidence that the difference between these two tenses is one of perfective vs. imperfective viewpoint aspect.[15] It is more likely that both tenses are unspecified for viewpoint aspect, since both are compatible with perfective as well as with imperfective interpretations, and with all situation types.

I now turn to a discussion of South German, whose use of the Perfect and the Preterite, in my view, is also representative of much of colloquial German. We will see that in South German, there is only one past tense, which is unspecified for viewpoint aspect.

South German: only one past tense. In South German, a secondary aspectual meaning of a past tense is unlikely because the Perfect has completely supplanted the Preterite. This phenomenon, called "Präteritumsschwund" ('preterite disappearance'), has been noted by many linguists (e.g., Dal 1966, Paul 1959, Vater 1997:3). I cite Paul as an illustration:

> Nachdem das umschriebene Perfekt sich ein bestimmtes eigenartiges Gebiet erobert und das einfache Präteritum daraus beinahe verdrängt hatte, ist die Entwicklung noch weitergegangen. In der Volkssprache ist es auch zur Verwendung für die Erzählung gelangt, wohl in ganz Deutschland, aber im ausgedehntesten Maße im Oberdeutschen. Hier ist es geradezu zur Alleinherrschaft gelangt . . . (Paul 1959:155)

> After the periphrastic Perfect had conquered for itself a certain characteristic territory, and had almost driven the simple Preterite out of there, the development went still further. In the vernacular it also gained use for narration, probably in all of Germany, but most extensively in Upper [= South] German. Here it has virtually attained a monopoly . . . [translation mine]

Thus, in South German, there is no Preterite tense.[16] As a consequence, the subtle differences between Perfect and Preterite cannot be exploited for viewpoint aspectual contrasts. To illustrate this, I review some circumstances under which a contrast between Perfect and Preterite exists in Standard German. We will see that no such contrasts exist in South German.

As mentioned above, in Standard German the Preterite but not the Perfect must be used to indicate simultaneity of two past situations in embedded clauses (example (23) above). Crucially, in South German, either the Perfect or the Present is used here (the Preterite may only occur with *sein* 'be,' as in (28b)). I illustrate with my dialect[17] (spelling as if Standard German):

(28) simultaneous past situations—South German

    a. Der Hans hat gewusst, dass es *regnet/geregnet hat* (*regnete).

       the Hans has known that it rain-PRES/rained has (*rain-PRET)

       'Hans knew that it was raining.'

> b. Der Hans ist früh aufgewacht. Heute *war* sein Geburtstag/*ist*
> the Hans is early up-woken today be-PRET his birthday/is
> sein Geb. *gewesen.*
> his birthday been
> 'Hans woke up early. Today was his birthday.'

Thus, the Preterite is not available in South German to express an imperfective viewpoint.[18]

Second, as also mentioned above (example (24)), in Standard German only the Perfect but not the Preterite can be used to refer to a completed future event. Here the Perfect also has to be used in South German, but this is irrelevant to my claim because the Preterite is not a possibility in the first place. Thus, in South German there is not even a possible contrast in this context.

Finally, Ehrich (1992) cites some Standard German examples from a past descriptive text in which replacing the Preterite with the Perfect or vice versa leads to a decline in acceptability or to a shift in meaning. However, in South German, the Perfect would be used throughout in such a text. This contrast is illustrated in (29) and (30). In the instance where use of the Perfect instead of the Preterite would lead to a shift (indicated by—>) from perfective past to perfect ('present relevance') meaning in Standard German, (29), the Perfect must be used in South German, (30), and crucially it does here have the perfective past meaning of the Standard German Preterite.

(29) Standard German   (Ehrich 1992:91)

> Am 30. September *übernahm* das Ehepaar Klören das Hotel
> at.the 30th Sept.   over-take-PRET the married.couple K. the hotel
> (—> *hat . . . übernommen*). Sie *brachten* das Gebäude auf den
> (—> has . . . over-taken)   they bring-PRET the building on the
> neuesten Stand (—> *haben . . . gebracht*) und *gaben* ihm eine
> newest stand (—> have . . . brought)   and give-PRET it a
> elegante Note (—> *haben . . . gegeben*).
> elegant note (—> have . . . given)
> 'On September 30, the Klörens took over the hotel. They brought it up to the state of the art, and gave it an elegant note.'

(30) South German (spelling as if Standard German)

Am 30. September *hat* das Ehepaar Klören das Hotel *übernommen*
At 30th September has the married.couple K. the hotel over-taken

(*übernahm). Sie *haben* das Gebäude auf den neuesten Stand
(*over-take-PRET) they have the building on the newest stand

gebracht und *haben* ihm eine elegante Note gegeben (*gaben)
brought (*bring-PRET) and have him an elegant note given (*give-PRET)

'On September 30, the Klörens took over the hotel. They brought it up to the state of the art, and gave it an elegant note.'

A comparison with Standard German thus supports the claim that South German has only one past tense, the Perfect, which also covers the functions of the Standard German Preterite.[19] Moreover, the South German Perfect, just like the Standard German Perfect, can convey imperfective as well as perfective viewpoints, as I will briefly show now.

Example (31) shows that it is pragmatic factors which are responsible for a perfective vs. imperfective interpretation. In this example, the viewpoint of the first clause depends on the following clause (spelling as if Standard German).

(31) South German Perfect (based on Musan's (2002:93) Standard German examples)

a. Der Hans *hat* im Garten *geschafft* und ist jetzt müde.
the Hans has in-the yard worked and is now tired
'Hans *(has) worked* in the yard and is tired now.' PERFECTIVE

b. Der Hans *hat* im Garten *geschafft* und (hat) das Telefon
the Hans has in-the yard worked and (has) the telephone
nicht gehört.
not heard
'Hans *was working* in the yard and didn't hear the phone.' IMPERF.

The next examples illustrate further that the South German Perfect is completely acceptable in contexts inviting an imperfective interpretation. In the first context, the subordinating conjunction *während* 'while' forces an imperfective (and simultaneous) interpretation. (32) contains atelic predicates, which are amenable to an imperfective interpretation anyway; (33) shows that an imperfective interpretation is even possible with telic predicates (accomplishments) (spelling as if Standard German).

(32) a. Während die Susi *gejoggt hat*, hat es angefangen zu regnen.
 while the Susi jogged has, has it started to rain
 'While Susi *was jogging*, it started to rain.'

 b. Wir sind gekommen, während die Susi *geschlafen hat*.
 we are come while the Susi slept has
 'We came while Susi was sleeping.'

(33) a. Während die Susi das Beet *umgegraben hat*, hat es angefangen
 while the Susi the garden-bed PART-dug has, has it started
 zu regnen.
 to rain
 'While Susi was digging the garden bed, it started raining.'

 b. Wir sind gekommen, während die Susi einen Kuchen *gebacken hat*.
 we are come while the Susi a cake baked has
 'We came while Susi was baking a cake.'

Recall also that atelic predicates receive a default imperfective interpretation. This imperfective interpretation is conveyed without any problems by the Perfect.

(34) Es ist Sonntag gewesen. Die Sonne *hat gescheint*, die Vögel *haben*
 it is Sunday been the sun has shined the birds have
 gesungen, und Susi *ist spazieren gegangen*.
 sung and Susi is walking gone
 'It was Sunday. The sun was shining, the birds were singing, and Susi was going for a walk.'

The examples presented in this subsection show clearly that the Perfect in South German may convey not only perfective, but also imperfective viewpoint. Therefore, it cannot be associated with a secondary viewpoint aspectual meaning, and does not constitute a grammatization of viewpoint aspect in South German.

1.4. Summary

In section 1 I have shown that German does not possess a grammatical category marking viewpoint aspect: German has neither an obligatory grammatical category dedicated to viewpoint aspectual meaning (such as the Dëne Imperfective/Perfective category, or the English Progressive), nor other grammatical categories, such as tense, with consistent secondary uses as viewpoint markers. In particular, both the Preterite and the Present, which have sometimes been analyzed as having a secondary imperfective meaning, can also freely express perfective meanings. Moreover, in South German (and probably colloquial German in general), where the Perfect is the only past and the Present the only nonpast tense[20], there are no competing forms for each tense meaning. Thus, in this dialect the differences between two competing tenses cannot be exploited to convey viewpoint aspectual nuances. I concluded with authors such as Musan (2002) that in German, and especially in South German, viewpoint is not grammatized either directly or indirectly via tense markers.[21]

In the second part of this chapter, I will demonstrate the consequences of the lack of viewpoint aspect in German. There are two consequences: first, viewpoint aspectual meanings can only be expressed indirectly at other grammatical levels; as we saw earlier, and will review below, in German telic predicates are used to convey perfective meaning. Second, I predict that because viewpoint aspect is the typical locus of grammatizing durativity, there is no category dedicated to the expression of durativity in the grammatical system of German. Lacking grammatical viewpoint aspect, German has no grammatical operation which affects durativity in a consistent manner—durativity is not grammatized.

2. DURATIVITY IS NOT GRAMMATIZED

Let us review our findings to this point. German does not have at its disposal a grammatical category of viewpoint aspect. We saw in Chapter Two on Dëne that an essential function of viewpoint aspect is to organize the sequencing of events in a discourse. If viewpoint aspect is not available in a language, some other grammatical device must be used in its place for this purpose.

Theoretically, there are several possibilities. A language could use some other type of inflection such as tense to convey event sequencing.

For example, French has two (or even three, if one includes the formal/literary register) tenses available for past tense reference: the Imparfait and the Passé Composé (and the Passé Simple). The Imparfait is an imperfective viewpoint, to indicate simultaneous events. The Passé Composé and the Passé Simple are perfective viewpoints, indicating sequential events (see Kamp and Rohrer 1983). We saw in section 1.3 above that this option is not available in German.

This leaves German with the option of using a situation type notion to indicate event sequencing. Again, there are two possibilities (ignoring stativity), durativity or telicity. Durativity could be associated with an imperfective viewpoint, i.e., to indicate simultaneous events. Or telicity could be associated with a perfective viewpoint, to indicate sequential events.

In German, telicity is used, indicating sequential events. (This was discussed in Chapter Two, section 3.1, and I will briefly review these facts in section 2.1 below.) And, as we saw in Chapter Four, telicity is pervasive and highly grammatized in German. I propose that these two facts are related. A grammatical marking of a (semantic) notion and its extensive use in the language go hand in hand. Moreover, a language will make use of grammatized notions to also convey related nongrammatized but universally required linguistic functions.

In the rest of this chapter, I will pursue the question of where durativity fits into the emerging picture of German. I will show that durativity is not grammatized in German, and that durativity of a predicate is not used to convey viewpoint-type meaning. Let us begin by reviewing the perfective viewpoint-type function of telicity in German.

2.1. *Telicity Conveys Viewpoint-Type Meaning*

In section 3.1 of Chapter Two I pointed out that, in general, situation type and viewpoint aspect have overlapping functions in terms of event sequencing in discourse (see Comrie 1976, Hopper 1982, Kamp and Rohrer 1983, Partee 1984, Dahl 1985, ter Meulen 1995). In German, telic predicates are usually interpreted as denoting perfective events. This is what Bohnemeyer and Swift (2004) call the "default perfective aspect" of telic predicates. Part of the default perfective meaning of telic predicates is that they indicate sequential (rather than simultaneous) events in discourse. I repeat here the example given earlier. The mini-discourse in (35a) contains the telic predicate *einen morschen Ast absägen* 'saw off a dead branch'; in contrast, example (35b) contains the atelic predicate *an einem morschen Ast sägen* 'sawing at a dead branch.'

(35) a. Susi *wollte*   den alten Apfelbaum beschneiden. Sie *sägte*   einen morschen
Susi *wanted* the old apple-tree prune   she *sawed* a   dead
   ATELIC   TELIC

Ast   *ab*. Es *fing an* zu regnen.
branch *off* it *started* to rain
             TELIC/inceptive

'Susi wanted to prune the old apple tree. She sawed off a dead branch. It started raining.' (<u>implied</u>: It started raining <u>after</u> Susi had sawed off the dead branch.)

b. Susi *wollte*   den alten Apfelbaum beschneiden. Sie *sägte*   eifrig (an einem
Susi *wanted* the old apple-tree prune   she *sawed* eagerly (at a
   ATELIC   ATELIC

morschen Ast).   Es *fing an* zu regnen.
dead   branch it *started* to rain
                     TELIC/inceptive

'Susi wanted to prune the old apple tree. She was sawing eagerly (at a dead branch). It started raining.' (<u>implied</u>: It started raining <u>while</u> Susi was sawing off the dead branch.)

In (35a), the event denoted by the last sentence is interpreted as following the telic *absägen* event, in (35b) it is interpreted as simultaneous with the atelic *sägen* event. Notice that the tense, Preterite[22], and the context are the same in both examples, thus the different viewpoints cannot be due to differences in verbal inflection, or in order of narration—they are due to differences in telicity, a situation type notion.

As also pointed out in Chapter Two, and in the discussion in section 1.1 of this chapter, perfectivity and telicity are not identical. A situation, particularly a telic situation, presented in perfective viewpoint is truly closed, and a simultaneous interpretation in narrative is quite unexpected, if not impossible. To telic situations without a morphological viewpoint marker (as in German), however, the option of a simultaneous/imperfective interpretation is easily available. Again, I repeat an earlier example (ex. (57) from Chapter Two) to illustrate: (36) shows an accomplishment situation in two contexts which force a simultaneous interpretation. The sentences are not ungrammatical or semantically odd. (See also examples (2b) and (4) in section 1.1 above.)

(36) a. Susi *sägte*   einen morschen Ast   *ab*, als   es anfing zu regnen.
       Susi *sawed* a   dead   branch *off* when it started to rain
                                                    TELIC

   'Susi was sawing off a dead branch when it started raining.'

   b. Während Susi einen morschen Ast   *absägte*, fing es an   zu regnen.
      while   Susi a   dead   branch *off-sawed* start₁ it start₂ to rain
                                                      TELIC

   'While Susi was sawing off a dead branch, it started raining.'

One could say, following Bohnemeyer and Swift (2004), that here a telic situation is presented in imperfective viewpoint rather than in the default perfective viewpoint. This is possible because, as shown above, German has no overt imperfective-perfective distinction.

In conclusion, perfectivity and telicity share the important properties of bounding an event, and of specifying sequentiality in discourse. German, which does not have an overt perfective (or imperfective) viewpoint, uses telic predicates to convey perfective-type meaning.

Now, unlike telicity, durativity is not used in German to convey viewpoint-type meaning. I claim that this is intimately related to the fact that durativity is not grammatized in German. In the next sections, I present evidence for the latter claim. We will first see that the durativity of German predicates can change without accompanying morphosyntactic change. Then I will show that those morphosyntactic changes which do accompany a situation type change do not mark durativity, but rather telicity. Finally, a comparison with Dëne reveals that the locus of grammatizing durativity in that language, namely overtly marked imperfective viewpoint, is missing from German.

2.2. Durativity Not Overtly Marked in German

Many German predicates are unspecified for durativity, and it depends on the context whether a given predicate is interpreted as durative or nondurative. Crucially, no morphosyntactic change correlates with a change from nondurative to durative interpretation or vice versa. The first example of this was already seen in section 3.2 of Chapter Four, where we examined semelfactive predicates. Achievements pattern identically. Let us begin by reviewing semelfactives.

2.2.1. Semelfactive vs. Activity (Single vs. Iterative Reading)

All languages contain predicates which denote a single occurrence of a punctual, atelic situation. German is no exception, e.g., *klopfen* 'knock,' *husten* 'cough,' *schlagen* 'strike.' However, unlike many languages including Dëne, the difference between a truly semelfactive, punctual interpretation (single occurrence), and an iterative durative interpretation is not marked overtly, but determined by context in German. This contrast is illustrated in (37) and (38).

(37) a. Ich habe ihn (einmal) geschlagen.
 'I hit him (once).'

b. Ich habe ihn (mehrmals/fünf Minuten lang) geschlagen.
 'I hit him (several times/for five minutes).'

(38) a. *ná*nighikár.
 ná#ne–i–ghe–i–Ø–kár
 th#th-th(sem.?)-CM-1s-cl-slap
 'I slapped him/it once.'

b. *hu*ghikár sį.
 h–*u*–ghe–i–Ø–kár sį
 ep-th(ser.?)-CM-1s-cl-slap assert
 'I slapped it repeatedly, I had gone through the process of slapping.'

In Dëne, verbal prefixes overtly mark the single-event vs. repeated-event interpretation. In German, the verb form stays the same, and only other elements in the context, e.g., adverbials, specify the interpretation. Likewise, I showed in section 3.2 of Chapter Four that telic particles can derive either an achievement (nondurative) or an accomplishment (durative) from a semelfactive base verb. In addition, I established in Chapter Four that particles affect telicity but not durativity. This is further evidence that the base verb is morphosyntactically unspecified for durativity.

(39) husten 'cough' (semelfactive)

a. Sie hat (#*in fünf Minuten*) gehustet. *atelic*
 'She coughed (#*in five minutes*).'

b. Sie hat *fünf Minuten lang* gehustet. => iterative *nondurative*
 'She coughed *for five minutes* (repeatedly).'

(40) **aus**husten 'cough out/up' (achievement or accomplishment)

    a. Sie hat (*in fünf Minuten*) den Staub/den Krümel ausgehustet.   *telic*
       'She coughed out/up   the dust/the   crumbs (*in five minutes*).'

    b. ??'Sie *hörte auf*, den Krümel auszuhusten.'   *nondurative?*
       ??'She *stopped* coughing out/up the crumb.'

    c. Sie *hörte auf*, den Staub auszuhusten.   *durative?*
       'She *stopped* coughing out/up the dust.'

Interestingly, the difference in durativity between semelfactives and activities or iterative semelfactives is usually not reflected in predicate decomposition. Both situation types are represented with the predicate *DO* (e.g., Rapp 1997a,b) or *ACT* (e.g., Rappaport Hovav and Levin 1998). For example, both semelfactive *and* iterative *husten* have the same lexical semantic structure *DO (x)* (or *ACT (x)*, depending on the author). The fact that these predicate decomposition structures—which are assumed to represent only those elements of a verb's meaning which are visible to the morphosyntax, i.e., which are grammatically relevant—do not represent the difference between semelfactive and iterative predicates implies that durativity is not grammatically relevant in atelic events.

In sum, we have empirical evidence that durativity is not overtly marked in atelic predicates in German. And lexical semantic theories often lack a formal distinction between durative and nondurative (atelic) predicates, providing general theoretical support that durativity is not part of the grammatically visible meaning of atelic verbs.

2.2.2. Achievement vs. Accomplishment

If we briefly reconsider example (40), we will see that here the difference between the (nondurative) achievement and the (durative) accomplishment interpretation is not marked overtly, either by the particle or by other elements. The context, in this case the meaning of the object, together with world knowledge determines durativity. Our knowledge of the world tells us that it usually (but not necessarily) takes just one cough to get rid of a single crumb, while it may take several coughs to get rid of a (small) amount of dust. Note that here we are not dealing with an object characteristic which is marked in the morphosyntax—both objects are quantized (definite singular).

It is the case with many telic verbs that nongrammatized object characteristics determine durativity. Here are just a few examples:

(41) abschlagen 'sever by striking' (achievement or accomplishment)

    a. Sie hat (*10 Minuten lang*) den Putz von der Wand abgeschlagen.   *durative*

       'She knocked/struck the plaster off the wall (*for 10 minutes*).'

    b. Sie *hat aufgehört*, den Putz von der Wand abzuschlagen.   *durative*

       'She *stopped* knocking/striking the plaster off the wall.'

    c. #Sie hat (*10 Minuten lang*) dem Angeklagten den Kopf abgeschlagen.   *nondurative*

       ('She knocked the head off the accused (*for 10 minutes*).')

    d. #Sie hat *aufgehört*, dem Angeklagten den Kopf abzuschlagen.   *nondurative*

       ('She *stopped* knocking the head off the accused.')

(42) fallen 'fall' (achievement or accomplishment)

    a. # Der Stein fiel *langsam* zur Erde.   *nondurative*

       ('The rock fell *slowly* to the ground.')

    b. Die Schneeflocke fiel *langsam* zur Erde.   *durative*

       'The snowflake fell *slowly* to the ground.'

    c. Die Temperatur fiel *langsam* auf Null Grad.   *durative*

       'The temperature *slowly* fell to zero degrees.'

    d. # Die alte Frau *hörte auf* zu fallen.   *nondurative*
       (ok only on iterative reading)

       ('The old woman *stopped* falling.')

    e. Die Temperatur *hörte auf* zu fallen. (no iterative reading)   *durative*

       'The temperature *stopped* falling.'

In (41), world knowledge tells us that it takes only a second to cut off someone's head, while it may take a while to get the plaster off the wall. In (42), *fallen* shows more and less durative uses[23] with and without an overt goal. Again, it is world knowledge that tells us that a snowflake and especially something like temperature may take longer to reach a certain point by falling.

This same claim, namely that durativity is determined by world knowledge and hence extralinguistic, has also been made by Verkuyl (1989, 1993) and Tenny (1994) for English.

In the next section, we will see an even more surprising phenomenon: a durative base verb can turn either into an accomplishment or an *achievement* particle verb. The latter pattern, i.e., the removal of durativity, is a completely unexpected modification of meaning.

2.3. Durativity Not Systematic in Particle Verb Formation

In Chapter Four, I showed that certain particles have a telicizing function, deriving telic from atelic predicates. If German has particles which affect the situation type notion of telicity, we might reasonably expect to find other particles which affect another situation type notion, such as durativity. However, particles do not affect durativity in any systematic way. While the durativity of the base verb and of the particle verb are often the same, there are also a number of cases in which achievements are derived from activities. Assuming that particles contribute a result state, thus telicity, the derivation of achievements from activities is completely unpredicted because in addition to adding a meaning component, particle verb formation here also *removes* a component of meaning (namely, durativity) from the verb.[24] The following are just a few examples.

(43) rennen 'run' (activity) —> **um**rennen 'knock over running' (achievement)

    a. #Sie ist *in einer Stunde* gerannt.   *atelic*
    (# 'She ran *in an hour*.')

    b. Sie *hörte auf* zu rennen.   *durative*
    'She *stopped* running.'

    c. Sie hat mich *in einer Sekunde* umgerannt.   *telic*
    'She knocked me over running *in one second*.'

    d. #Sie *hörte auf,* mich umzurennen.   *nondurative*
    (# 'She *stopped* knocking me over running.')

(44) blühen 'bloom' (activity) —> **aus**blühen 'finish blooming' (achievement)

    a. #Die Rosen haben *in einer Stunde* geblüht.   *atelic*
    (# 'The roses bloomed *in an hour*.')

b. Die Rosen *waren am* Blühen, als . . .   *durative*
   'The roses *were in the process of* blooming when . . .'

c. Die Rosen hatten *in einer Stunde* ausgeblüht.   *telic*
   'The roses had finished blooming *in one hour*.'

d. #Die Rosen *waren am* Ausblühen, als . . .   *nondurative*
   (# 'The roses *were* finish*ing* blooming when . . .')

(45) <u>fahren</u> 'drive, move, go, ride' (activity) —> **ab**<u>fahren</u> 'depart' (achievement)

a. #Der Zug ist *in einer Stunde* gefahren.   *atelic*
   (#'The train went/moved *in an hour*.')

b. Der Zug *hörte auf,* zu fahren.   *durative*
   'The train *stopped* going/moving.'

c. Der Zug ist *in einer Minute* abgefahren.   *telic*
   'The train departed *in a minute*.'

d. #Der Zug *hörte auf* abzufahren.   *nondurative*
   ('The train *stopped* departing.')

To illustrate that the removal of durativity is completely unpredicted, let us consider what a derivation as in examples (43)-(45) might look like in predicate decomposition theories. The manner-of-motion base verb would have a structure as in (46), the particle verb would be represented as in (47):

(46) <u>manner of motion base verb:</u> *fahren*

a. DO (x) or DO (x,y)   (Rapp 1997a)

b. [x ACT$_{<MANNER>}$]   (RH&L 1998)

(47) <u>causative directed motion particle verb:</u> *abfahren*

a. CAUSE (DO (x), GO (LOC (y,a), LOC (y,b)))   (Rapp 1997a)

b. [[x ACT$_{<MANNER>}$] CAUSE [BECOME [y <*PLACE/STATE*>]]]
   (RH&L 1998)

To paraphrase the structures in (47), the particle indicates the result location or state (i.e., not at the station); the manner of motion is in a causative relation to this result location or state. Neither the causative predicate nor the result predicate may express durativity. In fact, in Rappaport Hovav and Levin (1998) causativity seems to be the hallmark of accomplishments, thus we would expect *abfahren* etc. to be durative. And for Rapp (1997a,b) the predicates GO and DEV (from 'develop') have durative force, while BECOME is reserved for the punctual changes of state typical of achievements. But notice that in these examples, only the durative predicates appear in Rapp's notation. Neither Rappaport Hovav and Levin (1998) nor Rapp (1997a,b) have a way of representing the removal of durativity witnessed in the German examples.

Summing up, the derivation of achievements from activities through telicizing particles is unpredicted. This derivation only makes sense if durativity is not visible/accessible to the morphosyntax in German, and thus if durativity is not included in the lexical semantic structure of either simple or particle verbs in German.

Another explanation one might propose is that perhaps atelic verbs are subcategorized into two types, those which become achievements and those which become accomplishments, and that these two subcategories would not correspond to the semelfactive-activity distinction. But this idea is not supported by the facts. It turns out that the same verb can form either an achievement or an accomplishment, depending on which particle is used. Some instances of this can be found in the data given above, but I will discuss some more examples here. Consider *fahren*. In (45) we saw that this is an activity which combines with *ab* to become an achievement. (48) shows that *fahren* in combination with the particle *aus* is an accomplishment. The sentences (49) demonstrate the same variability with the verb 'fall.'[25]

(48) ausfahren 'move out (vehicle)': accomplishment

    a. Der Zug ist *in einer Minute* (aus dem Bahnhof) ausgefahren.   *telic*
       'The train moved out (of the station) *in one minute.*'

    b. Der Zug *war dabei* (aus dem Bahnhof) auszufahren, als . . .   *durative*
       'The train *was in the process of* moving out (of the station) when . . .'

(49) fallen 'fall': achievement
    abfallen 'fall off': achievement
    umfallen 'fall over': accomplishment

    a. Das Ei ist *in zwei Sekunden* (vom Nest) auf den Boden gefallen.   *telic*
       'The egg fell (from the nest) to the ground *in two seconds.*'

b. ??Das Ei *war dabei*, auf den Boden zu fallen, als . . .   *nondurative*
('The egg *was in the process of* falling to the ground when . . .')

c. Der Griff ist *in einer Minute* abgefallen.   *telic*
'The handle fell off *in a minute*.'

d. Der Griff *war dabei* abzufallen, als . . .   *nondurative*
(i) #'The handle *was in the process of* falling off when . . .'
(ii) 'The handle was *about to (would soon)* fall off when . . .'

e. Der Kran ist *in einer Minute* umgefallen.   *telic*
'The crane fell over *in a minute*.'

f. Der Kran *war dabei* umzufallen/*war am* Umfallen, als . . .   *durative*
(i) 'The crane *was in the process of* falling over when . . .'
(ii) ?'The crane *was about to* fall over when . . .'

Although at first glance it seems that the durativity test is positive in (49d), this is not really the case. If the *dabei sein* construction combines with *abfallen*, it does not mean 'be in the process of' but 'be about to,' which says nothing about the presence or absence of process.

These examples illustrate that the meaning of the base verb does not predetermine which kinds of derivations are possible. We therefore cannot use the base verb meaning to try to explain the unpredicted patterns away. A more promising way out of the dilemma may seem to subcategorize the particles into achievement- versus accomplishment-deriving ones. For example, one may stipulate that certain particles do not just add an endpoint to the event denoted by the verb, but that they also remove the process from the verb's meaning.

Unfortunately, this explanation is not available either, as the same particle is able to derive both kinds of telic verbs. For example, *um* forms accomplishments, e.g. *umgraben* 'turn over soil' and *umfallen* 'fall over' in (49), as well as achievements, *umrennen* 'knock over running,' (43), and *umfahren* 'knock over driving.' Similarly, *ab* and *aus* form both accomplishments, e.g., *ausfahren* 'move out (vehicle)' in (48) and *absägen* 'saw off,' and achievements, *ausblühen* 'finish blooming,' (44), and *abfahren* 'depart,' (45). It thus appears that particle verb formation is completely regular with respect to telicity (certain particles always derive telic verbs)[26] but irregular and unpredictable in terms of durativity.

In summary, then, we have seen in this section that particle verb formation does not obey the predictions of a situation type classification. The predicted pattern of semelfactives forming achievements seems no more frequent than the unpredicted pattern of forming accomplishments, and while the particles derive accomplishments (telic and durative) from activities (atelic and durative), they also, and unexpectedly, derive—nondurative—achievements from activities. From these facts I conclude that the durativity of the situation type classification is simply irrelevant to particle verb formation. More generally, I claim that particle verb formation provides evidence that, in terms of temporal-aspectual notions, German represents telicity but not durativity in the level of representation of verb meaning to which the morphosyntax has access. In other words, durativity is not grammatized in German.

2.4. *Discussion*

In section 2, I showed that durativity is not overtly marked in German. This can be seen from two facts. First, German verbs alternate between a durative and nondurative meaning without accompanying morphosyntactic change. German speakers seem to determine durativity based on their world knowledge. Second, a morphosyntactic process which does affect situation type—particle verb formation—only affects telicity systematically. Both of these fact indicate that the semantic notion of durativity is not grammatized in German.

We can now relate this finding on durativity with the finding on viewpoint aspect in section 1 of this chapter. Both viewpoint aspect and durativity are absent from the grammatical system of German. In contrast, both viewpoint aspect and durativity are strongly present in the grammatical system of Dëne. I propose that this is no coincidence. According to my hypothesis, (imperfective) viewpoint aspect is the prime locus of grammatizing durativity in a language, and if there is no grammatical viewpoint aspect, there is no grammatically relevant durativity either. In this sense, it is misleading to talk about durativity as a situation type notion. Durativity is rather a viewpoint notion. This will be elaborated in the next chapter.

Chapter Six
The Grammatization of Aspectual Notions

1. INTRODUCTION

In this chapter I will tie together the results from Chapters Two through Five and discuss their implications for the organization of aspect in the grammar of natural language. In particular, I will give an explanation for the ways in which situation-type aspectual notions are grammatized and propose a theoretical explanation for the patterns discovered in the examination of German and Dëne.

The central concern of this dissertation is to understand better how temporal-aspectual characteristics of predicates are grammatized in natural language. This very general question was narrowed down to an examination of the temporal-aspectual notions of durativity and telicity, which led to the revised research question given in (1), where "grammatized" is defined as in (2).

(1) *Revised Research Question*
How are telicity and durativity grammatized in natural language?

(2) *Grammatization*
A semantic notion/feature evident in a productive morphosyntactic contrast is *grammatized*.[1]

The empirical study of question (1) in German and Dëne yielded the following results: telicity is evident in productive morphosyntax, thus grammatized, in German but not in Dëne. Durativity is evident in productive morphosyntax, thus grammatized, in Dëne but not in German. But German and Dëne differ not only in which notion is grammatized, they also differ in the locus of grammatization, i.e., in the type of morphosyntax expressing the respective notion. The locus of grammatization of telicity in German is the VP domain. The locus of grammatization of durativity in Dëne is the IP domain. (3) summarizes the relevant morphosyntactic phenomena of each domain:

(3) *Summary of empirical results*

Durativity: IP domain (Dëne)
• obligatory and productive inflection for perfective or imperfective viewpoint
• imperfective has durative meaning
• imperfective incompatible with nondurative predicates
• (perfective marker *ghe-* predominantly with durative/cumulative verbs)
• no interaction with direct internal argument or its quantization
• viewpoint meaning fully compositional
Telicity: VP domain (German)
• particle verb formation creates telic predicates (so do goal PPs and result phrases)
• quantized direct internal argument required for telic interpretation
• quantized reference marked overtly on DPs
• telicity determines interpretation of attributive perfect participle
• special, noncompositional meanings may occur

Moreover, the examination of German and Dëne also showed that IP domain phenomena do not grammatize telicity, and that VP domain phenomena do not grammatize durativity. A relevant summary is provided in (4).

(4) *Summary of empirical results, continued*

IP domain: not telicity (Dëne)
• viewpoint marker (=CM) patterns do not correlate with telicity
• both viewpoints compatible with telic and atelic predicates
• perfective has completive, but not telic, meaning
VP domain: not durativity (German)
• particle verb formation does not affect durativity systematically
• durativity independent of (quantization of) internal argument
• durativity plays no role in interpretation of attributive participle

The Grammatization of Aspectual Notions

I propose that the empirical findings in these two very distinct languages indicate a cross-linguistic generalization. This generalization is my answer to the revised research question:

(5) *Aspect Grammatization Hypothesis* (to be revised)

> If *durativity* is grammatized, it is grammatized in the IP domain.
>
> If *telicity* is grammatized, it is grammatized in the VP domain.

(5) makes the strong and interesting claim that the patterns found in German and Dëne are no coincidence. It implies that telicity and durativity are very different notions, and that the two are necessarily grammatized in different morphosyntactic domains. (5) also immediately raises the question of a deeper motivation or explanation for this generalization. These issues will be addressed in section 2.

2. THE DIFFERENT NATURES OF TELICITY AND DURATIVITY

In this section I take a closer look at the nature of durativity and telicity, and motivate their different loci of grammatization from their different natures.

Durativity is in essence a temporal notion. It says something about the amount of time that a situation lasts (or that we conceptualize a situation to last). Telicity, on the other hand, is not temporal at all. Whether a situation is telic or not has nothing to do with how much time it takes. Telicity has something to do with whether there is a relevant change or effect (it is no coincidence that in predicate decomposition theories, telicity is expressed as a change of state, by *BECOME* or a similar predicate). Thus, telicity is in essence what Talmy (1976, 1988, 2000) and Croft (1998) call a "force-dynamic" notion, a notion that has to do with "the transmission of force relationships between participants in events" (Croft 1998:31).

For these reasons, it is not surprising that the grammatization patterns of telicity and durativity (as expressed in (5)) are very different. In fact, I propose to derive their different grammatization patterns from their different natures. I will propose that the nature of durativity requires AspP (of the IP domain) as grammatization locus, and that the nature of telicity requires VP as grammatization locus. This assumes a certain clause structure, which I will introduce first.

2.1. Clause Structure

I assume a clause structure in which all internal arguments of the verb are merged inside the VP. Following Kratzer (1996), I further assume a projection *v*P immediately dominating VP, which introduces the external argument of the verb (i.e., the external or subject argument) and the predicate's event argument (but see below). Finally, I assume that above *v*P, there is a functional projection AspP for viewpoint aspect and above that a functional projection TP for tense (Stowell 1996, Giorgi and Pianesi 1998, Kratzer 1998, Demirdache and Uribe-Etxebarria 2000, Matthewson 2002, Musan 2002).[2] This gives us the following structure (which is not meant to reflect linear order):

(6)
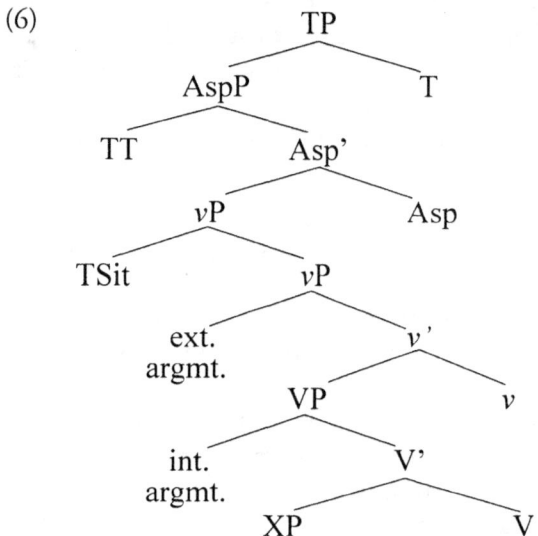

TP houses the function of tense, AspP the function of viewpoint aspect. Semantically, both tense and viewpoint aspect relate two times. One way of conceiving of the function of TP and AspP is that their heads are "dyadic spatiotemporal ordering predicates taking time-denoting phrases as arguments" (Demirdache and Uribe-Etxebarria 2000:162). In this way the syntax reflects directly what the semantics is doing: for example, semantically, viewpoint aspect relates the reference or topic time of a clause (TT) and the time of the situation (TSit) denoted by the *v*P. Syntactically, there is a corresponding element in Asp which takes TT and TSit (="EV-T" in Demirdache and Uribe-Etxebarria 2000) as its arguments.[3]

Demirdache and Uribe-Etxebarria assume, with Stowell (1996), that Kratzer's event argument *e* is time-denoting, and thus call it "EV-T" (=my TSit) rather than *e*.[4] Thus, on this view *v*P has a time argument (TSit, instead of *e*) and a nominal argument. VP has no time (or event) argument, only the standard thematic arguments.

Finally, as explained in Chapter One, I assume that the syntax manipulates only abstract roots and feature bundles, and that "lexical insertion" as well as interpretation happen post-syntactically (Halle and Marantz 1993, Marantz 1997). With this background in place, I can introduce my proposal.

2.2. Deriving the Loci of Grammatization

As just discussed, durativity is a temporal notion. Therefore, the most natural assumption is that those elements of the grammar which manipulate times grammatize this notion. The obvious candidates for this are TP and/or AspP, since they relate times (temporal arguments). AspP interacts with TSit, the time of the situation (and/or with *e*, see footnote 4); TP does not. Since durativity says something about the time of the situation, it must be grammatized in AspP rather than in TP.

As we also saw, telicity is a force-dynamic notion, not a temporal one. Thus, it is plausible to assume that it is grammatized in a domain or projection that is involved with argument structure: recall that I mean by force-dynamics "the transmission of force relationships between participants in events" (Croft 1998:31). What is crucial here is the phrase "between *participants* in events:" participants are usually expressed as arguments of a predicate. This means that a force-dynamic notion such as telicity affects argument structure.

Now, the VP is the projection which is crucially involved in force-dynamics/argument structure: it contains the internal argument, which is the argument on which change, or the effect of a situation, is "measured out" (Tenny 1987, 1994). Moreover, VP is distinguished from TP, AspP and *v*P in that it contains no temporal argument. Thus, VP is the most natural location for the grammatization of the force-dynamic notion of telicity.[5]

These considerations lead me to sharpen (5) as the hypothesis given in (7), and illustrated in (8). (7) makes the strong and interesting claim that AspP and VP are the *only* possible loci of grammatizing durativity and telicity, respectively. Again, this must be so because Asp is the only projection relating TSit and another time, and VP is the only projection where the direct internal argument is first merged.

(7) *Aspect Grammatization Hypothesis* (revised)

> If *durativity* is grammatized, it is grammatized in AspP.
>
> If *telicity* is grammatized, it is grammatized in VP.

(8)

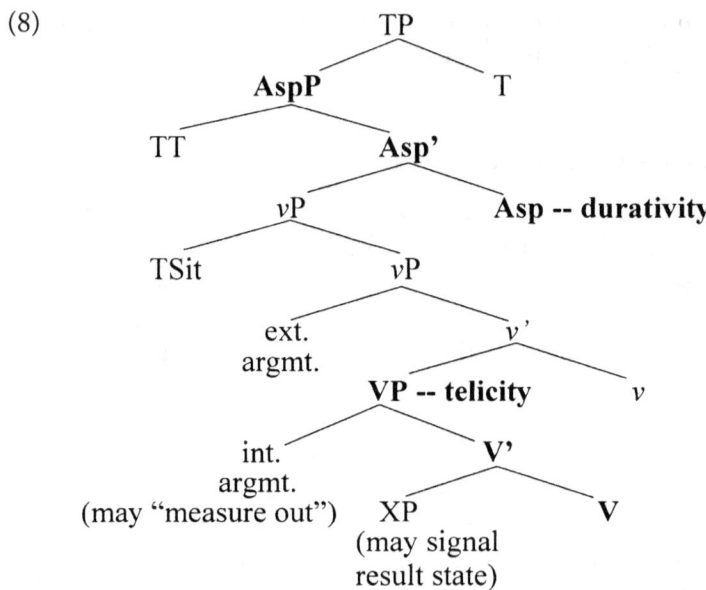

This proposal has a number of desired consequences. First, as already discussed, it derives the loci of grammatization of telicity and durativity: it is no coincidence that durativity is grammatized in Asp, because only Asp temporally orders TSit (or *e*). And only VP is a truly nontemporal projection, without temporal arguments. Instead, it contains the direct internal argument, which is critical to the force-dynamic nature of telicity.

Second, the proposal reflects an additional difference between durativity and telicity, namely that it is the Asp *head* which grammatizes durativity, but that it is the entire verb *phrase* which grammatizes telicity:

AspP has times as arguments; but these times are not expressed overtly. However, the Asp head may contain the overt morphosyntactic material necessary to express a grammatical contrast. Thus, a language grammatizes durativity only if there are contrasting Asp heads, i.e., if the language has different perfective and imperfective (or progressive, etc.) morphemes, typically realized as verb inflections. This is precisely the case in Dëne.

The VP is different because it has overt arguments and an overt head, all of which are able to express a grammatical, and more specifically, an argument structure, contrast. Such contrasts exist, for example, in German between telic particle verbs and atelic base verbs, or between quantized and nonquantized direct internal arguments.

Tying grammatization to an overt grammatical contrast is desirable for learnability reasons. It is only through overt morphosyntactic contrasts that a child can acquire a functional or semantic contrast housed in a certain projection. And indeed, this is just the flip side of grammatization. Examining the *grammatization* of durativity and telicity is another way of asking whether there are concrete morphosyntactic facts by which a child can determine whether her language grammatizes a given semantic notion.

The third desired consequence of my proposal is that it accounts for the characteristics of Dëne and German summarized in (3) and (4) above. In Dëne, durativity is grammatized through the imperfective viewpoint. My proposal ties the grammatization of durativity to viewpoint aspect, simply because durativity must be grammatized in Asp, and Asp heads the projection for viewpoint aspect. And the fact that durativity is grammatized in Asp explains the properties listed in (3) above, in particular, the fact that durativity does not interact with the direct internal argument or its quantization properties. This is so because Asp does not have overt (nominal) arguments.

Similarly, telicity is necessarily tied to VP simply because it does not express temporal but rather force-dynamic relations. Moreover, the fact that the grammatization of telicity is phrasal, as just discussed, explains the importance of Spec-VP and the sister of V in grammatizing telicity. Again, this is precisely what is found in German, as summarized in (3) and (4) above.

In sum, grammatizing durativity in AspP and telicity in VP is not only conceptually the most logical approach, taking into consideration the temporal nature of durativity and the force-dynamic nature of telicity. It also derives the characteristics given in (3) and (4) above, and correctly predicts that durativity is grammatized in a head but telicity in a phrase.

In the next two sections (section 3 and 4), I will discuss how my proposal given in (7) and (8) above can be implemented in a concrete way. This will further illustrate what I mean by "grammatization." I will then conclude the chapter by discussing implications and consequences of my proposal (section 5).

3. GRAMMATIZATION

I defined grammatization as the existence of a productive morphosyntactic contrast which manifests a semantic notion.[6] We have established that telicity is grammatized by contrasts in the VP, durativity by a contrast in Asp. But how precisely can this contrast be expressed? And how does the interface of the morphosyntax and the semantics work? In other words, what precisely is grammatization? I will sketch here one concrete way of implementing grammatization. The advantages and limitations of this implementation will give us further insight into grammatization, and into the nature of telicity and durativity.

Let me begin by considering what we would like the implementation to do. We would like it to derive the patterns found in Dëne and German, respectively. These languages differ not only in the projection that is involved (AspP vs. VP), but also in which elements of the respective projection are involved: the Asp head vs. the entire VP, i.e., the verb and its internal arguments. The contrast in Asp is affixal, the contrasts in the VP have to do with the presence or absence of argument XPs with certain meanings. Thus, the grammatization of telicity has to do with argument structure and linking, while the grammatization of durativity has to do with inflectional morphology.

One way to express a morphosyntactic contrast is through the presence vs. absence of a projection. This will not work for my proposal, however, because we can hardly say that VP is absent in languages without grammatized telicity. Telicity also cannot be tied to the presence of a sister of the verb or a Spec-VP: these elements also must have certain semantic characteristics in order to derive telicity. Finally, it is also unappealing to think that AspP might be absent in a language like German: the fact that different viewpoint interpretations, i.e., different orderings of TSit and TT are available, is straightforwardly accounted for if there is an AspP in the clause (compare Matthewson 2002 for a detailed argument for the existence of TP in a tenseless language).

Another way of expressing morphosyntactic contrast is through features. For example, grammatical person and number marking are expressed through phi-features on nominal constituents and the verb. A contrast exists if one head can bear at least two opposing features, or by the presence or absence of a feature. Since we need VP (and presumably also AspP) in both German and English, I assume that features are involved in the grammatization of telicity and durativity. Thus, I will formally express grammatization through a featural contrast in either Asp or V. Let's see how this works for AspP/durativity and VP/telicity.

3.1. [perf]/[impf] in AspP: Durativity

A contrast in inflectional morphology is usually expressed through features on the respective inflectional head. I will show here that the grammatization of durativity can be implemented as a featural contrast on the Asp head.

We know that Dëne has an overt contrast between imperfective and perfective viewpoint aspect: most verbs show the morphemes ("conjugation markers") *ghe-* or *the-* in the perfective, and Ø in the imperfective.[7] This overt contrast translates into the featural contrast [perf]/[impf] in Asp. Note that although only [perf] corresponds to overt—perfective—morphology, there still is a contrast, because the absence of the overt perfective morphology is interpreted as an imperfective form. This justifies associating the absence of perfective morphology with a feature [impf].

The features [perf] and [impf] then correspond to two different semantic definitions, perfective vs. imperfective, respectively. The perfective locates TSit within TT. This is compatible with any type of TSit. But crucially, the imperfective viewpoint specifies TT as being *included in TSit*. Formally, this is often expressed as proper inclusion, i.e., TT ⊂ TSit (e.g., Klein 1994, Musan 2002). Crucially, for a time TSit to be able to properly include another time (TT), TSit cannot consist of one time point only, but must be a true interval (a set of time points). Thus, the imperfective viewpoint can only select a TSit argument which consists of more than one time point. In other words, the [impf] Asp head comes with a selectional restriction for a durative TSit.

This is the way in which durativity of a predicate is built right into the definition of imperfective viewpoint, and thereby into [impf] Asp. Clearly, such a definition requires that durativity of a predicate be accessible to imperfective viewpoint. It also follows from such a definition that predicates which are not durative (or cannot be shifted to a durative meaning) are incompatible with imperfective viewpoint, and with [impf] Asp.

Let's illustrate with two Dëne examples, durative *ya#l–ti* 'talk/pray' and nondurative *ná#ne–(i–)Ø–kár* 'slap O once.' Following Rice (2000), I assume that the Dëne verb corresponds to an entire clause (see Chapter Two for discussion, and Chapter Three for arguments that *ghe-* etc. are viewpoint markers). Thus, the verb in (10) roughly translates into the clause given in (11).

(10) *ya#l–ti* 'talk/pray'—IMPERFECTIVE
 yasti sı̨
 ya#Ø–s–ł–ti   sı̨
 th#impf-1sS-cl-stem assert
 'I am talking/praying'

(11)

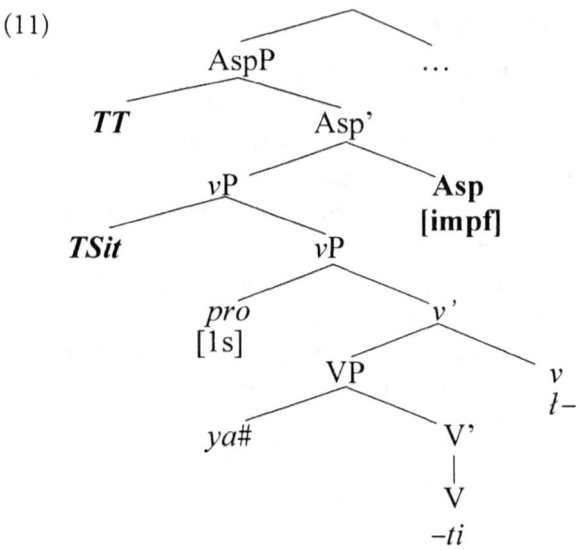

The Ø imperfective morphology means that AspP is headed by [impf], which contrasts with a possible [perf] perfective Asp head. [impf] in Asp means that the relation of TT and TSit is specified as TT ⊂ TSit. This yields the typical imperfective interpretation that the talking/praying event is viewed "from the inside" (Comrie 1976).[8] Crucially, TT ⊂ TSit is possible here because TSit consists of more than one time point, i.e., the situation is durative.

However, things are different if the event is nondurative. A verb denoting a nondurative situation is infelicitous in the imperfective. For example:

(12) *ná#ne-(i-)Ø-kár* 'slap O once'—IMPERFECTIVE

　＊ náneskár

　ná#ne-Ø-s-Ø-kár

　adv#th-<u>impf</u>-1s-cl-flat hand action

The time of Dëne 'slap once' is conceptualized as being very short; punctual, in fact. Let's assume that the TSit of a nondurative situation consists of a time point only (see Smith 1991). This makes it impossible to properly include another time into TSit. However, the imperfective viewpoint requires precisely such an inclusion. Thus, the imperfective viewpoint is by definition incompatible with nondurative situations, and (12) is ungrammatical. This account explains the pattern found in Dëne, namely that nondurative predicates cannot occur in the imperfective viewpoint (unless a durative reading is coerced, for example, by including an achievement situation's preliminary stages).

In sum, an overt morphosyntactic contrast between *ghe-* or *the-* and Ø corresponds to a featural contrast between [perf] and the absence of [impf] in Asp. [impf] is associated with imperfective viewpoint, which requires a durative TSit. Thus, [impf] Asp has a selectional restriction for a durative internal argument. This is how durativity is grammatized in Dëne.

Generalizing, I claim that the grammatization of durativity is mediated by imperfective viewpoint. It is expressed as a selectional restriction a head places on one of its arguments. This is the only possible, and therefore the most direct way, in which durativity may be grammatized at all. In other words, selectional restrictions of an imperfective (or progressive/durative/etc.) Asp head on Tsit is the only way in which durativity *can* be grammatized.

Using a featural contrast such as [perf]/[impf] in Asp, together with a suitable semantics, works well to express this, as long as [impf] is associated with a semantics in which TSit properly includes TT.

Let us now turn to the grammatization of telicity.

3.2. [delim]/Ø in VP: Telicity

One way in which German shows a morphosyntactic contrast is in the existence of many pairs of telic particle verbs and their atelic base verbs, e.g., *absägen* 'saw off' and *sägen* 'saw.' Can we express this difference through features?

Particles like *ab* 'off' signal a result state and thereby provide an inherent endpoint or limit for an event. Since this is part of their meaning, we could say that *ab* and other delimiting particles are lexically marked with a feature [delim] for "delimiting" (nondelimiting particles do not have this feature). The base verb, *sägen* 'saw,' is atelic. Again, this is a lexical characteristic of this verb. Therefore, we could say that this verb is lexically not marked as [delim], and that this results in an atelic interpretation. This is conveniently expressed by the contrast [delim]/Ø.

For the particle verb to have telic meaning, we have to assume that the particle imparts its feature [delim] onto the complex V. This could be implemented in one of two ways. First, we could assume that [delim] moves to V, thus marking the verb as telic. Alternatively we could exploit the fact discussed in Chapters One and Four that the particle and the verb form a domain in which special meanings are possible: recall that I follow Zeller's (2001) Distributed Morphology account of particle verbs, and that according to Zeller, the special domain formed by the verb and particle is defined as "structural adjacency." We could thus assume that being structurally adjacent allows the particle to impart the [delim] feature onto the verb, or that it enables the verb to access this feature. Again, the result is a telic complex verb. For the sake of concreteness, I will assume the latter rather than movement.

(13) situation aspectual composition of *ab* 'off' + *sägen* 'saw' —> *absägen* 'saw'

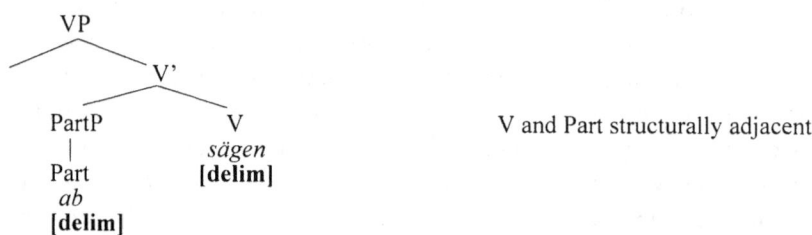

V and Part structurally adjacent

Another very important way in which telicity is grammatized in German is through the direct internal argument. Recall that German telic verbs require a quantized direct internal argument for a telic interpretation (rather than a nonquantized/cumulative direct internal argument, an *an*-PP, or no direct internal argument). Atelic verbs have no such requirements for an atelic interpretation. This is illustrated in (14) and (15).

(14) telic particle verb
Susi hat *den Ast/ *Holz/ *Äste/ *Ø/*an dem Ast/*Ø*
Susi has the branch/*wood/*branches/*Ø/*at the branch

in fünf Minuten abgesägt.
in five minutes off-sawn

'Susi sawed off *the branch/*wood/*branches/was sawing off on the branch* in five minutes.'

(15) atelic simplex verb
Susi hat fünf Minuten lang √*Holz/?das Holz/ *den Ast⁰/ √Ø*
Susi has five minutes long √wood/√the wood/*the branch/√Ø

√*an dem Ast* gesägt.
√at the branch sawn

'Susi sawed √*wood/√the wood/*the branch/√at the branch/√Ø* for five minutes.'

This might be formalized as the requirement that the direct internal argument also be specified as [delim] for a telic interpretation of the predicate.

The featural contrast [delim]/Ø works well to express this. Note that nominals with quantized reference have more structure—an overt determiner, a numeral, or even a measure phrase—than nominals with nonquantized/cumulative reference, which typically are determinerless. We could correlate the presence of additional structure with the presence of the feature [delim], and the absence of this structure with the absence of [delim], i.e., with Ø.[10] Again, this gives us a nice parallel between the overt forms and the types of features used. Moreover, using the same featural contrast [delim]/Ø on nominals as on verbs expresses semanticists' observation that quantization in the nominal domain is parallel to telicity in the verbal domain, e.g., Mourelatos (1978), Bach (1981, 1986), Krifka (1989, 1992). To sum up, we can comfortably assume that nominal constituents of a certain form (e.g., DPs) have a feature [delim], which corresponds to quantized reference in the semantics. Other nominal constituents (e.g., NPs) do not have this feature, which corresponds to nonquantized/cumulative reference in the semantics (see footnote 10).

Let us now see how we can capture the fact that the presence of a [delim] DP in Spec-VP is *required* for a telic interpretation. In other words, why is the type of structure shown in (16) required for a telic interpretation?

(16) situation aspectual composition of *den Ast absägen* 'saw off the branch'

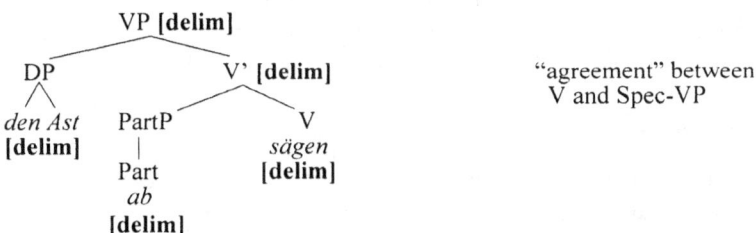

"agreement" between V and Spec-VP

What seems to be the case is that the V and its internal argument must "agree" in delimitedness. How can this be implemented?

First of all, we cannot assume that [delim] on the verb and on the nominal in Spec-VP are morphosyntactic features which enter into a minimalist checking relation (as in, e.g., Chomsky 1995, Chomsky 2000, Pesetsky and Torrego 2004): syntactic feature checking erases (uninterpretable) features. However, we must not lose [delim] on either V or Spec-VP to feature erasure, because both are *required* in the semantic component to derive a telic interpretation.

Thus, we must assume that [delim] is a semantic rather than a strictly morphosyntactic feature, i.e., it is a feature with semantic content. We can then say that it is the *meaning* of [delim] on V/VP which requires a [delim] argument in Spec-VP for a telic interpretation. However, the relation between [delim] on V/VP and on Spec-VP is not one of selectional restriction. Selectional restriction predicts that sentences where [delim] is present on the verb but not on the direct internal argument are semantically ill-formed. Instead, such sentences often are completely acceptable, but have an atelic interpretation:[11]

(17) Susi hat (#in einer Stunde) *Briefe geschrieben.*
   Ø [delim]
'Susi wrote letters (#in an hour).'

Instead, we must specify in the semantics of [delim] on V that it requires a "measuring out" argument (which would be merged in Spec-VP) for a telic interpretation. Such a semantics can be found, for example, in Verkuyl's (1993) definition of the verbal feature [+ADD TO], and in Krifka's (1989, 1992, 1998) and Ramchand's (1997) definitions of object-(and path-)to-event mapping properties. I assume that the feature [delim] on V is defined along these lines, without going into any detail here.

In conclusion, it is the semantics associated with the feature [delim] on V that requires a quantized DP in Spec-VP for a telic interpretation of VP. Representing this telicity-deriving semantics through a feature in the syntax reflects that this part of the meaning is grammatically relevant and responsible for morphosyntactic contrasts—it is grammatized.

3.3. Discussion

What can we learn from this implementation of grammatization through featural contrasts? First, we have seen that in both Dëne and German it is the semantics associated with a certain feature (or the absence of that feature) that is responsible for grammatical patterns. In my view, this expresses precisely that a semantic notion is grammatized.

Next, we notice a subtle difference if we compare the grammatization of durativity with that of telicity. In VP, the feature [delim] *derives* or *represents* telicity as the interpretation of the VP. In doing so, it affects argument structure (presence of a direct internal argument). In AspP, the contrast [perf]/[impf] represents inflectional morphology, whose meaning *accesses* durativity via something like selectional restrictions. Thus, we have subtly different grammatization devices in VP and AspP.[12] Finding different grammatization devices is not surprising, given that my definition of grammatization (existence of a morphosyntactic contrast) is quite broad.

4. NON-GRAMMATIZATION

The fact that my definition of grammatization is quite broad may suggest that anything can be interpreted as grammatized. In order to show that this is not the case, I now discuss non-grammatization of telicity and durativity. I will show in this section that my definition of grammatization allows us to distinguish clearly between grammatized and non-grammatized semantic notions. To make the discussion more concrete, I will again use the features [perf]/[impf] and [delim]/Ø in German and Dëne.

4.1. Telicity

4.1.1. No Feature [delim] in Dëne VP

Until now, I have focused on the relationship between the presence of a morphosyntactic contrast and a corresponding semantic contrast. Now let us consider the significance of the absence of a productive morphosyntactic contrast. In Dëne, there is no telicity-related morphosyntactic contrast in the VP, thus no grammatization of that notion.

To begin with Spec-VP, we know that nominal quantization is not marked overtly in Dëne. This means that there is no featural contrast (e.g., between [delim] and Ø) in nominal constituents. This correlates with an absence of determiners and number inflection.[13] The direct internal argument is unspecified for quantization, and therefore cannot grammatize telicity in Dëne.

Second, the sister of the verb, i.e., the position of German particles, has no productive role in marking telicity either. According to Rice (2000), whose clause structure I roughly follow (see Chapter Two), most of the Athapaskan preverbs (adverbial and prepositional disjunct prefixes) are adjuncts, i.e., not sisters, of the verb, as shown in (19) below. Thus, the aspectually relevant sister of the verb position is usually empty in Dëne. Moreover, even if some preverbs were sisters of the verb, this would not be a productive or transparent pattern. Most Dëne preverbs are highly opaque—nothing is known about their semantic contribution, aspectual or otherwise (an example of this is *ya#* in (18) below).[14] We thus do not have empirical grounds for proposing that Dëne preverbs are heads which are systematically marked with the presence or absence of a feature [delim]. I propose that preverbs cannot impart a feature [delim] on the verb, and in fact that there is no feature [delim] in the VP whatsoever. This is why telicity has no morphosyntactic correlates in Dëne. Telicity is purely semantic, i.e., it is part of the semantic but not of the morphosyntactic representation of telic verbs.[15]

To sum up, the absence of telicity-related morphosyntactic contrasts indicates that telicity is not grammatized in Dëne. This is expressed by the absence of a feature [delim] from the VP.

4.1.2. [perf] in AspP: Perfective Viewpoint

What Dëne does have is a contrasting feature [perf] in Asp. For example, the perfective form of *ya#ł–ti* 'talk/pray' contains the morpheme *ghe-*, which does not occur in the imperfective. We are thus justified in assuming that *ghe-* is specified for [perf]:

(18) *ya#ł–ti* 'talk/pray'—PERFECTIVE

yaghiłti nį

ya#ghe–i–ł–ti   nį

th#perf-1s-cl-stem past

'I talked/prayed'

(19)

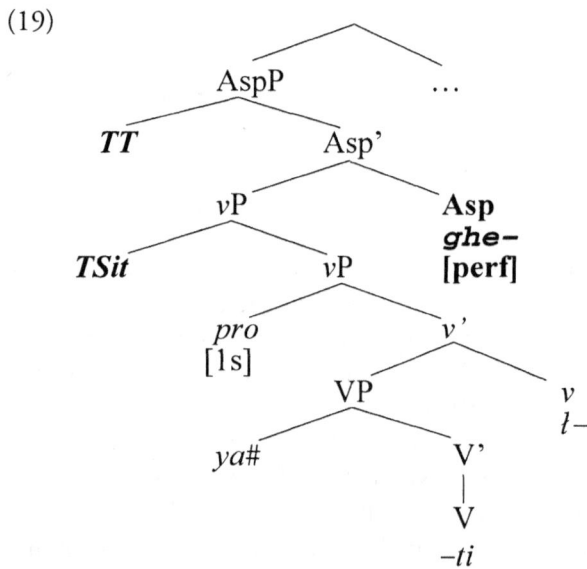

The feature [perf] is associated with a perfective semantics. As we saw in Chapter Two, the perfective viewpoint has special completive meaning in Dëne, as if to compensate for the absence of telicity. Also in Chapter Two, I proposed to account for the special completive meaning of the Dëne Perfective by including, along with TSit, a posttime of TSit into TT. Through its completive meaning, the Dëne perfective comes close to having a telic meaning.[16]

4.1.3. Summary

The fact that telicity is not grammatized in Dëne can be seen from the absence of telicity-related morphosyntactic contrasts in the VP. This was expressed through the absence of a (contrastive) feature [delim] from the constituents of the VP: the verb, the sister of the verb and the specifier of VP. On the other hand, the feature [perf] is active in the IP-domain AspP in Dëne, which gives us an overtly marked perfective viewpoint.

4.2. Durativity: No Features in German AspP

German verbs, or rather, clauses, may have an imperfective or a perfective interpretation, but no overt morphology corresponds to either viewpoint. Since viewpoints do exist in German, it is reasonable to assume that German has an AspP above VP/vP, but that Asp is not specified for imperfective or perfective. I propose that in German there is no viewpoint feature in Asp.[17] Thus, how TT and TSit are related in a German sentence is not determined by information in the Asp head—Asp is always empty in German, reflecting the absence of viewpoint aspect morphosyntax.[18] This means that, in principle (and abstracting away from pragmatic considerations), every German clause can have either a perfective or an imperfective interpretation, which is correct.

To illustrate, consider briefly the clause structure of a Perfect and a Preterite sentence in German. Recall that I argued in Chapter Five that both of these tenses are compatible with an imperfective as well as with a perfective interpretation. For the Perfect, I assume a structure as in Musan (2002), shown in (20a). The main verb moves to the Perfect head to obtain its participial form as well as an anterior meaning. Crucially, the perfect morphology is associated with the Perfect rather than with the Asp head, and Asp remains Ø. For the Preterite, I assume a structure as in (20b): again, the Asp head is empty; the Preterite morphology is located in T.

(20) a. German Present Perfect   (see Musan 2002:54)

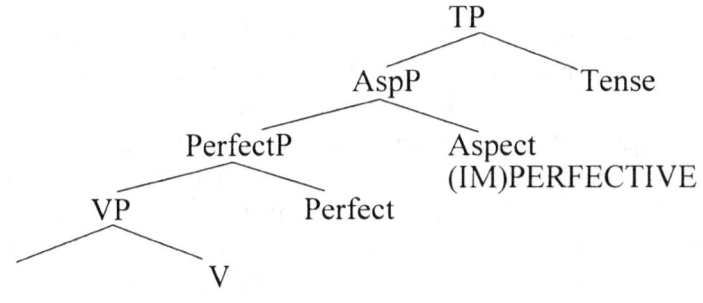

b. German Preterite

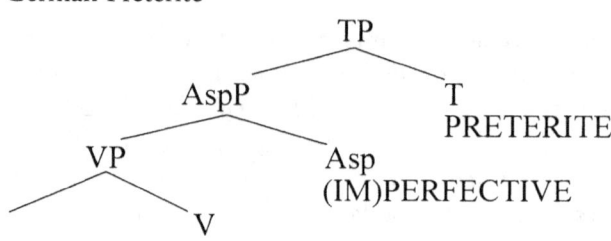

Since Asp is always empty in German, there is no morphosyntactic environment which requires an imperfective interpretation—which requires proper inclusion of TT in TSit. Therefore, German does not have morphosyntactic environments which are necessarily incompatible with a nondurative situation.

In sum, I argued in this section that durativity is not grammatized in German because the viewpoint head Asp is unspecified in this language. In other words, there is no intrinsic Asp head/feature which locates TT within TSit, and thus no grammatical contrast which accesses the durativity of a predicate.

4.3. (Non-)Grammatization: Discussion

I have considered the (non-)grammatization of semantic notions in some detail. It was confirmed that grammatization must be anchored in a productive morphosyntactic contrast, and that the lack of such a contrast indicates non-grammatization. If a contrast does exist, it gives formal expression to a semantic notion. This does not replace the semantics, but the semantics is now explicitly represented in the morphosyntax. Thus, when examining the grammatization of semantic notions, we should never expect to find purely formal, a-semantic facts. Otherwise, we would not be speaking about a semantic notion at all. Grammatizing a semantic notion always happens through what we might call a grammatico-semantic category or contrast.

We have also seen that there may be different grammatization devices. Durativity seems grammatized indirectly, mediated through imperfective viewpoint, while telicity seems to be compositionally derived from the VP elements, without mediation through another (grammatico-semantic) category. Moreover, durativity is grammatized via an inflectional/functional head, while telicity is grammatized via argument structure or linking.

Certainly, the nature of grammatization and the range of devices deserves further scrutiny. My study offers a first attempt, from which further

The Grammatization of Aspectual Notions

work may proceed. What I think of as undisputable is that grammatization, by its very nature, has two components: (i) a morphosyntactic contrast, and (ii) a semantic component (i.e., a semantics associated with the morphosyntactic contrast). If either of these components is missing, we cannot talk about grammatization of a semantic notion.

5. IMPLICATIONS, CONSEQUENCES, FURTHER WORK

I will conclude this chapter by discussing the implications of my study. At the heart of my dissertation is the finding that telicity is grammatized in VP, and durativity is grammatized in AspP:

(21) *Aspect Grammatization Hypothesis*

> If *durativity* is grammatized, it is grammatized in AspP.
>
> If *telicity* is grammatized, it is grammatized in VP.

(22)

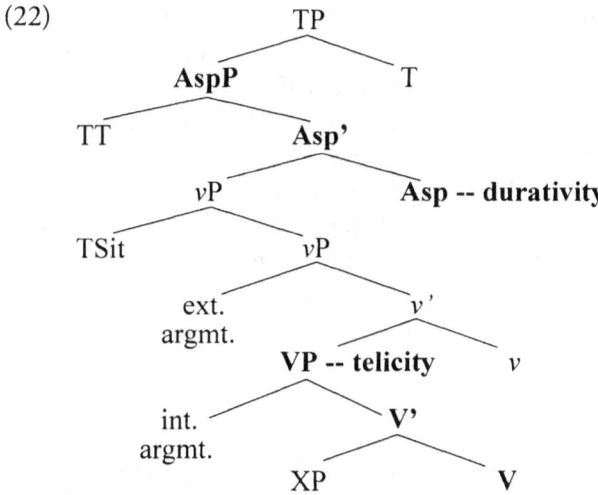

We saw that this proposal gives a natural explanation for the patterns observed in Dëne and German. I have argued that (21)/(22) express a cross-linguistic fact, i.e., that they express something about the organization of UG. I gave a motivation for my proposal from the temporal nature of durativity and the force-dynamic nature of telicity (section 2 above).

5.1. Theoretical Consequences

5.1.1. Telicity and Durativity Not Universal Grammatical Categories

The first and foremost consequence of my research is that neither telicity nor durativity are grammatical (or grammatico-semantic) categories in all languages. This sheds considerable light on the debates on the status of telicity and durativity, and the Vendler verb classes, in the literature. In particular, it helps us understand why some authors take durativity, or Vendler's achievement class, as universal (e.g., Dowty 1979, Ehrich 1992, ter Meulen 1995, Rapp 1997a,b, Levin and Rappaport Hovav 1998, Ramchand 2002), while others explicitly dismiss durativity or the achievement class as extra-linguistic (Verkuyl 1989, Tenny 1987, 1994, Klein 1994, etc.). My research makes the following contribution to this debate: one has to distinguish between the semantic notion of durativity and its grammatization. Semantically, durativity may well be universal. Grammatically, however, I maintain that durativity is not universal.

There is a similar consequence for telicity. As far as I know, with the exception of Smith (1991, 1996), linguists do not dispute the universal status of telicity. Again, I agree that all languages can express this kind of meaning. However, my study of Dëne supports Smith's finding that telicity is not grammatized universally. This means that theories which import telicity into the syntax (e.g., Borer 1994, 1998, Ramchand 1997, 2002, Kratzer 2004, and indirectly Hale and Keyser 1993) or the syntax-semantics interface (Dowty 1979, Grimshaw 1990, Rapp 1997a,b, Levin and Rappaport Hovav 1998, etc.) must be careful to allow for representations for languages which do not grammatize telicity. The work of Ritter and Rosen (1998, 2000) is along these lines, although see the next section for some criticism.

In sum, it is important to distinguish between a semantic notion and its grammatization. Theories representing these notions formally must allow for languages that grammatize them and those that do not.

5.1.2. Grammatization Loci

The second key finding of my research concerns the loci of grammatization: telicity in VP, durativity in AspP. Again, this has consequences for theories representing telicity and durativity formally. If those theories say something about the interface with the syntax, or are syntactic per se, durativity should be represented in or relating to AspP and telicity in or relating to VP and argument structure. (I gave an example of how this might be done in section 3 above.)

Lexical semantic predicate decomposition theories, which are usually understood as informing the argument/VP structure of a predicate, should

The Grammatization of Aspectual Notions

not differentiate accomplishments from achievements, e.g. through predicates such as *CAUSE* (Rappaport Hovav and Levin 1998) or *DEV* (Rapp 1997a,b). Rather, durativity should not be represented here at all. This is independently supported by the fact that, to the best of my knowledge, lexical decomposition theories represent durativity only in telic but never in atelic situation types. More specifically, the distinction between activities (durative) and semelfactives (nondurative) is not represented (semelfactives are usually not recognized as a separate situation type). However, this is inconsistent: either durativity should be represented for all predicate types, or for no predicate types. The lack of a formal durativity distinction for atelic predicates indicates that durativity is not a universal feature, and supports my suggestion to drop the representation of durativity altogether in these VP-related theories. See Verkuyl (1989, 1993) for a related criticism of the lexical decomposition theory in Dowty (1979).[19]

Similarly, a representation of durativity in the syntactic structure of VP is also inadequate. For example, Butt and Ramchand (2001), Ramchand (2002) assume a maximally tripartite shell structure for verbs/predicates:

(23)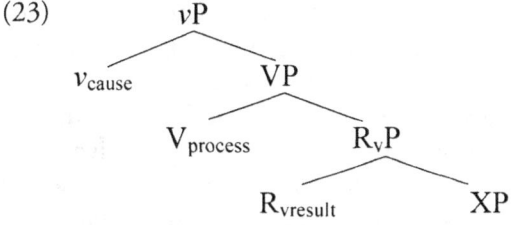

An accomplishment consists at least of $V_{process}$ and $R_{vresult}$; $V_{process}$ encodes the durativity component of accomplishments, via the process subevent. This is proposed to be universal, i.e., all accomplishments in all languages have at least this structure. However, German achievement particle verbs derived from activity base verbs would also be predicted to have the structure shown in (23): since they are telic, they are predicted to contain R_vP. Since they are derived from activity base verbs (which contain the $V_{process}$ projection), they must also contain $V_{process}$. But this structure is incorrect, since achievements are not durative and do not contain a process. The solution is to use durativity-neutral V instead of $V_{process}$, at least in languages like German, where durativity is not grammatized.

Next, grammatical theories of telicity should represent telicity in or relating to the VP and argument structure. The examination of German in Chapter Four and in section 3 of this chapter confirmed that telicity cannot simply be located in just one element of the VP. For example, we cannot simply tie telicity to the presence of an R_vP (see (23) above), since it is possible in German to derive telic particle verbs from telic base verbs. Assuming that particles are $R_{vresult}$ heads, their occurrence with telic base verbs should be blocked if all telic verbs, including morphologically simple ones, contained a single R_vP.[20]

We also cannot say that only telic predicates contain a (quantized) Spec-VP, or a "delimiting" FP above VP which is responsible for checking syntactic properties of the internal argument such as accusative case or definiteness (as in Borer (1994, 1998), Kratzer (2004), Ritter and Rosen (1998, 2000)). German contains clear evidence that Spec-VP/Spec-FP may be occupied (by an accusative-marked, definite nominal) in atelic VPs/clauses as well. What seems to be the case instead, at least in German, is that the semantic properties of V, the sister of V, and Spec-VP interact to derive a telic reading. I expressed this in section 3 as a semantic feature [delim].

5.1.3. Deconstructing (Eventive) Situation Types/Vendler Classes

The different ways and loci in which telicity and durativity are grammatized have an additional, more general theoretical consequence. Durativity emerges as a viewpoint feature, rather than a situation type feature. What does this do to the concept of situation type, or the Vendler verb classes?

I propose that, besides the distinction into events and states, situation types, or the Vendler classes, have no formal status.[21] The eventive situation types are a composite of telicity and durativity. However, my findings strongly suggest that these two semantic notions relate to the grammar in very different ways, and thus are not of the same kind. I claim that it is therefore impossible to derive any grammatically meaningful concepts or entities from their combination. We can either talk about telicity and the VP, or about durativity and the AspP. However, we cannot talk about the grammatization of (eventive) situation type, or its locus in the morphosyntax. As pointed out by Verkuyl (1989), the Vendler classes, or situation types, are useful as an ontological concept, but they are not useful for theories of aspect in natural language. What seems more useful, in light of my findings, is to talk about "inner and outer aspect" (e.g., Travis 1991, Verkuyl 1993), where inner aspect corresponds to telicity (in VP) and outer aspect corresponds to viewpoint aspect (and durativity) in AspP.

A distinction along these lines—i.e., inner aspect is telicity, not situation type—is supported by the affinities of (a)telicity and viewpoint found in the study of Dëne and German. First, both are involved in event sequencing in discourse, (24a). Telic clauses and perfective clauses suggest that the event denoted by the clause follows another event; atelic clauses and imperfective clauses suggest that the event denoted by the clause overlaps with another event. Second, (a)telicity determines the default viewpoint of a clause if viewpoint aspect is unspecified, (24b).

(24)

		inner aspect	outer aspect
a.	sequential events	telic predicate	perfective predicate
	overlapping events	atelic predicate	imperfective predicate
b.	default interpretation	telic predicate =>	default perfective reading
		atelic predicate =>	default imperfective reading

In sum, the study of the grammatization of telicity and durativity strongly suggests that these two notions are not on an equal footing linguistically, and that they do not lead to a cross-classification of eventive situations which is helpful to the study of aspect. It is more helpful to think in terms of inner aspect, which corresponds to (a)telicity, and outer aspect, which corresponds to durativity. Inner aspect, i.e., telicity, is grammatized in the VP, outer aspect in AspP.

5.2. Predictions: Grammatization Typology

My central proposal, the Aspect Grammatization Hypothesis given in (21) above, as well as the deconstruction of situation type into inner and outer aspect, makes several typological predictions. They predict four possible ways in which durativity and telicity may be grammatized: (i), a language grammatizes only outer aspect (durativity). (ii), a language grammatizes only inner aspect (telicity). (iii) a language grammatizes inner and outer aspect (durativity and telicity). (iv), a language grammatizes neither inner nor outer aspect (neither durativity nor telicity). I will briefly discuss aspectual properties of each type, and the classification of German, Dëne and English.

Type (i) is represented by a language like Dëne. Such languages lack inner aspect properties. They do not overtly mark quantization of direct internal arguments, and preverbs/particles are not transparently and productively involved in telicity. Finally, such languages lack overt result phrases.

Type (ii) languages look like German. Telicity/inner aspect is grammatized, but durativity is not. Such languages have no grammatical viewpoint aspect, but they have the inner aspect properties associated with the VP, such as overtly quantized nominal elements, which occupy Spec-VP. Also, in such languages the sister of V productively signals that the situation has an inherent endpoint or a "goal." In other words, such a languages will typically have productive delimiting particles/preverbs and/or result phrases.

Type (iii) is represented by a language like English. Here both outer and inner aspect, hence both durativity and telicity, are grammatized. According to the Aspect Grammatization Hypothesis, this means that such a language has the properties of both an "inner aspect" and an "outer aspect" language. However, since such a language does not lack grammatized telicity, I predict that it will not have a perfective viewpoint with a strong completive meaning. This is because there is no motivation for viewpoint aspect to compensate for the lack of telicity.

Finally, the predictions for type (iv) languages are most speculative. This would be a language without aspectual contrasts in AspP or VP, in other words: no overt viewpoint marking, no overt noun quantization and no productive delimiting particles/preverbs and/or result phrases. I can imagine two ways in which such a language might work. On the one hand, such a language may make finer aspectual distinctions such as inceptive, habitual, egressive, iterative, in order to convey some sort of aspect, which is important to event sequencing in discourse (perhaps Slavic languages are candidates for this type). On the other hand, such a language may lack grammatical aspect altogether and be a truly "aspect-less" language. How would such a language convey event sequencing in discourse? Of course, it is always possible to glean event sequencing from discourse factors, such as clause ordering (usually, an earlier clause denotes an earlier event) or the conjunctions used (e.g., *while*: simultaneous, *when*: sequential). But perhaps such a language might also convey event sequencing/aspectual information through grammatizing stativity, a topic put aside in this dissertation, or perhaps through grammatizing discourse notions such as topichood or referential tracking. To mind come the topic marking found in Philippine languages (see Li 1976), or switch-reference marking as in Chuave (Thurman 1978; see also Stirling 1993, Haiman and Munro 1983). Other devices of inter-clausal coherence are discussed in Givón (2001) and Longacre (1985).

It is also worth considering here whether tense may be able to play a role in event sequencing, or discourse structuring. While it is true (certainly in Dëne) that perfective viewpoint has a default past tense interpretation and imperfective viewpoint a default present tense interpretation, there does not appear to be a reverse correlation from tense to aspect. Nor is it obvious that tenses per se could contribute much to event sequencing. Of course, past tense clauses denote events which are over and present tense events do not, thus the event denoted by a past tense sentence would precede the event denoted by a present tense sentence. However, in a narrative, the tense usually does not change from past to present; narratives are usually all about past events, so tense would rarely if ever be used in this way.[22]

Obviously, these typological predictions need to be empirically tested on a range of languages. This is one way in which my examination of telicity and durativity in German and Dëne leads to a principled way of asking further research questions. More such questions are discussed in the next section.

5.3. Future Research

One topic for further work that immediately comes out of this dissertation is the grammatical representation of the situation type notion of stativity, which I put aside in the present work. There is already a large body of work on stativity, and the difference between individual-level and stage-level states (Milsark 1974, Carlson 1977, Kratzer 1995, Diesing 1992). However, this body of work is based mostly on English and related languages. It would be interesting to examine stativity in a wider variety of languages. Dëne would be a good candidate, since there are clear morphosyntactic differences between (positional) stative and nonstative verbs.

Next, a host of issues was brought up by the examination of Dëne and German in Chapters Two through Five. I will mention just a few here. In Dëne, it would be highly desirable to explore the role of preverbs further and compare them to the role of particles and prefixes in German. Dëne preverbs are a difficult topic, since many of them are completely opaque semantically, and since homophony among preverbs, as well as fusion, present added complications. Nonetheless, the continued collection and analysis of Dëne verbs may provide some insight. Another question brought up by the study of Dëne is nominal quantization. Dëne has an intricate system of number marking on the verb, as well as verb stem alternations by number (compare the 'sit down,' 'give,' 'kill' and 'arrive' examples in Chapters Two and Three and Appendix One). The relationship between these different number marking systems, and their impact on the type of reference of nominals, represents a fascinating topic for future research. Such research may also contribute new evidence to the unresolved question of whether it is the nominals or the pronominal affixes that are the syntactic arguments in Dëne.

In German, there are several issues that I could only touch upon or had to ignore in this dissertation. One is the status of goal PPs and resultative phrases. I believe that they occur in the same sister-of-verb position as particles and have the same function as far as telicity is concerned (see Spencer and Zaretskaya 1998 for a similar view, based on Russian and English). However, this idea needs to be supported by syntactic and semantic evidence. Another issue is the relationship of telicity to unaccusativity. My account, according to which all telic predicates have a direct internal argument, suggests that all intransitive telic predicates are in fact unaccusative. As mentioned in Chapter Four, there is a large overlap between unaccusativity and telicity criteria in German, and the status of these criteria, as well as the status of unaccusativity in German, is under debate (see Paul 1902, Andersson 1972, Grewendorf 1989, Ehrich 1992, Abraham 1995, Kaufmann 1995a). Further topics are a semantics for the feature [delim] on V, the semantic and syntactic status of bare plurals in German (e.g., Carlson 1977, Diesing 1992, de Hoop 1992, van Geenhoven 1998), and a semantic analysis of the *an*-construction.

Finally, I'd like to point out an observation I made in developing a definition for the Dëne Perfective. My definition makes use of a posttime, and this is reminiscent of the post-state used in the definition of the German Perfect in Musan (2002) and Klein (1994). While there are good reasons to maintain a difference between the Dëne Perfective and the category of perfect, the two are nonetheless similar, and an examination of the relation between the two, as well as between perfects and perfectives in general, would be of great interest.

5.4. Conclusion

When I embarked on this research, I was driven by an unease with the notion of durativity, and a general interest in First Nations, particularly Athapaskan, languages. Little did I expect to end up deconstructing situation type, or the Vendler verb classes, into inner and outer, or VP-domain and IP-domain, aspect. However, I think this conclusion is inevitable in light of my findings about durativity and telicity: they are fundamentally different notions, grammatized in fundamentally different ways.

Appendix One

DËNE VERBS AND TESTS

The verb themes are listed by situation type, and within each situation type in the same order as in Chapter Three. Where more than one stem is cited for a given verb theme, the first stem is the imperfective stem, the second is the perfective stem (and the third is the optative stem). First and third person singular imperfective and perfective forms are given for each verb to illustrate inflection.

This partial paradigm is followed by the aspectual tests: the 'almost' test for telicity/accomplishments, and four durativity tests (backgrounding, 'for X time', 'stop/finish', 'quickly/slowly'). Note that compatibility with the imperfective (in the paradigm section) also indicates durativity. Nondurative verbs either have a future/prospective interpretation in the imperfective, or they cannot occur in a "bare" imperfective form at all, but need a future marker (*xa* or *xasį*).

Glosses are kept fairly general, since the morphophonemic processes of the verb are not of primary interest here. Imperfective forms are glossed by an English gerund ("V-ing"), perfective forms by a simple past ("V-ed"). Note that subject and object affixes do not specify gender but that this is not always reflected in the translations and glosses. The complementizer *(?)ú* (glossed as "C") used in the first durativity test has a very general meaning something like 'and/when.'

Unless otherwise indicated (as *A. W.*), translations are unedited, as given by the native speakers. If a verb fails a certain test, this is indicated by one of the following symbols: *??, #, *. If a test is missing for a given verb, the test was not performed, or (in a very small number of cases) the results were inconclusive.

1.1 Accomplishments

√ completion reading with 'almost'
√ pass durativity tests (including compatibility with simple imperfective)

(1)

Theme	ł–bes (cl–stem) 'boil O'
1sg impf	hesbes 'I'm boiling O (something, e.g., meat)'
3 sg impf	yełbes 's/he's boiling it'
1sg perf	thiłbes 'I boiled it'
3sg perf	yéłbes 's/he boiled it'
'almost' test	k'ájëne bër thiłbes almost meat I-boiled-it 'I'm almost done cooking O by boiling, I'm almost finished boiling it'
durativity tests	ʔiłághe ts'údzáhi k'e hesbes–ú tsątsą́naze naréłtsër one hour P I-boiling-it-C phone again-it-rang 'while I was boiling meat for one hour, the phone rang again'
	ʔiłághe ts'údzáhi k'e bër thiłbes one hour P meat I-boiled-it 'for one hour, I boiled the meat'
	hesbes ʔanast'e I-boiling-it I-finished 'I'm finished boiling'
	ts'ethię́ thiłbes slowly I-boiled-it 'I boiled it slowly'

(2)

Theme	ná–na#ł–dą́ (adv-ʔ#cl-stem) 'mend O'
1sg impf	nánasdą́ 'I'm patching O' (sewing, needle and thread)
3 sg impf	nánayełdą́ 's/he is patching O'
1sg perf	nánathiłdą́ 'I patched it'
3sg perf	nánayéłdą́ 's/he patched O'
'almost' test	k'ájëne nánaʔethiłdą́ almost I-mended-something 'I almost finished sewing/patching it'

Appendix One

durativity tests	ʔı̨́łá dziné k'étł'á nánathiłdą́ one day duration-of I-mended-it 'for the whole day I patched it'
	nánasdą́ ʔanast'e I-mending-it I-finished 'I'm finished patching it'
	ʔı́ghą́ jis nánáthiłdą́ quickly mitt I-mended-it 'it didn't take me long to patch the mitt(s)'

(3)

Theme	**(ho–)ł–tsi, –tsį** ((ar/th-)cl-stem) 'make sg O'
1sg impf	yeh hostsi sį 'I'm making/building a house' (sį = assert)
3 sg impf	yeh hołtsi sį 's/he is making a house'
1sg perf	yeh hóthiłtsį nį 'I (had) made a house' (Note: there might not be a high tone on o)
3sg perf	yeh hółtsį ʔósą́ ? 'did s/he make a house?'
'almost' test	k'ájëne yeh hóthiłtsį sį almost house I-made-it assert 'I'm just about done making a house'
durativity tests	ʔı̨́łá nëne yoh hostsi xa one year house I-making fut 'I'll build a house in a year (it will be done in a year)'
	ʔı́ghą́ tth'áy thiłtsį quickly dish I-made-it 'I made the dish unexpectedly quickly, it didn't take me long to make the dish'

(4)

Theme	**Ø–da, –dagh** (cl-stem) 'eat (up) sg animal'
1sg impf	łue hesda sį 'I'm eating fish right now'
3 sg impf	łue heda 's/he is eating fish right now'
1sg perf	łue ghesdagh 'I ate up the/a fish' (this verb used with big portions)
3sg perf	ʔı̨́łághe łue yedagh 's/he ate (up) one fish'
'almost' test	k'ájëne łue ghesdagh sį almost fish I-ate-it assert 'I just about ate the fish (just about done)'

durativity tests	(?) tthidziné k'e łue hesda–ú tsątsą́naze déłtsër yesterday fish I-eating-it-C phone it-rang ['when I was eating fish the phone rang' -- A.W.]
	ʔíghą́ łue ghesdagh quickly fish I-ate-it 'I ate a fish real quick'

(5)

Theme	ʔu–ne–Ø–ye, –yą (ser/th-gd-cl-stem) 'pick (berries)'
1sg impf	ʔuneshe 'I am picking several O (=berries)'
3 sg impf	ʔuneye 's/he is picking berries'
1sg perf	ʔuneghiyą 'I picked berries' (Note: the *e* is sometimes heard as an *i*)
3sg perf	ʔuneghiyą 's/he picked berries'
'almost' test	k'ájëne jíe ʔuneghiyą sį almost berry I-picked-them assert 'I'm just about done picking berries'
durativity tests	tthidziné k'e ʔuneshe–ú tsątsą́naze déłtsër yesterday I-picking-them-C phone it-rang 'yesterday while I was picking berries the phone rang'
	ʔįłá dziné k'e ʔuneghiyą one day P I-picked-them 'I picked berries for one day'
	ʔuneshe ʔanast'e I-picking-them I-finished 'I'm finished picking berries' (containers are all filled up)
	ʔíghą́ ʔuneghiyą quickly I-picked-them 'I picked berries fast' (the container was full fast)

(6)

Theme	(ho–)ł–ghą ((ar/th-)cl-stem) 'make pl O'
1sg impf	ke sųłiné hesxą sį	'I'm making a pair/pairs of mocassins'
3 sg impf	yeh hoghą sį	's/he is making houses'
1sg perf	tth'áy ghighą sį	'I made several dishes'
3sg perf	yeh hoghįghą nį	's/he had made plural houses'

Appendix One 233

'almost' test	k'ájëne ke sųłiné ghighą sį almost mocassin I-made-them assert 'I have just about completed the pair of moccasins'
durativity tests	not elicited, except for compatibility with imperfective (see above)

(7)

Theme	ł–t'éth, –t'e (cl-stem) 'roast/bake O'
1sg impf	łue hest'éth sį 'I am roasting fish'
3 sg impf	łue hełt'éth sį 's/he is roasting fish'
1sg perf	bĕr thiłt'e 'I roasted meat'
3sg perf	bĕr thełt'e 's/he roasted meat'
'almost' test	k'ájëne bĕr thiłt'e sį almost meat I-roasted-it assert 'I'm just about done cooking meat'
durativity tests	tthidziné k'e łue hełt'éth–ú ʔenétthëdh yesterday fish I-roasting-it-C fire-went-out 'yesterday while s/he cooked/was cooking the fire went out'
	ʔįłághe ts'údzáhi k'e bĕr thiłt'e one hour P meat I-roasted-it 'I cooked meat for one hour, it tooke me one hour to cook the meat'
	bĕr hest'éth ʔanasdhën meat I-roasting-it I-finished 'I finished cooking meat'
	ʔíghą bĕr thiłt'e quickly meat I-roasted-it 'I cooked the meat fast' (it didn't take me long)

(8)

Theme	be–ká#ł–t'éth, –t'e (3O-P#cl-stem) 'cook (meal)'
1sg impf	bekast'éth 'I'm cooking (it), preparing food'
3 sg impf	bekałt'éth 's/he is cooking (it)'
1sg perf	bekáthiłt'e 'I cooked (it)'
3sg perf	bekáthełt'e 's/he cooked (it)'
'almost' test	k'ájëne bekáthiłt'e almost I-cooked 'I just about finished cooking'

durativity tests	ʔiłághe ts'údzáhi k'e bekathełt'e one hour P I-cooked 's/he cooked it in/for an hour'
	bekast'éth ʔanasdhën I-cooking I-finished 'I am finished cooking'
	ʔíghą bekáthiłt'e quickly I-cooked 'I cooked it fast/in a hurry'

(9)

Theme	**ta#ne–ł–t'éth, –t'e** (adv?#th-cl-stem) 'cook several O'
1sg impf	betanest'éth 'I'm cooking a batch of something'
3 sg impf	*not elicited*
1sg perf	łés taniłt'e sį 'I cooked a bunch of bannock'
3sg perf	łés tanįłt'e sį 's/he cooked a bunch of bannock'
'almost' test	k'ájëne łés taniłt'e sį almost bannock I-cooked-several assert 'I'm just about done cooking a batch of bannock'
durativity tests	łés tanest'éth–ú tsątsąnaze déłtsër bannock I-cooking-several-C phone it-rang 'as I was cooking lots of bannock the phone rang'
	ʔiłághe ts'údzáhi k'e łés taniłt'e one hour P bannock I-cooked-several 'in an hour I cooked lots of bannock'
	? łés tanest'éth–i ʔanast'e bannock I-cooking-several-Nomlz I-finished 'I'm finished cooking a bunch of bread/bannock'
	ʔíghą łés taniłt'e quickly bannock I-cooked-several 'I cooked lots of bannock in a short time/quickly'

(10)

Theme	**tł'o de–Ø–t'áth, –t'adh** (N th-cl-stem) 'cut grass (hay)'
1sg impf	tł'o dest'áth sį 'I'm cutting grass' (cutting a big hayfield, or mowing a lawn)
3 sg impf	tł'o det'áth sį 's/he is cutting grass'
1sg perf	tthidziné k'e tł'o deghit'adh nį 'I cut grass yesterday'

Appendix One

3sg perf	tł'o deghit'adh ni 's/he cut grass'
'almost' test	k'ájëne tł'o deghit'adh si almost grass I-cut assert 'I'm just about done cutting grass'
durativity tests	tł'o dest'áth–ú tsił hejër héja ni grass I-cutting-C snow ? it-start past 'while I was cutting grass it started to snow'
	ʔiłághe ts'údzáhi k'e tł'o deghit'adh one hour P grass I-cut 'I cut grass for one hour'
	tł'o dest'áth ʔanasdhën grass I-cut I-finished 'I'm finished cutting the grass'
	ʔíghą́ tł'o deghit'adh si quickly grass I-cut assert 'it didn't take me long to cut the grass'

Note: The full word for 'grass' is *tł'ogh*. Although the final consonant is missing in the examples in (10), I do not believe this noun is incorporated, because it always occurs verb-initially, rather than in position 7 for incorporated nouns. Loss of a word-final fricative is a fairly common process in Dëne.

(11)

Theme	ná#Ø–t'áth, –t'adh (adv#cl-stem) 'cut O up (into pieces)'
1sg impf	bër nást'áth si 'I'm cutting the meat into pieces'
3 sg impf	bër nát'áth si 's/he is cutting the meat into pieces'
1sg perf	bër nághit'adh si 'I cut the meat into pieces'
3sg perf	bër nághit'adh si 's/he cut the meat into pieces'
'almost' test	k'ájëne bër nághit'adh si almost meat I-cut-it assert 'I'm just about done cutting up the meat'
durativity tests	tthidziné k'e bër nást'áth–ú tsątsą́naze déłtsër yesterday meat I-cuting-up-C phone it-rang 'yesterday just while I was cutting (up) the meat the phone rang'
	... náke ts'údzahaze k'e k'ásba nághit'adh ... two minute P chicken I-cut 'I was doing something else then I came and cut up the chicken for two minutes' (needs context)
	ʔíghą́ bër nághit'adh quickly meat I-cut 'it didn't take me long to cut up the meat'

(12)

Theme	ɬ–t'ḗth, –t'adh (cl-stem) 'shape O with blade/cut O out'	
1sg impf	hestḗth	'I'm shaping it with a blade now' (e.g., cutting out mocassins)
3 sg impf	yeɬt'ḗth	's/he is shaping it with a blade'
1sg perf	ke sųɬiné thiɬt'adh	'I shaped/cut out mocassins'
3sg perf	ke sųɬiné theɬt'adh	's/he shaped/cut out mocassins'
'almost' test	k'ájëne ke thiɬt'adh sį almost mocassin I-cut-it-out assert 'I'm just about finished cutting out mocassins'	
durativity tests	tthidziné k'e ke hest'ḗth–ú tsątsą́naze déɬtsër yesterday mocassin I-cutting-it-out-C phone it-rang 'yesterday as I was cutting out the mocassins the phone rang'	
	ʔiɬághe ts'údzáhi k'e ke thiɬt'adh one hour P mocassins I-cut-it-out 'it took me an hour to cut out (a pair of) mocassins'	
	ke hestḗth–i ʔanasdhën mocassins I-cutting-it-out-Nomlz I-finished 'I'm finished cutting the mocassins out (all done)'	
	ʔíghą́ ke thiɬt'adh quickly mocassin I-cut-it-out 'it didn't take me long to cut out the mocassins'	

(13)

Theme	da#Ø–ʔá, –ʔą, –ʔaɬ (adv#cl-stem) 'put round solid O up there'
1sg impf	dzóɬ dathesʔá sį 'I am putting the ball there/up'
3 sg impf	dzóɬ dahʔá sį 's/he is putting the ball there/up'
1sg perf	dzóɬ dathiʔą sį 'I put the ball there'
3sg perf	dzóɬ datheʔą sį 's/he put the ball there'
'almost' test	k'ájëne tthe dathiʔą almost rock I-put-it-up 'I just about put the rock up there (I tried and just about got it where I wanted)'
durativity tests	tthe dathesʔá–ú náhestth'ër rock I-putting-it-up-C I-fell-down 'I fell down as I was putting a rock up there'

Appendix One

| | ?? sǫlághe ts'údzáhaze k'e dzół dathi?ą
five minute P ball I-put-it-up
'it took me 5 minutes to put the ball up there'
(speaker comment: but strange thing to say) |
|---|---|
| | ?ı́ghą́ dzół dathi?ą sı̨
quickly ball I-put it-up assert
'I put up the ball quickly' (quick movement) |

(14)

Theme	ná#Ø-?á, -?ą, -?ał (adv#cl-stem) 'take round solid O down'	
1sg impf	dzół nás?á	'I'm taking the ball down' (climbing down with it)
3 sg impf	dzół ná?á	's/he is taking the ball down'
1sg perf	(tthidziné k'e) dzół nághi?ą	'I took the ball down (yesterday)'
3sg perf	dzół nághį?ą	's/he took the ball down'
'almost' test	k'ájëne dzół nághi?ą
almost ball I-took-it-down
'I just about got the ball down' (almost finished)	
durativity tests	dzół nás?á–ú náhestth'ër
ball I-taking-it-down-C I-fell-down
'as I was taking down the ball I fell down'	
	?įłághe ts'údzáhi k'e dzół nághi?ą
one hour P ball I-took-it-down
'I took the ball down in an hour'	
	dzół nás?á ?anast'e
ball I-taking-it-down I-finished
'I'm finished taking the ball down'	
	?ı́ghą́ dzół nághi?ą
quickly ball I-took-it-down
'I took the ball down quickly'	

1.2. Activities

X   no completion reading with 'almost' (onset reading or unacceptable)
√   pass durativity tests

(15)

Theme	ł–yúł/l (cl-stem) 'blow O prolonged'
1sg impf	heshúł 'I'm blowing O'

3 sg impf	yeshúł 's/he keeps blowing at it'
1sg perf	ghishúl, ghishúł 'I blew (on) it prolonged, I had kept blowing (on) it'
3sg perf	yeghi̲shúl, yeghi̲shúł 's/he had kept blowing at it'
'almost' test	# k'ájëne ghishúl
durativity tests	tthidziné k'e t'és heshúł–ú tsa̲tsá̲naze déłtsër yesterday coal I-blowing-it-C phone it-rang 'yesterday as I was blowing the coals the phone rang'
	tthidziné k'e ʔi̲łághe ts'údzáhi k'e t'és ghishúl ... yesterday one hour P coal I-blew-it 'yesterday I blew the coals for one hour...' (needs context, e.g.: only then the fire started)
	# ʔí̲ghá̲ t'és ghishúl quickly coals I-blew-it (marginally: 'suddenly I blew the coals')

(16)

Theme	**Ø–tsagh** (cl-stem) 'cry'
1sg impf	hestsagh 'I'm crying'
3 sg impf	hetsagh 's/he's crying'
1sg perf	ghitsagh 'I cried'
3sg perf	ghi̲tsagh 's/he cried'
'almost' test	k'ájëne ghitsagh almost I-cried 'I almost cried' (but did not start)
durativity tests	tthidziné k'e hestsagh–ú tsa̲tsá̲naze naréłtsër yesterday I-crying-C phone again-it-rang 'yesterday while I was crying the phone rang again'
	ʔi̲ła dziné k'étł'á ghitsagh one day duration-of I-cried 'I cried for a whole day'
	hestsagh ʔanasdhën I-crying I-finished 'I finished crying, I shall cry no more, I did all my crying and now I'm finished, I'm totally cried out'
	# ʔí̲ghá̲ ghitsagh quickly I-cried

Appendix One

(17)

Theme	**Ø–t'áth, –t'adh** (cl-stem) 'cut O'
1sg impf	bĕr hest'áth sį 'I'm cutting this meat'
3 sg impf	bĕr het'áth sį 's/he is cutting the meat'
1sg perf	bĕr ghit'adh nį 'I had cut the meat'
3sg perf	yeghįt'adh nį 's/he had cut it'
'almost' test	# k'ájëne bĕr ghit'adh sį almost meat I-cut-it assert
durativity tests	tthidziné k'e bĕr hest'áth–ú tsątsánaze déłtsĕr yesterday meat I-cutting-it-C phone it-rang 'yesterday just while I was cutting the meat the phone rang'
	ʔįłághe ts'údzáhi k'e bĕr ghit'adh one hour P meat I-cut-it 'I was cutting the meat for one hour, it took me an hour to cut the meat'
	bĕr hest'áth–i ʔanast'e meat I-cutting-it-Nomlz I-finish 'I'm finished/I stopped cutting the meat'
	? ʔíghą́ bĕr ghit'adh sį quickly meat I-cut-it assert 'I went through the motion of cutting the meat quickly'

(18)

Theme	**yá#l–gus** (adv#cl-stem) 'jump prolonged'
1sg impf	yásgus 'I am jumping (continuously)'
3 sg impf	yálgus 's/he is jumping'
1sg perf	yághesgus 'I jumped, had been jumping (continuously)'
3sg perf	yághelgus 's/he jumped, had been jumping'
'almost' test	k'ájëne yághesgus almost I-jumped.cont 'I almost jumped (continuously)' (but I never did jump)
durativity tests	tthidziné k'e yásgus–ú tsątsánaze déłtsĕr yesterday I-jumping.cont-C phone it-rang 'yesterday while I was jumping (continuously) the phone rang'
	ʔįłághe ts'údzáhi k'e yághesgus one hour P I-jumped.cont 'I jumped for an hour'

	yásgus ʔanastʼe I-jumping.cont I-finish 'I'm done with jumping (for now)'
	ʔį́ghą́ yághesgus quickly I-jumped.cont 'I was jumping quickly, hopping'

(19)

Theme	**u–ł–tʼus** (ser/th-cl-stem) 'punch O repeatedly'
1sg impf	hustʼus 'I'm punching him/her/it (repeatedly)'
3 sg impf	*not elicited*
1sg perf	hughiłtʼus 'I punched O repeatedly'
3sg perf	*not elicited*
'almost' test	# kʼájëne hughiłtʼus almost I-punched-cont-it
durativity tests	tthidziné kʼe hustʼus–ú tsątsą́naze déłtsěr yesterday I-punching-cont-it-C phone it-rang ['yesterday while I was punching him/her/it (repeatedly) the phone rang' — A.W.]
	ʔįłághe tsʼúdzáhi kʼe hughiłtʼus ... one hour P I-punched-cont-it 'I punched him for a whole hour ...' (context needed, e.g.: until he gave up)
	hustʼus–i ʔanasdhën I-punching-cont-it-Nomlz I-finished 'I'm done punching him'
	? ʔį́ghą́ hughiłtʼus quickly I-punched-cont-it 'I hit him quickly' (speaker comment: seldom used)

(20)

Theme	**Ø–ził** (cl-stem) 'scream repeatedly/prolonged'
1sg impf	hessił 'I am screaming repeatedly/continuously'
3 sg impf	heził 's/he is screaming repeatedly'
1sg perf	ghiził 'I screamed repeatedly'
3sg perf	ghįził 's/he screamed repeatedly'

Appendix One 241

'almost' test	? k'ájëne ghizil almost I-screamed.cont 'I almost screamed for a long time' (but I didn't scream at all)
durativity tests	dëneyuaze ʔịłághe ts'údzáhi k'étł'á ghizil little-boy one hour duration-of he-screamed.cont 'the little boy screamed for one whole hour'
	dëneyuaze hezil ʔanat'e little-boy he-screaming.cont he-finish 'the little boy quit screaming'

(21)

Theme	**ne–ł–ʔị, –ʔị̇, –ʔị** (th-cl-stem) 'look at O'	
1sg impf	nesʔị	'I'm looking at O'
3 sg impf	yenełʔị	's/he's looking at O'
1sg perf	nighiłʔị̇	'I had looked at O'
3sg perf	yenighiłʔị̇	's/he had looked at O'
'almost' test	k'ájëne nighiłʔị̇ almost I-looked-at-it 'I almost looked at O' (I never did)	
durativity tests	thanakódhi nesʔį̣–ú tsątsąnaze narélts'ër car I-looking-at-it-C phone again-it-rang 'while I was looking at the car the phone rang again'	
	ʔịłághe ts'údzáhi k'e nighiłʔị̇ one hour P I-looked-at-it 'I looked at O for one hour'	
	nesʔị ʔanast'e I-looking-at-it I-finish 'I'm finished looking at it' (e.g.,TV program)	
	ts'ethiẹ nighiłʔị̇ carefully I-looked-at-it 'I looked at it thoroughly'	

(22)

Theme	**d–yēn** (cl-stem) 'sing'	
1sg impf	hesjën	'I'm singing'
3 sg impf	hejën	's/he's singing'
1sg perf	ghesjën	'I sang'

3sg perf	ghejën 's/he sang'
'almost' test	?? k'ájëne ghesjën almost I-sang 'I just about sang' (but I didn't) (speaker comment: doesn't make sense)
durativity tests	tthidziné k'e hesjën–ú tsątsánaze déɬtsër yesterday I-singing-C phone it-rang 'yesterday while I was singing the phone rang'
	ʔįɬághe ts'údzáhi k'e ghesjën one hour P I-sang 'I sang for an hour'
	hesjën ʔanast'e I-singing I-finish 'I'm done singing'
	# ʔįghą́ ghesjën quickly I-sang

(23)

Theme	**ya#ɬ–ti** (?#cl-stem) 'talk, pray'
1sg impf	yasti sį 'I'm talking/praying'
3 sg impf	yaɬti sį 's/he is talking/praying'
1sg perf	yaghiɬti nį 'I talked/spoke/prayed'
3sg perf	yaghįɬti nį 's/he talked/spoke/prayed'
'almost' test	k'ájëne yaghiɬti sį almost I-talked/prayed assert 'I was going to speak but I didn't' (I didn't get a chance to make my speech)
durativity tests	yasti nú tsątsánaze déɬtsër I-talking/praying past-C phone it-rang 'as I was talking/praying the phone rang'
	ʔįɬághe ts'údzáhi yaghiɬti one hour I-talked/prayed 'I spoke for one hour'
	yasti ʔanast'e I-talking/praying I-finish 'I finished praying/speaking, I stopped praying/quit talking'
	ts'ethię̈ yaghiɬti slowly I-talked/prayed 'I talked slowly'

Appendix One   243

(24)

Theme	**dzí#(dé?–)Ø–gha** (adv#(?-)cl-stem) 'sg walk around'
1sg impf	yísį dzíréssa sį 'I am walking around inside (the house)'
3 sg impf	yísį dzírégha sį 's/he is walking around inside'
1sg perf	tthidziné k'e dzíghigha nį 'yesterday I walked around'
3sg perf	tthidziné k'e dzíghįgha nį 'yesterday s/he walked around'
'almost' test	# k'ájëne yísį dzíghigha nį almost inside around-I-walked past
durativity tests	tthidziné k'e yísį dzíréssa–ú tsątsąnaze déłtsër yesterday inside around-I-walking-C phone it-rang 'yesterday while I was walking around inside the phone rang' ?įłághe ts'údzáhi k'e dzíghigha sį . . . one hour P around-I-walked assert 'I was walking around inside for one hour' (because . . .) * yísį dzíréssa ?anast'e inside around-I-walking I-finish ?íghą yísį dzíghigha nį . . . quickly inside around-I-walked past 'I was walking around inside quickly' (because...)

(25)

Theme	**u–Ø–kár** (ser/th-cl-stem) 'slap O repeatedly'
1sg impf	bek'eshích'elyį huskár 'I keep/am slapping the table'
3 sg impf	yukár 's/he keeps slapping it'
1sg perf	hughikár nį 'I (had) slapped (it) repeatedly, I had gone through the process of slapping'
3sg perf	yughįkár nį 's/he had gone through the process of slapping'
'almost' test	# k'ájëne hughikár almost I-slapped-cont-it (speaker comment: contradiction between done and not done)
durativity tests	bek'eshích'elyį huskár–ú tsątsąnaze déłtsër table I-slapping-cont-it-C phone it-rang 'as I was slapping the table the phone rang' ?įłághe ts'údzáhi k'e hughikár one hou P I-slapped-cont-it 'I slapped it for one hour'

	huskár ʔanastʼe I-slapping-cont-it I-finish 'I quit slapping'
	?? ʔíghą́ hughikár quickly I-slapped-cont-it (speaker comment: speed of hitting can't be specified)

(26)

Theme	**(u–)Ø–kə̌r** (ser/th-cl-stem) 'pat O'
1sg impf	łįchogh heskə̌r sį 'I'm patting the horse'
3 sg impf	łįchogh hekə̌r sį 's/he is patting the horse'
1sg perf	łįchogh (hu)ghikə̌r nį 'I patted the horse'
3sg perf	łįchogh (hu)ghįkə̌r 's/he patted the horse'
'almost' test	kʼájëne hughikə̌r almost I-patted-it 'I just about patted' (but I did not at all)
durativity tests	hotié łįchogh heskə̌r–ú ʔerelyël héja just horse I-patting-it-C thunder it-happened '(just) as I was petting the horse it thundered'
	ʔįłághe tsʼúdzáhi kʼe hughikə̌r one hour P I-patted-it 'I patted for one hour'
	heskə̌r ʔanastʼe I-patting-it I-finish 'I'm finished patting, I quit patting'
	ʔíghą́ hughikə̌r quickly I-patted-it 'I patted it quickly/hurriedly' (quick movements)

(27)

Theme	**na#Ø–ku(i)** (?#cl-stem) 'vomit'
1sg impf	nasku(i) 'I am in the process of vomiting'
3 sg impf	naku(i) 's/he is in the process of vomiting'
1sg perf	nathesku(i) 'I vomited'
3sg perf	natheku(i) 's/he vomited'

Appendix One

'almost' test	k'ájëne nátheskui almost I-vomited 'I just about vomited' (but I did not at all)
durativity tests	tthidziné k'e naskui–ú tsątsą́naze déɬtsér yesterday I-vomiting-C phone it-rang 'yesterday when I was vomiting the phone rang'
	? tthidziné k'e ʔįɬághe ts'údzáhi k'e nathesku yesterday one hour P I-vomited 'yesterday I was vomiting for one hour'
	# nasku ʔanast'e I-vomiting I-finish (speaker comment: end is unpredictable)
	# ts'ethię́ nathesku slowly I-vomited (speaker comment: can't be done slowly) (<u>Note</u>: ʔíghą́ is also bad)

(28)

Theme	**hú–the–Ø–gha, –ya, –yá** (?-CM-cl-stem) 'sg travel through/by'
1sg impf	húthessa sį 'I'm passing through'
3 sg impf	húxa sį 's/he passing through'
1sg perf	húthiya sį 'I passed through'
3sg perf	húya sį 's/he passed through'
'almost' test	k'ájëne Drumheller húthiya sį almost Drumheller I-traveled-through assert 'I almost passed through Drumheller' (I saw it from a short distance)
durativity tests	tthidziné k'e ją húthessa–ú tsiɬ hejër héja yesterday here I-traveling-through-C snow ? it-start 'yesterday when I was going through here it started to snow'
	ʔįɬághe ts'údzáhi k'e Tsádhekų́ę ts'ën húthiya one hour P Edmonton to I-traveled-through 'I travelled for one hour to Edmonton'
	#/* Drumheller húthessa ʔanast'e Drumheller I-traveling-through I-finish
	ʔíghą́ húthiya sį quickly I-traveled-through assert 'I went through/passed by quickly'

1.3. Achievements

X no completion reading with 'almost' (onset reading or unacceptable)
(√) pass some durativity tests (e.g., nonfuture imperfective)

(29)

Theme	**ts'e#Ø–dhi, –dhër** (adv#cl-stem) 'sg wake up'	
1sg impf	ts'enesthi	'I am (in the process of) waking up'
3 sg impf	ts'ehidhi	's/he is waking up'
1sg perf	ts'enidhër	'I woke up'
3sg perf	ts'enidhër	's/he just woke up' (i.e., s/he is awake now)
'almost' test	k'ájëne ts'enidhër almost s/he-woke-up 's/he's just about up' (but still sleeping, or has already started waking up)	
durativity tests	?iłághe ts'údzáhi k'e ts'enidhër one hour P s/he-woke-up 's/he woke up during this hour' or, in an operation/anaesthesia scenario: 's/he woke up in one hour/it took her one hour to wake up'	
	* ts'enesthi ?anast'e / ?anasdhën I-waking-up I-finish / I-finished	
	?íghą ts'enidhër quickly I-woke-up 'I woke up early' (cannot mean: 'I woke up quickly')	

(30)

Theme	**ní#Ø–gha, –ya, –yá** (adv#cl-stem) 'sg arrive'	
1sg impf	k'abí dé Tsádhekuę nínessa xa	'tomorrow I'll arrive in Edmonton' (*xa* = future/prospective marker)
3 sg impf	k'abí dé Tsádhekuę nígha xa	's/he will arrive in Edmonton tomorrow'
1sg perf	tthidziné k'e Tsádhekuę níniya ni	'yesterday I arrived in Edmonton'
3sg perf	tthidziné k'e Nora Tsádhekuę níniya	'yest. Nora arrived in Edmonton'
'almost' test	k'ájëne Tsádhekuę níniya almost Edmonton I-arrived 'I'm just about arriving in Edmonton' (I'm almost there)	
durativity tests	Tsádhekuę nínessa–ú tsił hejër héja Edmonton I-arriving snow ? it-start 'when I was arriving in Edmonton it started to snow'	

	# sǫlághe ts'údzáhi k'e Tsádhekų́ę níniya five hour P Edmonton I-arrived (can't mean: it took me 5 hrs to get to Edmonton)
	* nínessa ʔanast'e / ʔanasdhën I-arriving I-finish / I-finished
	ʔı́ghá́ níniya quickly I-arrived 'I got there quickly' (= event onset reading)

(31)

Theme	ná#ł–bes (, –bez) (adv#cl-stem) 'boil O (too) soft'
1sg impf	bĕr násbes sı̨ 'I'm boiling the meat soft'
3 sg impf	bĕr náłbes sı̨ 's/he is boiling the meat soft'
1sg perf	bĕr nághiłbez sı̨ 'I overboiled the meat (too soft)'
3sg perf	bĕr nághiłbez sı̨ 's/he overboiled the meat'
'almost' test	k'ájëne bĕr nághilbez . . . almost meat I-boiled-soft 'I just about overcooked the meat (but took it off the heat before it happened)' (. . . needs context)
durativity tests	? bĕr násbes-ú tsątsą́naze déłtsĕr meat I-boiling-soft-C phone it-rang ['as I was boiling the meat soft the phone rang' — A.W.]
	#/* ʔı̨łághe ts'údzáhi k'e bĕr nághiłbez one hour P meat I-boiled-soft
	#/* bĕr násbes ʔanast'e meat I-boiling-soft I-finish
	ʔı́ghá́ bĕr nághiłbez quickly meat I-cooked-soft 'I cooked the meat soft quickly' (not sure whether process or onset reading)

Note: The perfective stem of this verb varies between -*bes* and -*bez*.

(32)

Theme	Ø–ʔı̨́, –ʔı̨, –ʔı̨́ (cl-stem) 'see O'
1sg impf	k'ąbí dé hesʔı̨́ xa 'tomorrow I'm going to see O'
3 sg impf	k'ąbí dé yeʔı̨́ xa 'tomorrow s/he's going to see O'

1sg perf	ghes?į̂	'I saw O'
3sg perf	ye?į̂	's/he saw O'
'almost' test	# k'ájëne thanakódhi ghes?į̂ almost car I-saw-it ('I just about saw the car' (but I didn't); speaker comment: how can one say this? context?)	
durativity tests	# thanakódhi hes?į̂–ú tsątsánaze naréłtsër car I-seeing-it-C phone again-it-rang	
	?įłághe ts'údzáhi k'e ghes?į̂ one hour P I-saw-it 'I saw him/her for one hour (visited with him, talked to him)'	
	# hes?į̂ ?anast'e I-seeing-it I-finish (speaker comment: contradiction)	
	?į́ghą́ ghes?į̂ quickly I-saw-it 'I saw it/her/him just for a short time'	

Note: Although this verb theme is usually classed as "operative/durative" (i.e., as an activity), according to my tests it behaves more like an achievement ('come to see'/'spot') than an activity.

(33)

Theme	**he/te–ł–yú:ł, –yë́ł** (incept-cl-stem) 'throw solid round O once'	
1sg impf	dzół teshú:ł sį̂	'I am throwing the ball' (I'm ready to throw it: I'm going through the motions but I have not thrown it yet)
3 sg impf	dzół teshú:ł sį̂	's/he is throwing the ball' (s/he's ready to throw it)
1sg perf	dzół tishë́l sį̂	'I threw the ball (once)'
3sg perf	dzół téshël sį̂	's/he threw the ball (once)'
'almost' test	k'ájëne dzół tishë́l almost ball I-threw-it 'I just about threw the ball' (I went through the motion but didn't throw it yet: I changed my mind or I slipped)	
durativity tests	hotié dzół tishë́l–ú hutheskë́r just ball I-throwing-it-C I-slipped 'just as (after) I threw the ball I slipped'	
	# sǫlághe ts'údzáhaze k'e dzół tishë́l five minute P ball I-threw-it	
	#/* dzół heshúł ?anast'e / ?anasdhën ball I-throwing-it I-finish / I-finished	

	ʔíghą́ dzół tishël quickly ball I-threw-it 'I threw the ball quickly'

(34)

Theme	k'e#ne–Ø–yís, –yéz (?#th/CM-cl-stem) 'break elongated O in two'
1sg impf	dechën k'eneshís sį 'I am breaking the stick in two'
3 sg impf	dechën k'ehęyís sį 's/he is breaking the stick in two' (in progress "right now")
1sg perf	dechën k'eniyéz 'I broke the stick in two/in half'
3sg perf	dechën k'enįyéz 's/he broke the stick in two'
'almost' test	k'ájëne dechën k'eniyéz almost stick I-broke-it-in-two 'I just about broke the stick' (I tried but did not succeed)
durativity tests	(hotié) dechën k'eneshís–ú tsił hejër héja nį just stick I-breaking-it-in-two-C snow ? it-start past '(just) as/while I was breaking a stick it started snowing'
	?? ʔįłághe ts'údzáhaze k'e dechën k'eniyéz one minute P stick I-broke-it-in-two
	#/* dechën k'eneshís ʔanast'e / ʔanasdhën stick I-breaking-it-in-two I-finish / I-finished
	ʔíghą́ dechën k'eniyéz nį quickly stick I-broke-it-in-two past 'I had broken the stick fast' (it didn't take me long to do it)

(35)

Theme	ná#Ø–yís, –yéz (adv#cl-stem) 'break sg O'
1sg impf	dųhų́ tth'áy náshís 'I'm breaking the dish now'
3 sg impf	náyeyís 's/he's breaking it once'
1sg perf	tth'áy nághiyéz 'I broke the dish'
3sg perf	náyeghįyéz 's/he broke it once'
'almost' test	k'ájëne nághiyéz almost I-broke-it 'I just about broke it' (I might have dropped it on the floor but it did not break)
durativity tests	?? diri tth'áy náshís–ú tsątsą́naze déłtsër this dish I-breaking-it-C phone it-rang 'while I was busy breaking the dish the phone rang' (pragmatically strange)

	?? ?įlághe ts'údzáhi k'e nághiyéz one hour P I-broke-it
	??/* náshís ?anast'e / ?anasdhën I-breaking-it I-finish / I-finished
	? ?íghą́ nághiyéz quickly I-broke-it 'I was using it and it broke right away'

(36)

Theme	**ná–dá#Ø–yéz** (adv-distr#cl-stem) 'break pl O'
1sg impf	tth'áy náráshéz 'I'm breaking the dishes'
3 sg impf	tth'áy náráyéz xasį 's/he is going to break (the) dishes' (xa = future/prospective; sį = assert)
1sg perf	tth'áy nádáthiyéz sį 'I broke (the) dishes' (two or more)
3sg perf	tth'áy nárátheyéz sį 's/he broke the dishes'
'almost' test	k'ájëne tth'áy nádáthiyéz almost dish I-broke-them 'I just about broke the dishes' (but I never started/never did)
durativity tests	(hotié) tth'áy náráshéz–ú tsątsánaze déɬtsër (just) dish I-breaking-them-C phone it-rang '(just) when I broke the dishes the phone rang'
	?? ?įlághe ts'údzáhaze k'e tth'áy nádáthiyéz one minute P dish I-broke-them (speaker comment: nonsense to put time in it)
	?? ?íghą́ tth'áy nádáthiyéz quickly dish I-broke-them (speaker comment: nonsense to put time in it)

(37)

Theme	**(O yé) Ø–gha, –ya, –yá** ((PP) cl-stem) 'sg step (into O)'
1sg impf	ts'i yéssa sį 'I'm getting into the boat'
3 sg impf	ts'i yégha sį 's/he is getting into the boat'
1sg perf	ts'i yé ghiya sį 'I just got/stepped/walked into the boat'
3sg perf	ts'i yé ghiya sį 's/he got into the boat'
'almost' test	k'ájëne ts'i yéghiya sį almost boat I-stepped-in assert 'I just about got into the boat' (but I didn't)

Appendix One

| durativity tests | ts'i   yéssa–ú   huthesker
boat   I-stepping-into-C   I-slipped
'as I was getting into the boat I slipped' |
|---|---|
| | ?? ?iłághe ts'údzáhaze k'e ts'i   yéghiya   si
       one   minute   P boat I-stepped-in assert |
| | #/* ts'i   yéssa   ?anast'e / ?anasdhën
      boat I-stepping-in I-finish / I-finished
      (speaker comment: senseless) |
| | ?íghá   ts'i yéghiya   si
quickly boat I-stepped-in assert
'I got into the boat very quickly' |

(38)

Theme	he/te–Ø–gha, –ya, –yá (incept-cl-stem) 'sg leave' (lit., 'start to go')	
1sg impf	Tsádhekųę ts'én hessa/tessa sį	'I'm leaving to Edmonton (right now)'
3 sg impf	Tsádhekųę ts'én hegha xasį	's/he is going to leave to Edmonton'
1sg perf	tthidziné k'e Tsádhekųę ts'én hiya/tiya nį	'I left for E. yesterday' (nį = past marker)
3sg perf	tthidziné k'e Tsádhekųę ts'én téya/héya nį	's/he left for E. yesterday'
'almost' test	k'ájëne Tsádhekųę ts'én tiya . . .
almost   Edmonton   to   I-left
'I almost left to Edmonton . . .' (but, e.g., I changed my mind)	
durativity tests	# Tsádhekųę ts'én hessa-ú tsił hejër héja
Edmonton   to   I-leaving-C snow   ?   it-start
['as I was leaving for Edmonton it started snowing' — A.W.]	
	# ?iłághe ts'údzáhi k'e Tsádhekųę ts'én hessa xasį
one hour P Edmonton to I-leaving fut-assert	
	#/* Tsádhekųę ts'én hessa ?anast'e
Edmonton to I-leaving I-finish	
	?íghá Tsádhekųę ts'én tiya
quickly Edmonton   to   I-left
'I left for Edmonton early/soon/immediately'	

(39)

| Theme | be–ghá#ne–Ø–?á, –?ą, –?ał (3O-P#th/CM-cl-stem)
                                'give solid round O to' |
|---|---|

1sg impf	tthe beghánes?á	'I'm giving him/her a pipe'
3 sg impf	tthe yeghą́?á	's/he is giving him/her a pipe'
1sg perf	tthe begháni̜?ą	'I gave him/her a pipe'
3sg perf	tthe yegháni̜?ą	's/he gave him/her a pipe'
'almost' test	k'ájëne tthe begháni?ą almost pipe I-gave-it-to-him/her 'I just about gave him a pipe' (but I didn't)	
durativity tests	# tthe beghánes?á–ú tsą̀tsą́naze déɬtsër pipe I-giving-it-to-him/her-C phone it-rang	
	?? ?iɬághe ts'údzhi k'e tthe begháni?ą one hour P pipe I-gave-it-to-him/her	
	#/* tthe beghánes?á ?anast'e / ?anasdhën pipe I-giving-it-to-him/her I-finish / I-finished	
	?? ?ígha̧ tthe begháni?ą quickly pipe I-gave-it-to-him/her (speaker comment: not very common)	

(40)

Theme	ni#dí–∅–?á, –?ą, –?aɬ (N?#?-cl-stem) 'pick/lift up solid round O'
1sg impf	tthe nirés?á si̜ 'I am lifting a rock' (now)
3 sg impf	tthe nií?á si̜ 's/he is lifting a rock'
1sg perf	tthe nirí?ą si̜ 'I picked the rock up, I lifted the rock up'
3sg perf	tthe nirí?ą si̜ 's/he picked the rock up'
'almost' test	k'ájëne tthe nirí?ą si̜ almost rock I-lifted-up 'I just about lifted the rock' (e.g, I only thought about it, the rock was too heavy, etc.)
durativity tests	tthe nirés?á–ú tsą̀tsą́naze déɬtsër rock I-lifting-up-C phone it-rang 'as I was lifting the rock the phone rang'
	# sǫlághe ts'údzáhaze k'e tthe nirí?ą si̜ five minute P rock I-lifted-up assert
	#/* tthe nirés?á ?anast'e / ?anasdhën rock I-lifting-up I-finish / I-finished
	?ígha̧ tthe nirí?ą si̜ quickly rock I-lifted-up assert 'I picked the rock up quickly' (action of lifting is quick)

Appendix One

1.4. Semelfactives

X no completion reading with 'almost' (onset reading or unacceptable)
X fail all durativity tests

(41)

Theme	é–∅–t'ë́th, ∅–t'áth (sem/th-cl-stem, cl-stem) 'make one quick cut' (e.g., knife slips)
1sg impf	hést'ë́th xa 'I am going to cut it' (one quick cut)
3 sg impf	yít'ë́th xasį 's/he is going to cut it' (one quick cut)
1sg perf	sįlá thit'áth sį 'I cut my hand (accidentally)'
3sg perf	bįlá thet'áth 's/he cut his/her hand'
'almost' test	k'ájëne sįlá thit'áth almost my-hand I-cut-it 'I just about cut my hand'
durativity tests	tthidziné k'e sįlá thit'áth–ú tsątsą́naze déɬtsër yesterday my-hand I-cut-it-C phone it-rang 'yesterday just when (=after) I cut my hand the phone rang'
	# ʔįɬághe ts'údzahaze k'e thit'áth one minute P I-cut-it (speaker comment: no time can be specified for slashing)
	?? ʔį́ghą́ bër thit'áth quickly meat I-cut-it ('I cut the meat quickly'; speaker comment: ʔį́ghą́ not needed)

(42)

Theme	é–∅–ziɬ, ∅–zëɬ (sem/th-cl-stem, cl-stem) 'scream once'
1sg impf	héssiɬ (xa) 'I'm going to scream once' (* 'I'm screaming once')
3 sg impf	híziɬ xa 's/he is going to scream once'
1sg perf	thizëɬ 'I screamed once'
3sg perf	thezëɬ 's/he screamed once'
'almost' test	k'ájëne thizëɬ almost I-screamed-once 'I just about screamed' (but I did not scream at all)
durativity tests	# tthidziné k'e héssiɬ–ú tsątsą́naze déɬtsër yesterday I-screaming-once-C phone it-rang
	# ʔįɬághe ts'údzáhi k'étł'á thizëɬ one hour duration-of I-screamed-once (speaker comment: not good because *thizëɬ* suggests "just one little scream." It is very marginally possible as a one hour-long uninterrupted scream.)

	# héssił ʔanast'e
	I-screaming-once I-finish
	# ʔígha̧ thizël
	quickly I-screamed-once

(43)

Theme	é–ł–k'íth, ł–k'éth (sem/th-cl-stem, cl-stem) 'shoot O (with gun)'
1sg impf	k'a̧bí dé hésk'íth xasi̧ 'tomorrow I'm going to shoot it'
3 sg impf	k'a̧bí dé yíłk'íth xasi̧ 'tomorrow s/he's going to shoot it'
1sg perf	thiłk'éth 'I shot O'
3sg perf	yełk'éth si̧ 's/he shot O'
'almost' test	k'ájëne łi̧ thiłk'éth almost dog I-shot-it 'I just about shot the dog' (I missed or changed my mind, i.e., I never shot/hit it)
durativity tests	# łi̧ hesk'íth–ú tsa̧tsá̧naze déłtsër dog I-shooting-it-C phone it-rang
	# ʔiłághe ts'údzáhi k'e łi̧ thiłk'éth one hour P dog I-shot-it (speaker comment: it only takes a split second)
	# łi̧ hesk'íth ʔanast'e / ʔanasdhën dog I-shooting-it I-finish / I-finished
	? ʔígha̧ łi̧ thiłk'éth quickly dog I-shot-it ('I shot the dog fast')

Note: Speakers warn that this verb has strong sexual connotations in some contexts. In particular, the sexual meaning is prevalent in non-hunting contexts (e.g., indoors).

(44)

Theme	ha̧–tthi#de–l–tsa(gh), (adv-ʔ#th-cl-stem) ha̧–tthi#de–í–l–tsa(gh) (adv-ʔ#th-sem?-cl-stem) 'cry out in fear'
1sg impf	bech'á ha̧tthirestsagh si̧ 'I am crying out in fear of him'
3 sg impf	bech'á/yech'á ha̧tthireltsagh 's/he is crying out in fear of him'
1sg perf	bech'á ha̧tthiríthestsa(gh) 'I cried out in fear of him'
3sg perf	yech'á ha̧tthiréłtsa 's/he cried out in fear of him'

Appendix One 255

'almost' test	? k'ájëne hątthiríthestsa(gh) almost I-cried-out-in-fear ('I just about screamed out in fear')
durativity tests	(hotié) bech'á hątthirestsagh–ú tsątsą́naze déłtsër just of-him/her I-crying-out-in-fear-C phone it-rang '(just) as I was crying out in fear of him, the phone rang' (simultaneous events)
	# ʔįłághe ts'údzáhi k'e hątthiríthestsa one hour P I-cried-out-in-fear
	#/* hątthirestsagh ʔanast'e I-crying-out-in-fear I-finish
	?? ʔíghą́ bech'á hątthiríthestsa quickly of-him/her I-cried-out-in-fear (speaker comment: it's already quick without ʔíghą́)

Note: The stem-final consonant of this verb is often dropped.

(45)

Theme	é–ł–yúł, ł–yúł (sem/th-cl-stem, cl-stem) 'blow O once' (e.g., blow out candle)
1sg impf	héshúł xasį 'I'm going to blow it once'
3 sg impf	yíshúł xasį 's/he is going to blow it once'
1sg perf	thishúł 'I blew O once'
3sg perf	yéshúł 's/he blew O once'
'almost' test	k'ájëne bek'ák'áni thishúł almost candle I-blew-it-once 'I just about blew the light once' (but I didn't; perhaps I changed my mind or (for some reason) my wind stopped half way)
durativity tests	tthidziné k'e héshúł–ú tsątsą́naze déłtsër yesterday I-blowing-it-once-C phone it-rang 'yesterday as I was going to blow it (once), the phone rang'
	ʔįłághe ts'údzáhi k'e thishúł one hour P I-blew-it-once 'I blew for one hour (one uninterrupted blow)'
	# héshúł ʔanast'e I-blowing-it-once I-finish (speaker comment: nonsense/contradiction)
	ʔíghą́ thishúł quickly I-blew-it-once 'I blew it (once) quickly'

Note: This verb theme seems to undergo aspectual shift in some tests. With the time span 'one hour' it is interpreted as one uninterrupted, hour-long blowing event. With the 'almost' test, there is an onset reading

('I just about blew the light (once) but I changed my mind and didn't') and what might be an onset or a completion reading ('I just about blew the light (once) but my wind stopped half way and I didn't.'). Both of these unexpected readings are pragmatically extremely odd, which I take as an indication that they represent a nonbasic situation type. I take the verb theme to be basically a semelfactive because it cannot occur in a nonfuture imperfective, and because 'quickly' may only modify the event onset.

(46)

Theme	yá#l–gus, –gos (adv#cl-stem) 'jump once'	
1sg impf	yásgus	'I'm going to jump (once)'
3 sg impf	yélgus	's/he is going to jump (once)'
1sg perf	yásgos	'I jumped once'
3sg perf	yélgos	's/he jumped once'
'almost' test	k'ájëne yásgos almost I-jumped-once 'I almost jumped once' (I did not jump)	
durativity tests	tthidziné k'e yásgus–ú tsątsánaze déłtsër yesterday I-jumping-C phone it-rang * 'yesterday as I was jumping once the phone rang' √ 'yesterday while I was jumping continuously the phone rang'	
	# ?iłághe ts'údzáhi k'e yásgos one hour P I-jumped-once	
	# yásgu:s ?anast'e I-jumping-once I-finish	
	?įghą yásgos quickly I-jumped-once 'I jumped (once) right away'	

Note: The imperfective form of this verb is identical to the imperfective form of the verb 'jump continuously' (see (18) above). Therefore, the verb seems to pass the durativity tests which use the imperfective form. However, the tests are passed only on the meaning 'jump continuously', not on the meaning 'jump once'. One speaker seems to distinguish imperfective 'jump once' by a lengthened stem vowel (*-gu:s*). If this unambiguous form is used, the durativity tests are failed (see 'finish' test).

(47)

Theme	ná#ne–ł–t'us (adv#th-cl-stem) 'punch O once'	
1sg impf	nánest'us xasį	'I'm gonna punch him/it (once)'
3 sg impf	náyenełt'us xa	's/he is gonna punch him/it (once)'
1sg perf	nánighiłt'us	'I punched him/it (once)'
3sg perf	náyenighiłt'us	's/he punched him/it (once)'
'almost' test	k'ájëne nánighiłt'us almost I-punched-it-once 'I just about hit him' (I did not hit him at all)	

Appendix One 257

durativity tests	# tthidziné k'e nánest'us–ú tsątsánaze déltsër yesterday I-punching-it-once-C phone it-rang
	# ʔįłághe ts'údzáhi k'e nánighiłt'us one hour P I-punched-it-once
	# nánest'us ʔanast'e I-punching-it-once I-finish
	ʔį́ghą́ nánighiłt'us quickly I-punched-it-once 'I punched O quickly/immediately'

(48)

Theme	**ná#ne–(i–)Ø–kár** (adv#th-(ʔ-)cl-stem) 'slap O once'
1sg impf	náneskár xa 'I'm going to slap him/it once'
3 sg impf	bek'eshích'elyį nánekár xa 's/he is going to slap the table once'
1sg perf	nánighikár 'I slapped him/it once'
3sg perf	náyenighįkár 's/he slapped him/it once'
'almost' test	k'ájëne nánighikár almost I-slapped-it-once 'I almost slapped it' (but I did not)
durativity tests	# náneskár–ú tsątsánaze déltsër I-slapping-it-once-C phone it-rang
	# ʔįłághe ts'údzáhi k'e nánighikár one hour P I-slapped-it-once
	# náneskár ʔanas'te / ʔanasdhën I-slapping-it-once I-finish / I-finished
	?? ʔį́ghą́ nánighikár quickly I-slapped-it-once (speaker comment: *ʔį́ghą́* not needed)

(49)

Theme	**ní–na#ne–d–gha, –ya, –yá** (adv-iter#th-cl-stem) 'come back' (lit., 'arrive again/arrive back')
1sg impf	ninesda xasį 'I'm going to come back'
3 sg impf	k'ąbí dé nįda xa 's/he is going to come back tomorrow'
1sg perf	tthidziné k'e ninesja nį 'I came back yesterday'
3sg perf	nįja 's/he came back'

'almost' test	# k'ájëne ninesja almost I-came-back (speaker comment: the verb means that I came back already)
durativity tests	?? ninesda–ú tsątsąnaze déłtsë́r I-coming-back-C phone it-rang
	# ʔįłághe ts'údzáhi k'e ninesja one hour P I-came-back
	# ninesda ʔanas'te I-coming-back I-finish
	ʔį́ghą́ ninesja quickly I-came-back 'I came back soon' (I was not away for long)

(50)

Theme	**łeghá#ne–ł–dhi, –dhër** (?#th/CM-cl-stem) 'kill sg O'	
1sg impf	łį łeghánesthi	'I'm going to kill the/a dog'
3 sg impf	k'ąbí dé łegháyiłthi	'tomorrow s/he's going to kill it'
1sg perf	łeghániłthër	'I killed it'
3sg perf	łegháyenįłthër	's/he killed it'
'almost' test	k'ájëne łegháníłthër almost I-killed-it 'I just about killed it/her/him' (but I didn't; cannot mean: 'I just about finished killing it')	
durativity tests	# tthidziné k'e k'ásba łeghánesthi–ú tsątsąnaze déłtsë́r yesterday chicken I-killing-it-C phone it-rang (speaker comment: "strange to put the length in the killing")	
	?? ʔįłághe ts'údzáhi k'e łegháníłthër one hour P I-killed-it	
	?? łeghánesthi ʔanas'te I-killing-it I-finish	
	ʔį́ghą́ łegháníłthër quickly I-killed-it 'I killed it quickly'	

Appendix Two

GERMAN VERBS AND TESTS

The verbs are listed by situation type, and within each situation type as follows: particle verbs with *ab*, particle verbs with *aus*, particle verbs with *um*, simplex verbs. Note that the four (nonstative) situation types are followed by a last category "unspecified" (section 2.5), which contains verbs for which the situation type tests, and specifically the durativity tests, did not yield conclusive results.

For particle verbs, the meaning and situation type of the base verb are also indicated. For simplex verbs, the related particle verbs which are contained in the database are also listed, with their meaning and situation type. A question mark behind the situation type indicates that the classification is not completely clear. Finally, an example sentence illustrates whether the verb is obligatorily transitive or not.

This general information is followed by telicity and durativity tests: compatibility with 'in X time' (or sometimes with 'take an hour to VP') for telicity, and compatibility with 'stop VP-ing' or with a pseudo-progressive (see Chapter Five) for durativity. If a verb, or rather, VP, fails a certain test, this is indicated by one of the following symbols: ??, #, *. Note that my analysis focuses on the most common meaning of a given verb. Sometimes additional meanings are indicated in the form of a note.

Morpheme-by-morpheme glosses are not given, except where relevant. The reader should be aware that most German sentences are in the Present Perfect, while most of the English translations are in the simple past or the past progressive (see Chapter Five for discussion of the function of the German Perfect).

2.1. Accomplishments

√ pass telicity tests
√ pass durativity tests

(1)

Verb	**ABÄNDERN** 'make a (small) change to'
Related	ÄNDERN 'change something' (accompl.) UMÄNDERN 'change around' (accompl.)
transitivity	* Sie hat abgeändert. she has *ab*-changed　　　　　　　　　　(obligatorily transitive)
telicity test	Sie hat das Programm in zwei Minuten abgeändert. 'She made a change to the program in two minutes.'
durativity test	Sie hat aufgehört, das Programm abzuändern. 'She stopped making changes to the program.'

(2)

Verb	**ABARBEITEN** 'pay off/reduce by working'
Related	ARBEITEN 'work' (activity) AUSARBEITEN 'work out (details of)' (accompl.) UMARBEITEN 'work over, rework' (accompl.)
transitivity	* Sie hat abgearbeitet. she has *ab*-worked　　　　　　　　　　(obligatorily transitive)
telicity test	Sie hat die Schulden in einem Jahr abgearbeitet. 'She worked off her debts in one year.'
durativity test	Sie hat aufgehört, die Schulden abzuarbeiten. 'She stopped working off her debts.'

(3)

Verb	**ABBAGGERN** 'remove/level with an excavator'
Related	BAGGERN 'move dirt with a machine, excavate' (activity) AUSBAGGERN 'excavate' (accomplishment)
transitivity	* Sie hat abgebaggert. she has *ab*-excavated　　　　　　　　　(obligatorily transitive)
telicity test	Sie hat in einer Stunde die Sandbank abgebaggert. 'She removed the sandbank in one hour.'
durativity test	Sie hat aufgehört, die Sandbank abzubaggern. 'She stopped removing the sandbank.'

Appendix Two

(4)

Verb	**ABBAUEN** 'dismantle'
Related	BAUEN 'build' (accompl.) AUSBAUEN 'take out/extend' (accompl.) UMBAUEN 'remodel, rearrange' (accompl.)
transitivity	* Sie hat abgebaut. she has *ab*-built (obligatorily transitive)
telicity test	Sie hat das Gerüst in einer Stunde abgebaut. 'She dismantled the scaffold in an hour.'
durativity test	Sie hat aufgehört, das Gerüst abzubauen. 'She stopped dismantling the scaffold.'

Note: There is a different sense of *abbauen* ('decline mentally/physically', accompl.) which is intransitive.

(5)

Verb	**ABBRENNEN** 'burn down'
Related	BRENNEN 'burn' (activity) AUSBRENNEN 'burn out' (accompl.)
transitivity	Das Haus brennt (* die Wand) ab. the house burns (*the wall) *ab* Sie brennen das alte Haus ab. they burn the old house *ab* (intransitive; may form causative)
telicity test	Das Haus ist in einer Stunde abgebrannt. 'The house burned down in an hour.'
durativity test	? Das Haus ist am Abbrennen. 'The house is in the process of burning down.'

Note: Durativity tests are not completely felicitous with this verb. The intuition is to use atelic *brennen* 'burn' when emphasizing process/duration.

(6)

Verb	**ABHUSTEN** 'cough up, clear lungs/throat of something'
Related	HUSTEN 'cough' (semelf.) AUSHUSTEN 'cough up, cough out' (achievement or accompl.)
transitivity	Sie hat (den Schleim) abgehustet. (transitive; implied she has (the phlegm) *ab*-coughed object can be deleted)
telicity test	Sie hat in 5 Minuten den Schleim abgehustet. 'She cleared her throat of the phlegm in five minutes.'
durativity test	Sie hat aufgehört, den Schleim abzuhusten. 'She stopped clearing her throat of the phlegm.'

(7)

Verb	**ABKLOPFEN** 'knock/beat sth. off of sth.'
Related	KLOPFEN 'knock, hit, beat' (semelf.) AUSKLOPFEN 'clean by beating/knocking' (accompl.)
transitivity	* Sie hat abgeklopft. she has *ab*-knocked (obligatorily transitive)
telicity test	Sie hat in fünf Minuten den Schnee vom Mantel abgeklopft. 'She knocked the snow off the coat in five minutes.'
durativity test	Sie hat aufgehört, den Schnee vom Mantel abzuklopfen. 'She stopped knocking the snow off the coat.'

(8)

Verb	**ABKRATZEN** 'scrape off'
Related	KRATZEN 'scratch, scrape' (activity) AUSKRATZEN 'empty or hollow out by scraping' (accompl.)
transitivity	* Sie hat abgekratzt. she has *ab*-scratched (obligatorily transitive)
telicity test	Sie hat in einer Stunde die Farbe von dem Bilderrahmen abgekratzt. 'She scraped the paint off the picture frame in an hour.'
durativity test	Sie hat aufgehört, die Farbe von dem Bilderrahmen abzukratzen. 'She stopped scraping the paint off the picture frame.'

Note: This verb has an intransitive variant *abkratzen* 'die/snuff it' which is also telic.

(9)

Verb	**ABRENNEN** 'cover area by running'
Related	RENNEN 'run' (activity) UMRENNEN 'knock over by running' (achievement)
transitivity	* Sie hat abgerannt. she has *ab*-run (obligatorily transitive)
telicity test	Sie hat in einer Stunde alle Läden abgerannt. 'She hurried through all the stores in one hour.'
durativity test	? Sie hat aufgehört, die Läden abzurennen. 'She stopped hurrying through the stores.'

(10)

Verb	**ABSÄGEN** 'saw off'
Related	SÄGEN 'saw' (activity) AUSSÄGEN 'saw out' (accompl.)

Appendix Two 263

transitivity	* Sie hat abgesägt. she has *ab*-sawn	(obligatorily transitive)
telicity test	Sie hat in einer Stunde den Ast abgesägt. 'She sawed off the branch in an hour.'	
durativity test	Sie hat aufgehört, den Ast abzusägen. 'She stopped sawing off the branch.'	

(11)

Verb	**ABSCHREIBEN** 'copy'
Related	SCHREIBEN 'write' (accompl.) AUSSCHREIBEN 'write out' (accompl.) UMSCHREIBEN 'rewrite' (accompl.)
transitivity	Sie hat (die Lösung/die Hausaufgaben) abgeschrieben. she has (the solution/the homework) *ab*-written (variable)
telicity test	Sie hat in einer Stunde den Aufsatz abgeschrieben. 'She copied the essay in an hour.'
durativity test	Sie hat aufgehört, den Aufsatz abzuschreiben. 'She stopped copying the essay.'

Note: Without object, the verb patterns as an activity. I take the transitive, telic variant to be the basic one (see Rapp 1997b).

(12)

Verb	**ABSUCHEN** 'search an area'	
Related	SUCHEN 'look for, seek, search' (activity) AUSSUCHEN 'pick out/choose' (accompl.?)	
transitivity	* Sie sucht ab. she seeks *ab*	(obligatorily transitive)
telicity test	Sie hat in einer Stunde das Feld abgesucht. 'She searched the (entire) field in an hour.'	
durativity test	Sie hat aufgehört, das Feld abzusuchen. 'She stopped searching the field.'	

(13)

Verb	**ABWASCHEN** 'wash off'
Related	WASCHEN 'wash' (accompl.) AUSWASCHEN 'wash out' (accompl.)

transitivity	Sie hat (das Geschirr/*den Teller/*den Dreck) abgewaschen.
	she has (the dishes/*the plate/*the dirt) *ab*-washed
	(transitive; implied object can be deleted)
telicity test	Sie hat den Dreck in fünf Minuten abgewaschen.
	'She washed off the dirt in five minutes.'
durativity test	Sie hat aufgehört, den Dreck abzuwaschen.
	'She stopped washing off the dirt.'

(14)

Verb	**AUSARBEITEN** 'work out (details of)'
Related	ARBEITEN 'work' (activity)
	ABARBEITEN 'pay off/reduce by working' (accompl.)
	UMARBEITEN 'work over, rework' (accompl.)
transitivity	* Sie hat ausgearbeitet.
	she has *aus*-worked (obligatorily transitive, but see note)
telicity test	Sie hat den Plan in einem Jahr ausgearbeitet.
	'She worked out the plan in one year.'
durativity test	Sie hat aufgehört, den Plan auszuarbeiten.
	'She stopped working out the plan.'

Note: There is a different sense of *ausarbeiten* ('finish working', achievement) which is intransitive.

(15)

Verb	**AUSBAGGERN** 'excavate'
Related	BAGGERN 'move dirt with a machine, excavate' (activity)
	ABBAGGERN 'remove/level with an excavator' (accomplishment)
transitivity	* Sie hat ausgebaggert.
	she has *aus*-excavated (obligatorily transitive)
telicity test	Sie haben das Fundament in einer Stunde ausgebaggert.
	'They excavated the foundation in one hour.'
durativity test	Sie haben aufgehört, das Fundament auszubaggern.
	'They stopped excavating the foundation.'

Note: There is a different sense of *ausbaggern* ('finish excavating', achievement) which is intransitive.

(16)

Verb	**AUSBAUEN** 'take out/extend'
Related	BAUEN 'build' (accompl.)
	ABBAUEN 'dismantle' (accompl.)
	UMBAUEN 'remodel, rearrange' (accompl.)

Appendix Two 265

transitivity	Sie hat haben (das Haus/*den Motor) ausgebaut. they have (the house/*the engine) *aus*-built 'They built an addition to the house.', * 'They took out the engine.' (transitive; implied object can be deleted)
telicity test	Sie den Motor in einer Stunde ausgebaut. 'She took out the engine in an hour.'
durativity test	Sie hat aufgehört, den Motor auszubauen. 'She stopped taking out the engine.'

(17)

Verb	**AUSBRENNEN** 'burn down'
Related	BRENNEN 'burn' (activity) ABBRENNEN 'burn down' (accompl.)
transitivity	Das Auto brennt (* das Dach) aus. the car burns (*the roof) *aus* Sie brennen das alte Auto aus. they burn the old car *aus* (intransitive, may form causative)
telicity test	Das Auto/die Glühbirne ist in einer Stunde ausgebrannt. 'The car/lightbulb burned out in an hour.'
durativity test	? Das Auto ist am Ausbrennen. 'The car is in the process of burning out/completely.' ?? Die Glühbirne ist am Ausbrennen. The lightbulb is in the process of burning out.'

Note: Durativity tests are not completely felicitous with this verb. Moreover, durativity also depends on the object. *Ausbrennen* is more durative combined with *das Auto* 'the car' than with *die Glühbirne* 'the lightbulb'.

(18)

Verb	**AUSBRÜTEN** 'hatch out'
Related	BRÜTEN 'brood, hatch, sit' (activity)
transitivity	* Die Henne brütet aus. the hen hatches/sits *aus* (obligatorily transitive)
telicity test	Die Henne hat in einer Woche die Küken/Eier ausgebrütet. 'The hen hatched hatched out the chicks/eggs in one week.'
durativity test	Die Henne hat aufgehört, die Küken/Eier auszubrüten. 'The hen stopped hatching out the chicks/eggs.'

(19)

Verb	**AUSESSEN** 'empty, clear (by eating)'
Related	ESSEN 'eat' (accompl.)
transitivity	* Sie hat ausgegessen. she has *aus*-eaten (obligatorily transitive)
telicity test	Sie hat die Schüssel in einer Minute ausgegessen. 'She emptied the bowl in one minute.'
durativity test	Sie hat aufgehört, die Schüssel auszuessen. 'She stopped emptying the bowl.'

Note: There is an intransitive variant *ausessen*, which means 'finish eating' and which patterns as an achievement.

(20)

Verb	**AUSGRABEN** 'dig out'
Related	GRABEN 'dig, burrow' (activity) UMGRABEN 'turn over (soil), dig a garden bed' (accompl.)
transitivity	* Sie gräbt aus. she digs *aus* (obligatorily transitive)
telicity test	Sie hat in einer Stunde den Schatz ausgegraben. 'She dug out the treasure in an hour.'
durativity test	Sie hat aufgehört, den Schatz auszugraben. 'She stopped digging out the treasure.'

(21)

Verb	**AUSFAHREN** '(vehicle) move out of'
Related	FAHREN 'go (by vehicle), drive' (activity) ABFAHREN 'depart' (achievement) UMFAHREN 'knock over driving' (achievement)
transitivity	Der Zug ist (*den/dem Bahnhof) ausgefahren. the train is (*the train-station) *aus*-driven (intransitive)
telicity test	Der Zug ist in einer Minute (aus dem Bahnhof) ausgefahren. 'The train moved out (of the station) in one minute.'
durativity test	Der Zug hat aufgehört, (aus dem Bahnhof) auszufahren. 'The train stopped moving out of the station.'

Note: There is a transitive variant of *ausfahren* which is also an accomplishment. The meaning depends on the other constituents of the VP. For example: *die Antenne ausfahren* 'extend the antenna', *die Pakete ausfahren* 'deliver the parcels'.

Appendix Two

(22)

Verb	**AUSKLOPFEN** 'clean by beating/knocking'
Related	KLOPFEN 'knock, hit, beat' (semelf.) ABKLOPFEN 'knock/beat sth. off of sth.' (accompl.)
transitivity	* Sie hat ausgeklopft. she has *aus*-knocked (obligatorily transitive)
telicity test	Sie hat in fünf Minuten den Teppich ausgeklopft. 'She beat the rug clean in five minutes.'
durativity test	Sie hat aufgehört, den Teppich auszuklopfen. 'She stopped beating the rug.'

Note: There is an intransitive, achievement variant *ausklopfen* which means 'finish knocking'.

(23)

Verb	**AUSKRATZEN** 'empty or hollow out by scraping'
Related	KRATZEN 'scratch, scrape' (activity) ABKRATZEN 'scrape off' (accompl.)
transitivity	* Sie hat ausgekratzt. she has *aus*-scratched (obligatorily transitive)
telicity test	Sie hat in einer Minute die Schüssel ausgekratzt. 'She scraped out the bowl in a minute.'
durativity test	Sie hat aufgehört, die Schüssel auszukratzen. 'She stopped scraping out the bowl.'

(24)

Verb	**AUSRÄUMEN** 'clear out, empty'
Related	RÄUMEN 'clear (out), move' (accompl.?) UMRÄUMEN 'arrange/store differently' (accompl.)
transitivity	Sie hat (das Haus/das Zimmer) ausgeräumt. she has (the house/the room) *aus*-cleared/moved (variable)
telicity test	Sie hat das Zimmer in einer Stunde ausgeräumt. 'She cleared out the room in an hour.'
durativity test	Sie hat aufgehört, das Zimmer auszuräumen. 'She stopped clearing out the room.'

Note: Without object, the verb patterns as an activity. I take the transitive, telic variant to be the basic one (see Rapp 1997b).

(25)

Verb	**AUSSÄGEN** 'saw out'
Related	SÄGEN 'saw' (activity) ABSÄGEN 'saw off' (accompl.)
transitivity	* Sie hat ausgesägt. she has *aus*-sawn (obligatorily transitive)
telicity test	Sie hat in einer Stunde ein Herz ausgesägt. 'She sawed out a heart in an hour.'
durativity test	Sie hat aufgehört, ein Herz auszusägen. 'She stopped sawing out a heart.'

(26)

Verb	**AUSSCHREIBEN** 'write out'
Related	SCHREIBEN 'write' (accompl.) ABSCHREIBEN 'copy' (accompl.) UMSCHREIBEN 'rewrite' (accompl.)
transitivity	* Sie hat ausgeschrieben. she has *aus*-written (obligatorily transitive)
telicity test	Sie hat die Rede in einer Stunde ausgeschrieben. 'She wrote out the speech in an hour.'
durativity test	Sie hat aufgehört, die Rede auszuschreiben. 'She stopped writing out the speech.'

(27)

Verb	**AUSSUCHEN** 'pick out/choose'
Related	SUCHEN 'look for, seek, search' (activity) ABSUCHEN 'search an area' (accompl.)
transitivity	* Sie sucht aus. she seeks *aus* (obligatorily transitive)
telicity test	Sie hat in einer Stunde ein Rezept ausgesucht. 'She picked out a recipe in an hour.'
durativity test	? Sie hat aufgehört, ein Rezept auszusuchen. 'She stopped picking out a recipe.' Sie ist dabei, ein Rezept auszusuchen. 'She is in the process of picking out a recipe.'

Appendix Two

(28)

Verb	**AUSWASCHEN** 'wash out'
Related	WASCHEN 'wash' (accompl.) ABWASCHEN 'wash off' (accompl.)
transitivity	* Sie hat ausgewaschen. she has *aus*-washed (obligatorily transitive)
telicity test	Sie hat den Dreck in fünf Minuten ausgewaschen. 'She washed out the dirt in five minutes.'
durativity test	Sie hat aufgehört, den Dreck auszuwaschen. 'She stopped washing out the dirt.'

(29)

Verb	**UMÄNDERN** 'change around'
Related	ÄNDERN 'change something' (accompl.) ABÄNDERN 'make a (small) change to' (accompl.)
transitivity	* Sie hat umgeändert. she has *um*-changed (obligatorily transitive)
telicity test	Sie hat das Kleid in einer Stunde umgeändert. 'She changed around the dress in one hour.'
durativity test	Sie hat aufgehört, das Kleid umzuändern. 'She stopped changing around the dress.'

(30)

Verb	**UMARBEITEN** 'work over, rework'
Related	ARBEITEN 'work' (activity) ABARBEITEN 'pay off/reduce by working' (accompl.) AUSARBEITEN 'work out (details of)' (accompl.)
transitivity	* Sie hat umgearbeitet. she has *um*-worked (obligatorily transitive)
telicity test	Sie hat den Roman in einem Jahr umgearbeitet. 'She reworked/revised the novel in one year.'
durativity test	Sie hat aufgehört, den Roman umzuarbeiten. 'She stopped reworking the novel.'

(31)

Verb	**UMBAUEN** 'remodel, rearrange'
Related	BAUEN 'build' (accompl.) ABBAUEN 'dismantle' (accompl.) AUSBAUEN 'take out/extend' (accompl.)
transitivity	Sie haben (das Haus/*die Bühne) umgebaut. they have (the house/*the stage) *um*-built 'They remodeled the house.', * 'They rearranged the stage.' (transitive; implied object can be deleted)
telicity test	Sie haben die Bühne in einer Stunde umgebaut. 'They rearranged the stage in an hour.'
durativity test	Sie hat aufgehört, die Bühne umzubauen. 'She stopped rearranging the stage.'

(32)

Verb	**UMFALLEN** 'fall over'
Related	FALLEN 'fall' (achievement?) ABFALLEN 'fall off' (achievement) AUSFALLEN 'fall out' (achievement)
transitivity	* die Vase ist den Tisch umgefallen the vase is the table *um*-fallen (intransitive)
telicity test	Der Kran ist in einer Minute (langsam) umgefallen 'The crane fell over (slowly) in one minute.'
durativity test	Der Kran war dabei umzufallen/war am Umfallen, als... 'The crane was in the process of falling over when...'

Note: With smaller objects (e.g., *die Vase* 'the vase'), *umfallen* patterns more like an achievement.

(33)

Verb	**UMGRABEN** 'turn over (soil), dig a garden bed'
Related	GRABEN 'dig, burrow' (activity) AUSGRABEN 'dig out' (accompl.)
transitivity	?? Sie gräbt um. she digs *um* (transitive; implied object can be deleted)
telicity test	Sie hat in einer Stunde das Beet umgegraben. 'She dug the (entire) garden bed in an hour.'
durativity test	Sie hat aufgehört, das Beet umzugraben. 'She stopped digging the garden bed.'

Appendix Two

(34)

Verb	**UMNÄHEN** 'fold over and hem'
Related	NÄHEN 'sew' (accompl.)
transitivity	Sie hat *(die Hosenbeine) umgenäht. she has *(the pantlegs) *um*-sewn (obligatorily transitive)
telicity test	Sie hat die Hosenbeine in einer Stunde umgenäht. 'She shortened/hemmed the pantlegs in an hour.'
durativity test	Sie hat aufgehört, die Hosenbeine umzunähen. 'She stopped shortening/hemming the pantlegs.'

(35)

Verb	**UMPFLANZEN** 'plant somewhere else, transplant'
Related	PFLANZEN 'plant' (accompl.?)
transitivity	* Sie hat umgepflanzt she has *um*-planted (obligatorily transitive)
telicity test	Sie hat den Baum in einer Stunde umgepflanzt. 'She transplanted/moved the tree in an hour.'
durativity tests	? Sie hat aufgehört, den Baum umzupflanzen. 'She stopped transplanting the tree.' Sie ist dabei, den Baum umzupflanzen. 'She is in the process of transplanting the tree.'

Note: This verb also has some achievement characteristics.

(36)

Verb	**UMRÄUMEN** 'rearrange, store differently'
Related	RÄUMEN 'clear (out), move' (accompl.?) AUSRÄUMEN 'clear out, empty' (accompl.)
transitivity	Sie hat (das Haus/das Zimmer) umgeräumt. she has (the house/the room) *um*-cleared/moved (variable)
telicity test	Sie hat das Zimmer/die Möbel in einer Stunde umgeräumt. 'She rearranged the room/the furniture in an hour.'
durativity test	Sie hat aufgehört, das Zimmer/die Möbel umzuräumen. 'She stopped rearranging the room/the furniture.'

Note: Without object, the verb patterns as an activity. I take the transitive, telic variant to be the basic one (see Rapp 1997b).

(37)

Verb	**UMSCHREIBEN** 'rewrite'
Related	SCHREIBEN 'write' (accompl.) ABSCHREIBEN 'copy' (accompl.) AUSSCHREIBEN 'write out' (accompl.)
transitivity	* Sie hat umgeschrieben. she has *um*-written (obligatorily transitive)
telicity test	Sie hat die Rede in einer Stunde umgeschrieben. 'She rewrote (i.e., changed) the speech in an hour.'
durativity test	Sie hat aufgehört, die Rede umzuschreiben. 'She stopped rewriting the speech.'

(38)

Verb	**UMSCHÜTTEN** 'pour into something else'
Related	SCHÜTTEN 'pour' (accompl.)
transitivity	* Sie hat umgeschüttet. she has *um*-poured (obligatorily transitive)
telicity test	Sie hat das Wasser in fünf Minuten umgeschüttet. 'She poured the water into something else in five minutes.'
durativity test	Sie hat aufgehört, das Wasser umzuschütten. 'She stopped pouring the water into something else.'

Note: *Umschütten* can also mean 'spill/pour out (accidentally)' and then patterns as an achievement.

(39)

Verb	**ÄNDERN** 'change something'
Related	ABÄNDERN 'make a (small) change to' (accompl.) UMÄNDERN 'change around' (accompl.)
transitivity	* Sie hat geändert. she has changed (obligatorily transitive)
telicity test	Sie hat den Text in zwei Minuten geändert. 'She changed the text in two minutes.'
durativity test	Sie hat aufgehört, den Text zu ändern. 'She stopped changing the text.'

Appendix Two

(40)

Verb	**BAUEN** 'build'
Related	ABBAUEN 'dismantle' (accompl.) AUSBAUEN 'take out/extend' (accompl.) UMBAUEN 'remodel, rearrange' (accompl.)
transitivity	Sie hat (ein Haus/*einen Turm) gebaut. she has (a house/*a tower) built (transitive; implied object can be deleted)
telicity test	Sie haben das Haus in einem halben Jahr gebaut. 'They built the house in half a year.'
durativity test	Sie haben aufgehört, das Haus zu bauen. 'They stopped building the house.'

(41)

Verb	**ESSEN** 'eat'
Related	AUSESSEN 'empty, clear (by eating)' (accompl.)
transitivity	Sie hat (eine Mahlzeit/*eine Nuss) gegessen. she has (a meal/*a nut) eaten (transitive; implied object can be deleted)
telicity test	Sie hat das Stück Kuchen in einer Minute gegessen. 'She ate the piece of cake in one minute.'
durativity test	Sie hat aufgehört, das Stück Kuchen zu essen. 'She stopped eating the piece of cake.'

Note: Without object, the verb patterns as an activity. I take the transitive, telic variant to be the basic one (see Rapp 1997b).

(42)

Verb	**NÄHEN** 'sew'
Related	UMNÄHEN 'fold over and hem' (accompl.)
transitivity	Sie hat (ein Kleid) genäht. she has (a dress) sewn (variable)
telicity test	Sie hat das Kleid in einer Stunde genäht. 'She sewed the dress in an hour.'
durativity test	Sie hat aufgehört, das Kleid zu nähen. 'She stopped sewing the dress.'

Note: Without object, the verb patterns as an activity. I take the transitive, telic variant to be the basic one (see Rapp 1997b).

(43)

Verb	**PFLANZEN** 'plant'
Related	UMPFLANZEN 'plant somewhere else' (accompl.?)
transitivity	?? Sie hat gepflanzt. she has planted (obligatorily transitive)
telicity test	Sie hat den Baum in einer Stunde gepflanzt. 'She planted the tree in an hour.'
durativity test	? Sie hat aufgehört, den Baum zu pflanzen. 'She stopped planting the tree.' Sie ist dabei, den Baum zu pflanzen. 'She is in the process of planting the tree.'

Note: This verb also has some achievement characteristics.

(44)

Verb	**RÄUMEN** 'clear (out), move'
Related	AUSRÄUMEN 'clear out, empty' (accompl.) UMRÄUMEN 'rearrange, store differently' (accompl.)
transitivity	* Sie hat geräumt. she has cleared/moved (obligatorily transitive)
telicity test	Sie hat das Zimmer in einer Stunde geräumt. 'She cleared (out) the room in an hour.'
durativity test	?? Sie hat aufgehört, das Zimmer zu räumen. 'She stopped clearing (out) the room.' Sie ist dabei, das Zimmer zu räumen. 'She is in the process of clearing (out) the room.'

Note: This verb also has achievement characteristics. *Räumen* can also be used with a goal PP (e.g., *die Möbel in den Keller räumen* 'move the furniture into the basement') and then clearly patterns as an accomplishment.

(45)

Verb	**SCHREIBEN** 'write'
Related	ABSCHREIBEN 'copy' (accompl.) AUSSCHREIBEN 'write out' (accompl.) UMSCHREIBEN 'rewrite' (accompl.)
transitivity	Sie hat (einen Brief/einen Roman) geschrieben. she has (a letter/a novel) written (variable)
telicity test	Sie hat in einer Stunde den Brief geschrieben. 'She wrote the letter in an hour.'

Appendix Two 275

| durativity test | Sie hat aufgehört, den Brief zu schreiben. 'She stopped writing the letter.' |

Note: Without object, the verb patterns as an activity. I take the transitive, telic variant to be the basic one (see Rapp 1997b).

(46)

Verb	**SCHÜTTEN** 'pour'
Related	UMSCHÜTTEN 'pour into something else' (accompl.)
transitivity	* Sie hat geschüttet. she has poured (obligatorily transitive)
telicity test	Sie hat das Wasser in fünf Minuten in den Eimer geschüttet. 'She poured the water into the bucket in five minutes.'
durativity test	Sie hat aufgehört, das Wasser in den Eimer zu schütten. 'She stopped pouring the water into the bucket.'

(47)

Verb	**WASCHEN** 'wash'
Related	ABWASCHEN 'wash off' (accompl.) AUSWASCHEN 'wash out' (accompl.)
transitivity	Sie hat (die Wäsche/*das Kleid/*das Auto) gewaschen. she has (the laundry/*the dress/*the car) washed (transitive; implied object can be deleted)
telicity test	Sie hat den Pullover in fünf Minuten gewaschen. 'She washed the sweater in five minutes.'
durativity test	Sie hat aufgehört, den Pullover zu waschen. 'She stopped washing the sweater.'

2.2. Activities

X   fail telicity tests
√   pass durativity tests

(48)

Verb	**ARBEITEN** 'work'
Related	ABARBEITEN 'pay off/reduce by working' (accompl.) AUSARBEITEN 'work out (details of)' (accompl.) UMARBEITEN 'work over, rework' (accompl.)

transitivity	Sie hat (* den Pullover) gearbeitet.
	she has (*the sweater) worked (intransitive)
telicity test	#Sie hat in einer Woche/Stunde (an dem Pullover) gearbeitet.
	# 'She worked (on the sweater) in one week/hour.'
durativity test	Sie hat aufgehört, (an dem Pullover) zu arbeiten.
	'She stopped working (on the sweater).'

(49)

Verb	**BAGGERN** 'move dirt with a machine, excavate'
Related	ABBAGGERN 'remove/level with an excavator' (accompl.)
	AUSBAGGERN 'excavate' (accompl.)
transitivity	Sie hat (* den Sand) gebaggert.
	she has (*the sand) excavated (intransitive, except for fake objects)
telicity test	# Sie hat in einer Woche (in der Keplerstraße) gebaggert.
	# 'She did excavating (in the Kepler Street) in one week.'
durativity test	Sie hat aufgehört, (in der Keplerstraße) zu baggern.
	'She stopped excavating (in the Kepler Street).'

Note: With a fake object, such as *ein Loch* 'a hole', *baggern* patterns as a telic, accomplishment predicate.

(50)

Verb	**BLÜHEN** 'bloom'
Related	AUSBLÜHEN 'finish blooming' (achievement)
transitivity	* Die Rose blüht eine Blüte., *Die Wiese blüht Blumen.
	the rose blooms a blossom the meadow blooms flowers (intransitive)
telicity test	# Die Rose hat in einer Stunde geblüht.
	# 'The rose bloomed in one hour.' (ok on an onset reading: 'start blooming')
durativity test	Die Rose hat aufgehört zu blühen.
	'The rose stopped blooming.'

(51)

Verb	**BRENNEN** 'burn'
Related	ABBRENNEN 'burn down' (accompl.)
	AUSBRENNEN 'burn out' (accompl.)

Appendix Two

transitivity	* Das Feuer brennt ein Haus., *Die Kerze brennt eine Flamme. the fire burns a house the candle burns a flame (intransitive)
telicity test	# Das Haus/Feuer hat in einer Stunde gebrannt. # 'The house/fire burnt in one hour.' (ok on an onset reading: 'start burning')
durativity test	Das Haus/Feuer hat aufgehört zu brennen. 'The house/fire stopped burning.'

Note: With a goal PP, the predicate is telic and transitive, e.g.: *ein Loch in den Teppich brennen* 'burn a hole into the carpet'.

(52)

Verb	**BRÜTEN** 'brood, hatch, sit'
Related	AUSBRÜTEN 'hatch out' (accompl.)
transitivity	Die Henne brütet (*ein Ei). the hen hatches/sits (*an egg) (intransitive)
telicity test	# Die Henne hat in einer Stunde gebrütet. # 'The hen hatched/sat in one hour.'
durativity test	Die Henne hat aufgehört zu brüten. 'The hen stopped hatching/sitting.'

(53)

Verb	**FAHREN** 'go (by vehicle), drive'
Related	ABFAHREN 'depart' (achievement) AUSFAHREN '(vehicle) move out of' (accompl.) UMFAHREN 'knock over driving' (achievement)
transitivity	Der Zug/Susi fährt (langsam). the train/Susi goes (slowly) Sie fährt (das Auto) in die Garage. she drives (the car) into the garage (variable)
telicity test	# Sie ist in einer Stunde (langsam/im Nebel/Eisenbahn) gefahren. # 'She drove (slowly/in the fog/went by train) in an hour.'
durativity test	Die Eisenbahn/Susi hat aufgehört zu fahren. 'The train/Susi stopped going/driving.'

Note: With a goal PP (e.g., *nach Berlin* 'to Berlin') the predicate is telic. It is also telic with a fake object, e.g., *einen Umweg fahren* 'drive a detour', *100km (weit) fahren* 'drive 100 km's'.

(54)

Verb	**FLIEGEN** 'fly'
Related	ABFLIEGEN 'fly off, take off' (achievement) AUSFLIEGEN 'fly away, leave the nest' (achievement)
transitivity	Die Schwalbe fliegt (schnell). the swallow flies (quickly) Sie fliegt (den Hubschrauber) nach Berlin. she flies (the helicopter) to Berlin (variable)
telicity test	# Die Schwalbe ist in einer Stunde (schnell) geflogen. # 'The swallow flew (quickly) in an hour.'
durativity test	Die Schwalbe hat aufgehört (schnell) zu fliegen. 'The swallow stopped flying (quickly).'

Note: With a goal PP (e.g., *nach Berlin* 'to Berlin') the predicate is telic. It is also telic with a fake object, e.g., *einen Umweg fliegen* 'fly a detour', *1000km (weit) fliegen* 'fly 1000 km's'.

(55)

Verb	**GRABEN** 'dig, burrow'
Related	AUSGRABEN 'dig out' (accompl.) UMGRABEN 'turn over (soil), dig a garden bed' (accompl.)
transitivity	Sie gräbt (in der Erde/*die Erde). she digs (in the soil/*the soil) (intransitive)
telicity test	# Sie hat in einer Stunde (in der Erde/im Garten) gegraben. # 'She dug (in the soil/in the garden) in an hour.'
durativity test	Sie hat aufgehört, (in der Erde/im Garten) zu graben. 'She stopped digging (in the soil/in the garden).'

Note: There is a transitive variant which patterns as an accomplishment: *ein Loch/einen Tunnel/eine Grube graben* 'dig a hole/a tunnel/a pit'. Some of the objects of this variant are "fake" objects, but others are not.

(56)

Verb	**JAGEN** 'hunt, chase'
Related	ABJAGEN 'take sth. from someone after a chase' (achievement)
transitivity	Sie jagt (einen Hirsch/*einen Verbrecher). she hunts (a stag/*a criminal) (transitive; implied object can be deleted)
telicity test	# Sie hat in einer Stunde den Hirsch gejagt. # 'She hunted the stag in an hour.'

Appendix Two 279

durativity test	Sie hat aufgehört, den Hirsch zu jagen. 'She stopped hunting the stag.'

Note: With a source/goal PP, the predicate is telic, e.g. *die Maus aus dem Haus jagen* 'chase the mouse out of the house'. The goal PP and the direct object determine the predicate's meaning, including durativity. For example, *die Maus aus dem Haus jagen* is durative, but *den Ball ins Netz jagen* '(mightily) kick the ball into the net' is nondurative.

(57)

Verb	**KRATZEN** 'scratch, scrape'
Related	ABKRATZEN 'scrape off' (accompl.) AUSKRATZEN 'empty or hollow out by scraping' (accompl.)
transitivity	Sie hat mich/sich gekratzt. she has me/herself scratched Sie hat an der Wand gekratzt. she has at the wall scratched (variable)
telicity test	# Sie hat (mich) in einer Stunde gekratzt. # 'She was scratching (me) in an hour.'
durativity test	Sie hat aufgehört, (mich/an der Wand) zu kratzen. 'She stopped scratching (me/on the wall).'

(58)

Verb	**RENNEN** 'run'
Related	ABRENNEN 'cover area by running' (accompl.) UMRENNEN 'knock over by running' (achievement)
transitivity	Sie ist (*die Straße) gerannt. she is (*the road) run (intransitive, except for fake objects)
telicity test	# Sie ist in einer Stunde (schnell/hin und her) gerannt. 'She ran (quickly/back and forth) in one hour.'
durativity test	Sie hat aufgehört, (schnell/hin und her) zu rennen. 'She stopped running (quickly/back and forth).'

Note: With a goal PP such as *ins Haus* 'into the house', *rennen* patterns as a telic predicate, probably an accomplishment. With a fake object, such as *den ganzen Weg* 'the entire way', *rennen* also patterns as telic/accomplishment.

(59)

Verb	**SÄGEN** 'saw'
Related	ABSÄGEN 'saw off' (accompl.) AUSSÄGEN 'saw out' (accompl.)
transitivity	Sie hat (Holz/*das Brett) gesägt. she has (wood/*the board) sawn (intransitive, except for fake objects)

telicity test	# Sie hat in einer Stunde (draußen/Holz) gesägt. # 'She was sawing (outside/wood) in an hour.'
durativity test	Sie hat aufgehört zu sägen. 'She stopped sawing.'

Note: With an object of creation, or with a result phrase, a transitive accomplishment predicate is formed. E.g., *ein Muster in die Tür sägen* 'saw a pattern into the door' (object of creation); *ein Rohr in zwei Teile sägen* 'saw a pipe into two pieces' (result phrase).

(60)

Verb	**SCHLAFEN** 'sleep'
Related	AUSSCHLAFEN 'sleep until well rested' (achievement)
transitivity	Das Kind schläft (*das Bett). the child sleeps (*the bed) (intransitive, except for fake objects)
telicity test	# Das Kind hat in einer Stunde geschlafen. # 'The child slept in an hour.' (ok only on an event onset reading: 'fall asleep')
durativity test	Das Kind hat aufgehört zu schlafen. 'The child stopped sleeping.'

(61)

Verb	**SUCHEN** 'look for, seek, search'
Related	ABSUCHEN 'search an area' (accompl.) AUSSUCHEN 'pick out/choose' (accompl.?)
transitivity	* Sie sucht. she seeks (usually transitive)
telicity test	# Sie hat in einer Stunde den Schlüssel gesucht. # 'She was looking for the key in an hour.'
durativity test	Sie hat aufgehört, den Schlüssel zu suchen. 'She stopped looking for the key.'

2.3. Achievements

√ pass telicity tests
X fail most durativity tests

(62)

Verb	**ABBRINGEN** '(manage to) get sth. off of sth., talk someone out of sth.'
Related	BRINGEN ' bring' (achievement or accompl.) AUSBRINGEN ' deliver verbally, propose' (achievement or accompl.) UMBRINGEN ' kill' (achievement)

Appendix Two 281

transitivity	* Sie hat abgebracht. she has *ab*-brought (obligatorily transitive)
telicity test	Sie hat den Fleck in fünf Minuten von der Bluse abgebracht. 'She managed to get the stain off the blouse in five minutes.'
durativity tests	# Sie hat aufgehört, den Fleck von der Bluse abzubringen. # 'She stopped managing to get the stain off the blouse.'

(63)

Verb	**ABJAGEN** '(manage to) snatch sth. from someone'
Related	JAGEN 'hunt, chase' (activity)
transitivity	* Sie hat abgejagt. she has *ab*-hunted (obligatorily (di)transitive)
telicity test	Sie hat ihm die gestohlene Handtasche in einer Stunde abgejagt. 'She managed to snatch the stolen purse from him in an hour.'
durativity test	?? Sie hat aufgehört, ihm die gestohlene Handtasche abzujagen. ?? 'She stopped snatching the stolen purse from him.'

(64)

Verb	**ABFAHREN** 'depart'
Related	FAHREN 'go (by vehicle), drive' (activity) AUSFAHREN '(vehicle) move out of' (accompl.) UMFAHREN 'knock over driving' (achievement)
transitivity	Der Zug ist (*den/dem Bahnhof) abgefahren. the train is (*the train station) *ab*-driven (intransitive)
telicity test	? Das Schiff/Susi hat eine Stunde gebraucht, um abzufahren. ? 'It took the ship/Susi one hour to depart.'
durativity test	# Das Schiff/Susi hat aufgehört abzufahren. # 'The train/Susi stopped departing.'

Note: There is a transitive, telic variant of *abfahren*. The meanings and durativity depend on the other constituents of the VP. For example: *den Schutt abfahren* 'take away the debris', *den Reifen abfahren* 'wear down the tire', *von der Autobahn abfahren* 'leave the highway'.

(65)

Verb	**ABFALLEN** 'fall off'
Related	FALLEN 'fall' (achievement?) AUSFALLEN 'fall out' (achievement) UMFALLEN 'fall over' (accompl.?)

transitivity	* der Haken ist die Wand abgefallen	
	the hook is the wall *ab*-fallen	(intransitive)
telicity test	Der Haken ist in einer Minute abgefallen.	
	'The hook fell off in a minute.'	
durativity test	# Der Haken hat aufgehört abzufallen.	
	# 'The hook stopped falling off.' (ok on an iterative reading)	

(66)

Verb	**ABFLIEGEN** 'fly off, take off'	
Related	FLIEGEN 'fly' (activity)	
	AUSFLIEGEN 'fly away, leave the nest' (achievement)	
transitivity	Das Flugzeug ist (*den/dem Flughafen) abgeflogen.	
	the airplane is (*the airport) *ab*-flown	(intransitive)
telicity test	Das Flugzeug hat 30 Sekunden gebraucht, um abzufliegen.	
	'It took the airplane 30 seconds to take off.'	
durativity test	# Das Flugzeug hat aufgehört abzufliegen.	
	# 'The airplane stopped taking off.'	

Note: There is also a transitive variant of *abfliegen*, which means 'fly over an area, cover/patrol an area by plane' and which patterns as an accomplishment.

(67)

Verb	**AUSBLÜHEN** 'finish blooming'	
Related	BLÜHEN 'bloom' (activity)	
transitivity	* Die Rose blüht eine Blüte aus.	
	the rose blooms a blossom *out*	(intransitive)
telicity test	Die Rose hat in einer Stunde ausgeblüht.	
	'The rose finished blooming in one hour.'	
durativity test	# Die Rose hat aufgehört auszublühen.	
	# 'The rose stopped finishing blooming.'	

(68)

Verb	**AUSFALLEN** 'fall out'	
Related	FALLEN 'fall' (achievement?)	
	ABFALLEN 'fall off' (achievement)	
	UMFALLEN 'fall over' (accompl.?)	
transitivity	* der Zahn ist den Mund ausgefallen	
	the tooth is the mouth *aus*-fallen	(intransitive)

telicity test	Der wacklige Zahn ist in einer Stunde ausgefallen. 'The wiggly tooth fell out in an hour.'
durativity test	# Der wacklige Zahn hat aufgehört auszufallen. # 'The wiggly tooth stopped falling out.' (ok on an iterative reading)

(69)

Verb	**AUSFLIEGEN** 'fly away, leave the nest'
Related	FLIEGEN 'fly' (activity) ABFLIEGEN 'fly off, take off' (achievement)
transitivity	Die Schwalbe fliegt (*das Nest) aus. the swallow flies (*the nest) *aus* (intransitive)
telicity test	Die Schwalbe ist in 10 Sekunden (aus dem Nest) ausgeflogen. 'The swallow left/flew out of the nest in 10 seconds.'
durativity test	# Die Schwalbe hat aufgehört auszufliegen. # 'The swallow stopped flying out.' (ok on an iterative reading)

Note: There is a transitive variant of *ausfliegen*, which means 'fly someone out of an area' and which is also telic.

(70)

Verb	**AUSSCHLAFEN** 'sleep until well rested/finish sleeping'
Related	SCHLAFEN 'sleep' (activity)
transitivity	Sie schläft (sich/ihren Rausch /*Kopfschmerzen/* den Frust) aus. she sleeps (herself/her drunkenness/*headaches/*the frustration) *aus* (intransitive, except for fake objects and *Rausch*)
telicity test	Sie hat (sich) in einer Stunde ausgeschlafen. 'She caught enough sleep/finished sleeping in an hour.'
durativity test	# Sie hat aufgehört, (sich) auszuschlafen. # 'She stopped catching enough sleep/finishing sleeping.'

(71)

Verb	**UMBRINGEN** 'kill'
Related	BRINGEN ' bring' (achievement or accompl.) ABBRINGEN ' (manage to) get sth. off of sth., talk someone out of sth.' (achievement) AUSBRINGEN 'deliver verbally, propose' (achievement or accompl.)
transitivity	* Sie hat umgebracht. she has *um*-brought (obligatorily transitive)

telicity test	Das Gift hat ihn in 10 Sekunden umgebracht. 'The poison killed him in 10 seconds.'
durativity tests	# Das Gift/Sie hat aufgehört, ihn umzubringen. # 'The poison/She stopped killing him.' (ok on an iterative reading) # Das Gift/?Sie ist dabei, ihn umzubringen. '# The poison/?She is in the process of killing him.'

Note: This predicate also has some durative characteristics.

(72)

Verb	**UMFAHREN** 'knock over driving'
Related	FAHREN 'go (by vehicle), drive' (activity) ABFAHREN 'depart' (achievement) AUSFAHREN '(vehicle) move out of' (achievement)
transitivity	* Sie fährt um. she drives *um* (obligatorily transitive)
telicity test	Sie hat in 10 Sekunden das Verkehrsschild umgefahren. 'She knocked over the traffic sign in 10 seconds.'
durativity test	# Sie hat aufgehört, das Verkehrsschild umzufahren. # 'She stopped knocking over the traffic sign.' (ok on an iterative reading)

(73)

Verb	**UMKOMMEN** 'die, perish'
Related	KOMMEN (achievement?)
transitivity	Sie kommt (*ihr Leben) um. she comes (*her life) *um* (intransitive)
telicity test	Sie ist in fünf Minuten umgekommen. 'She died/perished in five minutes.'
durativity test	# Sie hat aufgehört, umzukommen. # 'She stopped dying/perishing.' (ok on an iterative reading) # Sie war dabei, umzukommen, als … # 'She was in the process of dying/perishing when …'

(74)

Verb	**UMRENNEN** 'knock over running'
Related	RENNEN 'run' (activity)

Appendix Two

	ABRENNEN 'cover area by running/hasten through something' (accompl.)
transitivity	* Sie hat umgerannt. she has *um*-run (obligatorily transitive)
telicity test	Sie hat in 10 Sekunden den Papierkorb umgerannt. 'She knocked over the waste basket in 10 seconds.'
durativity test	# Sie hat aufgehört, den Papierkorb umzurennen. 'She stopped knocking over the waste basket.'

(75)

Verb	**FALLEN** 'fall'
Related	ABFALLEN 'fall off' (achievement) AUSFALLEN 'fall out' (achievement) UMFALLEN 'fall over' (accompl.?)
transitivity	Der Stein fällt (*den/dem Brunnen). the rock falls (*the well) (intransitive)
telicity test	Der Stein ist in 30 Sekunden auf den Grund des Brunnens gefallen. 'The rock fell to the bottom of the well in 30 seconds.'
durativity test	# Der Stein hat aufgehört, (auf den Grund des Brunnens) zu fallen. # 'The rock stopped falling (to the bottom of the well).'

Note: Fallen usually occurs with an overt goal or/and source argument. If this argument is nonovert, it is usually implied, and the predicate is still telic: *fallen* by itself usually means 'fall to the ground'. *Fallen* is also telic with a fake object, e.g., *100m (tief) fallen* 'fall 100 meters'.

(76)

Verb	**KOMMEN** 'come'
Related	UMKOMMEN 'die, perish' (achievement)
transitivity	Sie kommt (*den/dem Zaun). she comes (*the fence) (intransitive)
telicity test	Sie ist in fünf Minuten zum Zaun gekommen. 'She came to the fence in five minutes.'
durativity test	# Sie hat aufgehört, zum Zaun zu kommen. # 'She stopped coming to the fence.' (ok on an iterative reading) Sie war dabei, zum Zaun zu kommen, als ... 'She was in the process of coming to the fence when ...'

Note: Kommen also has some durative characteristics. Durativity depends on the other elements in the VP. To take an extreme example, *zu Bewusstsein kommen* 'come to (consciousness)' patterns as an accomplishment.

2.4. Semelfactives

X   fail telicity tests
(X) have an iterative reading with durativity tests

(77)

Verb	**HUSTEN** 'cough'
Related	ABHUSTEN 'cough up, clear lungs/throat of something' (accompl.) AUSHUSTEN 'cough up, cough out' (achievement or accompl.)
transitivity	Sie hat (*einen Husten/??Schleim/*Luft/*Blut) gehustet. she has (*a cough/??phlegm/*air/blood) coughed (intransitive)
telicity test	# Sie hat in fünf Minuten gehustet. # 'She coughed in five minutes.'
durativity test	Sie hat aufgehört zu husten. 'She stopped coughing.' (iterative reading only)

(78)

Verb	**KLOPFEN** 'knock, hit, beat'
Related	ABKLOPFEN 'knock/beat sth. off of sth.' (accompl.) AUSKLOPFEN 'clean by beating/knocking' (accompl.)
transitivity	Sie hat (an die Tür) geklopft. she has (at the door) knocked (intransitive, except for fake objects)
telicity test	# Sie hat in fünf Minuten (an der Tür) geklopft. # 'She knocked (on the door) in five minutes.'
durativity test	Sie hat aufgehört, (an der Tür) zu klopfen. 'She stopped knocking (on the door).' (iterative reading only)

(79)

Verb	**SCHLAGEN** 'strike, hit, beat'
Related	ABSCHLAGEN 'sever by striking' (achievement or accompl.) AUSSCHLAGEN 'knock/beat out' (achievement or accompl.) UMSCHLAGEN 'turn over' (achievement or accompl.)
transitivity	* Sie hat geschlagen. she has struck/hit (transitive; implied object can be deleted)
telicity test	# Sie hat in fünf Minuten den Hund geschlagen. # 'She beat the dog in five minutes.'
durativity test	Sie hat aufgehört, den Hund zu schlagen. 'She stopped beating the dog.' (iterative reading only)

2.5. Situation Type/Durativity is Unclear

In this section I list the verbs for which durativity tests yield inconclusive results.

(80)

Verb	**ABSCHLAGEN** 'sever by striking'
Related	SCHLAGEN 'strike, hit, beat' (semelf.) AUSSCHLAGEN 'knock/beat out' (achievement or accompl.) UMSCHLAGEN 'turn over, turn around/change' (achievement or accompl.)
transitivity	* Sie schlägt ab. she strikes *ab* (obligatorily transitive)
telicity test	Sie hat in einer Stunde den Putz (von der Wand) abgeschlagen. 'She knocked the plaster off the wall in an hour.'
durativity test	Sie hat aufgehört, den Putz von der Wand abzuschlagen. 'She stopped knocking the plaster off the wall. # Sie hat aufgehört, dem Angeklagten den Kopf abzuschlagen. # 'She stopped knocking the head off the accused.' (ok on an iterative reading)

Note: Durativity depends on the object.

(81)

Verb	**AUSBRINGEN** 'deliver verbally, propose' (achievement or accompl.)
Related	BRINGEN ' bring' (achievement or accompl.) ABBRINGEN ' (manage to) get sth. off of sth., talk someone out of sth.' (achievement) UMBRINGEN ' kill' (achievement)
transitivity	* Sie hat ausgebracht. she has *aus*-brought (obligatorily transitive)
telicity test	Sie hat (nur) 10 Sekunden gebraucht, um einen Toast auf ihn auszubringen. 'It (only) took her 10 seconds to toast/propose a toast to him.'
durativity tests	?? Sie hat aufgehört, einen Toast auf ihn auszubringen. ?? 'She stopped toasting/proposing a toast to him.' Sie ist dabei, einen Toast auf ihn auszubringen. 'She is in the process of toasting/proposing a toast to him.'

(82)

Verb	**AUSHUSTEN** 'cough up, cough out'
Related	HUSTEN 'cough' (semelf.) ABHUSTEN 'cough up, clear lungs/throat of something' (accompl.)
transitivity	Sie hat *(den Schleim/den Staub/die Fliege) ausgehustet. she has *(the phlegm/the dust/the fly) *aus*-coughed (obligatorily transitive)
telicity test	Sie hat in 5 Minuten den Staub/den Krümel ausgehustet. 'She coughed up the dust/the crumb in five minutes.'
durativity test	?? Sie hat aufgehört, den Krümel auszuhusten. ?? 'She stopped coughing up the crumb.' Sie hat aufgehört, den Staub auszuhusten. 'She stopped coughing up the dust.'

Note: Durativity depends on the object. Also note that there is an (intransitive) variant *(sich) aushusten*, which means 'finish coughing' and which patterns as an achievement.

(83)

Verb	**AUSSCHLAGEN** 'knock/beat out'
Related	SCHLAGEN 'strike, hit, beat' (semelf.) ABSCHLAGEN 'sever by striking' (achievement or accompl.) UMSCHLAGEN 'turn over' (achievement or accompl.)
transitivity	* Sie schlägt aus. she strikes *aus* (obligatorily transitive)
telicity test	Sie hat ihm in einer Sekunde einen Zahn ausgeschlagen. 'She knocked out one of his teeth in one second.'
durativity test	Sie hat aufgehört, das Feuer auszuschlagen. 'She stopped beating the fire dead.' # Sie hat aufgehört, ihm einen Zahn auszuschlagen.. # 'She stopped knocking out one of his teeth.'

Note: Durativity depends on the object. Also note that *ausschlagen* has additional, less transparent meanings, e.g., 'bud (trees)', 'kick out (horse)'. The latter seems to describe a semelfactive, i.e., atelic, situation. I treat this as an exception.

(84)

Verb	**UMSCHLAGEN** 'turn over'
Related	SCHLAGEN 'strike, hit, beat' (semelf.) ABSCHLAGEN 'sever by striking' (achievement or accompl.) AUSSCHLAGEN 'knock/beat out' (achievement or accompl.)

transitivity	* Sie schlägt um.
	she strikes *um* (obligatorily transitive)
telicity test	Sie hat in einer Sekunde die Seite/das Hosenbein umgeschlagen.
	'She turned over the page/the pantleg in one second.'
durativity test	Sie hat aufgehört, das Hosenbein umzuschlagen.
	'She stopped turning over the pantleg.'
	?? Sie hat aufgehört, die Seite umzuschlagen.
	?? 'She stopped turning over the page.'

Note: Durativity depends on the object. Also note that that there is an intransitive variant of *umschlagen*: *das Wetter schlägt um* 'the weather is changing'. On this meaning, *umschlagen* seems to pattern as an achievement.

(85)

Verb	**BRINGEN** 'bring' (achievement or accompl.)
Related	ABBRINGEN ' get sth. off of sth., talk someone out of sth.'
	(achievement)
	AUSBRINGEN ' deliver verbally, propose' (achievement or accompl.)
	UMBRINGEN ' kill' (achievement)
transitivity	* Sie bringt (zum Bahnhof).
	she brings (to-the station) (obligatorily transitive)
telicity test	Sie hat den Koffer in fünf Minuten zum Bahnhof gebracht.
	'She brought the suitcase to the station in five minutes.'
durativity tests	# Sie hat aufgehört, den Koffer zum Bahnhof zu bringen.
	# 'She stopped bringing the suitcase to the station.'
	Sie ist dabei, den Koffer zum Bahnhof zu bringen.
	'She is in the process of bringing the suitcase to the station.'

Appendix Three

THE DËNE PROGRESSIVE

Progressive verb themes have a CM *ghe-* and a stem suffix *-ł*. The distinction between imperfective and perfective viewpoints is often neutralized: Many of them have no distinct imperfective and perfective (and optative) forms. If they have a CM, it is *ghe-*, but *ghe-* does not necessarily convey perfective meaning. Consider a few examples:

(1) a. verb theme: *da–ł–te–ł* (?-cl-stem-prog) 'be holding O' (Cook 2004)
    daghesteł   'I'm holding it'   (IMPF)
    daghiłteł   'I have been holding it'   (PERF)
    dawasteł   'I shall hold it up'   (OPT)

   b. verb theme: *ghe–d–gha–ł* 'be walking'   (Cook 2004)
    ghesał   'I am walking'   (PROG/IMPF)
    ghigał   'I am coming'   (PROG/PERF?)
    —   (PROG/OPT)

   c. verb theme: *ghe–l–ge–ł* 'be crawling'   (Elford & Elford 1998:127)
    ghesgoł   'I am crawling'   (PROG)
    —   (PERF)
    —   (OPT)

   d. verb theme: *ya#ghe–l–ti–ł* 'keep on talking (while walking)'
                                                                                  (Cook 2004)
    yaghestił   'I am talking (while walking)'   (PROG)
    —   (PERF)
    —   (OPT)

e. verb theme: *ya#ł–ti–ł* 'keep on talking' (Elford & Elford 1998:312)
   yastił   'I keep on talking'   (PROG)
   —   (PERF)
   —   (OPT)

(1a) above is the only Progressive theme I have seen which may occur in both viewpoints and the Optative mode. Note that *ghe-* occurs in both viewpoints. (1b) looks like it has a Perfective and an Imperfective, however, first person singular is the only Perfective form that seems to exist, and it does not have a perfective meaning. Usually only one form exists, as in (1c-e), and it cannot be ascertained of this form whether it is Imperfective or Perfective. Rather, it seems to be simply "Progressive." This suggests that the Progressive is a subsituation aspect, with more specific meaning than the Imperfective and Perfective (and Optative).

It is difficult to determine whether the Progressive is a viewpoint or a situation aspect. Rice (2000:290) says it is both: "The progressive defines an event that is ongoing or in progress at the reference time [= TT]. It refers to reference time, making it a kind of viewpoint, but also to the internal states of that time, making it a kind of situation type." Corresponding to this is the double marking in Slave with both a (viewpoint) CM and a derivational (=lexical aspect/situation type) suffix. Cook (2004) argues that in Dëne the Progressive is a derivational aspect, for two reasons. First, it is by far not as productive as the Imperfective and Perfective viewpoints (and the Optative mode), and second, both the *ghe-* prefix and the *ł*–suffix are derivational. Cook takes *ghe-* to be derivational or "thematic" in the Progressive because it does not convey the usual viewpoint meaning (i.e., perfective) and because it is optional (cf. (1e) above).

The one Progressive theme in my database is 'be walking.' This theme is atelic (no completion reading with 'almost') and passes some durativity tests but fails others. This suggests that Progressive verbs have a narrower meaning than Imperfective activities.

(2) tthidziné k'e ją ghesał t'ú tsił hejër héja.
    tthidziné k'e ją   ghe–s–gha–ł   t'ú   tsił   hejër héja
    yesterday here CM-1s-sg go-prog and/when snow ?   it-started
    'Yesterday while I was walking through here it started to snow.'

Appendix Three

(3) # ʔįłághe ts'údzáhi k'e ghesał sį.
   ʔįłághe ts'údzáhi k'e ghe–s–gha–ł   sį
   one   hour   P   CM-1s-sg go-prog assert
   (intended: 'I am walking for one hour.')

(4) # ghesał ʔanast'e.
   ghe–s–gha–ł   ʔa–na#s–t'e
   CM-1s-sg go-prog th-th#1s-stem
   (intended: 'I finished/stopped walking.')

Perhaps (3) and (4) are infelicitous because a Progressive verb emphasizes what is going on right at the Topic Time and does not look beyond that particular moment. One could perhaps say that it focuses an "inner," "in-progress at TT" phase of an activity. Thus, although this verb theme passes some durativity tests and fails the 'almost' test, it should not be considered a standard activity.

I conclude that the Dëne Progressive is less productive and more specific in meaning than the Imperfective viewpoint. Progressive verb themes have durative characteristics but are not standard activities. The Dëne Progressive is best considered a derivational subsituation aspect.

Notes

NOTES TO CHAPTER ONE

1. This example is unacceptable for semantic rather than for syntactic reasons. I use # rather than * to indicate semantic oddity.
2. Smith (p.c.) suggests that the study of process might give results quite different from those involving durativity. Clearly, this is a topic for further research. A preliminary study of the grammatization of process in German suggests that just like durativity, it is not grammatized in this language (Wilhelm 2000, 2001).
3. See Steinitz (1981:29–30): "Die Grammatik beschreibt nur solche semantischen Distinktionen, die mit syntaktischen und/oder morphologischen, d.h. hier mit grammatischen Distinktionen korrelieren." [= 'The grammar describes only those semantic distinctions which correlate with syntactic and/or morphological distinctions, i.e., with distinctions which here are called grammatical.']
4. I thank Darin Howe for this example. As mentioned, matters are actually more complex, and different phonological theories account for the relationship between phonetics and phonology in different ways.
5. This term is from Smith (1991). Other terms are *Aktionsart* (Kratzer 1998), *temporal constitution* (François 1985, Krifka 1989), *event-type* (Pustejovsky 1991), *lexical aspect*.
6. Smith (1991) defines viewpoints slightly differently. Roughly, viewpoints hold of an interval which is specified as to whether or not it includes the initial, the final, and internal moments of the respective situation time. This interval is usually identical with the reference time/TT. It is not identical with TT in sentences with perfect tenses or with embedded clauses.

    Also, I only discuss what Smith calls the "general imperfective." Other types of imperfective viewpoints are the progressive and the resultative (Smith 1991:175ff; see also Comrie 1976 for types of imperfectives).
7. In embedded clauses, the privileged time may be a time established by the tense of the matrix clause, rather than TU. For example: *Peter phoned me*

five minutes ago. He said [that he <u>had</u> (*has) locked himself out and <u>needed</u> (??needs) my help].

8. This can be formalized as follows, where P is a predicate, ⊏ is the proper part relation and ⊕ is the join or sum operation in a complete join semi-lattice:
    (i) quantized reference: $\forall e, e'\ [P(e) \land P(e') \rightarrow \neg e' \sqsubset e]$ (Krifka 1992, 1998)
    (ii) cumulative reference: $\forall e, e'\ [P(e) \land P(e') \rightarrow P(e \oplus e')]$

    Krifka (1992) also shows that predicates with quantized reference will have a "set terminal point." I believe that the inherent endpoint of telic predicates is one kind of "set terminal point," but that a set terminal point can also be provided in other ways. See the discussion of "boundedness" immediately below.

9. The term found more commonly in the literature is "subevent," but this is misleading as many subevents are states.

10. Idioms also present a challenge to the lexicalist hypothesis.

11. It should be noted that DM embraces the syntactic, "piece"-based view of morphology that I criticized earlier. However, by assuming a distributed lexicon and late insertion, DM seems to be able to deal with many of the problems encountered by the "piece"-based view. See Zeller (2001) for discussion.

NOTES TO CHAPTER TWO

1. Some verbs may also occur in progressive form, but the progressive is not productive in Dëne. According to Comrie (1976) and Smith (1991), progressive viewpoint is a subtype of imperfective viewpoint. See Appendix Three for the progressive in Dëne.

2. *www.ethnologue.com* estimates only 4,000 speakers.

3. It is unclear at this point whether nominal constituents are best analyzed as NPs or DPs (with a zero D) in Dëne. For simplicity, I will call them NPs. See Chapter Six for some speculations.

4. Cook (2004) observes that sometimes the disjunct prefixes fuse as if they were conjunct. I will not concern myself with these exceptions, other than noting them where they occur in my examples.

5. One empirical argument that the stem and the lexical items function as a unit is that the iterative prefix (*na#* in Dëne), which is located between a lexical preverb and the stem, takes scope not only over the stem, but over the stem-preverb combination. Thus, in Slave, *téhkǫyetła* 's/he went out of the water again' cannot mean 'she went out of the water and went again into the water,' it denotes a repeated going out of the water (Rice 2000:76f).

6. See Hale (2001) for a different approach to the surface order that does not involve movement.

7. The meaning of this stem is very abstract. The gloss used here is from Axelrod (1993), who discusses the cognate Koyukon stem.

Notes to Chapter Two

8. In terms of DM, one would say that certain vocabulary items with different feature specifications have the same phonological form. It is not always clear in Dëne/Athapaskan languages whether one deals with two or more distinct but homophonous vocabulary items, or whether there is only one vocabulary item with a very general (underspecified) meaning/function/feature specification.
9. The absence of a position 2 subject prefix indicates a third person (i.e., nonlocal) subject.
10. To maintain this generalization for verb themes without overt classifiers, we assume that they have a "Ø-classifier," as in table 3 and the examples above.
11. The paradigms also show several morphological and phonological processes: there is the variation between *s-* and *i-* for first person singular. *i-* occurs in the perfective form of verbs which have a *ɬ-* or Ø classifier, *s-* occurs elsewhere. Next, the alternation between *ne-* and vowel nasalization (plus raising) for second person singular is conditioned by the preceding morpheme. The "nasalization allomorph" of the second person singular prefix occurs after a CV conjunct prefix, *ne-* elsewhere. Phonological fusion in the conjunct domain is illustrated further in (8a, c), where the underlying three-consonant sequence *s-ɬ-t* in the 1sg form must be reduced to two because Dëne only allows CVC syllables. Similarly, the two adjacent vowels *e* and *i* are merged into one, as in (8b). In other cases, segments are inserted to fulfill the requirement of a minimally two-syllable surface structure. Thus, *he* is inserted in the first and *h* in the second form in (9a). The actual morphophonemics of conjunct prefixes can be complex. For accounts, see Cook (2004), Causley (1996), and Hargus and Tuttle (1997) for a pan-Athapaskan discussion and proposal. Compare also McDonough's (1990) account of Navajo.
12. Rice (2000) offers a different view. See Chapter Three for discussion.
13. A brief note about these paradigms: the 1dl/pl and 2dl/pl forms are glossed 'we (two)' and 'you (two)' respectively because dual rather than plural is the default interpretation. A disjunct prefix $dá_9$# is often (but not always) used for a plural reading. Similarly, a prefix he_5- is used in 3dual and the prefix $dá_9$# (often plus *he-*) in 3pl forms. The exact conditions under which these prefixes occur await further research. See Cook (2004) for some discussion. Optative forms are not my primary concern and are difficult to elicit. This is why I do not have complete optative paradigms.
14. The nasal feature (N) and other surprising elements in some third person forms are discussed in Chapter Three.
15. A third, hard-to-pinpoint type of perfective marking is sometimes seen as changes in position 2 or 3 morphemes. This is also discussed in Chapter Three.
16. Making a similar argument, Rice (2000) provides a Slave example of a future perfective.
17. Both of these verbs can also mean 'stop' in other contexts, see section 3.2.2 below.

18. What is indicated as "implied" was discussed with consultants. The translation of (22b), as all translations, is unedited. A native English speaker might prefer 'in a year' rather than 'for a year' here. Dëne does not have distinct expressions for 'in X time' and 'for X time' (see section 3.2.1).
19. Some speakers use *yeh* rather than *yoh* for 'house.'
20. This claim does not necessarily extend to stative verbs, as it seems that not all stative verbs are marked for viewpoint aspect in Dëne. One group, positional stative verbs, do show an imperfective-perfective distinction: they have the CM pattern *the-* (Impf.)/*ghe-* (Perf.), as well as stem changes (see section 2.3.3). Other stative verbs are described as having a Ø-/Ø- or a Ø-/* CM pattern (cf. Bortolin 1998), which suggests that here the viewpoint distinction is neutralized or simply nonexistent. However, some verbs of the latter verb class do seem to have a Ø-/*ghe-* viewpoint distinction after all, see, e.g., the 1sg Impf. form *desgai* vs. the 1sg Perf. form *deghesgai* taken from a paradigm given in Cook (2004); unfortunately, no translations are given.
21. We will see shortly that (33) is an activity while (32) is an accomplishment.
22. Recall that all translations are unedited, including the 'for a year' translation in (34b).
23. Smith (p.c.) suggests that French and Dëne might be similar. The French viewpoints are discussed in Smith (1991).
24. See Wilhelm (2003) for a formal semantic account of the Dëne perfective, utilizing the "posttime" notion.
25. ϕ and $\neg\phi$, see also Klein's (1994) 'source state' and 'target state,' and the BECOME ϕ representation of telic situations in predicate decomposition theories (Jackendoff 1990, Rappaport Hovav and Levin 1998, etc.).
26. The presence of the CM *the-* can be detected by a high-tone reflex in third person forms: *néda* 's/he sat down.' See Chapter Three for detailed discussion.
27. As already pointed out by Kamp & Rohrer (1983), the function of tense and viewpoint aspect can only adequately be dealt with at the text level, and not in terms of truth conditions on individual sentences. They show for French that the "choice of the tense form depends on the function that the sentence in which it occurs has in a text" (p. 253). My discussion of the event ordering functions of the Dëne viewpoints should be understood in this spirit.
28. Other aspectual means are used in addition to the imperfective and perfective, but Axelrod herself says that the "modes" (=viewpoints) are the most important devices used in event ordering and backgrounding (see p. 172, 174, 178).
29. The difference between telicity and perfectivity is already noted in Andersson (1972), who argues at length that particle verbs are not perfective but telic. See Chapter Five for details.
30. Recall that translations throughout are as provided by the Dëne speakers, and were not edited.

31. My guess is that even where only one translation was given, [NP *k'e*] might have been translated with the other meaning on a different occasion.
32. An expression is general if it is unspecified with respect to a particular distinction. An expression is ambiguous if it has two (or more) readings (see Cruse 1986). For example, while *bat* is ambiguous between 'winged mammal' and 'baseball equipment,' *kick* is general regarding whether there is one kick or several kicks.
33. The other two items behave similarly to *ʔanat'e*:
    (i) ʔanasdhën (V_{tr}): NP or (imperfective) VP + *ʔanasdhën* (often used with transitive verbs)
    'I'm finished it, I'm finished V-ing, I quit V-ing'
    (ii) kút'a: *kút'a* + (perfective) VP
    'that's enough, that's it'
34. Mass nouns require a measure phrase to become countable.
35. As in English, Dëne mass nouns are not countable without a measure phrase (Wilhelm 2005):
    (i) # sǫlághe bĕr
    (five meat)

NOTES TO CHAPTER THREE

1. For the sake of simplicity, I will adhere to the traditional terminology in discussing verb theme categories. This does not mean that I adopt the view of the Athapaskan verb (theme) underlying this terminology (see Chapters One and Two).
2. The aspectual-semantic reality of the categories is even more doubtful for the stative themes, which all correspond to one situation type (state) and whose theme categories do not seem to correlate with any semantic aspectual characteristic.
3. "T" symbolizes obstruents; *oo* = [u].
4. Conservative *bez* is sometimes heard.
5. Li (1946) is based on fieldwork carried out in 1928.
6. The fifth CM, *wa-*, which marks "optative" mood, is irrelevant to my discussion.
7. Some earlier work has endowed the CM's with situation aspectual meaning, for example, Krauss (1969) and Young and Morgan (1987). However, Axelrod (1993), after careful study, cannot find such meaning for the CM's in Koyukon.
8. Thus, from a strictly morphological perspective, there are only four distinct classes.
9. Rice further shows that when semelfactives are "refocused" as activities (they then denote plural patients or events), they take the CM *gh-*, as predicted

10. The *the-* CM is deleted after a conjunct prefix but leaves a high-tone reflex in third person forms (Cook 2004). For example, see (5b), (7b).
11. This verb is heard with a voiceless or voiced stem-final consonant in the Perfective.
12. This verb theme has stem alternation by number, i.e., the stem with a dual subject is –*ké/–ke*, and –*tth'i/–tth'i* with a plural subject.
13. Some speakers have reanalyzed the classifier and stem of this verb theme as Ø–*shúl*. The third person Imperfective may contain an additional (irregular) thematic prefix *i-*. The initial *h* in some of the examples is epenthetic. *ghwa-* (instead of *wa-*) is the conservative Optative morpheme.
14. The stem-final consonant is sometimes heard as a voiced segment *l*.
15. Cook (2004) proposes that with a *d-* or *l-* classifier, **n* may sometimes show up as *i-* in at least third person, but this *i-* seems quite irregular and is poorly understood, and does at this point not present solid evidence for the presence of **n*.
16. The observation by Cook (2004) that H and N sometimes also occur in Imperfective verb forms presents a further problem for this proposal.
17. This verb theme has stem alternation by number, i.e., the stem with a dual subject is –*ké/–ke*, and –*tth'i/–tth'i* with a plural subject.
18. Of course, explicitly bounded atelic predicates, such as *work for 2 hours*, also have quantized reference. The proposal in (14) does not apply to such derived quantization.
19. This argument exploits the well-known "imperfective paradox" (e.g., Dowty 1979, Parsons 1990, Landman 1992).
20. The question arises why the Imperfective marker is not cumulative *ghe-*. Also, note that on this argument, it is surprising that in English, imperfective viewpoint is marked overtly by the progressive form.
21. For an analysis of stativity in Dëne, see Bortolin (1998). Also see the work of Smith (1991) on Navajo.
22. The Imperfective becomes even clearer as a durativity test when used in a sentence which provides the background for another event. See Appendix One for such examples.
23. I assume the CM is *the-* because of the occurrence of a high tone in third person forms, e.g., *ʔanayildhën* 's/he is done.' See section 2.2.1 for discussion of H in third person.
24. The related verb theme Ø–*zil* (CM pattern Ø/*ghe-*) 'scream repeatedly/continuously' is felicitous in durative contexts.
25. After some discussion, speakers conceded that a very marginal interpretation of (18b) is an hour-long uninterrupted scream. However, this may just have been said to please me, and a Dëne speaker would probably never utter

Notes to Chapter Three

a sentence like (18b). The time span expression headed by *k'e* was deemed even worse than that with *k'étł'á* in (18b).

26. Recall that *the-* is regularly deleted after a conjunct prefix.
27. I have heard this word as either *k'ájëne* or *k'ásjëne* in Cold Lake. Bortolin (1998), who worked in La Loche, Saskatchewan, has *k'asjëne*.
28. Several stems may be given due to stem variation by viewpoint/mode.
29. See discussion of these under 'semelfactives' and in section 3.3.2 below.
30. Several stems may be given due to stem variation by viewpoint/mode.
31. Several stems, or themes, may be given due to morphological variation by viewpoint/mode.
32. Speakers warn that this verb has strong sexual connotations in some contexts. In particular, the sexual meaning is prevalent in non-hunting contexts (e.g., indoors).
33. This theme seems to undergo aspectual shift in some tests. With the time span 'one hour' it is interpreted as one uninterrupted, hour-long blowing event. With the 'almost' test, there is an onset reading ('I just about blew the light (once) but I changed my mind and didn't') and what might be an onset or a completion reading ('I just about blew the light (once) but my wind stopped half way and I didn't.'). Both of these unexpected readings are pragmatically extremely odd, which I take as an indication that they represent a nonbasic situation type. I take the verb theme to be basically a semelfactive because it cannot occur in a nonfuture Imperfective, and because 'quickly' may only modify the event onset. See Appendix One for details.
34. The high tone is unlikey to stem from deletion of the CM *the-*, for two reasons: (i), H shows up in all persons, while the H reflex of *the-* only shows up in third person, (ii), there is no conjunct prefix which could trigger *the-* deletion.
35. Axelrod (1993:35ff) comes to a similar conclusion. She writes about Koyukon: "The *le-* (=*the-*) perfective is used with semelfactive, bisective, conclusive, continuative, distributive, perambulative, most reversative, some transitional, and some momentaneous derivatives. The *ghe-* perfective is used with durative, consecutive, repetitive, directive-repetitive, persistive, progressive, customary, neuter, some reversative, and some momentaneous derivatives. The *Ø-* is used in some transitional and some momentaneous derivatives, and the *ne-* perfective prefix is used exclusively with momentaneous derivatives. [. . .] It is difficult to imagine a single semantic characterization underlying each of these groupings."
36. The idea that CM choice marks situation type appears even more problematic in light of some facts from Cook (2004). Cook gives examples of verbs which seem to be able to occur with both *the-* and *ghe-* in the perfective: *dathes?á* 'I put it up' (impf), *dathi?ą* 'I have put it up' (perf), *daghi?ą* 'I had put it up' (perf) or *horésk'ą* 'I start a fire,' *horéthiłk'ą* 'I have made a fire'

(a fire is still on) (perf), *horéghiłk'ën* 'I had made a fire' (there is no fire) (perf). I suspect that the *ghe*-perfective is derived from the *the*-perfective, thus is a "perfective of a perfective," just as seen in stative verbs. But clearly, further research is needed to understand these patterns.

37. A fourth subsituation aspect, the inchoative, which occurs with stative verbs, is not discussed.
38. Conative situations are usually considered atelic. Judging from the English translations of the Slave conative examples (e.g., 's/he shot at O,' Rice 2000:162), they denote atelic situations. If I am right that these conative predicates are really atelic, the CM *ne-* is not predicted.
39. Some stative verb themes may occur in a similar subsituation aspect, the *inchoative* or *transitional*. Among other morphology, inchoatives show a conjunct high tone or a conjunct prefix *í-* (Cook 2004):

    (i) a. dígay   cf. delgai
                de–í–d–gay   de–l–gai
                th-inch-cl-white inch   th-cl-white
                'it is turning white'   'it is white'
        b. dík'ǫs   cf. delk'os
                de–í–d–k'ǫs   de–l–k'os
                th-inch-cl-red inch   th-cl-red
                'it is turning red'   'it is red'

According to Rice (2000), inchoative and transitional are two separate subsituation aspects. Perhaps they are merged in Dëne.

40. I also have one example where a nonfuture Imperfective is acceptable: *yehełt'us sı̨* 'he is beating him up right now.' Further research is needed to determine whether this example indeed is an instance of the *he–ł–t'us* verb theme, and if so, whether this theme truly is an achievement.
41. The stem vowel of this verb sounds quite long to me, almost like [yú:ł]. In Cold Lake Dëne, the difference between full vowels and reduced schwa is sometimes reflected in vowel length (Cook, p.c.).
42. This verb theme may contain a semelfactive prefix *i-*. However, it is also possible that the vowel *i* here is simply the result of assimilation (*ne–> ni*), and that there is no prefix *i-* at all. The same is true for 'punch O once' in example (40).
43. Several stems may be given due to stem variation by viewpoint/mode.
44. I do not have aspectual tests for this verb theme. I added it to the list for the sake of completeness.
45. Speakers warn that this verb has strong sexual connotations in some contexts. In particular, the sexual meaning is prevalent in non-hunting contexts (e.g., indoors).
46. Cook (2004) also notes a seriative prefix *i-* as well as a homophonous semelfactive prefix *i-*. Considering that a third conjunct prefix *i-* is proposed as a reflex in third person (with *l-/d-*classifiers) of historical *ŋ or *ɲ, an accurate

interpretation of conjunct *i-* prefixes becomes nearly impossible, and I will simply gloss them with a question mark.

47. In Midgette's theory, we would expect verbs with *a-* to have a *y-* (=*ghe-*) CM and verbs with Ø or *yi-* to have a *s-* (=*the-*) CM in the perfective. However, Midgette does not give perfective examples.
48. Recall that Dëne nouns are also not marked for definiteness. The only way to specify a noun as unambiguously definite in the NP/DP is by using a demonstrative pronoun, for example: *diri łés* 'this bread' (Elford and Elford 1998:397). See also footnote 51.
49. The English translation does not reflect that there are several pieces of meat. While an event onset reading of 'almost' is also possible, the crucial thing is the event completion reading, which can only occur in accomplishments.
50. This sentence was judged completely acceptable with *horelyų* 'all,' which presumably makes the plural entity quantized.
51. A predominantly quantized interpretation of objects may have an independent cause in the object marking system of the language. It seems to me that unless the "unspecified object" prefix *?e-* is used, objects tend to have a specific interpretation in Dëne (a definite/specific interpretation of arguments not marked with *a-* (= Dëne *?e-*) has been established for Navajo in Willie 1991). This specificity might imply quantization in most cases. However, there are no good formal accounts of either specificity or its relationship to quantization in the semantics literature. Moreover, the interpretation of objects (and other arguments) in Dëne requires careful study. In principle, objects not marked with *?e-* can have an indefinite, nonspecific, narrow-scope reading (Wilhelm 2005). I leave these issues for further research.
52. In general, it is problematic to call semelfactives "telic," see Smith (1991). If semelfactives are not telic (but only punctual), the correlation between perfectivity and telicity in Navajo breaks down completely.
53. Bortolin (1998) also uses semantic tests.

NOTES TO CHAPTER FOUR

1. Most German examples are main clauses in the present perfect tense, and are of the form [S Aux O (Adjunct) V], where Aux is a finite form of 'have' or 'be,' and V is in past participle form. They are so similar to English that after example (1a), I omitted a word-by word gloss. Examples that differ from this format do have a word-by-word gloss.
2. The reading here is that the children fell asleep after one hour, not that they were in the process of falling asleep during the hour. This ingressive interpretation is typical of achievements, which are telic nondurative predicates.
3. An acceptable interpretation can be achieved here by coercing these predicates to mean 'begin V-ing,' which is a shift to a telic meaning.

4. Ehrich (1992), Abraham (1995), and Rapp (1997a,b) call telic predicates resultative predicates.
5. The suffix *-en* here is the infinitive suffix.
6. The perfect participle can also be used attributively of the single argument of intransitive stative, i.e., atelic, predicates, as shown in (i). I assume that these single arguments are internal arguments (cf. Rapp 1997a,b).
    (i) die Stadt, die am Rhein liegt—die am Rhein gelegene Stadt
       the city rel at-the Rhine lies the at-the Rhine lain city
       'the city which is situated by the Rhine'—'the city situatted by the Rhine'

   For intransitive verbs, this suggests that the attributive perfect participle is a diagnostic of unaccusativity, as argued by Grewendorf (1989) for German and by Levin and Rappaport Hovav (1995) for English, rather than of telicity/resultativity (but see Abraham 1995, Kaufmann 1995a,b for different views).
7. In fact, the key role which telicity plays in the patterning of the perfect participle has led linguists like Leiss (1992) to propose a category of "resultative" verb forms in German. According to Leiss, this category, which consists of a form of *sein* 'be' plus the perfect participle, is restricted to telic ("perfective/terminative" in her terminology) verbs and has "ergative syntax." By "ergative syntax," she means that the resultative can be formed with objects of transitive and subjects of intransitive (telic) verbs. Here are Leiss's examples:
    (i) The verbal category of resultative: *sein* + perfect participle of telic verbs (Leiss 1992:170)
        a. transitive telic verbs:
           Das Fenster *ist geöffnet.*
           'The window is open.' (lit., ' The window *is opened.*')
        b. intransitive telic verbs:
           Das Paket *ist angekommen.*
           'The parcel has arrived.' (lit., 'The parcel *is arrived.*')

   This proposal is not uncontroversial because it cuts across the standard classification of German verb forms: forms like (ia) are traditionally classed as a type of passive ("Zustandspassiv," i.e., stative or resultative passive), while (ib) is traditionally considered a type of present perfect. I do not take a stand on this issue, but the mere fact that a special category for only telic verbs has been proposed, indicates how important a factor telicity is in the grammar of German. In fact, Leiss finds that aspectuality (i.e., telicity) is a "verbal phenomenon" which is ubiquitous in the verbal system of German: it "colours all verbal categories in the narrower sense of the term [. . .]: tense, voice, and mode" (Leiss 1992:22; translation mine).
8. According to Rapp (1997b), verbs with an incremental theme are optionally intransitive, other verbs are obligatorily transitive. However, I do not find this generalization completely accurate. (i) below contains the German

translation of Dowty's (1991) famous example of an incremental theme, but the intransitive variant is quite bad. Also, the object in (12) is an incremental theme according to a test suggested by Rapp: compatibility with *zur Hälfte* 'by half' (shown in (ii) below). Nonetheless, (12) is completely ungrammatical without object.
    (i)   Sie hat *(den Rasen) gemäht.
         'She mowed *(the lawn).'
    (ii) Sie hat den Ast *zur Hälfte* abgesägt.
         'She sawed off the branch *by half*.'

9. There are some potential English counterexamples to this claim in the literature. For example, *The parade passed the house, John entered the icy water (very slowly), The crowd exited the auditorium (in 21 minutes)* (Declerck (1979), Dowty (1991), cited in Jackendoff 1996). Here the subject seems to "measure out" the event as much as the object does. It is beyond the scope of this dissertation to deal with such counterexamples. I simply note that in German, these examples do not easily translate into transitive clauses, and where they do, passivization is difficult. These facts indicate that at least in German, Tenny's claim seems to hold up:
    (i)   ??Die Parade passierte das Haus.
         ('The parade passed   the house.')
         vs.
         √Die Parade zog   an dem Haus vorbei.
          the parade went at the   house past
         'The parade moved past the house.'
    (ii) #John betrat   das eisige Wasser (sehr langsam).
         ('John entered the icy   water   (very slowly).')
         vs.
         √John stieg   (sehr langsam) in   das eisige Wasser.
         'John stepped (very slowly)   into the icy   water.'
    (iii) Das   Publikum (/??die Menschenmenge) verließ den Saal
         'The audience (/??the crowd)   exited the auditorium
                         (nachdenklich   /??in 21 Minuten).
                         (deep in thought/??in 21 minutes).'
    (iv) ??Der Saal   wurde   vom   Publikum/von der
            The auditorium became by-the audience/ by   the
                           Menschenmenge verlassen.
                           crowd   left
         ('The auditorium was exited/left by the audience/crowd.')

10. Nouns preceded by a definite article may also have *generic* reference. For example:
    (i)   *Die Liebe* beflügelt *den Menschen.*
         the love   BE-wings the human
         'Love gives wing to humanity.'

11. This sentence is grammatical under a coerced quantized reading of *Pudding* 'three portions of pudding.'
12. This generalization predicts that VPs with objects bearing dative or genitive case cannot denote a telic situation. Preliminary evidence suggests that this prediction is correct:
    (i) Susi hat *dem Lehrer* √eine Stunde lang/#in einer Stunde geholfen/ gedankt.
    'Susi helped/thanked *the.DAT teacher* √for an hour/#in an hour.'
    (ii) Susi hat √eine Stunde lang/#in einer Stunde *des Verstorbenen* gedacht.
    'Susi commemorated *the.GEN deceased* √for an hour/#in an hour.'
13. Filip (1989) calls the atelic interpretation 'progressive.' However, the fact that the examples with partitive objects are incompatible with 'in X time' (and compatible with 'for X time') clearly shows that (a)telicity is involved. Filip has no explanation for the patterning of the 'in/for X time' test, but has to make the unusual assumption that compatibility with 'in/for X time' is a test for perfective vs. imperfective viewpoint. In my analysis of the *an* construction as atelic, the 'in/for X time' test remains a telicity test. And it is the atelicity of the *an* construction which is responsible for a default imperfective/progressive interpretation.
14. For the doubtful, here is syntactic evidence that the elements affecting telicity are located in the VP. Topicalization, (i), shows syntactic constituent status. VP status is shown by an extraposed clause, (ii), which must adjoin to a VP (Haider 1993).
    (i) a. [*Das neue Buch lesen*] will   Susi heute nicht.
           the new book read   wants Susi today not
           'Susi does not want to *read the new book* today.'
        b. [*Die Kiste unter den Tisch geschoben*] hat Susi gestern schon.
           the box   under the table pushed   has Susi yesterday already
           'Susi has *pushed the box under the table* already yesterday.'
    (ii) a. [[Das Buch *t* lesen,]$_{VP}$ das Peter ihr geschenkt hat,]$_{VP}$
            the book   read   REL Peter her given   has
            will Susi heute nicht.
            wants Susi today not
            '*Read the book which Peter gave her*, Susi does not want to do today.'
         b. [[An dem Pullover t gestrickt,]$_{VP}$ den sie Peter schenken will,]$_{VP}$
            at the sweater   knitted   REL she Peter give   wants
            hat Susi schon lange   nicht mehr.
            has Susi already longtime not   anymore
            'For a long time now, Susi has not *knitted on the sweater she wanted to give to Peter*.'

c. [[Die Kiste unter den Tisch *t* schieben,]ᵥₚ der voll mit Spinn-
the box under the table push REL full with spider-
weben ist,]ᵥₚ will wohl keiner.
webs is wants probably noone
'Noone seems to want to *push the box under the table that is full of cobwebs.*'

15. As the term suggests, (inseparable) prefixes always have to be bound to the base verb. Furthermore, they are unstressed while particles are stressed. Since stress is assigned to the (first) stem, this means that particles but not inseparable prefixes are treated as stems by the phonology.

    Prefix verb formation is usually treated as word formation (i.e., as nonsyntactic), since prefixes do not behave like stems, are always bound, and are, in many cases, semantically bleached. They also affect argument structure differently from particles. For a comparison of prefixes and particles, see Stiebels and Wunderlich (1994) and Wurmbrand (1998).

16. Note that due to a confusion between viewpoint and situation aspect verbal prefixes and particles are often called "perfectivizing" in traditional sources. See Chapter Five for arguments against a perfective analysis.

    Some traditional sources also attempt to class different prefixes and particles as indicating different "Aktionsarten." A frequently cited example is *er-blühen* 'blossom/start blooming' vs. *ver-blühen* 'wither/finish blooming,' where the former is said to be of ingressive/inchoative and the latter to be of egressive/terminative Aktionsart (e.g., Flämig 1965, Dal 1966, Duden 1984). However, there is no systematic correspondence of any morpheme with any Aktionsart—Aktionsarten are purely semantic distinctions in German (see Steinitz 1981 for detailed arguments).

17. The primary concern of most work on particle verbs is to find a structural analysis which accounts for their lexical vs. syntactic characteristics, and/or their effects on argument structure.

18. Other particles, such as *mit* '(along) with' and *nach* 'after' do not contribute to telicity, but are aspectually neutral. I only discuss "telicizing" particles.

19. German does not have very good durativity tests, or rather, the tests are often inconclusive. I am using the durativity test that I have found to be most reliable: compatibility with *aufhören* 'stop' on a noniterative reading (see section 3.3). *Aufhören* is followed by a nonfinite VP, as shown in (28b) and (29b). I will omit the word-by-word gloss from subsequent *aufhören* examples.

20. This verb can also mean 'die' and then patterns as an achievement.

21. I am not concerned here with another meaning of *aushusten* 'finish coughing,' which also patterns as an achievement.

22. Although *Schleim* and *Staub* are mass nouns, they have quantized reference when combined with a definite determiner. In this context, they refer to a certain amount of phlegm or dust, an amount that still is unlikely to be removed by one cough.

23. This verb has additional, less transparent meanings, e.g., 'bud (trees),' 'kick out (horse).' The latter seems to describe a semelfactive, i.e., atelic, situation. This is the only exception I have found to the particle *aus* deriving telic verbs.
24. *Bauen* often is also telic without overt object, cf. (i). Following Rapp (1997b), I take this to mean that in these cases the verb is transitive with an implied object, rather than intransitive.
    (i) Sie haben in einem Jahr gebaut.
    'They built (implied: a house/*a tower/*a model airplane) in one year.'
25. In *ausbauen* in the sense of 'extend,' *aus* has a less concrete meaning, best represented by *BE (x)*.
26. A location reading (e.g., the event takes place in the sandbox) is excluded because here *in* assigns accusative case, which unambiguously identifies it as a goal rather than location PP.
27. In the examples with a time span adverbial, the event occurs after 'X time,' and there is little or no associated process which occurs during 'X time.' This is typical of achievements, which are telic nondurative predicates.
28. This sentence is acceptable on an atelic iterative interpretation of repeated bringing events. However, each individual bringing event is still an achievement.
29. This sentence is acceptable on an atelic iterative interpretation of repeated coming events. However, each individual coming event is still an achievement.
30. Stiebels (1996) and Zeller (2001) present evidence for semantic regularity even in the putative less transparent cases of particle verb formation. Often the meaning of a particle verb is at least partially predictable from the semantic class of the base verb.
31. Also, in a diachronic study of English, Brinton shows that certain particles (e.g., *up, down, off, over, out, through, away*) express "the goal or endpoint of a situation" (Brinton 1988:163), i.e., that they contribute telicity. While Brinton does not agree that these particles are "resultative," I believe this is simply due to the fact that she has a more restricted understanding of this term.
32. Should it turn out that truly external arguments can also influence telicity in German (see footnote 9 above), this would not threaten my view of the grammatization of telicity in the VP domain. External arguments originate in *v*P, which is part of the VP domain.

NOTES TO CHAPTER FIVE

1. But even in Slavic languages, it is not always clear whether these verb pairs encode a viewpoint or a situation type distinction. See, for example, Spencer and Zaretskaya (1998) for a large class of Russian prefixed verbs which are telic rather than perfective.

2. I am only considering the indicative forms of a verb, and am ignoring the subjunctive and imperative forms, which are even less likely to express viewpoint aspect.
3. Sometimes *beim* is used instead of *am*. The choice between the two is partly lexicalized, probably with regional differences (Duden 1984), but as Delisle (1985) shows, there are also true syntactic and semantic differences between *beim* and *am*. These differences are irrelevant to our concerns.
4. The perfect is preferred over the Preterite (*Was machte er?*) in spoken German. In South German, the Preterite is impossible (see section 1.3.2 below.)
5. In the Rhineland/Cologne area the *am* construction (choice (b)) is productive and widespread, similar to the English progressive, and allows for non-compounded objects in addition to the verb (Duden 1984, Stiebels, p.c.), so that (9b-d) below are grammatical.
6. See Dal (1966) for a concise overview of the historical development of the Modern German tense system.
7. Presumably, on such a proposal a perfective interpretation of a Present or Preterite clause must be attributed to some aspectual shift or coercion.
8. I ignore here the present tense meaning of the Present Perfect, because it is irrelevant to the argument.
9. The fact that one has to work harder to obtain the present tense reading in (12a) than in (12b) has to do with the person of the subject. As Wunderlich (1970) explains, self-commentary is pragmatically odd in most contexts.
10. The ability of the Present in much of spoken German to express present as well as future meaning is reflected in a theoretical and empirical debate on the status of the Present and the Future, respectively. In particular, there is a controversy on whether the Future is purely modal or does indeed also have a (future) tense function. See Wunderlich (1970), Vater (1975), Leiss (1992), and Brons-Albert (1982) and Matzel and Ulvestad (1982) for empirical studies.
11. Of course, a future reading also arises from the constellation TSit $\subseteq$ TT & TT > TU. TT > TU is another subcase of TT $\neg<$ TU. See Musan (2002) for details on the Present Tense.
12. As far as I can see, imperfective TT $\subset$ TSit would also be possible.
13. Ehrich also specifies a default condition that TT be included in the time of the result state of a telic predicate.
14. The difference between perfectives and perfects, and in particular between the Dëne Perfective and perfects in other languages, is an exciting topic for further work. Certainly, my account of the Dëne Perfective in Chapter Two implies that this viewpoint is more "perfect-like" than other perfective viewpoints. However, there are good reasons to believe that the Dëne Perfective really is a perfective rather than a perfect. For example, as opposed to perfects, its meaning is not primarily stative (see Smith 1991, Musan 2002

on stativity of perfects), and unlike perfects (compare English) it is used in narration.

15. It is beyond the scope of this dissertation to account for the subtle differences between the Present Perfect and the Preterite. See Musan (2002) for a thorough analysis.

16. The interested reader is referred to the cleverly constructed, amusing mystery novels by ex-linguist Wolf Haas (see references), who deliberately writes in Austrian German, a South German dialect. These novels nicely illustrate the exclusive use of the Perfect, even with stative verbs and the copula *sein* 'be.'

17. My variety of South German lies on the boundary of Low Alemannic and Swabian. Phonologically, it is very similar to Low Alemannic. (*http://www. uni-marburg.de/dsa/dtdialekte.html*)

18. The Perfect also cannot be used in Standard German to indicate a posterior relation between two past events. In this context, the Preterite is obligatory, e.g., (i). However, in South German not the Preterite but either the Perfect or Present is used here, (ii). This contrast illustrates further the absence of the Preterite from South German.

   (i) <u>Posterior use—Standard German</u>: (Ehrich 1992:69)
      a. Hans wartete darauf, dass der Bus *kam*   (*gekommen ist).
         Hans wait-PRET on   that the bus come-PRET (*come is)
         'Hans was waiting for the bus to come.'
      b. Die Kinder waren leise, damit der Vater nicht
         the children were quiet, so-that the father not
         aufwachte   (*aufgewacht ist).
         up-wake-PRET (*woken-up is)
         'The children were quiet so that the father would not wake up.'

   (ii) <u>Posterior use—South German</u>:
      a. Der Hans hat darauf gewartet, dass der Bus *kommt*   (*kam).
         the Hans has on   waited   that the bus come-PRES (*come-PRET)
         'Hans was waiting for the bus to come.'
      b. Die Kinder sind leise gewesen, damit der Vater nicht
         the children were quiet been   so-that the father not
         aufgewacht ist (*aufwachte).
         up-woken is (*up-wake-PRET)
         'The children were quiet so that the father would not wake up.'

19. A formal analysis of the meaning of the German Perfect, which could easily be extended to the South German Perfect, can be found in Musan (2002).

20. I ignore here the present tense meaning of the Present Perfect, because it is irrelevant to the argument.

21. Since the only place where South German shows stronger evidence for this claim than Standard German is in the absence of the Preterite (section 1.3), I will from now on assume that viewpoint aspect is not grammatized in

German in general. The reader who is not convinced may restrict my claim to South German.
22. In South German, the entire discourse would be in the Perfect.
23. Also note that different durativity tests yield different results. While *langsam* is fine in (42b), *aufhören* and 'for X time' are both pretty bad in this example, cf. (i)–(ii). This contrasts with telicity, for which usually all tests yield the same results.

    (i) #Die Schneeflocke *hörte auf*, zur Erde zu fallen.
         'The snowflake *stopped* falling to the ground.'
    (ii) #Die Schneeflocke fiel *5 Sekunden lang* zur Erde.
         'The snowflake fell to the ground *for 5 seconds*.'

24. Smith (p.c.) points out that the derivation from activity to achievement, where the achievement means something like 'begin V-ing' or 'stop V-ing,' is frequently found in language. However, these derivations seem to be of a different type, since result states are not involved. I leave a comparison of these kinds of derivations and particle verb formation to future research. Potentially, the unsystematicity of durativity is much more widespread than believed.
25. Because the *aufhören* 'stop' test is rarely good with nonagentive subjects, I use instead compatibility with pseudo-progressive *dabei sein* to test for durativity in these examples.
26. Particle verb formation is also regular with respect to aspectually neutral particles such as *mit* '(along) with' in that the aspectual class remains unchanged, i.e., the particle verb is of the same aspectual class as the base verb.

NOTES TO CHAPTER SIX

1. Recall that this is not to be confused with *grammaticalization/grammaticization*, in the sense of the diachronic development of a grammatical element, often through semantic bleaching of a lexical element (e.g., Lehmann 1982, Traugott and Heine 1991, Bybee et al 1994).
2. Other FPs may be present, but these are irrelevant to my topic, and I remain agnostic about them.
3. Note that in the theory of Demirdache and Uribe-Etxebarria (2000), the lower argument of TP and Asp respectively is not its complement but the specifier of its complement. Moreover, it is assumed that projections can have multiple specifiers, e.g., both TSit and the verb's external argument are specifiers of vP. I adopt these assumptions without discussion.
4. This is not a standard assumption. Usually, events are not thought of as time intervals. For example, a definition of events as times would not be able to distinguish between two completely simultaneous events. We may thus have to assume that the argument in Spec-vP is *e* after all, and use something like a temporal trace function (e.g., Krifka 1992) or a running time function to

convert the event into a time. Kratzer (1998), Matthewson (2002) propose that this running time function is part of what the Asp head does, in addition to locating the running time with respect to the reference or topic time. The difference between these two assumptions is irrelevant to my proposal, since on both views it is Asp which relates TSit to TT.

5. This view coincides with the insight expressed in lexical decomposition theories. Such theories, which are intended to inform argument structure, represent telicity as a change of state (formally, *BECOME [STATE (x)]*). And crucially, the argument of which the change of state is predicated is linked as the direct internal argument (i.e., the VP-internal DP) in the syntax.

6. Recall from Chapter One that this parallels the "grammatization" of phonological features. A phonological feature is also only part of the grammar of a language if it is manifested in a contrast in that language.

7. Positional stative verbs have the pattern *the*-imperfective, *ghe*-perfective. I suggested in Chapter Three that these verbs are derived from perfective forms of nonstative verbs. They could thus be treated similarly to actual perfective nonstative verbs. However, stative verbs are beyond the scope of this dissertation. I also exclude from the analysis here verbs which potentially have the pattern *ne*-imperfective, *ne*-perfective. See Chapter Three for discussion.

8. I am not concerned here with how a present, past or future tense interpretation is obtained in Dëne. In the theory I am assuming, tense is represented as a relation of time of utterance (TU) and TT, and this relation is anchored in the syntactic projection TP. TU is a specifier of TP, and TT is the specifier of its complement. The status of TP has not been explored for Dëne, but certainly not every sentence has an overt element in T. I refer the interested reader to Matthewson (2002, 2005) and Wiltschko (2003) for two different views on the status of TP in tenseless languages.

9. The unacceptability of *den Ast* here is due to the fact that atelic base verbs usually have different selectional restrictions than the particle verbs derived from them. However, the unacceptability of *den Ast* has nothing to do with its being quantized or definite.

10. The typical nonquantized (count) nominal is a bare plural, without determiner. Consequently, we might say that nonquantized (count) nominals are NPs and quantized nominals are DPs. Compare the following paradigm of count nouns:

    (i) some ways of marking quantized reference on count nouns

type of DP/NP	type of reference	example	determiner
sg definite	quantized	*der Ast* 'the branch'	*der*
pl definite	quantized	*die Äste* 'the branches'	*die*
sg indefinite	quantized	*ein Ast* 'a branch'	*ein*
pl indefinite	cumulative	*Äste* 'branches'	Ø

11. Such examples also constitute empirical evidence against the assumption that [delim] on V is uninterpretable and must be checked: a derivation like (17) in which this feature cannot be "checked" does not crash, but converges—with an atelic interpretation.
12. In a way, what happens in VP is a more direct grammatization, because there is no mediation through another grammatico-semantic notion such as viewpoint aspect. In another way, it is less direct, because telicity cannot simply be associated with *one* morpheme or form, as can durativity (see Smith 1991 on telicity).
13. Assuming that it is the function of determiners to convey such meanings as definiteness and quantization, it is an interesting issue for further research whether nominals in Dëne are NPs and not DPs.
14. As discussed in Chapters Two and Three, one reason for this is that their semantic contribution cannot be isolated from that of other opaque elements of a verb.
15. The 'almost' test in Dëne is a semantic test that is sensitive to the semantic representation of telicity, rather than to its grammatized representation.
16. A formal semantic account of the completive meaning of the Dëne perfective is given in Wilhelm (2003).
17. Smith (1991) proposes that sentences with neither a perfective nor an imperfective morpheme have a *neutral viewpoint*. The neutral viewpoint allows for a simultaneous/overlapping interpretation like the imperfective, and it allows for a closed/nonoverlapping interpretation like the perfective, but it does not allow for the preliminary ('about to') interpretation which is typical of imperfective viewpoints. I do not adopt this proposal, for the following reason: we know that in German, situation type/telicity influences whether a sentence receives a perfective or an imperfective interpretation. It is not clear to me how the influence of telicity can be accounted for if Asp is already specified for a viewpoint, namely neutral viewpoint.
18. Of course, one could also simply say that German has no AspP at all. But see Matthewson (2002, 2005) for arguments why an empty projection is preferable over the complete absence of the projection in such cases.
19. Again, Smith (p.c.) suggests that if process rather than durativity were used to distinguish accomplishments from achievements (and perhaps activities from semelfactives), as is done in Pustejovsky (1991, 1995), the results of a grammatization study might be different, and allow for a representation in the VP. See Chapter One, section 1.2, for why I chose to focus on durativity rather than process. The grammatization of process is a topic for further research.
20. Moreover, German aspectually neutral particles, which are not discussed in this dissertation, behave morphosyntactically identically to bounding particles. They thus must also be sisters of the verb, but they cannot be instances of an R_vP. This is one reason why in section 3 I chose to implement the

grammatization of telicity through the presence of a feature on VP elements, rather than through the presence alone of these elements.
21. Recall that the status of stativity is not addressed in this dissertation.
22. Perfect "tenses," e.g., the past perfect, can order an event as preceding another. However, perfects are not pure tenses, they are at best a mix of tense and viewpoint aspect (see Comrie 1976, Smith 1991, Musan 2002), and I believe it is the viewpoint component of perfects which is responsible for the anteriority effect.

Bibliography

Abraham, Werner. 1995. *Deutsche Syntax im Sprachenvergleich. Grundlegung einer typologischen Syntax des Deutschen.* Tübingen: Gunter Narr.
Anderson, Stephen R. 1992. *A-Morphous Morphology.* Cambridge: Cambridge University Press.
Andersson, S.G. 1972. *Aktionalität im Deutschen.* Uppsala: S. Academiae Ubsaliensis.
Axelrod, Melissa. 1993. *The Semantics of Time. Aspectual Categorization in Koyukon Athabaskan.* Lincoln, Nebraska: University of Nebraska Press.
Bach, Emmon. 1981. On Time, Tense, and Aspect: An Essay in English Metaphysics. In *Radical Pragmatics*, ed. Peter Cole, 63–81. NY: Academic Press.
———. 1986. The Algebra of Events. *Linguistics and Philosophy* 9:5–16.
Baker, Mark. 1985. The Mirror Principle and Morphosyntactic Explanation. *Linguistic Inquiry* 16:373–416.
———. 1988. *Incorporation: A Theory of Grammatical Function Changing.* Chicago: Chicago University Press.
Bar-el, Leora, Peter Jacobs, and Martina Wiltschko. 2001. A [+interpretable] Number Feature on Verbs: Evidence from Squamish Salish. In *Proceedings of the West Coast Conference on Formal Linguistics 20*, 43–55. Somerville, MA: Cascadilla Press.
Bauer, Laurie. 2001. *Morphological Productivity.* Cambridge: Cambridge University Press.
Behagel, Otto. 1907[4]. *Die Deutsche Sprache.* Wien/Leipzig: Tempsky/Freytag.
Benware, Wilbur A. 1993. Representing Prepositions: New High German *um*. *Linguistics* 31:135–157.
Bierwisch, Manfred. 1983. Semantische und konzeptuelle Repräsentation lexikalischer Einheiten. In *Untersuchungen zur Semantik*, ed. Rolf Ruzicka and Wolfgang Motsch, 61–99. Berlin: Akademie Verlag.
Blom, Corrien. 2002. The Diachrony of Complex Predicates in Dutch: a Case Study in the Grammaticalization and the Stability of the Particle Verb System. Paper presented at the Workshop on Complex Predicates, Particles and Subevents, September 30–October 2, Konstanz University, Germany.

Bohnemeyer, Jürgen, and Mary Swift. 2004. Event realization and aspectual interpretation. *Linguistics and Philosophy* 27:263–296.

Booij, Geert. 2002a. *The Morphology of Dutch*. Oxford: Oxford University Press.

———. 2002b. Constructional Idioms, Morphology, and the Dutch Lexicon. *Journal of Germanic Linguistics* 14:301–29.

Borer, Hagit. 1994. The Projection of Arguments. In *University of Massachusetts Occasional Papers* 17. GLSA, University of Massachusetts, Amherst.

———. 1998. Deriving Passive Without Theta Roles. In *Morphology and its Relation to Phonology and Syntax*, ed. Steven G. Lapointe et al., 60–99. Stanford, CA: CSLI Publications.

———. 2004. The Grammar Machine. In *The Unaccusativity Puzzle*, ed. Artemis Alexiadou et al. Oxford: Oxford University Press.

Bortolin, Leah. 1998. *Aspect and the Chipewyan Verb*. M.A. thesis, University Calgary, AB.

Brinton, Laurel J. 1988. *The Development of English Aspectual Systems: Aspectualizers and Post Verbal Particles*. Cambridge: Cambridge University Press.

Brons-Albert, Ruth. 1982. *Die Bezeichnung von Zukünftigem in der gesprochenen deutschen Standardsprache*. Tübingen: G. Narr.

Butt, Miriam, and Gillian Ramchand. 2001. Building Complex Events in Hindi/Urdu. Paper presented at the Workshop on the Syntax of Predication, ZAS, November 2001, ZAS, Berlin, Germany.

Bybee, Joan. 1985. *Morphology : a Study of the Relation Between Meaning and Form*. Amsterdam: John Benjamins.

Bybee, Joan, Revere Perkins, and William Pagliuca. 1994. *The Evolution of Grammar. Tense, Aspect, and Modality in the Languages of the World*. Chicago: The University of Chicago Press.

Carlson, Gregory N. 1977. Reference to kinds in English. Ph.D. dissertation, University of Massachusetts, Amherst.

Carlson, Lauri. 1981. Aspect and Quantification. In *Syntax and Semantics 14: Tense and Aspect*, ed. Philip J. Tedeschi and Annie Zaenen, 31–64. New York: Academic Press.

Causley, Trisha. 1996. Featural Correspondence and Consonant Coalescence in Athapaskan. Ms. (Generals Paper), University of Toronto, ON.

Chierchia, Gennaro. 1998. Plurality of mass nouns and the notion of „semantic parameter." In *Events and Grammar*, ed. Susan Rothstein, 53–103. Dordrecht: Kluwer.

Chomsky, Noam. 1970. Remarks on Nominalization. In *Readings in English Transformational Grammar*, ed. Roderick A. Jacobs and Peter S. Rosenbaum, 184–221. Waltham, Mass: Ginn.

———. 1995. *The Minimalist Program*. Cambridge: MIT Press.

———. 2000. Minimalist Inquiries: The Framework. In *Step by Step. Essays on Minimalist Syntax in Honor of Howard Lasnik*, ed. Roger Martin et al., 89–155. Cambridge, Mass: MIT Press.

Chung, Sandra, and Alan Timberlake. 1985. Tense, Aspect, and Mood. In *Language Typology and Syntactic Description III: Grammatical Categories and the Lexicon*, ed. Timothy Shopen, 202–258. Cambridge: Cambridge University Press.

Comrie, Bernard. 1976. *Aspect*. Cambridge: Cambridge University Press.

———. 1985. *Tense*. Cambridge: Cambridge University Press.

Cook, E.-D. 2004. *A grammar of Dëne Sųłiné (Chipewyan)*. Winnipeg: Algonquian and Iroquoian Linguistics (Memoir 17: Special Athabaskan Number).

Corbett, Greville. 2000. *Number*. Cambridge: Cambridge University Press.

———. 1991. *Gender*. Cambridge: Cambridge University Press.

Croft, William. 1998. Event Structure in Argument Linking. In *The Projection of Arguments: Lexical and Compositional Factors*, ed. Miriam Butt and Wilhelm Geuder, 21–63. Stanford, CA: CSLI Publications.

Cruse, D.A. 1986. *Lexical Semantics*. Cambridge: Cambridge University Press.

Dahl, Östen. 1985. *Tense and Aspect Systems*. Oxford: Blackwell.

Dal, Ingerid. 1966. *Kurze deutsche Syntax*. Tübingen: Max Niemeyer Verlag.

Davidson, Donald. 1966. The Logical Form of Action Sentences. In *The Logic of Decision and Action*, ed. Nicholas Rescher, 81–95. Pittsburgh: University of Pittsburgh Press.

de Hoop, Helen. 1992. *Case Configuration and Noun Phrase Interpretation*. (Groningen Dissertations in Linguistics 4). Groningen: Grodil.

Declerck, Renaat. 1979. Aspect and the Bounded/Unbounded (Telic/Atelic) Distinction. *Linguistics* 17:761–94.

Delisle, Helga. 1985. *Am/Beim* Progressive Constructions in German. In *The Twelfth LACUS Forum, 1985*, 215–24. Lake Bluff, IL: LACUS.

Demirdache, Hamida, and Myriam Uribe-Etxebarria. 2000. The Primitives of Temporal Relations. In *Step by Step. Essays on Minimalist Syntax in Honor of Howard Lasnik*, ed. Roger Martin et al., 157–86. Cambridge, Mass: MIT Press.

Depraetere, Ilse. 1995. On the Necessity of Distinguishing Between (Un)boundedness and (A)telicity. *Linguistics and Philosophy* 18:1–19.

DiSciullo, Anna-Maria, and Edwin Williams. 1987. *On the Definition of Word*. Cambridge, Mass: MIT Press.

Diesing, Molly. 1992. *Indefinites*. Cambridge, Mass.: MIT Press.

Dowty, David R. 1979. *Word Meaning and Montague Grammar*. Dordrecht: Reidel.

———. 1991. Thematic Proto-Roles and Argument Selection. *Language* 67:547–619.

Duden. 2001. *Deutsches Universalwörterbuch*. Mannheim: Dudenverlag.

———. 1984. *Duden, Vol. 4: Grammatik (4th ed.)*. Ed. by G. Drosdowski. Mannheim: Duden Verlag.

Durie, Mark. 1986. The Grammaticization of Number As a Verbal Category. *Proceedings of the Twelfth Annual Meeting of the Berkeley Linguistics Society*, 355–370. University of Berkeley, CA.

Ehrich, Veronika. 1992. *Hier und Jetzt. Studien zur lokalen und temporalen Deixis im Deutschen*. Tübingen: Niemeyer.

Elford, Leon, and Marjorie Elford. 1998. *Dene (Chipewyan) Dictionary*. Prince Albert, Sask.: Northern Canada Mission Distributors.

Fagan, Sarah M.B. 1992. *The Syntax and Semantics of Middle Constructions. A Study With Special Reference to German*. Cambridge: Cambridge University Press.

Filip, Hana. 1989. Aspectual Properties of the AN-Construction in German. In *Tempus—Aspekt—Modus*, ed. Werner Abraham and Theo Janssen, 259–92. Tübingen: Niemeyer.

Flämig, Walter. 1964. Zur Funktion des Verbs. I. Tempus und Temporalität. *Deutsch als Fremdsprache* 1(4):1–8.

———. 1965. Zur Funktion des Verbs. III. Aktionsart und Aktionalität. *Deutsch als Fremdsprache* 2(2):4–12.

François, Jacques. 1985. Aktionsart, Aspekt und Zeitkonstitution. In *Handbuch der Lexikologie*, ed. Christoph Schwarze and Dieter Wunderlich, 229–49. Kronberg: Athenäum.

Gil, David. 1993. Nominal and Verbal Quantification. *Sprachtypologie und Universalienforschung* 46:275–317.

Giorgi, Alessandra, and Fabio Pianesi. 1998. *Tense and Aspect. From Semantics to Morphosyntax*. Oxford: Oxford University Press.

Givón, Talmy. 2001. *Syntax*, vol. II (revised edition). Amsterdam: John Benjamins.

Goldberg, Adele. 1995. *Constructions. A Construction Grammar Approach to Argument Structure*. Chicago: University of Chicago Press.

Government of Alberta. 2004. *Alberta: First Nations Population, Summary December 2003*. Strategic Services, Alberta Aboriginal Affairs and Northern Development. Retrieved at: *http://www.aand.gov.ab.ca/AAND.asp?lid=133*

Grewendorf, Günther. 1989. *Ergativity in German*. Dordrecht: Foris.

Grice, H.P. 1975. Logic and Conversation. In *Syntax and Semantics 3: Speech Acts*, ed. Peter Cole and Jerry L. Morgan.

Grimshaw, Jane. 1990. *Argument Structure*. Cambridge, Mass: MIT Press.

Haas, Wolf. 1996. *Auferstehung der Toten*. Reinbek bei Hamburg: Rowohlt.

———. 1997. *Der Knochenmann*. Reinbek bei Hamburg: Rowohlt.

———. 1998. *Komm, süßer Tod*. Reinbek bei Hamburg: Rowohlt.

———. 1999. *Silentium!* Reinbek bei Hamburg: Rowohlt.

———. 2001. *Wie die Tiere*. Reinbek bei Hamburg: Rowohlt.

Haider, Hubert. 1993. *Deutsche Syntax—generativ*. Tübingen: Gunter Narr.

Haiman, John, and Pamela Munro 1983. *Switch-Reference and Universal Grammar: Proceedings of a Symposium on Switch Reference and Universal Grammar, Winnipeg, May 1981*. Amsterdam: John Benjamins.

Hale, Ken. 2001. Navajo Verb Stem Position and the Bipartite Structure of the Navajo Conjunct Sector. *Linguistic Inquiry* 32:678–93.

Hale, Ken, and Samuel J. Keyser. 1993. On Argument Structure and the Lexical Expression of Syntactic Relations. In *The View From Building 20*, ed. Ken Hale and Samuel J. Keyser, 53–109. Cambridge, Mass: MIT Press.

Halle, Morris, and Alec Marantz. 1993. Distributed Morphology and the Pieces of Inflection. *The View From Building 20*, ed. Ken Hale and Samuel J. Keyser, 111–176. Cambridge, Mass: MIT Press.

Hargus, Sharon, and Siri G. Tuttle. 1997. Augmentation as Affixation in Athabaskan Languages. *Phonology* 14:177–220.

Harley, Heidi, and Rolf Noyer. 1999. State-of-the-Article: Distributed Morphology. *Glot* 4:3–9.

Higginbotham, James. 1985. On Semantics. *Linguistic Inquiry* 16:547–93.

Hinrichs, Erhard. 1985. *A Compositional Semantics for Aktionsarten and NP Reference in English.* Ph.D. dissertation, Ohio State University.

Hoekstra, Teun. 1988. Small Clause Results. *Lingua* 74:101–39.

Hopper, Paul, ed. 1982. *Tense-Aspect: Between Semantics and Pragmatics.* Amsterdam: John Benjamins.

Horn, Laurence R. 1972. *On the Semantic Properties of Logical Operators in English.* Ph.D. dissertation, UCLA. Distributed by Indiana University Linguistics Club, Bloomington.

Hundsnurscher, Franz. 1968. *Das System der Partikelverben mit "aus" in der Gegenwartssprache.* Göppingen: Kümmerle.

Jackendoff, Ray. 1990. *Semantic Structures.* Cambridge, Mass: MIT Press.

———. 1996. The Proper Treatment of Measuring Out, Telicity, and Perhaps Even Quantification. *Natural Language and Linguistic Theory* 14:305–54.

———. 1997. *The Architecture of the Language Faculty.* Cambridge, Mass: MIT Press.

Kamp, Hans, and Christian Rohrer. 1983. Tense in Texts. In *Meaning, Use, and Interpretation of Language*, ed. Rainer Bäuerle et al., 250–69. Berlin: Walter de Gruyter.

Kari, James. 1979. *Athabaskan Verb Theme Categories: Ahtna.* (Alaska Native Language Center Research Papers 2). Fairbanks: Alaska Native Language Center.

———. 1989. Affix Positions and Zones in the Athapaskan Verb Complex: Ahtna and Navajo. *International Journal of American Linguistics* 55:424–54.

Kaufmann, Ingrid. 1995a. O- and D-Predicates: A Semantic Approach to the Unaccusative-Unergative Distinction. *Journal of Semantics* 12:377–427.

———. 1995b. What Is an (Im-)possible Verb? Restrictions on Semantic Form and Their Consequences for Argument Structure. *Folia Linguistica* 29:67–103.

Kenny, Anthony. 1963. *Action, Emotion and Will.* New York: Humanities Press.

Kiparsky, Paul. 1998. Partitive Case and Aspect. In *The Projection of Arguments*, ed. Miriam Butt and Wilhelm Geuder, 265–307. Stanford, CA: CSLI Publications.

Klein, Wolfgang. 1994. *Time in Language.* London: Routledge.

———. 2002. On Times and Arguments. Paper presented at *Sinn und Bedeutung VII*, October 3–5, 2002, University of Konstanz, Germany.

Kratzer, Angelika. 1995. Stage-Level and Individual-Level Predicates. In *The Generic Book*, ed. Gregory N. Carlson and Francis Jeffry Pelletier, 125–175. Chicago: University of Chicago Press. (First published 1988 in *Genericity in Natural Language*, ed. Manfred Krifka, 247–284. SNS-Bericht 88-42, University of Tübingen.)

———. 1996. Severing the External Argument From Its Verb. In *Phrase Structure and the Lexicon*, ed. Johan Rooryck and Laurie Zaring, 109–37. Dordrecht: Kluwer.

———. 1998. More Structural Analogies Between Pronouns and Tenses. In *Proceedings of Semantics and Linguistic Theory VIII*, 92–110. Ithaca, NY: Cornell University.

———. 2004. Telicity and the Meaning of Objective Case. In *The Syntax of Time*, ed. Jaqueline Guéron and Jaqueline Lecarme, 389–424. Cambridge, Mass: MIT Press.

Krauss, Michael E. 1969. On the Classifiers in the Athabaskan, Eyak, and Tlingit Verb. *Indiana University Publications in Anthropology and Linguistics* 23/24.

Krifka, Manfred. 1989. *Nominalreferenz und Zeitkonstitution. Zur Semantik von Massentermen, Pluraltermen und Aspektklassen*. Munich: Fink.

———. 1992. Thematic Relations as Links Between Nominal Reference and Temporal Constitution. In *Lexical Matters*, ed. Ivan Sag and Anna Szabolcsi, 29–53. Stanford: CSLI Publications.

———. 1998. The Origins of Telicity. In *Events and Grammar*, ed. Susan Rothstein, 197–235. Dordrecht: Kluwer.

Landman, Fred. 1992. The Progressive. *Natural Language Semantics* 1:1–32.

Lehmann, Christian. 1982. *Thoughts on Grammaticalization: A Programmatic Sketch*, vol. 1. (Arbeiten des Kölner Universalien-Projekts Nr. 48) University of Cologne.

Leiss, Elisabeth. 1992. *Die Verbalkategorien des Deutschen*. Berlin: Walter de Gruyter.

Levin, Beth, and Malka Rappaport Hovav. 1995. *Unaccusativity*. Cambridge, Mass: MIT Press.

Levinson, Stephen C. 1983. *Pragmatics*. Cambridge: Cambridge University Press.

Li, Charles N., ed. 1976. *Subject and Topic*. New York: Academic Press.

Li, Fang-Kuei. 1946. Chipewyan. In *Linguistic Structures of Native America*, ed. Cornelius Osgood, 398–423. New York: Johnson Reprint Corporation (Viking Fund Publications in Anthropology 6).

Lieber, Rochelle. 1992. *Deconstructing Morphology: Word Structure in Syntactic Theory*. Chicago: University of Chicago Press.

Link, Godehard. 1983. The logical analysis of plural and mass nouns: a lattice-theoretic approach. In *Meaning, Use, and Interpretation of Language*, ed. Rainer Bäuerle et al., 302–323. Berlin: de Gruyter.

Löbner, Sebastian. 1988. Ansätze zu einer integralen semantischen Theorie von Tempus, Aspekt und Aktionsarten. In *Temporalsemantik: Beiträge zur Linguistik der Zeitreferenz*, ed. Veronika Ehrich and Heinz Vater, 163–191. Tübingen: Niemeyer.

Longacre, Robert. 1985. Sentences as Combinations of Clauses. In *Language Tyypology and Syntactic Description*, vol. II, ed. Timothy Shopen, 235–286. Cambridge: Cambridge University Press.

Lüdeling, Anke. 1998. *On Particle Verbs and Similar Constructions in German*. Ph.D. dissertation, University of Stuttgart, Germany.

Marantz, Alec. 1997. No Escape from Syntax: Don't Try Morphological Analysis in the Privacy of Your Own Lexicon. *U Penn Working Papers in Linguistics* 4:201–25.

Matthewson, Lisa. 2002. On Universality and Variation in Tense Systems. Talk given in the University of Calgary Linguistics Colloquium Series, 4 October 2002, Calgary, Alberta.

———. 2005. On the Absence of Tense on Determiners. *Lingua* 115:1697–1735.

Matzel, Klaus, and Barne Ulvestad. 1982. Futur I und futurisches Präsens. *Sprachwissenschaft* 7:282–328.

McDonough, Joyce. 1990. *Topics in the Phonology and Morphology of Navajo Verbs*. Ph.D. dissertation, University of Massachusetts, Amherst.

Mezhevich, Ilana. 2003. English Resultatives: State Versus Location. Paper presented at the 2003 Annual Meeting of the Canadian Linguistic Association/Association Linguistique Canadienne, June 2003, Dalhousie University, Halifax, Nova Scotia.

Midgette, Sally. 1996. Lexical Aspect in Navajo: The Telic Property. In *Athabaskan Language Studies. Essays in Honor of Robert W. Young*, ed. Eloise Jelinek et al., 305–30. Albuquerque: University of New Mexico Press.

Milsark, Gary. 1974. *Existential Sentences in English*. Ph.D. dissertation, MIT, Cambridge, Mass. Distributed by Indiana University Linguistics Club.

Mithun, Marianne. 1988. Lexical Categories and the Evolution of Number Marking. In *Theoretical Morphology*, ed. Michael Hammond and Michael Noonan, 211–234. San Diego: Academic Press.

Moens, Marc. 1987. *Tense, Aspect, and Temporal Reference*. Ph.D. dissertation, University of Edinborough.

Mohanan, Tara, and Lionel Wee, eds. 1999. *Grammatical Semantics*. Stanford, CA: CSLI Publications.

Mourelatos, Alexander P.D. 1978. Events, Processes, and States. *Linguistics and Philosophy* 2:415–34.

Musan, Renate. 2002. *The German Perfect*. Dordrecht: Kluwer.

Neeleman, Ad, and Fred Weerman. 1993. The Balance Between Syntax and Morphology: Dutch Particles and Resultatives. *Natural Language and Linguistic Theory* 11:433–75.

Parks, Douglas R. 1976. *A Grammar of Pawnee*. New York: Garland.

Parsons, Terence. 1990. *Events in the Semantics of English*. Cambridge, Mass: MIT Press.

Partee, Barbara. 1984. Nominal and Temporal Anaphora. *Linguistics and Philosophy* 7:243–86.

Paul, Hermann. 1902. Die Umschreibung des Perfektums im Deutschen mit haben und sein. *Abhandlungen der philologisch-logischen Klasse der königlichen bayerischen Akademie der Wissenschaften XXII*, vol. I. München, 161–210.

———. 1959. *Deutsche Grammatik*. Halle (Saale): VEB Max Niemeyer Verlag.

Pesetsky, David, and Esther Torrego. 2004. Tense, Case, and the Nature of Syntactic Categories. In *The Syntax of Time*, ed. Jaqueline Guéron and Jaqueline Lecarme, 495–538. Cambridge, Mass: MIT Press.

Pinker, Steven. 1989. *Learnability and Cognition: The Acquisition of Argument Structure*. Cambridge, Mass: MIT Press.

Piñón, Christopher. 1995. *An Ontology for Event Semantics*. Ph.D. dissertation, Stanford University, CA.

Pustejovsky, James. 1991. The Syntax of Event Structure. In *Lexical and Conceptual Semantics*, ed. Beth Levin and Steven Pinker, 47–82. Cambridge, Mass.: Blackwell.

———. 1995. *The Generative Lexicon*. Cambridge, Mass: MIT Press.

Ramchand, Gillian. 1997. *Aspect and Predication*. Oxford: Clarendon Press.

———. 2002. A Particle Theory of Light Verbs. Paper presented at the Workshop on Complex Predicates, Particles, and Subevents, September 30–October 2, 2002, University of Konstanz, Germany.

Rapp, Irene. 1997a. *Partizipien und semantische Struktur*. Tübingen: Stauffenberg.

———. 1997b. Fakultativität von Verbargumenten als Reflex der semantischen Struktur. *Linguistische Berichte* 172:490–529.

Rappaport Hovav, Malka, and Beth Levin. 1998. Building Verb Meanings. In *The Projection of Arguments. Lexical and Compositional Factors*, ed. Miriam Butt and Wilhelm Geuder, 97–134. Stanford: CSLI Publications.

Reichenbach, Hans. 1947. *Elements of Symbolic Logic*. London: Macmillan.

Rice, Keren. 1989. *A Grammar of Slave*. Berlin: Mouton de Gruyter.

———. 2000. *Morpheme Order and Semantic Scope*. Cambridge: Cambridge University Press.

Rice, Sally, and Valerie Wood. 2002. Variation in Language Decay: Some Dialectal Differences in Dëne Sųłiné (Chipewyan). Paper presented at *WSCLA 7* (Workshop on Structure and Constituency in the Languages of the Americas), March 22–24, University of Alberta, Edmonton.

Ritter, Elisabeth, and Sara Thomas Rosen. 1998. Delimiting Events in Syntax. In *The Projection of Arguments. Lexical and Compositional Factors*, ed. Miriam Butt and Wilhelm Geuder, 135–164. Stanford: CSLI Publications.

Ritter, Elisabeth, and Sara Thomas Rosen. 2000. Event Structure and Ergativity. In *Events as Grammatical Objects*, ed. James Pustejovsky and Carol Tenny, 187–238. Stanford, CA: CSLI Publications.

Ryle, Gilbert. 1949. *The Concept of Mind.* London: Barnes and Noble.
Saxon, Leslie. 1986. *The Syntax of Pronouns in Dogrib (Athapaskan): Some Theoretical Consequences.* Ph.D. dissertation, University of California, San Diego.
———. 1989. Lexical Versus Syntactic Projection: The Configurationality of Slave. In *Athapaskan Linguistics: Current Perspectives on a Language Family,* ed. E.-D. Cook and Keren Rice, 379–406. Berlin: Mouton de Gruyter.
Singh, Mona. 1991. The Perfective Paradox: Or How to Eat Your Cake and Have it Too. *Proceedings of the Seventeenth Annual Meeting of the Berkeley Linguistics Society,* 469–479. University of Berkeley, CA.
Smith, Carlota. 1991. *The Parameter of Aspect.* Dordrecht: Kluwer. (2nd edition: 1997)
———. 1996. Aspectual Categories in Navajo. *International Journal of American Linguistics* 62:227–263.
———. 1999. Activities: States or Events? *Linguistics and Philosophy* 22:479–508.
Speas, Margaret. 1984. Navajo Prefixes and Word Structure Typology. In *Papers from the January 1984 MIT Workshop in Morphology (MIT Working Papers in Linguistics* 7), 86–109. Cambridge, Mass: MIT Department of Linguistics.
———. 1990. *Phrase Structure in Natural Language.* Dordrecht: Kluwer.
Spencer, Andrew, and Marina Zaretskaya. 1998. Verb Prefixation in Russian as Lexical Subordination. *Linguistics* 36:1–39.
Steinitz, Renate. 1981. *Der Status der Kategorie „Aktionsart" in der Grammatik (oder: Gibt es Aktionsarten im Deutschen?).* Berlin (Ost): Zentralinstitut für Sprachwissenschaft (*Linguistische Studien Reihe A* 76).
Stiebels, Barbara. 1996. *Lexikalische Argumente und Adjunkte.* Berlin: Akademie Verlag.
Stiebels, Barbara, and Dieter Wunderlich. 1994. Morphology Feeds Syntax: the Case of Particle Verbs. *Linguistics* 32:913–68.
Stirling, Lesley. 1993. *Switch-Reference and Discourse Representation.* Cambridge: Cambridge University Press.
Stowell, Timothy. 1996. The Phrase Structure of Tense. In *Phrase Structure and the Lexicon,* ed. Johan Rooryck and Laurie Zaring, 277–291. Dordrecht: Kluwer.
Talmy, Leonard. 1976. Semantic Causative Types. In *Syntax and Semantics 6: The Grammar of Causative Constructions,* ed. Masayoshi Shibatani, 43–116. New York: Academic Press.
———. 1988. Force Dynamics in Language and Cognition. *Cognitive Science* 12:49–100.
———. 2000. *Toward a Cognitive Semantics.* Cambridge, Mass: MIT Press.
Taylor, Barry. 1985. *Modes of Occurrence.* Oxford: Blackwell.
Tenny, Carol. 1987. *Grammaticalizing Aspect and Affectedness.* Ph.D. dissertation, MIT, Cambridge, Mass.
———. 1994. *Aspectual Roles and the Syntax-Semantics Interface.* Dordrecht: Kluwer.
ter Meulen, Alice G. 1995. *Representing Time in Natural Language. The Dynamic Interpretation of Tense and Aspect.* Cambridge, Mass: MIT Press.

Thurman, R. 1978. *Interclausal Relations in Chuave.* M.A. Thesis, UCLA.

Traugott, Elizabeth Closs, and Bernd Heine, eds. 1991. *Approaches to Grammaticalization.* (2 vols.) Amsterdam: John Benjamins.

Travis, Lisa. 1991. Derived Objects, Inner Aspect and the Structure of VP. *Proceedings of the North Eastern Linguistics Society* 22. GLSA: University of Massachusetts, Amherst.

———. 1994. Event Phrase and a Theory of Functional Categories. In *Proceedings of the 1994 Annual Conference of the Canadian Linguistic Association (Toronto Working Papers in Linguistics)*. University of Toronto, Ontario.

van Geenhoven, Veerle. 1998. *Semantic Incorporation and Indefinite Descriptions.* Stanford, CA: CSLI Publications.

van Hout, Angeliek. 2000. Event Semantics in the Lexicon-Syntax Interface: Verb Frame Alternations in Dutch and their Acquisition. In *Events as Grammatical Objects*, ed. Carol Tenny and James Pustejovsky, 239–282. Stanford, CA: CSLI Publications.

Van Valin, Robert D. 1990. Semantic Parameters of Split Intransitivity. *Language* 66:221–60.

———, ed. 1993. *Advances in Role and Reference Grammar.* Amsterdam: John Benjamins.

Vater, Heinz. 1975. Werden als Modalverb. In *Aspekte der Modalität*, ed. Joseph Calbert and Heinz Vater, 71–148. Tübingen: Narr.

———, ed. 1997. *Zu Tempus und Modus im Deutschen.* Trier: Wissenschaftlicher Verlag Trier.

Vendler, Zeno. 1957. Verbs and Times. *Philosophical Review* 66:143–160. [Reprinted in Vendler, Z. 1967. *Linguistics in Philosophy.* New York: Cornell University Press]

Verkuyl, Henk. 1972. *On the Compositional Nature of the Aspects.* Dordrecht: Reidel.

———. 1989. Aspectual Classes and Aspectual Composition. *Linguistics and Philosophy* 12:39–94.

———. 1993. *A Theory of Aspectuality. The Interaction between Temporal and Atemporal Structure.* Cambridge: Cambridge University Press.

Wilhelm, Andrea. 2000. Event and Verb Types in German. Generals Paper, University of Calgary.

———. 2001. Categories of Lexical Aspect in German. Paper presented at the Seventh Germanic Linguistic Association Conference (GLAC 7), April 21–23, 2001, Banff, Alberta.

———. 2003. Quasi-Telic Perfective Aspect in Dëne Sųłiné (Chipewyan). *Proceedings of SALT (Semantics and Linguistic Theory) 13*, 310–327. Cornell University, Ithaca, NY.

———. 2005. Bare nouns and number in Dëne Sųłiné. *Proceedings of SULA (Semantics of underrepresented languages in the Americas) 3.* GLSA, University of Massachusetts, Amherst.

Willie, MaryAnn. 1991. *Navajo Pronouns and Obviation.* Ph.D. dissertation, University of California, San Diego.
Willie, MaryAnn, and Eloise Jelinek. 2000. Navajo as a Discourse Configurational Language. In *The Athabaskan Languages: Perspectives on a Native American Language Family*, ed. Theodore Fernald and Paul Platero, 252–87. Oxford: Oxford University Press.
Wiltschko, Martina. 2003. On the Interpretability of Tense on D and its Consequences for Case Theory. *Lingua* 113:659–696.
Wunderlich, Dieter. 1970. *Tempus und Zeitreferenz im Deutschen.* München: Max Hueber Verlag.
Wurmbrand, Susi. 1998. Heads or Phrases? Particles in Particular. In *Phonology and Morphology of the Germanic Languages*, ed. Wolfgang Kehrein and Richard Wiese, 267–296. Tübingen: Niemeyer.
Young, Robert. 2000. *The Navajo Verb System: an Overview.* Albuquerque, NM: University of New Mexico Press.
Young, Robert, and William Morgan. 1987. *The Navajo Language: A Grammar and Colloquial Dictionary.* Albuquerque, NM: University of New Mexico Press.
Zeller, Jochen. 2001. *Particle Verbs and Local Domains.* Amsterdam: John Benjamins.
Zwicky, Arnold. 1985. How to Describe Inflection. *Proceedings of the Eleventh Annual Meeting of the Berkeley Linguistics Society*, 372–386. University of Berkeley, CA.
———. 1992. Some Choices in the Theory of Morphology. In *Formal Grammar: Theory and Implementation*, ed. Robert Levine, 327–371. Oxford: Oxford University Press.
http://www.uni-marburg.de/dsa/dtdialekte.html (June 2003).

Author Index

A

Abraham, Werner, 6, 139f, 147, 228, 304n4, 304n6
Anderson, Stephen R., 18
Andersson, S.G., 139f, 166, 168–70, 184, 228, 298n29
Axelrod, Melissa, 22, 35, 44, 55, 70, 73–5, 77, 121, 296n7, 298n28, 299n7, 301n35

B

Bach, Emmon, 2, 15, 62, 215
Baker, Mark, 18, 29
Bar-el, Leora, 121
Bauer, Laurie, 7
Behagel, Otto, 57, 151, 172
Benware, Wilbur, 156
Bierwisch, Manfred, 7
Blom, Corrien, 163
Bohnemeyer, Jürgen, 56f, 171, 179, 191, 193
Booij, Geert, 19
Borer, Hagit, 2, 17, 145, 222, 224
Bortolin, Leah, 22, 58, 78–80, 88, 90–2, 97, 99, 128f, 298n20, 300n9, 301n27, 303n53
Brinton, Laurel, 308n32
Brons-Albert, Ruth, 309n10
Butt, Miriam, 17, 223
Bybee, Joan, 7, 29, 311n1

C

Carlson, Gregory, 5, 227f
Carlson, Lauri, 2

Causley, Trisha, 297n11
Chierchia, Gennaro, 63
Chomsky, Noam, 17f, 215
Chung, Sandra, 12
Comrie, Bernard, 2, 10f, 39, 41, 46, 54, 166, 185, 191, 212, 295n6, 296n1, 314n22
Cook, E.-D., 18, 23, 25–27, 30, 33, 40f, 44f, 55, 64, 75f, 81–5, 87f, 107, 110, 113, 115, 117f, 291f, 296n4, 297n11, 298n20, 300n10, 300n15–16, 301n36, 302n39, 302n41, 302n46
Corbett, Greville, 73, 121
Croft, William, 205, 207
Cruse, D.A., 299n32

D

Dahl, Östen, 54, 173f, 191
Dal, Ingerid, 151, 166f, 172, 175, 186, 307n16, 309n6
Davidson, Donald, 13f, 16
de Hoop, Helen, 228
Declerck, Renaat, 305n9
Delisle, Helga, 174, 309n3
Demirdache, Hamida, 12, 206f, 311n3
Depraetere, Ilse, 16
DiSciullo, Anna-Maria, 18
Diesing, Molly, 227f
Dowty, David R., 2–5, 7f, 15f, 58, 61, 65, 135, 222f, 300n19, 305n8–9
Duden, 6, 57, 151, 166f, 172, 176, 307n16, 309n3, 309n5

Durie, Mark, 121

E
Ehrich, Veronika, 2, 8, 136, 139f, 176–79, 181–83, 187, 222, 228, 304n4, 309n13
Elford, Leon, 115, 130, 291f, 303n48
Elford, Marjorie, 115, 130, 291f, 303n48

F
Fagan, Sarah M.B, 2
Filip, Hana, 119, 147, 306n13
Flämig, Walter, 6, 151, 166f, 172, 176, 181, 307n16
François, Jacques, 295n5

G
Giorgi, Alessandra, 12, 206
Givón, Talmy, 226
Goldberg, Adele, 19
Grewendorf, Günther, 228, 304n6
Grice, H.P., 47
Grimshaw, Jane, 2, 222

H
Haas, Wolf, 310n16
Haider, Hubert, 306n14
Haiman, John, 226
Hale, Ken, 28, 222, 296n6
Halle, Morris, 19, 150, 207
Hargus, Sharon, 84, 297n11
Harley, Heidi, 19, 150
Higginbotham, James, 13
Hinrichs, Erhard, 2
Hoekstra, Teun, 19, 150, 163
Hopper, Paul, 54, 191
Horn, Laurence R., 47
Hundsnurscher, Franz, 156

J
Jackendoff, Ray, 2, 7, 16, 19, 107, 156, 298n25, 305n9

K
Kamp, Hans, 41, 54, 191, 298n27
Kari, James, 18, 22, 28, 30, 53, 70–3, 76–8, 80, 90, 121

Kaufmann, Ingrid, 228, 304n6
Kenny, Anthony, 1
Keyser, Samuel J., 222
Kiparsky, Paul, 119
Klein, Wolfgang, 7f, 10, 12, 35, 51, 69, 135, 176, 185, 211, 222, 228, 298n25
Kratzer, Angelika, 5, 12f, 17, 145, 176, 206f, 222, 224, 227, 295n5, 312n4
Krauss, Michael E., 35, 299n7
Krifka, Manfred, 15, 62f, 88f, 123, 145, 147, 151, 164, 215f, 295n5, 296n8, 311n4

L
Landman, Fred, 39, 300n19
Lehmann, Christian, 7, 311n1
Leiss, Elisabeth, 151, 166f, 304n7, 309n10
Levin, Beth, 2, 7f, 16, 135, 156, 162, 195, 199, 222f, 298n25, 304n6
Levinson, Stephen C., 47
Li, Charles N., 226
Li, Fang-Kuei, 26, 53, 76–8, 80, 84, 87f, 299n5
Lieber, Rochelle, 18
Link, Godehard, 63
Löbner, Sebastian, 178
Longacre, Robert, 226
Lüdeling, Anke, 151

M
Marantz, Alec, 19, 29, 150, 207
Matthewson, Lisa, 206, 210, 312n4, 312n8, 313n18
Matzel, Klaus, 309n10
McDonough, Joyce, 297n11
Mezhevich, Ilana, 148
Midgette, Sally, 22, 49f, 58, 70, 78, 90, 120, 125–28, 303n47
Milsark, Gary, 227
Mithun, Marianne, 121
Moens, Marc, 2
Mohanan, Tara, 7
Morgan, William, 18, 35, 80, 299n7
Mourelatos, Alexander P.D., 2, 5, 215
Munro, Pamela, 226

Author Index

Musan, Renate, 2, 12, 42, 143, 175, 177–79, 182, 184f, 188, 190, 222, 211, 219, 228, 309n11, 309n14, 310n15, 310n19, 314n22

N
Neeleman, Ad, 19, 150
Noyer, Rolf, 19, 150

P
Parks, Douglas R., 9
Parsons, Terence, 2, 5, 13, 51, 185, 300n19
Partee, Barbara, 54, 191
Paul, Hermann, 57, 151, 166f, 172, 186, 228
Pesetsky, David, 215
Pianesi, Fabio, 12, 206
Pinker, Steven, 7, 16
Piñón, Christopher, 2
Pustejovsky, James, 2–4, 7, 14, 16, 135, 295n5, 313n19

R
Ramchand, Gillian, 2, 8, 15, 17, 135, 216, 222f
Rapp, Irene, 2, 8, 16, 135, 139, 141–43, 152, 156, 195, 198f, 222f, 304n4, 304n6, 304n8, 305n8, 308n25,
Rappaport Hovav, Malka, 2, 7f, 16, 135, 155f, 162, 195, 199, 222f, 298n25, 304n6
Reichenbach, Hans, 13, 176
Rice, Keren, 18, 22, 26, 28–31, 70, 78–80, 83, 85f, 88, 90f, 99, 108–10, 113, 121, 123, 128f, 211, 217, 292, 296n5, 297n12, 297n16, 299n9, 302n38–9
Rice, Sally, 23, 25
Ritter, Elisabeth, 2, 17, 145, 222, 224
Rohrer, Christian, 41, 54, 191, 298n27
Rosen, Sarah Thomas, 2, 17, 145, 222, 224
Ryle, Gilbert, 1

S
Singh, Mona, 51

Smith, Carlota, 2–5, 7f, 10–6, 22, 35f, 39, 44, 47, 49, 51f, 54, 58, 68, 70, 78, 90f, 97, 110, 125–28, 153, 157, 166, 170, 185, 212, 222, 295n2, 295n5–6, 296n1, 298n23, 300n21, 303n52, 309n14, 311n24, 313n12, 313n17, 313n19, 314n22
Speas, Margaret, 28, 84
Spencer, Andrew, 148, 156, 162f, 227, 308n1
Steinitz, Renate, 1, 150, 166–68, 295n3, 307n16
Stiebels, Barbara, 19, 150f, 156, 160, 162, 307n15, 308n30, 309n5
Stirling, Lesley, 226
Stowell, Timothy, 185, 206f
Swift, Mary, 56f, 171, 179, 191, 193

T
Talmy, Leonard, 205
Taylor, Barry, 1
Tenny, Carol, 2, 8, 145, 152f, 163, 197, 207, 222, 305n9
Timberlake, Alan, 12
Torrego, Esther, 215
Tuttle, Siri, 84, 297n11

U
Ulvestad, Barne, 309n10
Uribe-Etxebarria, Myriam, 12, 206f, 311n3

V
Van Valin, Robert D., 2, 163
Vater, Heinz, 186, 309n10
Vendler, Zeno, 1–5, 13, 15, 58, 153, 222, 224, 228
Verkuyl, Henk, 3, 8, 145, 197, 216, 222–24

W
Wee, Lionel, 7
Weerman, Fred, 19, 150
Wilhelm, Andrea, 4, 64, 295n2, 298n24, 299n35, 303n51 313n16
Williams, Edwin, 18
Willie, MaryAnn, 303n51
Wiltschko, Martina, 312n8
Wood, Valerie, 23, 25

Wunderlich, Dieter, 19, 150f, 172, 177f, 307n15, 309n9–10
Wurmbrand, Susi, 19, 150, 307n15

Y
Young, Robert, 18, 35, 44, 80, 299n7

Z
Zaretskaya, Marina, 148, 156, 162f, 227, 308n1
Zeller, Jochen, 20, 150f, 213, 296n11, 308n30
Zwicky, Arnold, 18

Subject Index

A

Ablaut *see* Stem: changes
Accomplishments, 1, 3–5, 14, 16, 39, 49, 56–8, 61, 65–7, 72, 79f, 88, 90f, 96–101, 106–08, 127, 153–60, 162, 195–97, 223, 230–37, 260–75, 329n19
Accusative, 119, 135, 146–48, 163f, 224, 308n27
Achievements, 1, 3–5, 14, 56, 67, 72, 74, 79, 88, 90f, 96–100, 102–04, 108–11, 156–58, 161f, 180f, 195–201, 222f, 246–52, 280–85, 287–89, 311n24, 313n19
Activities, 1, 3–5, 14, 16, 49, 51, 56, 58, 61, 65, 72, 79, 89–91, 98–102, 106–08, 117f, 153–56, 162, 193–95, 197–201, 223, 237–45, 275–80, 293, 311n24, 313n19
Adjuncts, 28, 146–48, 163, 174, 217, 303
lexical adjuncts/adjunction, 156, 158, 162
Adverbial prefix, 27, 31, 105, 109, 117, 217
Agent, agentivity, 3f, 311n25
Ahtna, 22, 70–8, 118, 125, 128
Aktionsart, 14, 166f, 170, 178, 295n5, 307n17
'almost' test, 65–8, 95–7, 99, 106f, 120–24, 229, 292f, 301n33, 303n49, 313n15
am (Ven sein) construction, 173–75, 309n2, 309n5
an construction, 119f, 146f, 228, 306n13

Anterior, anteriority, 143, 181, 219, 314n22
Argument structure, 10, 16, 156, 160, 207, 209f, 216, 220, 222f, 307n18, 312n5
Arguments *see* Adjuncts, Event argument, External argument, Internal argument, Predicate decomposition, Lexical semantics, Goal
Asp/AspP, 10, 205–13, 216, 218–22, 224–26, 311n3, 313n18
Aspect, 11–17, 205, 208, 221
  see also Aspectual classes, Imperfective, Perfect, Perfective, Progressive, Subsituation aspect, Viewpoint aspect
  aspectual shift, 58, 97, 211, 255n, 301n33, 303n3, 309n7
  inner and outer aspect, 224–26
  lexical aspect *see* Situation type(s)
Aspectless language, 226
Aspects (Athapaskan), 70–7, 107, 118, 128
Aspectual classes, 1–5, 79, 224f
  see also Aktionsarten, Aspects, Situation types, Verb theme categories
Atelicity:
  imperfective function, 164, 171, 179, 189, 225
  vs. progressive, 306n13
Athapaskan, 18, 20, 22f, 25f, 28–31, 35, 44, 58, 68–70, 72, 74, 79f, 90, 95, 99, 101, 110, 118, 121, 125, 128–31, 217, 297n8, 297n11, 299n1

331

B

Backgrounding, 36, 41f, 55, 67, 298n28
Bounds/Bounding/Bounded/Boundary, 16, 39, 41, 43, 52–4, 57, 67, 148, 165, 169f, 193, 296n8, 313n20
see also Endpoints

C

CM patterns, 52, 71, 78, 204, 298n20, 301n36, 312n7
see also Conjugation markers, Inceptive aspect, Seriative
and situation type, 78–88, 100, 102, 108, 117f, 129f, 299n7, 301n36
and quantization, 88–90, 108, 118
example paradigms, 81f
of accomplishments in Dëne, 100f, 108
of achievements in Dëne, 102–04, 108
of activities in Dëne, 101f, 108, 117f
of semelfactives in Dëne, 104–06
Case and telicity, 17, 119, 146–48, 163, 224, 306n12
Cancellation (implicature), 39, 41, 170f
Causative head, 17
Causative/Causing event, 3f, 198
Change of state/location, 15f, 51, 67, 135, 140, 144, 147f, 205, 298n25, 312n5
Checking of features, 215, 224, 313n11
Chuave, 226
Classes/classification:
see also Conjugation markers, Situation types, Vendler verb classes
aspectual *see* Aspectual classes
lexical, 22, 70, 72, 74, 78, 99
morphological, 22, 69, 72f, 78, 80, 90, 104f, 108, 129, 167, 299n8
semantic, 69, 72, 80, 108, 129, 151, 167
temporal-aspectual *see* Aspectual classes
Classifiers, 27–33, 83–6, 297n10, 300n13, 300n15, 302n46
Clause structure, 17f, 28f, 205–07, 217–20
Clitics (Dëne postverbal), 36f, 54
Coerced/coercion, 37, 183, 213, 303n3, 306n11, 309n7

Completion of event *see* Entailments, Perfective: Dëne perfective: completive meaning
Conative, 110, 113–16, 302n38
Conjugation markers (CMs), 27, 32–4, 71, 77–119, 204, 211, 291f, 299n6
see also CM patterns
and quantization, 88–90, 108, 118, 204
and situation type, 78–80, 90, 108, 118, 129
cooccurring morphemes, 80, 108–18
distribution, 78, 100–05, 116f
ne- not a CM/peculiarities, 86–8
status as viewpoint markers, 83–6, 88
*the-*deletion and high tone, 83f, 87, 111, 298n26, 300n10, 300n16, 300n23, 301n26
Conjunct prefixes/domain, 27f, 31, 83–5, 88, 111, 296n4, 297n11, 300n10, 301n26, 301n34, 302n39, 302n46, 303n46
see also Classifiers, Object prefixes, Subject prefixes, Thematic (prefixes)
Construction Grammar, 19
Contrast, 6f
absence, 64, 172, 177, 181, 186f, 217–19
featural, 210–16, 218
morphosyntactic, 22, 39, 42, 68f, 102, 203, 208–10, 213, 216f, 220f
phonological, 7, 312n6
semantic, 217, 221
Count nouns, 63f, 123, 312n10
Cumulative *see* Quantization

D

DP vs. NP, 215, 296n3, 312n10, 313n13
dabei sein construction, 173f, 200, 311n25
Dative, 135, 147f, 163, 306n12
Default:
override/shift of, 57, 177, 180f
tense, 176f, 180f, 226
viewpoint aspect/interpretation, 56f, 164, 171, 179f, 189, 191, 193, 225, 306n13

Definiteness, 63f, 123, 145, 195, 224, 303n48, 303n51, 305n10, 307n23, 312n10, 313n13
[delim] feature, 213–18, 224, 228, 313n11, 314n20
Delimiting, 57, 151, 162, 194, 197, 204, 213, 224, 226
Dëne/Dëne Sųłiné, 21–34, 74–7, 211–13, 217–19
  see also Aspects, Clitics, Conjugation markers, Inceptive, Inchoative, Imperfective: Dëne, Modes, Perfective: Dëne, Progressive: Dëne progressive, Seriative, Stem, Tense: Dëne tense marking, Verb theme categories
  morpheme co-occurrence patterns, 80, 108–18
  nouns, 64f
  telicity in Dëne, 58–68, 211–13
  verb (structure), 26–34, 211f, 217f, 297n11
    see also Conjunct prefixes, Disjunct prefixes, Stem:verb stem, Subject prefixes, Thematic (prefixes)
Derivation/derivational, 6, 18, 28, 34, 70–4, 76f, 80, 110, 117, 129f, 168, 171, 292f
Diachronic/diachrony, 7, 90, 163, 308n32, 309n6, 311n1
Direct objects and telicity, 119–25, 144–48, 152, 163, 204, 214–17, 308n25
  see also Internal arguments, Quantization
Discourse Representation theory, 15
Discourse-pragmatics, 41f, 54–8, 67, 131, 171, 188, 190f, 224–26, 298n27
  see also Backgrounding, Event ordering, Foregrounding, Simultaneous events, Sequential events
Disjunct prefixes/domain, 27f, 30f, 108–10, 118, 217, 227, 296n4–5, 297n13
  see also Adverbial prefix, Distributive prefix, Incorporated noun, Postposition, Iterative prefix
  determining CM patterns, 108–10

ná#, 117
Distributed Morphology, 19, 26, 31, 150, 207, 213, 296n11, 297n8
Distributive prefix *dá#*, 27, 64, 124, 297n13
Domains, 4, 10, 19, 29, 150, 176, 213, 215
  see also Conjunct, Disjunct, IP domain, Situation Type, VP domain
Durativity/durative, 3–6, 10, 16f, 36–9, 71, 73, 91, 108, 127, 166, 177, 180f, 204f, 207–09, 221, 223, 293, 313n19
  see also CM pattern, Grammatization, Imperfective, Particle verbs
  grammatization, 8–10, 35, 39, 43, 67, 102, 118f, 203–05, 207–09, 211–13
  non-grammatization, 10, 164f, 190f, 193, 199, 201, 204, 219–21
  syntax/syntactic representation, 223
  tests (Dëne), 37f, 91–5, 97–9, 177, 229, 300n22
  tests (German), 153, 157, 200, 259, 307n20, 311n23, 311n25
  variable/unspecified, 134, 158, 161, 163, 193–201, 311n24, 223
Dutch, 163

E
Endpoints, 39, 44, 49, 51, 53, 163, 169f, 200, 226, 296n8 308n32
  see also Bounds
English, 169, 225f
Entailments, 2, 21, 35, 39, 43f, 47–53, 67, 170f
Event argument/*e*, 13f, 17, 206–08, 311n4
Event ordering/sequencing, 41, 43, 54–7, 67, 171, 191–93, 224–27, 298n27–28, 314n22
Event type *see* Situation type
External arguments, 11, 17, 135, 206, 305n9, 308n33, 311n3
Extralinguistic, 8, 197, 222

F
Features, 7, 9, 17, 210–20, 224, 228, 312n6, 313n11, 314n20
French, 41, 172, 191, 298n23, 298n27

334 Subject Index

Force-dynamic, 10, 205, 207–09, 221
Foregrounding, 41, 55
'finish Ving' *see* Terminative expressions
'for an hour' *see* Time span expressions
Future, 12, 36f, 70, 75f, 92, 95, 105, 111, 113, 172, 175–80, 182f, 187, 229, 297n16, 309n10–11

G

General meaning *see* Unspecification
German, 6, 166–68, 172–75
    see also Durativity: tests (German), Particle verbs, Particles: German particles, Telicity: tests
    colloquial, 176, 181, 185, 190
    constituency tests, 150, 306n14
    dialects, 310n16–17
        South German, 134, 165f, 172, 176, 178f, 181, 186–90, 309n4, 310n16–19, 310n21, 311n22
    lack of viewpoint aspect, 56–8, 172–90
    tense, 172, 175–90, 309n6, 310n18
Germanic, 163, 175
Goal (argument/phrase/PP), 136, 147f, 156, 160, 162f, 204, 226f, 308n27, 308n32
Grammatization, 6–8, 39, 136, 203–5, 205, 208, 207–16, 220f, 295n5, 311n1, 313n12
    see also Conjugation markers, Contrast, Durativity: grammatization, Features, IP domain, Imperfective, Non-grammatization, Productivity, Situation type: grammatization, Telicity: grammatization, Typology, VP domain, Verb theme categories
    locus, 9, 35, 68, 134, 190, 193, 201, 203–05, 207–09, 222–24

H

Habitual, 41, 226
Hindi, 51

I

IP domain, 8, 10, 18, 136, 165, 204f, 219
    see also Asp/AspP, VP domain

Idioms/idiomatic, 18, 30, 151, 163, 296n10
Imperfective, 11f, 211f, 220
    see also Backgrounding, Default aspect/interpretation, Discourse-pragmatics, Durativity: tests (Dëne), Entailments, Event ordering, Perfective, Simultaneous situations/events
    Aktionsart, 165, 168–71
    and durativity, 21, 35–9, 43, 67, 125, 128, 177, 183, 204, 211–13
    cumulative reference, 89
    Dëne Imperfective, 34–43
    incomplete situations/events, 36, 39–41
    vs. tense, 175–91
Imperfective paradox, 300n19
Implicature, 47, 171
'in an hour' *see* Time span expressions
Inceptive aspect/prefix, 32, 56, 80, 104, 110–13, 115, 117, 192, 226
Inchoative aspect/prefix, 302n37, 302n39
Incorporated noun, 27, 31, 235n
Incremental theme, 147, 304n8, 305n8
Indefinite *see* Definiteness
Individual-level, 13, 227
Inflection, 6, 18, 26, 28, 31f, 34, 63f, 125f, 165, 171–73, 175, 204, 209–11, 216f, 220
    see also IP domain
Inner aspect, 224–26
Internal arguments, 17, 135f, 142–146, 148, 155, 163f, 204, 206f, 209, 214–17, 224f, 228, 304n6, 312n5
    see also Direct objects, Unaccusative
Iterative prefix *na#*, 27f, 296n5

K

Koyukon, 22, 35, 55, 70, 73–7, 118, 125, 128, 296n7, 299n7, 301n35

L

Lexical *see* Derivational, Thematic
Lexical aspect *see* Situation type(s)
Lexical semantics/analysis, 7, 156, 158, 160–62
    see also Predicate decomposition

Subject Index

lexical semantic structures, 2, 16, 152, 156, 160, 162, 195, 198f, 222f, 312n5
Lexicalism/lexical vs. syntactic, 18–20, 296n10

M

Mandarin, 46, 51
Manner adverbs, 91–5, 97f
Mass nouns, 62–4, 123, 145, 158, 299n34–35, 307n23
Measuring out, 145, 163, 207, 216, 305n9
Methodology, 9f, 22, 25, 70, 79f, 129f, 151–53, 303n53
Mode/Modes, 21, 27, 32–4, 70, 74, 76–8, 292, 298n28, 304n7
Momentaneous verb themes, 71, 87f
Motion/motion verbs, 144, 147f, 162f, 198
  Athapaskan, 71–4, 77, 79, 86f, 101f, 104f, 126f

N

Navajo, 8, 22, 35, 49f, 58, 68, 70, 90, 120, 125–28, 297n11, 300n21, 303n51–52,
Neuter verbs *see* Stative verbs
Non-grammatization, 58–69, 133f, 217–21
  see also Durativity: non-grammatization, Grammatization, Quantization: non-grammatization, Telicity: non-grammatization, Unspecification, Viewpoint aspect: absent/not grammatized in German
Nonpast, 175f
Number, 63f, 121, 210, 217, 227, 297n13
  stem alternations (verb), 121, 227, 300n12, 300n17
  see also Plural-stem verbs

O

Object selection, 148, 156, 159, 160
Objects *see* Direct objects and telicity, Internal arguments, Unselected objects, Unspecified object
Object prefixes, 27, 29, 32, 119–21, 229, 303n47, 303n51

Obligatoriness, 173, 175, 204
Optative, 32f, 34, 70, 74–6, 80, 87f, 101, 229, 291f, 297n13, 299n6, 300n13
Outer aspect, 224–26
Overlapping events *see* Simultaneous events/situations

P

Participle (perfect), 135, 140–45, 204, 304n6–7
Particle verbs, 19, 133–35, 149–63, 168, 213
  and durativity, 197–201, 204
  and telicity, 150–63, 200, 204
  not perfective, 168–171, 298n29
Particles:
  Dëne postverbal particles *see* Clitics
  German particles, 57, 149–63, 167f, 213, 226f
    aspectually neutral particles, 151, 307n19, 311n26, 313n20
    delimiting/resultative/telic, 135f, 151, 153–63, 194, 197, 204, 213, 226, 308n32, 313n20
    not perfective markers, 168–71, 307n17
Passive, 72, 143f, 304n7, 305n9
  Vorgangspassiv, 143f
  Zustandspassiv, 143, 304n7
Past participle *see* Participle (perfect)
Past tense/time, 11–13, 134, 165f, 169, 172, 175f, 181–91
  see also, Perfect, Preterite
Perfect, 134, 165, 172, 175f, 181–91, 219, 295n6, 304n7, 309n8, 309n14, 310n14–15, 310n18–20, 314n22
  see also Anteriority, Participle (perfect), Posttime, Preterite
  relation to perfective viewpoint, 228, 309n14
Perfect participle *see* Participle (perfect)
Perfective, 11–13, 211
  see also Bounds, Conjugation markers, Default aspect/interpretation, Discourse-pragmatics, Entailments, Event ordering,

Foregrounding, Imperfective,
Posttime. Sequential situations/
events
and telicity, 53–8, 67, 139, 168–71, 192,
298n29, 308n1
and tense, 183, 188, 191
Dëne Perfective, 34f, 43–53, 83–7,
302n36
completive meaning/completed
events, 21, 35, 40, 43–53, 58,
67, 204, 218, 313n16
obscures telicity, 21, 35, 67, 69, 119,
125
perfectivity test, 170f
relation to perfect, 228, 309n14
Perfective Aktionsart, 167–171
Phases, 3f, 127, 293
Philippine languages, 226
Plural, 63f, 124, 145, 297n13, 299n9,
303n50, 312n9
bare plural, 145, 228, 312n10
Plural-stem verbs, 120–23
see also Number: stem alternations (verb)
Postposition, 26f, 32, 58f, 92
Posttime/poststate/TPost, 51–3, 67, 185,
218, 228, 298n24
Pragmatics *see* Discourse-pragmatics
Predicate decomposition, 4, 16f, 152, 156,
160, 162, 195, 198f, 222f,
298n25, 312n5
see also Lexical semantics
Prefix verbs/prefixes (German), 57, 150,
167f, 170f, 227, 307n16
Prefixes *see* Conjunct prefixes, Disjunct prefixes, Prefix verbs/prefixes (German), Thematic (prefixes)
Present perfect *see* Perfect
Present tense/time, 11f, 172f, 175–81, 190,
309n11
Preterite, 134, 165, 172f, 175f, 219f,
310n15, 310n18
see also Event ordering, Imperfective,
Perfect, Perfective, Simultaneous
events
Präteritumsschwund, 186
vs. imperfective viewpoint, 175, 181–90
Preverbs *see* disjunct prefixes

Process, 3, 14, 16, 67, 92, 156, 200, 223,
295n2, 308n28, 313n19
Process head, 17, 223
Progressive, 11f, 16, 37, 39, 57, 97, 133, 169,
172, 185, 190, 209, 213, 259,
295n6, 300n20, 301n35, 306n13
Dëne Progressive, 76–8, 291–93, 296n1
German paraphrases/pseudo-progressives, 172–75, 200, 259, 309n2,
309n5, 311n25
Pronominal arguments, 227
Prospective interpretation, 37, 92, 95, 177,
229
Punctual, 67, 157, 167, 177f, 193f, 212,
303n52

Q

Quantization, 15f, 88–90, 108, 118f,
296n8, 300n18
noun/object quantization, 62–5, 89,
135, 145–48, 163, 195, 209,
215, 217, 225–27, 303n50–51,
307n23, 312n10, 313n13
and telicity, 62–4, 119–25, 145f,
152, 163f, 204, 214–16
non-grammatization, 88f, 118f
'quickly' *see* Manner adverbs

R

Reference time *see* Topic time
Result:
head, 17, 223f, 313n20, 314n20
location, 160, 163, 198f
state, 3, 52f, 133, 135, 140, 148, 153,
155–58, 160, 162f, 198f, 213,
223, 311n24
Resultative, 148, 167, 156–58, 162f, 204,
225f, 227, 295n6, 304n4,
304n7, 308n32
Root and suffix, 28, 70f, 74f, 90, 291
Russian, 46, 169f, 227, 308n1

S

Selectional restrictions, 14, 39, 211, 213,
216, 312n9
Semantics vs. Syntax/Grammar, 7f, 139,
157, 222

Subject Index 337

as means of expression, 21, 65, 99, 125, 173
in judgements, 295n1
representation, 2, 8f, 21f, 65, 217, 220, 295n3, 313n15
Semelfactive, 5, 66, 79, 82, 88, 104–06, 116f, 156–58, 299n9, 302n42, 302n46, 303n52
tests, 96–8, 157, 301n33
Separable prefixes *see* Particles: German particles
Sequential events/situations, 43, 54–7, 67, 171, 186, 189, 191–93, 225f
see also Default aspect/interpretation, Event ordering
Seriative, 79, 82, 89, 113, 115–18, 157, 302n46
Simultaneous events/situations, 36, 41f, 54–6, 67, 182f, 186, 191f, 225f
see also Default aspect/interpretation, Event ordering
Situation time/TSit, 12, 35f, 41–4, 51–3, 176f, 179f, 181f, 206f, 211–13, 295n6, 309n11–12, 311n3, 312n3
Situation type(s), 5, 10f, 13–7, 70, 91
see also Accomplishments, Achievements, Activities, Bounds, Change of State, Default aspect/interpretation, Discourse-pragmatics, Durativity, Grammatization, Part structure, Predicate decomposition, Process, Quantization, Result State, Semelfactives, States, Subevents, Telicity, Vendler verb classes, Viewpoint aspect
and conjugation markers, 78–80, 90, 108, 118, 129
and event ordering, 55–7, 191, 224f
connection with viewpoint aspect, 21, 35, 53–8, 125f, 128, 133f, 136, 164, 166–71, 190f, 201, 224f, 308n1
deconstruction of, 224f, 228
derivations
accomplishment > accomplishment, 158–61

achievement > achievement, 161f
activity > accomplishment, 153–56
activity > achievement, 197–201, 311n24
semelfactive > achievement/accomplishment, 156–58, 194f, 201
grammatization, 22, 70, 79
Slave (Slavey), 22f, 26, 70, 79, 86, 109f, 113, 128f, 292, 296n5, 297n16, 302n38
Slavic, 166, 168, 226, 308n1
see also Russian
Stage-level, 13, 227
States/Stativity, 1, 4f, 13f, 16, 79, 140, 153, 226f, 298n25, 300n21, 310n14, 312n5
see also Change of state, Individual-level, Result state, Stage-level
Stative verbs, 34, 71, 126f, 227, 298n20, 299n2, 302n36–37, 302n39, 304n6
positional stative verbs, 52f, 71, 79, 89f, 312n7
Stem:
alternations by number, 121, 227, 300n12, 300n17
changes, 34, 52, 70f, 79, 86, 140, 256, 291, 298n20
modes, 76f
suffix/suffixation patterns, 28, 70f, 74–6, 90, 101, 128, 291
verb stem, 18, 26–30, 32, 70, 229, 296n5, 300n13
'stop V-ing' *see* Terminative expressions
Subevents, 16, 156, 160, 163, 223, 296n9
Subject prefixes, 27, 29, 31f, 64, 83–6, 229, 297n9, 297m13
Subjects *see* External arguments
Subsituation aspect, 80, 104, 108, 110–18, 166–68, 292f, 302n37, 302n39
Superlexical aspect *see* Subsituation aspect

T
Telicity, 3, 5, 10f, 14–7, 147, 150–63, 165, 168–71, 192f, 197, 204f, 207–09, 221f, 304n4, 304n7

see also Bounds, Change of state, Default aspect/interpretation, Direct objects and telicity, Endpoints, Event ordering, Particles: German particles, Perfective, Quantization, Result, Resultative, Sequential events, Transition

and perfectivity, 44, 49, 53–8, 67, 133, 139, 164, 171, 179, 190–93, 224f, 298n29, 308n1

grammatization, 8, 10, 70, 158, 162, 169f, 191, 203–05, 207–09, 213–16

non-grammatization, 10, 58–69, 118f, 217–19

obscured/supplanted in Dëne, 57f, 61, 65, 67, 69

syntax/syntactic representation, 17, 145, 222–24, 314n20

tests, 3, 58–62, 95–9, 135–140, 150, 229, 259

Template morphology, 18, 26–8

Tense, 11–3, 133f, 165, 175–91, 206, 226f, 295n6–7, 298n27, 314n22

see also Future, German: tense, Nonpast, Past tense/time, Perfect, Present tense/time, Preterite

Dëne tense marking, 36, 312n8

Tests *see* 'Almost' test, Cancellation, Constituency tests, Durativity:tests, Methodology, Perfective: test, Semelfactive: tests, Telicity: tests, Terminative expressions, Time span expressions, VP: tests

Terminative expressions, 45, 47, 61f, 65, 92–5, 311n25

Thematic (prefixes), 18, 27, 30–32, 34, 40, 71, 87f, 101f, 105, 110, 115, 292, 300n13

Time span expressions, 3f, 37f, 58–61, 65, 92, 136–39, 150, 298n18, 301n33, 306n13, 308n28

Topic Time/TT, 12, 35f, 41–4, 51, 53, 176f, 179–82, 185, 206, 211–13, 292f, 295n6, 309n11–13, 311n3, 312n8

Transition, 14, 16, 53, 153

Transitivity issues, 152f, 156, 259, 304n8, 308n25

Typology (of aspect grammatization), 8, 225–27

U

Unaccusative, 142, 145, 228, 304n6

Universal/UG, 2, 8–10, 90, 99, 145, 221–23

Universal grinder and packager, 107

Unselected objects, 148, 156

Unspecification, 61, 158, 163, 171, 185, 193f, 217, 219f, 299n32

see also Non-grammatization

Unspecified object prefix, 120f, 303n47, 303n51

Utterance time/TU, 11f, 35, 41f, 176–82, 309n11, 312n8

V

v/vP, 17, 28f, 206f, 308n33, 311n3–4

VP/VP domain, 8–10, 17f, 109, 135f, 148, 152, 163–65, 204f, 207–09, 219, 221–25, 308n33, 313n20, 314n20

tests (German), 306n14

Vendler verb classes, 1, 224f

see also Accomplishments, Achievements, Activities, Aspectual classes, States

Verb classes *see* Classes

Verb stem *see* Stem: verb

Verb theme, 30–2, 296n5, 299n1

Verb theme categories, 70–8, 90, 99, 101f, 104f, 108, 125f, 128, 299n1

Viewpoint aspect, 11–3, 165, 176, 204, 295n6

see also Default aspect/interpretation, Discourse-pragmatics, Event Ordering, Imperfective, Perfective, Progressive, Unspecification

absent/not grammatized in German, 56–8, 133f, 164–66, 169, 171–90, 219–21, 225, 310n21

and tense, 35f, 175–91

Subject Index

connection with situation type, 21, 35, 53–8, 125f, 128, 133f, 136, 164, 190f, 201, 224f
Dëne viewpoint aspect, 27, 32–53, 83–88

neutral viewpoint aspect, 313n17
vs. situation type, 166–71, 308n1

W

World knowledge, 158, 195–97, 201

For Product Safety Concerns and Information please contact our EU
representative GPSR@taylorandfrancis.com
Taylor & Francis Verlag GmbH, Kaufingerstraße 24, 80331 München, Germany

www.ingramcontent.com/pod-product-compliance
Lightning Source LLC
Chambersburg PA
CBHW071758300426
44116CB00009B/1125